58421

LISTENING TO THE PEOPLE'S VOICE

LISTENING TO THE PEOPLE'S VOICE

ERUDITE AND POPULAR LITERATURE IN NORTH EAST BRAZIL

MARK DINNEEN

KEGAN PAUL INTERNATIONAL
London and New York

First published in 1996 by
Kegan Paul International
UK: P.O. Box 256, London WC1B 3SW, England
Tel: (0171) 580 5511 Fax: (0171) 436 0899
E-mail: books@keganpau.demon.co.uk
Internet: http://www.demon.co.uk/keganpaul/
USA: 562 West 113th Street, New York, NY 10025, USA
Tel: (212) 666 1000 Fax: (212) 316 3100

Distributed by
John Wiley & Sons Ltd
Southern Cross Trading Estate
1 Oldlands Way, Bognor Regis
West Sussex, PO22 9SA, England
Tel: (01243) 779 777   Fax: (01243) 820 250

Columbia University Press
562 West 113th Street
New York, NY 10025. USA
Tel: (212) 666 1000   Fax: (212) 316 3100

Printed in Great Britain

British Library Cataloguing in Publication Data
Dinneen, Mark Andrew
Listening to the People's Voice: Erudite and Popular Literature in North East Brazil
I. Title
869.09981

ISBN 0-7103-0545-1

Library of Congress Cataloging-in-Publication Data
Dinneen, Mark.
Listening to the people's voice: erudite and popular literature in
North East Brazil/ Mark Dinneen.
304 p. 23.4 cm.
Includes bibliographical references and index.
ISBN 0-7103-0545-1
1. Brazilian literature--Brazil, Northeast--History and criticism. 2. Popular literature--
Brazil, Northeast-- History and criticism.   3. Chapbooks, Brazilian--History.
4. Nationalism and literature--Brazil, Northeast. 5. Regionalism in literature.
6. Suassuna, Ariano--Criticism and interpretation. I. Title.
PQ9691.N59D5 1996

869.09'9813--dc20

95-44325
CIP

FOR MY FATHER,

AND IN MEMORY OF MY MOTHER

ACKNOWLEDGEMENTS

I am grateful to the British Academy, whose support enabled much of the research for this work to be carried out, and to the Instituto Joaquim Nabuco, in Recife, which gave vital assistance in Brazil. Mr Mike Gonzalez and Professor John Gledson gave valuable comments in the early stages of the work, and thanks are also due to Angelina Clariana-Piga, Gladys Iglesias, Denise Silva and Professor Peter Ucko for all

ILLUSTRATIONS

Page i, *The Story of Adam and Eve According to Elias Soares* by Ciro Fernandes. Page iii, *Flautist* by Marcelo Soares. Page vi, *'Repentistas'* by Marcelo Soares. Page viii, *Saint Francis* by Jota Borges. Page 17, *Lampião Fights the Devil* by Marcelo Soares. Page 149, *Forró (Popular Dance)* by Marcelo Soares. Page 272, *The Man Who Turned Into A Goat* by Dila. Page 280, *The Mother of the Oppressed* by Marcelo Soares. Page 294, *The Example Made of the Son Who Killed His Parents to Gain His Inheritance* by Jota Borges.

CONTENTS

INTRODUCTION: THE DEBATE AROUND
THE QUESTION OF NATIONAL CULTURE

i] Erudite culture and popular culture in Brazil

At the end of 1994, Ariano Suassuna, one of Brazil's foremost dramatists and novelists, was named as Minister of Culture for the state of Pernambuco. He quickly announced that his priority whilst in office would be to establish policies which would support and promote the traditional folk and popular art forms emanating from rural North East Brazil, to include drama, ceramics, engraving, folk music and popular literature. The artistic community in the North East was divided by Suassuna's approach. Some voiced support for him, whilst others condemned him for imposing what they saw as a narrow, retrograde and discriminatory policy towards the arts, and demanded recognition for cultural pluralism within the region. This represents one more stage in the long, ongoing debate on the ways in which erudite art and popular art might be brought together in order to affirm a distinctly regional cultural identity. Suassuna has dedicated most of his writing career to that problem. His ideas and literary work will be the focus of this study, for they represent the major contribution made in recent decades to the rich, regionalist literary tradition in the Brazilian North East.

However, Suassuna's theories on culture must be understood as the crystallisation of many ideas and attitudes elaborated in previous eras. Successive generations of Brazilian writers have attempted to incorporate expressions of popular culture and folklore into their work. The relationship between erudite 'high' culture and popular cultural expressions has been dynamic, its emphasis shifting over time in response to political and social factors, as much as to literary stimuli. This work will explore that process; a process which has produced literature of outstanding quality and originality, but which has also frequently embodied the contradictions inherent in the schemes of cultural nationalism and regional affirmation which have provided inspiration for so many of the writers concerned. Although much has now been written on the relationship between high culture and popular culture in Europe and the United States, relatively little research has been produced on the specific forms which the debate has taken in Brazil, and the particular ways in which they have helped to shape the country's erudite literature.

No where in Brazil has literary regionalism proved to be more dynamic and resilient, or programmes to promote regional art and culture formulated more clearly and consistently, than in the North East. That regionalism has constantly been fed by a rich variety of expressions of popular culture, which have endured due to the particular nature of the North East's historical development. Examining the principal transitions that North East literature has undergone in accordance with changing perceptions of national culture, regional identity and popular culture can contribute greatly to an understanding of the historical development of the region's literature, and of the tendencies and traits that still characterise much of it today.

One of the strongest expressions of North East popular culture is that of *folheto* verse; pamphlets of poetry produced, distributed and consumed by the poorest sectors of the region's population. The richness and variety of this poetry has long attracted the interest of erudite writers. Given its accessibility as one of the few printed forms that has developed out of popular oral tradition, readily available and easily collected in chap-book form, it is not surprising that it has become such important raw material for many regionalist writers, for whom it serves as a tangible link between their own formal, literary culture and the rich popular culture of the rural and urban masses. It is for this reason that the present work concentrates particularly on the relationship between erudite literature and popular pamphlet poetry, for no where has the interaction between 'high' culture and popular culture been clearer, or can be more readily examined. As the symbolic expression of the lived reality of those subaltern sectors of society, the frequently magic world presented in this popular poetry can only be understood in its relationship to the everyday social experience of those sectors. Through the symbolic universe of their poetry, the poor represent and discuss their daily struggles and conflicts. The poetry covers virtually all aspects of their experience, from religious faith to conflict on the land, and changing attitudes towards sexual and family relations to humorous anecdotes.

Writers such as Jorge Amado and Ariano Suassuna, have received much acclaim for their work which utilises the forms and themes of popular pamphlet poetry, but in their writing the popular material is divorced from the social context within which it is rooted, and is recreated into new forms with new meaning. Many of the popular perceptions and aspirations underlying the original poetry are lost. This is a major difficulty of the long held objective of creating an art that will be both national and popular, for no such grafting is possible without radical change in the significance of the original material. New interpretations and presentations of popular culture have been provided by a succession of erudite writers in the Brazilian North East, each influenced by new concepts and viewpoints relating to the crucial question of regional and national identity. As a result, the poor themselves have appeared in the literature of the region in a variety of guises: helpless victims in the work of Raquel de Queiroz, picturesque and inventive in the novels of Amado, and deeply religious and noble

2

in the writing of Suassuna. The contribution of these authors to North East regionalism, and the approach towards popular culture that they have adopted, will be examined in later chapters. Before looking in detail at Brazil, however, it is necessary to provide some context to the involvement of the erudite writer with popular culture and folklore. Briefly sketching out the way thinking on national culture and popular culture has developed through time can shed light on the changing attitudes of successive generations of Brazilian writers towards those issues, and suggest ways in which Brazilian popular culture may be understood.

ii] The debate around the ideology of national culture

The origins of the present-day concept of national culture - based on the notion of a state unified by fundamental common characteristics, such as race, language, shared beliefs or perceptions - are generally traced to the late eighteenth century. The German Romantics, seeking to elaborate a theoretical basis for the unity of the numerous German states and free cities then existing, are frequently seen as the first to develop the conception of a national spirit, a force providing cohesion among certain selected populations and contrasting them with others. It was a concept that went on to play a crucial role in the processes of consolidation of nation-states in Europe in the nineteenth century, and of increasingly intense political and economic competition between them.

Those emerging nation-states, however, were also characterised by sharp divisions of social class, and concomitant cultural divisions which intellectuals and writers of the nations concerned had to confront in their deliberations on the question of national culture. Even in the 1770s, long before German unification, the participants of the *Sturm und Drang* literary and philosophical movement, which included Goethe and Herder, had recognised such cultural stratification within society, deliberately emphasising in their work the particular traits which appeared to differentiate regions, communities or individuals. Reacting against the neoclassical view of reason, erudition and decorum as the basis for cultural expression, they advocated a free role for the creative imagination, emphasising subjectivity, spontaneity, intuition and passion in opposition to pure intellect, tendencies which clearly signalled the emergence of Romanticism. They also explain why, of all the social classes, it was the peasantry for whom they expressed most admiration. Clearly, they did not look upon the life of the rural poor with any real understanding, such was the distance that separated them, but rather with a sense of romantic attachment, seeing in the peasant's communal way of life, his continual interaction with the natural environment and

3

his daily practical labour, an existence that seemed in many ways more authentic and fulfilling than their own. Their intellectual activity only appeared to condemn them to isolation and spiritual malaise. (1)

It was that search for an artistic expression which sprang directly from the emotions and the imagination which explained the argument of Johann Gottfried Von Herder that the purest art was that of the *volk*, the poor, illiterate sectors of the population, comprising peasants, day labourers and artisans. At a time when most of the privileged, learned classes regarded folk poetry and song with total contempt, Herder argued that it represented a more natural and spontaneous expression of human feeling than the dry, artificial and scholarly creations of erudite writers. He sensed that the latter had become increasingly isolated from daily, mainstream social life and from the mass of the population, making their work frequently seem superfluous or reclusive, whilst the poetry of the *volk* issued from an active community within which it functioned as a vital social force. These ideas led Herder to argue that folk art was the true expression of the national spirit or soul, and therefore provided the basis for the most valuable national literature. Two hundred years later, remarkably similar views would form the conceptual foundation for the *Movimento Armorial* in the Brazilian North East.

The whole debate on the relationship between high culture and popular culture must therefore be understood first and foremost as the product of a particular historical era. The process of conceptualisation and definition of national culture was necessarily accompanied by consideration of the contributions made by each social class, and the relationships between those classes. Vastly differing attitudes to the problem can be traced in Europe throughout the nineteenth century. In the early decades, for example, many Romantic writers showed the same attraction to peasant life as Herder had done. Troubled by what they saw as the suffocation of free creativity by the mercenary nature and cold regimentation of industrial society, and by the growing divorce they detected between creative capacity and normal, daily productive capacity, they viewed peasant culture as a realm where balance, harmony and cohesion still existed. This vision found numerous forms of expression, varying considerably from one writer to another. In Britain, for example, Walter Scott collected, studied and even rewrote folk-tales and folk-songs, whilst carefully maintaining his distance from the rural communities that produced them, whereas Wordsworth, seeing in those communities a set of alternative, more positive values, not only idealised the peasantry in much of his work, but also attempted to overcome his own sense of separation from them by making an effort, albeit fitful, to integrate himself into their culture, seeking to adopt their living patterns

4

and perceptions of the world, and to write a type of folk poetry with which they might identify. According to one critic, such extreme romantic idealisation imbues much of the resulting work with "an element of pastoral masquerade." (2)

In the latter part of the century, Matthew Arnold presented a rather different conception of culture, essentially seen as high culture, embodying the highest qualities of human sensibility and intellectual achievement, the guardians of which would therefore have to be a highly educated and refined elite. The common people, now the proletariat rather than the peasantry, had little part to play. Submerged in ignorance, they constituted a threat to the perfect, civilised culture that Arnold envisaged. With the dissolution of aristocratic cultural values in the wake of accelerating capitalist development, Arnold attempted to counteract the "anarchy" he perceived in the new patterns of life and thought that were emerging with an elitist ideal of culture. (3) Similar arguments would be proposed by many other intellectuals in the present century, during which the whole discussion on the question of culture continued to intensify, eventually to become an arena of vigorous and highly contentious debate.

The development of the debate must therefore be seen as one response by bourgeois thought to the increasingly glaring contradictions inherent in the development of modern capitalism; contradictions which provided inspiration for a vast range of artistic expression. On the one hand is capitalism's promise of progress and modernisation, with the rapid expansion of urban, industrial society, systems of mass production creating greater material wealth than ever before and huge advances in technological development. Indeed, the bourgeois intellectual, privileged in society by his or her specialised education and professional formation, appears as a living symbol of that progress. That situation is perhaps the core of the personal contradiction of the intellectual: how to relate critically to a social environment that has formed them, structured their perceptions and apparently favoured them in significant ways. On the other hand however, are the striking contradictions within capitalist development which appear to negate that promised progress. The huge wealth generated has been accompanied by stark inequality and exploitation, conditions which have provided the inspiration for countless novels of social protest, like those of the nineteenth century Realist authors such as Dickens (1812-1870) and Elizabeth Gaskell (1810-1865). A very sophisticated and highly structured social and economic framework has emerged, apparently permitting a high level of social integration, and yet the antagonistic social divisions intrinsic to that framework have continued to foment tension and conflict. The rapid process of modernisation and technological advancement has provided undoubted benefits, but the consequent destruction of traditional patterns of collective life frequently instils a sense of loss, of dehumanisation, a key aspect of much Romantic literature of the nineteenth century.

Concern for the break-up of communal forms of life recurs in the work of many cultural critics of the present century. F.R. Leavis, for example, views the demise of traditional, organic community life as leading to the fragmentation of cultural practice and production. What he sees as the essentially harmonious order of pre-capitalist society has been destroyed, and with it the common, unified culture shared by all sectors within the community, to be replaced by a degraded mass culture which has led to a fall in cultural standards. (4) Many other writers have concentrated their attention on the expansion of mass society, arguing that if, on the one hand, the rapid social changes and advances in technology that have occurred during the past one hundred years have opened up new possibilities for social development, on the other they have led to the consolidation of a stereotyped, monotone mass culture which smothers original, creative expression. Again, however, widely differing responses to the question have been presented. For some conservative critics, the major negative effect of the expansion of mass society has been the standardisation of cultural expression and consequent decline in quality that has resulted, for they consider cultural production to be the natural domain of an enlightened and highly specialised elite. José Ortega y Gasset for example, writing in the 1920s when the organised, urban working classes had become a major social and political force in most European countries, including Spain, decried the encroachment of the masses into new spheres of social and cultural life, previously the domain of a privileged minority, threatening individuality and quality. Even the writer now had to create with low level, popular tastes in view. (5) Others however, like Richard Hoggart, writing in the 1950s, were more concerned with the corrosive effects that mass culture had on traditional, independent working-class culture than on that of the learned, leisured elite. (6)

In recent decades writers and scholars in Europe and the United States have shown increasing interest in the question of popular culture and its role in contemporary urban, industrial society. To some, the term popular culture is essentially synonymous with the mass culture industry, operating through powerful media such as radio, television, the popular press and the cinema. For others, the term refers to a complex of subcultures of certain, generally underprivileged, sectors within modern society, such as working-class youth or ethnic communities. The conclusions that have resulted from such research have been as varied as the approaches used. The participants in the Frankfurt School of the

1930s and 40s, for example, viewed popular culture with pessimism, seeing it dominated by a powerful culture industry which commercialises and trivialises production, ensuring that it remains essentially conservative and passive. (7) Other scholars, however, have indicated more positive qualities within forms of popular culture, particularly when understood in terms of subcultures, which, they argue, have retained a capacity for original creative expressions which frequently assert resistance to the dominant culture of the wider society.(8)

There is no doubt, however, that the whole debate that has developed around the problem of culture has added a dynamic new dimension to social analysis. Earlier, studies on the development of society tended to place heavy emphasis on economic and political factors, with cultural activity relegated to a secondary position, attractive perhaps, but not regarded as an essential component of historical development in the way that economic or political processes are. Now, however, more realistic recognition is given to the importance of cultural processes in that overall development. This has been stimulated by the specific contributions of the different approaches and ideological positions within the debate, and, more importantly, by the polemic that has taken place between them.

Empirical sociology and anthropology, for example, have focused attention on the multiplicity of forms of cultural manifestations, and this, though frequently resting on description rather than penetrative analysis, has at least stimulated serious interest as to the real significance of diverse cultural practices that were previously dismissed as simple diversion or mere frivolity. On the other hand, a vital contribution has been made by the various lines of Marxist thought. No one has been more influential in this area than Antonio Gramsci, who cast aside the mechanical models of other Marxists in which basic economic factors rigidly determine the nature of all other activity in society, and highlighted instead the influence that ideas and cultural practices have in shaping the very structure of society. Particularly important is his concept of hegemony, the process by which one class asserts its particular values and perceptions as the dominant ones in a given society, therefore helping it to preserve the economic and social structures which benefit it. Notably though, Gramsci argued that such ideological control was never total, for if part of the consciousness of the subordinate classes was determined by dominant class ideology, another part was shaped by their practical experiences of life and work in an exploitative society, and so held revolutionary potential. In this sense, popular cultural expressions can be creative and critical, rather than merely passive. (9)

Such thinking has provided considerable stimulus for the study of the role of ideology in cultural life, and neo-Marxist writers have gone on to study the different spheres of cultural activity and production as arenas of ideological dispute, articulating the desire either to reproduce or transform the existing relations of production that characterise a particular socio-economic formation. Of contemporary Marxist thinkers, special mention must be made of Raymond Williams, whose work added significant new dimensions to cultural theory. One of his major contributions was the analysis of the problematical concepts which underpin all discussion on culture, showing how words like art, class and culture itself have developed and changed through history, parallel to social change. His work also emphasised the analysis of literary works within the broader orbit of cultural studies, establishing the links between those works and the forms of consciousness and types of social structures that prevail within the historical conjuncture at which they are produced. (10)

Studies of cultural phenomena have advanced dramatically during the present century. Cultural practice no longer tends to be viewed as an isolated, capricious activity, peripheral to fundamental socio-economic development, but rather as an integral part of that development. Furthermore, high culture and popular culture are not seen as separate realms, but instead are generally perceived as having a dynamic, dialectical relationship, the interaction, and sometimes tension, between them greatly helping to explain the content, and even in some cases the form, of the expressions which each produces.

iii]   The debate in Brazil

The quest for a national form of expression has been a major dynamic force throughout the historical development of literature in Latin America. It has been an integral part of the affirmation of a distinctly national identity that has arisen from the experience of colonialism and neo-colonialism. Sometimes it has manifested itself in carefully considered theories or even programmes of action, and at others it has been expressed in a more unconscious way, as in the case of many literary works which, without necessarily being intentionally nationalistic, can still be seen to express a latent nativism in their treatment of local themes, human subjects and environment.

Examples of that process can be found in every Latin American country. The case of Peru is particularly striking, for there cultural nationalism has had to confront the problem of integrating two very distinct, even conflicting, cultures; the European and the Indian. In the 1920s, José Carlos Mariátegui addressed himself to the problem of the elaboration of a national literature, recognising that, regardless of their quality, Peru's *indigenista* works were still essentially a bourgeois form of expression with indigenous content, and that only the mass of the population, Indians and mestizos, could ultimately produce an authentic indigenous literature. Nonetheless, he concluded that the early decades of the century had seen writers responding in an increasingly critical way to the colonial patterns of thought which still persisted, and that there were indications of a new generation creating a literature more sensitive to the nation's particular problems and to the life and culture of the Indian population. (11) Some decades later, José María Arguedas, convinced that an authentic Peruvian culture had to be founded on that of the Indian, dealt with the more specific problem of how the erudite writer could penetrate Indian culture in order to write convincingly about it. Indignant at the way many novelists portrayed the Indians, documenting their life at such a distance that their social and cultural practices appeared dramatic or picturesque but essentially incomprehensible, Arguedas wrote arguably the most outstanding Indianist literature of Latin America, based on an intuitive understanding of Quechua cultural tradition that was rooted in his upbringing within an Indian community. (12) Most of Peru's *indigenista* authors did not write from the same experience however. The Indianist stories of Ventura García Calderón and Enrique López Albújar, for example, have many qualities, not least of which is the recognition given to the distinctive attributes of Indian life and culture, which are documented in detail, but the reader is constantly aware of the great distance between the world view of the author and that of his Indian subjects, viewed with paternalism by García Calderón and with sympathetic curiosity by López Albújar. (13)

A similar nationalising tendency can be traced through the literary history of Brazil, where numerous writers have contributed to the debate on the problem of national identity and how authentically Brazilian art forms might be produced. Like his or her Spanish-American counterparts, the Brazilian intellectual has been placed in an acute predicament as a result of the nation's experience of colonialism and neo-colonialism. Brazilian by birth, yet with his or her perceptions, beliefs and modes of expression largely formed by European cultural tradition, the writer has been beset with the need to elaborate an alternative cultural system truly capable of expressing the distinctive qualities of the nation. The result has been a continuous effort to adapt Western models and tendencies to the particular natural and human realities of Brazil, and, arguably, it is that effort which has provided Brazilian literature with its main dynamism. Numerous approaches to literary nationalism have been attempted, involving formal experiments, linguistic innovations or the incorporation of typically Brazilian themes and popular cultural expressions. As might be expected, such deliberate, at times programmed nationalism, has often resulted in artificiality, with the effort to create a work of national content given priority over ideas, arguments, creative imagination and aesthetic quality. Nonetheless, it may be asserted that some of Brazil's finest literature has resulted from the continued attempts by writers to express a national consciousness and document and discuss in their work the particular qualities and problems of Brazilian life. As Antônio Cândido comments however, there is little sense in condemning or extolling this literary nationalism *per se*, for it has arisen as a necessary response to specific historical conditions. (14) Instead, studies must examine critically the way that process has shaped the works that have emerged, identifying both positive qualities added and limitations imposed.

It is within the context of this search for national identity and self-expression that the debate on the question of high culture and popular culture in Brazil must be understood; a debate that has been given particular significance as a result of the nation's imbalance pattern of historical development. Instead of organic socio-economic development from within, the experience of colonialism and dependency has led to fragmentary, uneven growth stimulated mainly from without. As a result, a highly stratified society has emerged, ridden with racial and cultural divisions, acute contrasts between social classes and severe regional imbalances. Such stark divisions obviously make the concept of a national culture extremely problematical.

However, the divide between high and popular culture is not always explicitly acknowledged. So many works on Latin American cultural history concentrate almost exclusively on the high arts, such as erudite literature, painting and music, that the reader might easily forget that such works are the product of the cultural activities and practices of a minority, often a very small minority. (15) Literature offers a very extreme example. One critic, David Haberly, estimates that the active consumers of erudite literature in Brazil did not exceed one percent of the national population between 1822 and 1950, and that even in 1973, Jorge Amado's *Teresa Batista Cansada de Guerra* achieved record sales with approximately 250,000 copies sold, equalling about 0.53 percent of the national population in the over twenty age group. (16) The vast majority of the population, therefore, lives, works and conducts its social relationships within a very different cultural environment. It is an environment where alternative modes of artistic expression prevail, popular forms of dance, drama, carnival, music, poetry and story-telling that have been passed down through the generations, emphasising collective activity rather than individual expression, and oral transmission rather than the written word. Such expression has provided vital source material for those erudite writers seeking to integrate their work into the broader society and culture of their native land. Their problem is finding ways of achieving that by assimilating aspects of popular culture into an erudite work of literature.

Nowhere are social and cultural contrasts more apparent than in the North East of Brazil, *o Nordeste*, formed by the nine states of Bahia, Sergipe, Alagoas, Pernambuco, Paraíba, Rio Grande do Norte, Piauí, Ceará and Maranhão. The first region colonised by the Portuguese, it has a strong elite cultural tradition, jealously guarded by a minority, generally linked to the bourgeoisie and the old landowning aristocracy, whilst the mass of rural and urban poor produce their own, very distinct cultural expressions. Rich folkloric forms of song, dance, poetry and legend have remained vigorous in the North East, particularly in rural areas where they are deeply rooted in traditional, less fluid patterns of life, whilst they have declined or even disappeared in many other regions of the country.

For the first two centuries of the colonial period, the North East was the major centre of economic activity in Brazil, with agricultural production, essentially of sugar, providing considerable prosperity for the oligarchy. By the end of the seventeenth century however, sugar production was in decline and the axis of the colonial economy had moved south. Since then, the growing political, economic and cultural influence of states such as Minas Gerais, São Paulo and Rio de Janeiro has produced a defensive reaction from the dominant classes of the North East, anxious to protect the distinctive culture of their region against the increasing domination of other areas. The result has been the long series of attempts to affirm North Eastern regional identity which are traced in the present work. Through them there runs a line of continuity. In broad terms, all of them attempt to confront the contradictions inflicted on the region as a result of Brazil's particular pattern of development by promoting and reinforcing the particular qualities of North East life and culture in opposition to what is perceived as the expanding cosmopolitanism of the South. It will be seen, however, that the forms within which those efforts have been expressed have varied considerably, developing in accordance with changing perceptions of cultural nationalism, regional identity and the popular culture which so frequently provides the raw material for the affirmation of a distinctive North East identity.

Some North Eastern intellectuals did play a part in political movements pressurising for secession in the nineteenth century, but generally they have limited themselves to asserting the right and need of the North East to maintain a strong degree of cultural autonomy. The tension generated by the conflict of interests between regionalism and broader, national cultural trends, especially when the latter are perceived as emanating from the growing cultural hegemony of the Centre-South, has often manifested itself in polemics between writers of the North East and their counterparts further South. However, regionalist thought need not necessarily negate projects to elaborate a national culture. The majority of North Eastern intellectuals have not seen any fundamental contradiction between regionalism and nationalism, but instead have tended to consider the reinforcement of regional culture as strengthening rather than undermining Brazilian culture as a whole. The characteristic features of the region, they argue, are distinctly native properties which can counterbalance the external cultural tendencies and influences transplanted into Brazil. It is an argument which has a long history, stretching back into the early decades of the last century, and which is still voiced today. In the 1970s, Ariano Suassuna, speaking of the aims of the *Movimento Armorial*, the latest in the line of North Eastern movements promoting the region's culture and which is studied in a later chapter of this work, emphasised the role of himself and other participants in fortifying the bases of Brazilian culture, so that

> "(...) anything that comes to us from abroad becomes, not an influence that smothers us, turning our culture into a mass culture, a flat and monotonous cosmopolitanism, but something that enriches our culture upon being incorporated." (17)

In similar vein, the critic Afrânio Coutinho sees literary regionalism as demonstrating the rich variety of Brazilian culture, but in no way indicating national disintegration, for the divisions are counteracted by strong forces of unity, such as a common language, perceptions and patterns of behaviour. (18) In this sense, the relationship between regionalism and nationalism can be understood as one particular aspect of a major paradox inherent to Latin America as a whole: that of a vast continent which at one level appears unified, but at another, is characterised by sharp contrasts.

Coutinho is one of many critics who emphasise the emergence of a national cultural expression in Brazil as an essentially natural process that began from the earliest moments of colonialism. The cultural inheritance of the mother country was shed as the colonists adapted to the new environment and, of necessity, devised new patterns of life, methods of work and forms of expression. (19) In recent decades however, a number of scholars, such as Dante Moreira Leite, Carlos Guilherme Mota and Darcy Ribeiro, have produced research on the ideological underpinning of notions such as national culture and national character. (20) The dominant classes which have been the beneficiaries of Brazil's unbalanced pattern of development have had to seek ways of justifying and perpetuating the socio-economic processes and structures inherent to it. A wide-ranging and increasingly sophisticated ideology of national culture has resulted, developing through the decades, and functioning to interpret the acute contradictions, tensions and conflicting social forces generated in the course of Brazil's historical development in such a way as to harmonise them with the dominant order. Within this scheme, antagonistic forces are given new definition and value so as to neutralise their threat and integrate them into the overall process of national development. The ideology of national culture promotes the notion of homogeneity and unity under an all-embracing, abstract national identity. It presents an image of all the diverse forces that have emerged in the course of Brazilian history peacefully coexisting as component parts of a natural, harmonious order, and so legitimises existing socio-economic structures and the position of the dominant classes within them.

Moreira Leite and Mota show that this ideological framework has become so powerful and pervasive that it has structured the bulk of work produced in Brazil in the arts and social sciences during the past century. Relatively few intellectuals have managed to free themselves from the conceptual constraints imposed by it, and those that have have often been marginalised, or even forced into exile at times, as a result. Many writers engaged in the task of forging a national literature have participated, consciously or unconsciously, in that process of elaboration of an ideological national culture, and the concepts and patterns of thought integral to it are visible in their work. At times, however, consciousness of social contradictions becomes so sharp as to rupture those ideological concepts, and works of considerable critical tension result. A striking example is da Cunha's *Os Sertões* (1902), referred to in chapter 3, a work which, whilst assimilating the notions of climatic and racial determinism prevalent at the time, still offers one of the most powerful critical studies of Brazilian society ever produced. (21) Da Cunha's observations and experiences in the North East backlands whilst working as a journalist covering military operations against the messianic community of Canudos, contradicted his preconceived notions about the peasants of the region.

Popular culture, the cultural activity of the most deprived sectors of Brazilian society, has been a key element in the ideological process of cultural integration. Despite its own considerable contradictions, it is an alternative culture to that of the dominant classes. It is rooted in, and inseparable from, the particular material conditions of existence of the poorest classes of Brazilian society, and so its expressions are produced, disseminated and consumed according to very specific patterns and moulded by a particular world view. It therefore has the potential to challenge and undermine dominant ideology, and, as will be seen in chapter 4, it was that potential that the radical *Movimento de Cultura Popular* attempted to cultivate in the North East in the early 1960s, in order to raise political awareness. However, other movements, organisations and institutions have played a more conservative role, functioning to patronise and control popular cultural expressions and integrate them into the overall process of national development, neutralising their conflictive quality in the process. It is in this way that popular culture may be understood as an arena of conflict. Within it, a constant struggle is in progress between, one the one hand, the attempts to appropriate popular cultural practices and expressions and incorporate them into a broad scheme of national culture, and on the other, the resistance put up by the social forces behind those practices and expressions.

Many writers of the Brazilian North East have participated in that conflict, some quite consciously, others perhaps drawn in unwittingly through their simple desire to create a literature representative of regional reality. As the cultural expression of the vast majority of the inhabitants of the North East, popular culture has frequently been used to provide the symbols epitomising the distinctive qualities of the region. Implicit in this is the recognition by the writers concerned that their own cultural development and forms of expression have been largely shaped from outside by dominant metropolises, and the feeling that true Brazilian culture is really rooted in the lives of the poor masses, seemingly the sector of the population least affected by cosmopolitan cultural trends. This view has provided the basis for the many arguments that have emerged in the North East over the years proposing that popular culture be defended against the advance of industrial mass culture, so as to conserve it as a unique part of national patrimony. Programmes have even been elaborated outlining means by which the survival of popular cultural expressions might be ensured. Such ideas were central to the thought of Gilberto Freyre in the 1920s, and are also a vital component in that of Ariano Suassuna in the 1990s.

The work of Suassuna, and the *Movimento Armorial* which he founded, is an important phase in a long regionalist tradition in the arts in the Brazilian North East, and one more phase in the continuing debate on the issues of national culture, high culture and popular culture. It must be understood in this historical context, for many of the ideas which motivate Suassuna's work have acquired their deep roots through decades of intellectual and artistic activity in the region. The *Movimento*

Armorial revitalised those ideas, and, like the regionalist movements that preceded it, it made its own original contribution to North East art and literature. The most striking aspect of that contribution was the attempt to fuse erudite literature with North East popular literature, essentially the ballad or *romanceiro* tradition which still survives amongst the poorest sectors of the region's population.

The results of that attempt, exemplified by the plays and novels of Suassuna himself, will be analysed in chapter 4 of this work. However, the contradictions in Suassuna's approach towards popular culture are also significant. The whole topic of popular culture has long been politically sensitive in Brazil, and Suassuna's activities in the field during the period of military dictatorship in the 1970s made him a controversial figure. As political circumstances began to change in Brazil at the end of the decade, with the preparations for the return of democratic government, there began a new phase of the debate on the issue of national culture and the role of popular culture, and criticism of Suassuna mounted. The problematic nature of the debate was highlighted when in 1981, expressing disillusion, he withdrew from public life and stopped writing for several years.

The changing political circumstances in Brazil, and corresponding changes in the cultural environment, have presented new challenges to the writer, but also new opportunities. Alternative ways of working with popular culture continue to be sought, expressing, as before, different political positions and different strategies for confronting the ongoing process of transformation of all forms of popular cultural expression. Regionalism in Brazil has undoubtedly changed in recent decades in response to the expansion of the mass media and the culture industry throughout the country, but it remains a significant force in Brazilian art and literature. One of the most acclaimed Brazilian novels of the 1980s, João Ubaldo Ribeira's *Viva o Povo Brasileiro*, (1984), re-examines the question of national identity and explores the myths that have served to construct it. Significantly, Ribeira returns to such familiar regionalist themes as messianism and *candomblé* as he highlights the contradictions that have existed throughout Brazilian history between national myths and the experience and aspirations of the poor masses of the North East. The late 1980s also saw Ariano Suassuna resume his writing career, attempting to complete the trilogy of Armorial novels which he left interrupted in 1981. Amid the changes, continuities are to be found. Literary regionalism continues to produce a variety of ideologically divergent works, and the assimilation of popular forms of expression remains an important part of that creative process. Above all, the relationship between the erudite and the popular continues to be contradictory and controversial.

NOTES

1   R. Pascal, *The German Sturm und Drang* (Manchester University Press, Manchester, 1955), pp.71-86

2   V.G. Kiernan, 'Wordsworth and the People', in *Marxists on Literature*, edited by David Craig (Pelican, Harmondsworth, Middx, 1975), pp.174-175

3   Matthew Arnold, *Culture and Anarchy* (Cambridge University Press, Cambridge, 1984)

4   F.R. Leavis, *Mass Civilisation and Minority Culture* (The Minority Press, Cambridge, 1930)

5   José Ortega y Gasset, *La rebelión de las masas* (Espasa-Calpe Argentina SA, Buenos Aires, 1941)

6   Richard Hoggart, *The Uses of Literacy* (Penguin, Harmondsworth, Middx, 1963)

7   M. Jay, *The Dialectical Imagination: A History of the Frankfurt School and the Institute of Social Research 1923-50* (Little Brown, Boston, 1973)

8   See, for example, S. Hall and T. Jefferson (eds), *Resistance Through Rituals* (Hutchinson, London, 1976), passim

9   Antonio Gramsci, *Selections from Prison Notebooks* (Lawrence and Wishart, London, 1982), pp.12-13 and 55-60

10 Raymond Williams, *Keywords* (Fontana, Glasgow, 1979); and *The Country and the City* (Chatto and Windus, London, 1973)

11 José Carlos Mariátegui, *Siete ensayos de interpretación de la realidad peruana* (Editorial Universitaria, Santiago de Chile, 1955), pp.246-260

12 José María Arguedas, *Formación de una cultura nacional indoamericana* (Siglo Veintiuno, México DF, 2nd ed, 1977), pp.183-197

13 Ventura García Calderón, *La venganza del cóndor* (Mundo Latino, Madrid, 1922); Enrique López Albújar, *Cuentos andinos* (Juan Mejía Baca, Lima, 1965)

14 Antônio Cândido, *Formação da Literatura Brasileira*, Vol 1, (Martins, São Paulo, 1964), p.29

15 See for example: F. de Azevedo, *Brazilian Culture* (Hafner, New York, 1971); Jean Franco, *The Modern Culture of Latin America* (Pall Mall, London, 1967); C.C. Griffen (ed), *Concerning Latin American Culture* (Russell and Russell, New York, 1967)

16 D. Haberly, *Three Sad Races* (Cambridge University Press, Cambridge, 1983), p.5

17 Ariano Suassuna, *O Movimento Armorial* (Editora Universitária, Universidade Federal de Pernambuco, Recife, 1974), p.63

Introduction

18   See: Afrânio Coutinho, *A Tradição Afortunada: O Espírito de Nacionalidade na Crítica Brasileira* (José Olympio, Rio de Janeiro, 1968), and Conceito da Literatura Brasileira (Vozes, Petrópolis, 1981)

19   Afrânio Coutinho, *Conceito*, passim

20   See: Dante Moreira Leite, *O Caráter Nacional Brasileiro* (Livraria Pioneira Editora, São Paulo, 1976); Carlos Guilherme Mota, *Ideologia da Cultura Brasileira* (Editora Ática, São Paulo, 1980); Darcy Ribeiro, *Os Brasileiros: 1 Teoria do Brasil* (Vozes, Petrópolis, 1978)

21   Euclides da Cunha, *Os Sertões*, in Vol 2 of *Obras Completas*, edited by A. Coutinho (José Aguilar, Rio de Janeiro, 1966)

2
POPULAR POETS AND TALES OF THE PEOPLE

i]   The popular culture of North East Brazil

As was indicated in the Introduction, the term popular culture has been used in a number of different senses in Brazil, varying according to ideological position and historical circumstances, and one objective of this study will be to explore those differences, and the divergent approaches to questions of culture that they have produced from erudite writers.

It will be seen that some of the approaches have been sharply antagonistic, at times resulting in bitter disputes between writers and scholars involved with popular culture. The polemical nature of concepts of *cultura popular* must always be borne in mind. Indeed, it has frequently formed part of political programmes in Brazil. Governments have manipulated concepts of popular culture in the process of developing cultural policies aimed at promoting national integration, including the military regime that governed between 1964 and 1985, as will be seen in a later chapter. On the left, some writers developed the notion of popular culture as a means for raising the political consciousness of the subaltern sectors of Brazilian society. Within this scheme, many popular artistic traditions maintained by those sectors are rejected as alienated and reactionary, and what is proposed instead is a politically revolutionary popular culture that will be rooted in the aspirations and desire for change of the poor and oppressed. The result is a view of popular culture as it should be, according to the political perspective of the writer, rather than an attempt to understand it as it actually is. (1)

In addition, usage of the term in Brazil frequently overlaps with those of *cultura de massa* and *folclore*, further hindering definition. On the one hand, popular culture is used to refer to cultural forms, largely disseminated by the mass media, which are seen to be imposed on the subaltern classes, creating homogeneity by subsuming attempts at independent or dissenting expression. On the other, popular culture as folklore generally refers to the cultural processes that are normally associated with more communal, traditionally organised societies, such as peasant communities. Unlike mass culture, folk culture is seen as a set of traditional practices, developed, shared and perpetuated by a community for its own use. (2) However, because the emphasis is on tradition, folk practices tend to be seen as vestiges of a bygone era, in need of protection and preservation, thus denying the vitality and dynamism of expressions of popular culture. It will be seen in a later chapter that that view has featured prominently in some of the regionalist movements in the North East of Brazil, which have looked back nostalgically on the past. A flexible approach is clearly needed in examining the myriad of popular cultural expressions in Brazil, which are constantly changing their form, significance, and systems of production, distribution and reception in response to broader social, economic and cultural changes. A rigid definition must be avoided if that essential dynamism, and the contradictions that it generates, are to be understood.

In clarifying the meaning of popular culture in North East Brazil as used in this study, we can begin with a basic proposition: that the term will here refer to all cultural activity of those classes from that region that are economically and socially subordinate, and that the practices and products which result from that activity are initially developed by those classes to meet their own needs and give expression to their own values, concerns and experiences. Essentially, the poorest sectors of society are both the producers and consumers of the resulting cultural expressions. For some cultural critics, this is the vital distinction between popular culture, produced by the poor for the use of the poor, and mass culture, which is produced by a minority for sale to a mass of the population, composed of all social classes. (3) However, such a rigid division is simplistic, and an important qualification is needed. Popular artistic expressions traditionally associated with the rural interior of North East Brazil are constantly appearing in new locations, where the process of production is modified and a new public found. There are, for example, many popular singers or *cantadores* who have long sung improvised verses in fairs and market places throughout the North East, collecting money where they can, who in recent years have found new audiences and greater financial reward by performing on radio and recording their work. The popular poets who are dealt with in this chapter have traditionally printed the cheap leaflets of their verses on small handpresses for sale in the streets and markets of the region, but now, with production costs too high for some poets to meet, cultural and educational institutions, seeking to promote popular arts and crafts, sometimes arrange and finance the printing. Such forms of expression are highly fluid, constantly adapting to new circumstances, so that, with any given form of popular art, several different types of production and consumption may be in operation at the same time. Clearly, such differences are likely to produce concomitant differences in the thematic content of the resulting work. It will be seen that frequent attempts have been made by some scholars and writers to distinguish between those popular forms deemed to be 'authentic' and others perceived to be corrupted or distorted by economic or social factors, but such an approach makes impossible any understanding of the process of continual change that is a vital characteristic of popular culture.

Many cultural critics have turned to Gramsci, and most

specifically his concept of hegemony, as a way of dealing with the transformations and contradictions evident in forms of popular expression like those mentioned here. This approach sees popular culture as neither purely oppositional culture from below, nor as a dominant culture imposed from above, but as a space or site of struggle between dominant and subordinate ideological perspectives, values and cultural forms. This forms the basis for one of the most thorough studies of Latin American popular culture produced to date, by W. Rowe and V. Schelling, who, in their analysis of a wide range of cultural expressions from the region, highlight the role played by culture in either contesting or justifying social relationships, and the link between culture and relationships of power. They conclude that, despite its contradictions, popular culture can still retain an emancipatory force. (4)

Many of these points will be discussed as we look in detail at the popular poetry of the Brazilian North East, a form of literature with a long tradition, now undergoing significant changes which are seen as degeneration by some, and inevitable development by others.

ii]   **Origins: the *romanceiro* tradition and the emergence of the *folheto***

The popular poetry, legends, tales and songs of North East Brazil are essentially the product of a centuries old oral tradition, still maintained in the region today. Since the late nineteenth century however, popular ballads have been printed in the form of chap-books, or *folhetos*. It is this form that will be the main object of study in this chapter. Since the whole process of production, distribution and consumption of the *folheto* has long been an integral part of the social life of the poorest sectors of North Eastern society, particularly the rural communities of the interior, it offers a penetrating insight into the perceptions and social experience of those sectors, through an interweaving of myth, fable, popular history, anecdote and critical commentary. The dynamism that this process of production had attained by the 1950s, clearly shown by the number of professional poets and print-shops in the North East, and the volume of *folheto* sales, demonstrates its success as a means of popular expression. That success has meant that the *folheto* has attracted increasing attention from erudite writers, as mentioned in the Introduction.

The origins of the poetic tradition embodied in the *folheto* can be traced right back to the epic poetry that was common in many parts of Medieval Europe. Known as *cantares de gesta* in Spain, this was a poetry essentially aristocratic in character, consisting of long, narrative eulogies to the exploits of chivalrous heroes. Menéndez Pidal argues that, with the decay of feudalism in Spain, and emergence of the mercantilistic nation state, this increasingly anachronistic heroic poetry declined, leaving behind certain formal traditions and thematic fragments which were incorporated into the newly developing ballads. Shorter, more immediate and tailored for a wider audience, these ballads were passed on orally, constantly refashioned through a process of addition and omission, to suit the purposes of more extensive sectors of the population. (5) There thus evolved a popular poetic tradition, looked upon by the masses as their common property; their own system of communication through which to express their perception of the world around them, and debate the problems it posed for them. C.C. Smith notes how, through popularisation, the Iberian ballad developed a critical quality, often expressing dissent against the established moral and social order in a cynical or satirical tone. (6) By the sixteenth century, this popular poetry was being transcribed into simple printed leaflets in many parts of Europe - *pliegos sueltos* (Spain), *Littérature de colportage* (France) and *Literatura de cego* (Portugal) - establishing a dynamic and enduring popular tradition, easily adapted in Brazil during the nineteenth century. Whilst popular memory and oral transmission preserved this poetic tradition for the poor, the sixteenth century also saw many attempts by erudite writers to imitate the popular ballad, often so studiously that their poems, in the words of J.G. Cummins:

> (...) are in some cases indistinguishable in form, theme
> and style from the lyrics which they consciously
> emulate. (7)

So, although the ballad, or *romanceiro*, tradition is essentially of anonymous, folk origin, the interweaving of the erudite with the popular has been a recurring feature of its development through the centuries. This situation obviously makes the usage of the term popular semantically problematical at times, and highlights the inadequacy of relying on a purely intrinsic study of such texts in order to arrive at an interpretation of their significance. Only by studying them in their social context, with particular attention to production, distribution and consumption, can one reach the wider understanding necessary to draw fundamental distinctions between popular and erudite literature, and recognise their conflicting qualities.

Carried to the New World by the Spanish and Portuguese colonists, the popular ballad tradition began a new phase in its process of development and diffusion, undergoing modifications appropriate to the new environment. Different regions produced new variations, such as the varieties of the *corrido* found in Argentina, Mexico and Nicaragua, and fusion of the European inheritance with local themes and perspectives. Once again, such ballads, passed on orally among the populace, either through song or verse recitation, and thus continually being altered in the process, inspired a number of erudite literary works, such as *Martin Fierro* (1872), by José Hernández, based on the anonymous oral poetry of the Argentinean gaucho.

It is the work of Luis da Câmara Cascudo that provides the most thorough documentation of how this development of a popular literary tradition proceeded in Brazil. Although other scholars have pointed out the links between Brazil's *folheto* of popular verse and the earlier forms of pamphlet literature found in various parts of Europe (8), Câmara Cascudo rightly emphasises the Iberian roots of the tradition, tracing how stories such as *Donzela Teodora* and *Roberto do Diabo*, long popular in Spain and Portugal, were appropriated by Brazil's rural population, and modified through the years, in details of content, versification and dialect, in accordance with local taste. (9) Popular Brazilian versions eventually found their way into print with the *folhetos* of North Eastern poets like Leandro Gomes de Barros and João Martins de Athayde. (10) Alongside these traditional ballads imported from Europe, others of native creation emerged, some still borrowing heavily from the European sources, but others of much more independent creation, like the ballads composed by the *vaqueiros*, based on their experiences tending the herds.(11) In his *Literatura Oral no Brasil*, Câmara Cascudo shows how numerous different sources, both external and internal, provided elements that became fused over time, constantly reshaping existing popular stories and poems, and creating new ones. (12)

It was among Brazil's rural population that the popular poetic tradition took root. With the territory organised on the basis of a plantation system of agricultural production from the early days of colonialism, the patterns of rural life that emerged as a result, with scattered, relatively isolated communities, close knit and existing on the basis of collective forms of work and social relations, embodied their own particular expressions of folk culture. Such expressions, therefore, developed as an integral and inseparable element of a particular way of life. Traditional crafts, today simply seen as quaint pastimes, were then natural work practices of the community, and their art forms were ritual celebrations, an affirmation of their vision of the world, and of their specific cultural identity. Numerous sources were assimilated by the collective mind, reshaped to its own needs, and handed on as part of the community's cultural patrimony, thereby serving to reinforce the values and customs held dear by its members.

As has been seen, the popular ballad, first oral, and then in the printed *folheto* form, was a dynamic element in that process. It constituted, not simply an instrument for entertainment, but a natural part of the daily, working life of the rural population, and a medium through which to affirm the values that underpinned it. In answering the question as to how so many traditional stories were able to live on generation after generation, Câmara Cascudo states that:

> They brought to the people the living sentiments of their spiritual desires. In those poor pages they relived the enchantment of virtue and the punishment of detested vices. There was no other literature which could rival it in order to dispute its monopoly. (13)

Life for the peasant population was undoubtedly oppressive. The suffocating socio-economic structure of rural Brazil was maintained by the brutal despotism of the landowners, and this, complemented by the more specific abuse of power associated with the relations of dependency that characterised the patriarchal plantation system, severely limited the peasants' possibilities of instigating social action under their own initiative. Too often nostalgic romanticism has painted over the poverty and exploitation that was always part and parcel of traditional rural life in Brazil. Nevertheless, the nature of that life, and of the work practices at its centre, did allow the population a greater degree of control over its cultural behaviour and production than is the case with other subordinate social sectors. Furthermore, it might be argued that the difficulty in initiating concrete social action made autonomous cultural expression all the more important as a means for articulating protests, interests and aspirations. (14)

In rural Brazil, cultivating the fields or tending cattle, working solitarily or in small groups, relatively free of direct supervision, was conducive to the recitation of stories, poems and anecdotes, whilst the broader, communal way of life reinforced the significance of such cultural practices as an expression of collective perspectives and a collective identity. Work and cultural practice were inseparable, exemplified by the *mutirão*, when peasants, relying heavily on subsistence agriculture, would work collectively on one another's plots, and then celebrate the days work with a night of song, dance, stories and poems. (15) Furthermore, for a long time this degree of autonomous cultural expression was relatively unhindered by direct intervention from state institutions and organisations, mainly because the state machinery remained too weak to exert its full authority in the remoter rural areas, and was thus obliged to devolve its power to major local landowners, or *coroneis*.

The preservation for so long of that same basic socio-economic structure in the North East, and with it of many aspects of traditional rural life and work, largely explains how old forms of folk expression, like popular poetry, continued to flourish in the region, whilst declining in other areas of Brazil where the process of change was more rapid. For the rural inhabitants of the North East, illiterate, often isolated and lacking other means of communication, the recital of poems, stories and news became a vital aspect of life, interpreting their local environment and linking it to the wider world. As Câmara Cascudo asserts, anonymity was always a crucial characteristic of this oral literature, with any traces of individual authorship being eliminated in the course of transmission, so that it was regarded as collective property, created and propagated by everyone, and not the personal work of one individual.(16)

Nevertheless, many popular poets or *cantadores* did achieve fame in the North East, mainly through their skill and virtuosity in composing improvised verses in duels, or *desafios*, with other poets. Such poets travelled round the plantations and villages of the rural interior of the North East, singing and challenging rivals to duels. Monetary reward was rare, and they continued to rely on work on the land or with cattle for their sustenance. Robert Rowland has traced how this situation began to change at the end of the nineteenth century, with the gradual emergence of fully professional poets and *cantadores*, and sees it as a consequence of the social dislocation in the rural North East that was induced by external economic changes. Pressure to meet the increasing demand of the growing industrial centres led landowners to increase productivity by taking over more land for cash crops or pasture, at the expense of subsistence plots for the peasantry, and by demanding more labour from the peasant families living on their land. The result was a decline in the living standard of the peasant, for any increase in money income derived from his extra paid labour was swallowed up by price rises, and his access to the traditional outlet of subsistence farming became increasingly limited. (17) Under such pressures, more and more peasants began to seek other forms of livelihood, some emigrating to the towns in search of work, and others turning to banditry or messianism. Poetry and *cantoria* provided another alternative, as poets began to discover that the donations they could collect at a *desafio*, or the income received from the sale of cheap *folhetos* of their poems, could compete very favourably with a living scraped from the land. This is a significant point, showing that for the rural poor of the North East popular poetry is not just an amusing pastime, but rather a craft or profession, as valid as any other, or as Antônio Arantes describes:

(...) a profession which in that area is socially recognised, being the object of expectations, sanctions and specific representations. (18)

The date of the publication of the first *folheto* of popular literature in Brazil is disputed. It is probable that they were produced occasionally in newspaper print-shops from the mid-nineteenth century onwards. However, it was in the context of this process of professionalisation of the peasant-poet that the *folheto* became firmly established as a popular art form in the North East, and there is general agreement that by the last few decades of the nineteenth century poets like Leandro Gomes de Barros and Silvino Pirauá de Lima were producing pamphlets of their work in small print-shops in the region, and making a living by travelling around towns and villages selling them.

Obviously, the transcription into print of an oral tradition did imply certain changes in the development of the popular literature concerned. The process of communication itself increased in complexity with the introduction of the printed word to complement and reinforce the traditional oral transmission by recitation or song. More significantly, printing obviously entailed a far more sophisticated procedure of production. The need for capital to pay for printouts, and for a more efficient process of distribution and commercialisation as the popularity of the *folheto* grew throughout the North East, led to the emergence of specialised publishers (*editores*) and travelling salesmen (*folheteiros*), both deriving their livelihood largely from popular poetry. Nevertheless, this was an expansion and a development of the existing popular literary tradition, rather than a radical break. Essentially, printing merely complemented the oral tradition underlying it, rather than replaced it. Although Câmara Cascudo states that the *folheto* gradually drew away from oral literature, because printing gave the material concerned a fixed, static form that contrasted with the ever changing versions resulting from oral transmission, (19) there is considerable evidence to show that, in fact, the printed pamphlet developed in close, constant interaction with popular oral tradition. Orally transmitted stories, poems, anecdotes and news items continued to be a major source of inspiration for *folhetos*, which, being destined for rural communities where the majority were still illiterate, were still written for the purpose of being read out aloud. The traditional rhyme and metre patterns of oral verse were retained in the *folheto* with that intention in mind. The poet or *folheteiro* would recite his *folheto* aloud in the market place, crucial for stimulating interest and attracting potential customers, and the peasants who purchased a copy would take it back to their villages for communal, rather than private, reading. Manuel Diégues Júnior describes this procedure:

> The members of the family would gather after dinner, seated round a lamp. The lack of electricity meant that the lamp was the focal point for the family: parents, children, brothers and sisters, cousins, etc. And reading the pamphlet stories or poems would become the motive for the family gathering. The literate member of the family would be the reader. And in that way the story would be passed on. (20)

In fact, these readings did not just involve members of the family, but included other members of the community as well.

Its close proximity to the oral tradition was thus a vital factor in the development of the *folheto* as a communal art, belonging to the culture of a whole, and extensive, sector of the Brazilian population. Although to some extent enjoying special prestige in their community on account of their wider knowledge and literacy, or semi literacy, the peasant poet remains very much an integral member of it, sharing common origins, experience and economic and social position. Even today, when the production of the *folheto* has changed in significant ways and it has spread to new audiences in different environments, a considerable number of poets in the North East still trace their origins to peasant communities of the rural interior. (21) In fact, in marked contrast to the erudite writer, his role of poet has traditionally reinforced his position and participation in the community rather than distancing him from it, for, as will be seen, the thematic content of his work, and its process of diffusion among its public, has long served to re-emphasise the common pattern and experience of life linking him with others of his social class.

iii] The development of the *folheto* tradition and the traditional *folheto*

It will be shown later that the patterns of production, distribution and consumption of the *folheto* have changed significantly in recent decades, but the form developed strongly in the course of this century to meet the needs of a traditional public, composed mainly of low-paid workers and subsistence farmers of the same background as the poet himself. Today, those sectors continue to provide a significant, although reduced, percentage of *folheto* consumers. If the poet was to sell his work to that public, it was vital for him to remain keenly responsive to their perceptions, tastes and aspirations. The oral tradition of such communities was vital for that purpose, as a means for communicating the common attitudes and problems of its members within a shared, instantly recognised system of language and symbols. Thus, even in *folheto* form, popular literature in the Brazilian North East has continued to be held, not so much as the product of individual creativity, but rather as a common property, a common inheritance open to the participation of all, that reaffirms the values and identity of the sectors concerned. The emergence of the *folheto* did not automatically bring with it a new concept of personal, individualised creativity. It is true that poets have often complained of plagiarism and abuse of their rights of authorship by unscrupulous *editores*, (22) but this is generally motivated by the need to secure and protect the income from their work, rather than by a desire for public recognition for their artistic achievements. In fact, as one source affirms, it has been quite common practice for a poet to sell his rights of authorship outright to an *editor*, losing with the transaction any rights to have his name on the cover of the resulting *folheto*:

> The majority of our popular poets never appear to have given great importance as to whether or not their *folhetos* carried their own names. Some did have the custom of printing their names on them, but most did not. Those who paid to have their folhetos printed could put their name on the cover. If they sold their rights of authorship however, their name would generally disappear and only that of the printer-publisher would remain on the chap-book. This did not greatly concern the poet, for the most important thing for him was that his *folhetos* should sell and provide him with his livelihood. The fact that he was the sole creator of that literary work does not appear to have been uppermost in his mind, nor in those of his readers. (23)

The same source goes on to suggest that it has been the growing interest shown by scholars and erudite writers in popular literature, analysing it according to formal literary values of individual style and sensibility, that has stimulated an increasing preoccupation over authorship on the part of some popular poets in recent decades. (24)

Some poets were able to save enough capital to invest in a small handpress with which to print their own work, plus the *folhetos* of other poets, thus becoming *editores*. A few, like João Martins de Athayde and José Bernardo da Silva, were even able eventually to establish quite large print-shops, employing a few hands, which became the centre of publication for scores of other poets. These crude workshops, technically very simple, long dominated the production of cheap *folhetos* of popular verse in the North East. The vast majority of poets have been unable to own their own means of publication however, and so have to rely on the *editores*, who, as has been seen, were traditionally other poets of greater resources. Those able to afford it might pay a lump sum to have a pre-determined number of copies printed, usually a few thousand, but for most such financial resources were out of the question. They therefore had to come to an alternative arrangement with the *editor*, usually what is referred to as payment by *conga*. The poet handed over his poem to the editor to publish, receiving as payment a fixed number of copies, or *conga*, usually about 10% of the first printout, which he could sell himself. In this transaction, generally a simple verbal agreement, the poet would frequently lose all rights of authorship to the *editor*, who was free to sell the bulk of the printout himself, and run off subsequent copies for sale as he pleased. Such a transaction strongly favoured the *editor* and, inevitably, the poets quite frequently complained of exploitation. Nonetheless, the significant fact is that this traditional system of *folheto* production, still existing on a very limited scale, has always been essentially a local process, centred in workshops owned and controlled by members of the same social origins as the poet and his public. Within this scheme, the same social class directs publication, controlling decisions such as how many copies to print and what format and design to use, even though external constraints, such as limitation of resources and censorship by the authorities, might considerably influence these. Generally working on a tight budget, *editores* would always attempt to ensure that they only printed *folhetos* that would receive the approval of the traditional public, and so register good sales, sometimes testing out the market first by printing a small number of copies of a *folheto* and seeing how well they sold in the market, before risking a larger printout. (25) This would act as another mechanism for keeping *folheto* production responsive to the tastes and needs of its intended public.

Likewise, the process of distribution of the *folheto* was for a long time controlled by the same sectors. *Folheteiros* or resellers, very often also poets, would buy *folhetos* in bulk from a print-shop (*folhetaria*), and travel around markets and towns in the North East selling them at a small profit. Most poets have been *folheteiros* at some stage, particularly early on, and this experience of direct contact with the public, reading out *folhetos* aloud and encouraging sales, would serve to keep him in close touch with his customers, maintaining the immediate rapport that has long been a crucial characteristic of his art, and enabling him to develop his skill with the popular dialect, metre and rhyme patterns that it entails. Typically, the *folheteiro*, having attracted an audience, would recite a poem, adding comments, jokes and gestures to heighten interest and tension, and stop a few verses from the end, calling upon people to buy a copy to discover how the story finished. Public performance has therefore traditionally been a crucial aspect of *folheto* poetry. The whole act of recital and selling would depend on an affirmation of the fellow feeling existing between the *folheteiro* and the audience, and of their common identity with the values and experiences expounded by the poem. Antônio Arantes emphasises this point:

> (...) being able to recite *folheto* poetry is not simply a question of having the ability to read. One has to know how to do it, and do it in an entertaining way. It's important therefore, if not essential, that the readers and the public possess the same sense of humour, the same social base and similar views of the world. This is true for both poets and resellers. (26)

Unlike the erudite writer, therefore, the traditional *poeta-folheteiro* is not a special individual separated from the rest by his particular skill and creativity, but on the contrary, has depended for his success on his ability to reaffirm his links with his public, forged by shared experience and perception. In this sense, such orality has long continued to be a vital aspect of popular poetry, even in the form of a printed pamphlet. This whole process of direct communication would be reinforced by the frequent participation of the audience, making comments and jokes, cheering and requesting particular themes. Like the *cantador*, the *poeta-folheteiro* became an integral part of the typical open market of the North East town, where the lower income sectors of the population would purchase most of their necessities. The sale of the *folheto* thus developed as a social activity, intimately linked to other aspects of the daily life of the poor.

It is significant to note that, in further contrast with the case of erudite literature, the traditional pattern of production of the *folheto* is not divided into a series of highly specialised and clearly differentiated activities. Most small *editores* are also poets, and most poets are *folheteiros*. Quite a few individuals have worked at all three tasks at different stages of their lives, like Leandro Gomes de Barros and Francisco Chagas Batista. (27) Family labour would frequently be used to help with the tasks of printing, folding the *folhetos* together and selling. A poet would therefore be quite likely to participate in the whole production process of a *folheto*, from its writing, through its printing, right up to the final act of promotion and sale in the market place. (28) To repeat, this whole process traditionally has been organised and controlled by the same social class. At its height in the 1940s and 1950s it achieved considerable dynamism. There were scores of print-shops of varying size throughout the North East, a complex network of resellers, numbering hundreds, and sales far exceeding those of erudite novels. To quote one source:

> In that decade [1940-50], José Bernardo da Silva's print-shop published a minimum of 12,000 *folhetos* per day. These are astonishing numbers if compared with the numbers of copies printed for editions of erudite literary works. (29)

Today, the traditional public for the *folheto*, the poorest sectors of North East society from which most poets themselves originate, has been joined by new middle-class consumers. For the traditional public, the *folheto* is still one of the few forms of literature with which he or she is likely to have contact, and, in the era before the spread of radio and television throughout the North East, was probably the most vital medium between their own immediate world and the wider world outside. It is in this sense that the *folheto* has frequently been described as a form of popular journalism, reinterpreting external events according to the world view of the rural and urban poor. Some poets have specialised in this type of journalistic poetry, like José Soares (1914-1981), from Paraíba, who called himself the *poeta-repórter*, and who produced numerous *folhetos* based on news items, such as *A Cheia do Capibaribe*, relating the effects of floods in Recife in 1977, and *Acabou a Gasolina? Ou a Gasolina Acabou?*, about the shortage of petrol in Brazil the same year. He sold 60,000 copies of a *folheto* on the resignation of President Quadros in 1961, and another 40,000 of a *folheto* on the assassination of President Kennedy in 1963. (30) The best selling *folhetos* were apparently those dealing with the death of Getúlio Vargas, one, written by Francisco Sales Areda, reputedly selling over 300,000. (31) Even with the radio and television, however, *folhetos* of such events have sold rapidly and in quantity, demonstrating that it is not merely news of the event that attracts the public, but rather the way in which the news is conveyed, written within a literary tradition and interpreted according to a world view with which it identifies. As one poet asserts, the *folheto* has served as the peasant's own system of communication:

> The people of the backlands learn of important events via the radio, or through being told about them by others, but they only actually believe them when they appear in a *folheto* (...) If the *folheto* confirms that they happened, then they happened. (32)

Consequently, alongside this mediatory role, the *folheto* has also served to confirm and re-emphasise shared experience and perceptions of daily community life, through the repetition of commonly known and instantly recognisable conventions of theme, language, symbol and metaphor. All these can be endlessly repeated in rearranged forms to confirm the group's cultural identity and values. The traditional public thus recognises the *folheto* as something related intimately to their concrete lives, helping them to define them in terms of their past and present, and debating the problems that affect them daily. It is in this sense that it can be described as a communal rather than an individual product. Having purchased the *folheto*, the consumer would take it back home, where it would normally be read collectively, and then kept for future readings. Often, members of the community would memorise it, at least in part, and a process of oral transmission would start again.

The *folheto*, therefore, has long been a pole of identity for the poor of the North East, and its content expresses first and foremost collective attitudes towards their physical and social environment, and the problems it poses for them at all levels. Entertainment is certainly one of its key attributes, but its significance for its public goes far deeper than this. An infinite array of sources has been used by the poet, borrowing from the traditional stories and legends of oral literature, seen in such *folhetos* as *A História de Carlos Magno e Os Doze Pares de França* by João Lopes Freire, and *O Cavaleiro Roldão* by Antônio Eugênio da Silva, and from the endless stream of contemporary news, tales and anecdotes, national and international. All such material is refashioned by the poet to give it direct significance for his public. As Ariano Suassuna states:

> (...) whilst maintaining its Brazilian roots, the *folheto* does
> not shut out what comes from outside. On the contrary,
> it welcomes everything, from the tales of oral tradition
> to the theatrical pieces performed in circuses, or the
> films shown in cinemas which the poets occasionally see,
> and which are recreated in the same lively and unique
> way as the most traditional stories are. (33)

Some scholars analysing the thematic content of *folheto* verse have established a basic distinction between traditional themes, most of which can be traced back to the Iberian romance, and contemporary themes concerned with events and personalities that have captured the imagination of the mass of the North East population, or with issues and problems that it confronts in daily life. The work of Manuel Diégues Júnior serves as an example:

> (...) In both the traditional ballad and todays *literatura de*

31

cordel, we can highlight the existence of two fundamental types of theme: the traditional themes, which have been passed on from the *romanceiro*, initially conserved in the memory and today transmitted through *folhetos* - and in this category we can place such narratives as those which deal with Charlemagne, the twelve knights, Oliveiros, Joan of Arc, Malasartes, etc; and the themes based on events and affairs which have occurred at a given time and have made an impact on the population (...) today, with modern means of communication, events with an international repercussion are also included. (34)

It will be argued later that the dynamism of the *folheto* as a form of expression and of communication can largely be explained by the ability it has retained through the decades to respond to new problems affecting the poet's community, making use of new sources and assimilating new themes. There is an abundance of *folhetos* dealing with contemporary issues such as the exploitation of rural workers, inflation, migration from the countryside to the cities and the difficulties of urban life. These will be discussed later. However, as will be seen in chapter 4, Suassuna has tended to ignore such contemporary social themes and has concentrated his attention either on popular poetry linked directly to the medieval European romance, or that which recalls earlier periods of *sertão* history, such as the numerous *folhetos* dealing with banditry (*cangaço*) and messianism.

Of particular interest to Suassuna is the popular verse of religious content, that with the longest tradition of all. Ballads and stories relating the lives of Christ, the Virgin and the Saints, recounting miracles and narrating tales of moral example flourished in Medieval Europe, and such themes constantly recurred in new forms, written and oral, for centuries afterwards, and became firmly established in Brazil during the colonial period. Despite their differing content, all such work served to extol Christian faith and values and condemn what was perceived as immoral behaviour and profanity. Many *folhetos* in North East Brazil have developed this theme, often recreating biblical material. Manuel Caboclo e Silva, for example, a poet from Pernambuco, opens his *folheto* entitled *A Sentença de Jesus e A Morte dos Apóstolos*, instructing the reader in the example of Christ and his twelve apostles, with the following verses:

> Olhai as aves do céu
> pela janela da vida
> tanta maldade dos homens

tanta fúria desmedida!
Açoitaram o Bom Jesus
morreu cravado na cruz
com tão grande sofrimento
depois subiu para o céu
coberto com um fino véu
diz o Novo Testamento.

A sentença de Jesus
já estava preparada
escrita em letras de arame
com testemunha assinada
quando reinava o Império
do governo de Tibério
fez Herodes o movimento
da fonte do paganismo
sofrendo o cristianismo
diz o Novo Testamento. (35)

Look at the birds in the sky, through the window of life. So much evil by man, and so much rage! They flogged good Jesus. He died nailed to the cross, suffering greatly, and afterwards he rose to heaven, covered with a fine veil, according to the New Testament. Jesus' sentence was already prepared, written in harsh letters. His destiny was already sealed, during the reign of the empire governed by Tiberius, when Herod, acting like a pagan, made Christianity suffer, according to the New Testament. (35)

In similar vein, another Pernambuco poet, José Pacheco da Rocha, opens his poem, *Os Sofrimentos de Cristo*, with a request for Divine inspiration to help him convey in his work the example of Christ:

Oh! Jesus meu Redentor
dos altos Céus infinitos
abençoai meus escritos
por vosso divino amor
leciona um trovador
com divina inspiração
para que vossa paixão
seja descrita em clamores
desde o princípio das dôres
até a ressurreição.

Dentro do livro sagrado

São Marcos com perfeição
nos faz a revelação
de Jesus crucificado
foi prêso e foi arrastado
cuspido pelos judeus
por um apóstolo dos seus
covardemente vendido
viu-se amarrado e ferido
nas cordas dos fariseus. (36)

*Oh! Jesus my redeemer, in the high infinite heavens, bless my writing, with
your divine love. Give instruction to the ballad singer, with divine inspiration,
so that your martyrdom can be described with fervour, from the first sufferings
to the resurrection. In the sacred book, Saint Mark, with perfection, tells us
about Jesus being crucified. He was imprisoned and then dragged along, spat
upon by the Jews, having been cowardly betrayed by one of his apostles. He was
tied up by the Pharisees' ropes, and wounded. (36)*

The betrayal, trial and execution of Christ are described in the verses that
follow, ending with the resurrection.

In addition to such traditional religious material, local sources
have frequently been employed by poets to convey the same simple
Christian messages. New examples are found within Brazil itself to
promote the values of Christian life and the comfort and strength of
religious faith, the most notable being Padre Cícero Romão Batista,
(1844-1934). A priest from Ceará who became renowned in the region for
his miraculous powers and divine prophesies, and who developed a
fanatical following, Padre Cícero has become the subject of scores of
folhetos, in which he is represented as the protector of the poor of the
North East interior. In *Nascimento, Vida e Morte do Padre Cícero*, Apolônio
Alves Dos Santos, born in Paraíba in 1926, describes the help and
comfort the priest offered to the sick, poor and destitute who sought his
assistance at his church in Juazeiro do Norte, in Ceará. Faith in Padre
Cícero can ward off adversity, the poet asserts, mentioning certain
miracles to illustrate his point:

Dizem que um certo dia
uma onça no caminho
emboscou um velho e ele
valeu-se do meu padrinho
e a onça transformou-se
em um simples cabritinho. (37)

They say that one day, on a road, a puma ambushed an old man, and he appealed to our priest, and the puma was transformed into a harmless little goat. (37)

Several miracles performed by Padre Cícero are described in subsequent verses, demonstrating how the priest put his divine power at the service of the most vulnerable sectors of the population, who constantly faced hunger, drought and disease. The death of Padre Cícero has not diminished his influence, argues the poet, for he still remains a source of strength and protection for all, including the poet himself:

> Agora canonisou-se
> quebrando todos encantos
> está na corte divina
> rogando por nossos prantos
> e protegendo o poeta
> Apolônio Alves dos Santos. (38)

Now he has been canonised, breaking the spell that made him a man, and he's up in the divine court, pleading on behalf of our sorrows, and protecting the poet, Apolônio Alves dos Santos. (38)

Images throughout these *folhetos* reinforce the notion of Padre Cícero as the embodiment of divine power, as seen in *A Voz do Padre Cícero* by Enoque José de Maria:

> O Padre Cícero virá
> para todo mundo ver
> o seu manto cor do céu
> chegará resplandecer
> de cada lado uma luz
> vê-se o manto Jesus
> nessa hora aparecer. (39)

Padre Cícero will come back, for everyone to see. His heavenly coloured mantle will shine brilliantly. Everywhere there will be light, and the mantle of Jesus, at that moment will appear. (39)

The prophesies of the priest are detailed in the following verses, recalling again religious literature of previous centuries. The corrupt, godless behaviour of humankind will bring havoc and disaster on earth, and only turning to God and repenting can bring the hope of salvation:

Meu Padrinho nos avisava
à noite no seu sermão
dizendo para os romeiros
da Virgem da Conceição:
-Meus filhos cuidem de rezar
que não tardará chegar
os anjos da perdição
São os anjos do diabo
que chegam no fim da era
fazendo tanto milagre
que todo mundo os venera
semeando fome e sede
são iguais os capa verde
correios da besta fera (40)

Padre Cícero warned us, at night in his sermon, saying to the pilgrims of the Virgin of the Immaculate Conception: "my children, make sure you pray, for soon the angels of perdition will arrive. They are angels of the devil, who arrive at the end of the era, performing so many miracles that everybody worships them, but they bring hunger and drought, and are like demons, the messengers of the devil himself." (40)

Appeals to Padre Cícero for absolution and protection are at times coupled with others to the Virgin, requesting compassion, as in *A Morte de Meu Padrinho Cícero* by Manoel Rodrigues Tenório, who, having described the death of the priest and the impact of the event on the local population, ends his poem with the following verses:

Adeus meu padrinho Cícero
dai-no a santa benção
perdoai nossos pecados
dai-nos força, amor e calma
proteção a nossa alma
no reino da salvação

Adeus meu padrinho Cícero
Adeus querido pastor
Adeus Juazeiro de graça
que nos dê força e valor
Adeus varão predileto
vinde, vinde ao deserto
sêde nosso defensor

(...)

Vou terminar meu trabalho
pedindo a Virgem das Dores
que nos livre dos castigos
como mãe dos pecadores
dos males que vem a terra
da fome, da peste e guerra
dos demônios traidores. (41)

Goodbye my Padre Cícero, give us a holy blessing and forgive us for our sins. Give us strength, love and peace, and protection for our souls in the kingdom of salvation. Goodbye my Padre Cícero, goodbye beloved pastor. Goodbye blessed Juazeiro. May you give us strength and courage. Goodbye to a man most beloved. Watch over our dry North East and be our protector. I'm going to finish my work, asking the Virgin of compassion to free us from punishment, as the mother of all sinners, and from the evils found on earth, like hunger, plagues and war, and from treacherous demons. (41)

The back cover of the *folheto* contains a prayer underlying the theme of the need for faith, allegedly written by Padre Cícero in 1925 and entitled *Oração Milagrosa de Nossa Senhora de Monserrate*. It gives the assurance that anyone using the prayer will receive protection from misfortune and states:

E necessário ter fé, porque não havendo fé não ha
milagre nem salvação. (42)

It is necessary to have faith, because without faith there are no miracles and no salvation. (42)

The devil frequently appears in these *folhetos* of religious theme, attempting to win over souls through trickery or force, only to be defeated by divine intervention, often from the Virgin herself. In *A Surra que o Padre Cícero Deu no Diabo* by Antônio Caetano, it is Padre Cícero under instruction from the Virgin who thwarts the devil's attempt to carry off a young girl, the *folheto* ending with the following verses:

Nossa Senhora pediu
pelo seu Divino Manto
-Cícero livra aquela moça
que a salvação eu garanto
leve consigo a verdade

da Santíssima Trinidade
e o Divino Espírito Santo

A moça agradeceu
a Jesus crucificado
viva Nossa Mãe das Dores
Mãe do Verbo Encarnado
viva a voz do Padre Eterno
que me tirou do inferno
por ser Divino e Sagrado

Viva o Menino Jesus
que foi nascido em Belém
viva o senhor São José
viva os Santos também
viva o Padre Cícero Romão
que me deu a proteção
para todo sempre. Amen. (43)

Our Blessed Lady asked, with the authority of the Divine: "Cícero, free that girl, for I guarantee her salvation, may she carry with her the truth of the holy trinity, and the holy divine spirit." The girl thanked Christ the martyr, and blessed our Mother of Compassion, the mother of the word of God, saying: "long live the power of our eternal father who saved me from hell, because he's divine and holy. Blessed be the child Jesus, born in Bethlehem. Blessed be Saint Joseph, and the other saints as well, and long live Padre Cícero Romão, who gave me protection, for ever and ever. Amen." (43)

The poor are often praised in the *folhetos* for retaining their faith despite all the suffering they endure, whilst those guilty of blasphemy or profane behaviour are punished. In recent years, Frei Damião, still preaching in the North East backlands, or *sertão*, has become a popular figure in *folheto* poetry, fulfilling a similar role to that of Padre Cícero, as the embodiment of divine power and protector of the poor. Those doubting the word of Frei Damião are shown to suffer punishment and humiliation until they repent, as in *folhetos* such as *Estória de um Crente que Foi Castigado por Frei Damião*, by Amaro Cordeiro, in which a man who derides the alleged powers of Frei Damião finds that he suddenly loses control of the lorry which he is driving. It swerves off the road and turns over. The experience leads him to find Frei Damião and beg forgiveness, and the *folheto* ends with the familiar message of many such poems:

Vamos cada qual rezar
pedindo ao Pai da nação
que ampare os católicos
que mendigam o pobre pão
não desampare os fiéis
que crer em Frei Damião

Frei Damião diz ao povo
que procure se afastar
das ilusões infernais
cada qual cuide em rezar
porque está muito perto
deste mundo se acabar. (44)

Let each one of us pray, asking our father of the nation to protect all catholics who beg for daily bread, and not to forsake the faithful who believe in Frei Damião. Frei Damião tells the people they should try to turn away from infernal fantasies, and all should ensure they pray, for the end of the world is nigh. (44)

Similar examples are given in other *folhetos,* such as *O Homem que Atirou em Frei Damião e Virou num Urubú,* by Manoel Seráfim, and *O Exemplo da Crente que Profanou de Frei Damião e Virou Macaca,* by Olegário Fernandes, in which a woman who claims that Frei Damião is a false prophet is converted into an ape and is only returned to her normal state after repenting in front of the friar.

Many *folhetos* relate miracles in order to warn the reader to seek forgiveness for their sins and find salvation in God. A typical example is *A Santa que Falou Profetizando,* by José Costa Leite, born in Paraíba in 1927, which tells of a statue of the Virgin in a church in a town near Belo Horizonte which miraculously spoke to a priest. The Virgin prophesied that the rest of the present century would see hunger and disease increase as a punishment for man's rejection of God:

No ano 86
a crise é de fazer dó
para castigar o povo
que só vive no forró
a pobreza com fadiga
aperta tanto a barriga
que as tripas chegam dá nó

No ano 87
fica tudo diferente

ninguém se lembra de Deus
só se fala em matar gente
do povo se acaba a fé
tem gente que zomba até
de Deus Pai Onipotente. (45)

In the year 1986, the crisis will bring pain, punishing the people who simply like to have a good time. Poverty will wear them down, stomachs will be tightened, and intestines tied into knots. In the year 1987, everything will be different. Nobody will remember God, and all the talk will be of killing people. The people's faith will disappear, and there will even be those who mock God the all powerful father. (45)

1999 will bring judgement from God, and the Virgin demands that all should repeat the *Oração de São Jorge* to reaffirm their faith and beg salvation. Again, the prayer is included on the back cover of the *folheto*. Other poems tell of miracles that have taken place as a result of such faith, such as *Os Milagres da Virgem da Conceição*, by José Soares, already mentioned, which lists the miracles, such as the curing of illnesses, conceded by the Virgin to believers. New material is constantly being incorporated into the tradition of religious *folheto* verse, such as the visit of Pope John Paul II to Brazil in 1980, but the same fundamental message constantly recurs: the search for divine protection against hardship and suffering in life, and ultimately for salvation, through the rejection of sin and confirmation of faith. A few poets specialise in religious *folhetos* of this type, such as João de Cristo Rei, born in 1900 in Paraíba, who assumed his new name in fulfilment of a promise he made when praying to be cured of a serious illness. He became personally acquainted with Padre Cícero in the early 1930s and dedicated himself to composing poems through which to convey the teaching of the priest.

Most of the chivalric romances still found in *folheto* form in the Brazilian North East, extolling the valour and loyalty of medieval knights, are linked to this tradition of religious teaching. Tales of Charlemagne and his twelve peers are the most popular examples in Brazilian popular verse. Their military campaigns, described in the poems, are motivated by the desire to spread the Catholic faith, and the Virgin constantly protects the knights in their efforts. In one version of *A História da Carlos Magno e Os Doze Pares*, by João Lopes Freire, the poet writes:

Carlos Magno prontificou
a trabalhar para Deus
mostrando sua coragem

combatendo os ateus
por isto era inspirado
para defesa dos seus

Lutava contra os pagãos
que em Deus não acreditava
e seu poder tão fecundo
cada dia aumentava
ele só queria com ele
quem primeiro se batizava. (46)

Charlemagne declared that he would work for God, showing his courage by fighting against atheists, and this work inspired him, to defend his people. He fought against the pagans, who did not believe in God, and his prodigious power grew every day. He was only interested in those who became baptised. (46)

There are many popular poems dealing with the life of Charlemagne, as noted by Câmara Cascudo, (47) and one is quoted by Suassuna in his novel, *A Pedra do Reino*, where the narrator, Quaderna, recalls how it fired his imagination when he heard it for the first time as a young boy, and how he related it to his dreams of the North East *sertão* as an enchanted kingdom of chivalrous values. (48) Several scholars of popular literature have commented on the ways in which the *folheto* poet links the material of such ancient romances to *sertão* society, the most notable being the work of Jerusa Pires Ferreira, showing how in many *folhetos* the medieval world of kingdoms, kings and vassals becomes associated with the relations of domination and subordination in the rural North East. A process of affinity is achieved by the poet's manipulation of the original themes, recreating them within a new language and symbolic system proper to the culture of the rural poor of the North East. (49) Câmara Cascudo notes the same process in his comparisons of early European versions of popular stories, such as *História do Roberto do Diabo* and *A Nova História da Princesa Magalona*, with twentieth century Brazilian versions. He refers to significant changes that have occurred in the narrative, writing of *História do Roberto do Diabo*, for example:

Many episodes, included by the Spanish editor in 1509, were omitted in later editions. These changes responded to local taste, likes and dislikes, or standard habits or customs of the time which would end up being expressed in the gestures of the hero, in pleasing harmony with the environment in question. (50)

The picaresque tradition of sixteenth century Iberian literature is another source that has been adapted over the centuries by the popular poet of Brazil. Many *pícaros*, often referred to as *quengos* or *amarelos*, have become popular figures of *folheto* literature, triumphing over adversity and enemies through cunning and trickery. The oldest of these characters, still found in Brazilian popular verse, is undoubtedly Pedro Malazartes, who featured in many traditional stories of the Iberian Peninsula. (51) One such *folheto* is *As Diabruras de Pedro Malazartes*, by Expedito Sebastião da Silva, born in Ceará in 1928, narrating how Malazartes avoids work and relies on his wits to get what he wants:

> O Pedro enquanto criança
> foi cheio de diabruras
> devido a isso tornou-se
> campeão das travesuras
> foi um ente absoluto
> entre todas criaturas
>
> (...)
>
> Quando tornou-se rapaz
> só vivia a vadiar
> se deitava numa rede
> se balançando a cantar
> dizendo: não sou jumento
> pra morrer de trabalhar. (52)

When a child, Pedro was full of pranks, and so he became champion of tricks. He was unique among God's creatures. As a young lad, he liked to laze around, lying in a hammock, singing as it rocked, and saying: "I'm not some beast of burden, who's going to die of work." (52)

As in other poems of this type, the artfulness of the *pícaro* eventually enables him to win status and power. In this case, Malazartes deceives a king in order to win his jealously guarded daughter. In an ending typical of such *folhetos*, he finally marries the princess and inherits the kingdom. Other *pícaros*, distinctly Brazilian, have emerged in *folheto* literature of the North East over time, the best known being Canção de Fogo and João Grilo. (53) Typically, these characters are poor, weak and sickly, but survive, and even prosper, in a hostile world through their cunning. The first verses of *Proezas de João Grilo*, by João Martins de Athayde (Paraíba, 1880-1959), serve as an example:

João Grilo foi um cristão
que nasceu antes do dia
criou-se sem formosura
mas tinha sabedoria
e morreu depois da hora
pelas artes que fazia

(...)

Porem João Grilo criou-se
pequeno, magro e sambudo
as pernas tortas e finas
a boca grande e beiçudo
no sitio onde morava
dava notícia de tudo. (54)

João Grilo was a Christian who was born prematurely, and he was far from attractive when he grew up, but was very wise. He died much later than he should have done, because of the tricks he performed. He grew up, however, small, thin and sickly, and his bow legs were spindly. He had a big mouth and thick lips. In the place where he lived, he knew everything and spread the gossip.(54)

The triumph of the *pícaro*, invariably over those of greater wealth or social status, avenges the poor for abuses suffered, and their deception is seen as a justifiable strategy for those who have no other means to defend their dignity in a world of greed and dishonesty. In *A Vida de Canção de Fogo e o seu Testamento*, by Leandro Gomes de Barros, Canção de Fogo says to a new acquaintance:

Quer ir comigo, acompanhe-me
faço-lhe observação
e nem há de ser ladrão
ser esperto nos negócios
isso é uma obrigação. (55)

If you want to go with me, accompany me, I'll tell you this: "you don't have to be a thief, but be an expert at deals and tricks, that's absolutely crucial." (55)

God will understand their need and forgive their actions, Canção de Fogo goes on to explain. In similar fashion, the Christian faith of João Grilo is emphasised in the *folheto* by Athayde already cited, as when the character gives a demonstration of his sharp thinking by outwitting his teacher at school through a series of questions relating to religious belief:

> Um dia perguntou ao mestre:
> o que é que Deus não vê
> o homem vê qualquer hora?
> diz ele: não pode ser
> pois Deus vê tudo no mundo
> em menos de um segundo
> de tudo pode saber
>
> João Grilo disse: qual nada
> quêde os elementos seus?
> abra os olhos, mestre velho
> que vou-lhe mostrar os meus
> seus estudos se consomem
> um homem ver outro homem
> só Deus não ver outro Deus. (56)

One day he asked the teacher: "what is it that God can't see, but man sees all the time?" The teacher replied: "there is nothing, for God sees the whole world in less than a second, and knows about everything." João Grilo said: "what do you mean, nothing? You, with all your learning! Open your eyes, old teacher, and I'll teach you something. All your learning isn't enough. A man can see another man, but God cannot see another God." (56)

The triumph of the *pícaro* in a trial of questions and answers is a device commonly employed in such *folhetos*, and has a long tradition in popular stories and legends. Of all the figures of *folheto* poetic tradition, it is the *pícaro* that Ariano Suassuna has most utilised in his work, with, for example, João Grilo serving as the main protagonist in his best known play, *Auto da Compadecida*. It will be seen in chapter 4 how Suassuna contrasts the simple faith of João with the hypocrisy of other characters of greater social status within the play, in order to develop the Christian message of the work.

Another figure of popular literature employed by Suassuna and other Armorial writers is that of the *cangaceiro*, the popular bandit. The theme of popular banditry in the North East dates from the nineteenth century, and although the last bands of *cangaceiros* had by and large disappeared from the *sertão* by the 1940s, *folhetos* of their adventures, especially of Lampião and Antônio Silvino, still appear today. Silvino is generally presented as a very romantic and sympathetic character, who assisted the poor and later repented of his life as a bandit. Lampião appears more ruthless and violent in most *folhetos*, with numerous verses relating torture, rapes and murders committed by him. At times he appears as a sadist who enjoys violence for its own sake, and who appears to have forgotten the ideals of honour and justice which originally motivated his actions. Rodolfo Coelho Cavalcante, a poet born in Alagoas in 1917, writes in *Lampião - O Terror do Nordeste*:

> Lampião nunca sorriu
> Para os seus dentes mostrar
> Quando sorria era o ódio
> Sua senha de matar
> Nasceu para ser carniceiro
> Foi o Nero brasileiro
> Que se pode registrar. (57)

Lampião never smiled, never revealed his teeth. If he ever grinned it was with hate, the indication that he was about to kill, for he was born to be a butcher, the Nero of Brazil, that's what we can record here. (57)

Nevertheless, the bandits are rarely condemned outright by the poet. As in the case of the *pícaro*, their actions are understood within the context of an unjust and corrupt society. Lampião and Silvino are seen as having been forced into banditry by the need to avenge a crime committed against their families. In *Lampião, O Rei do Cangaço* by Antônio Teodoro do Santos, born in Bahia in 1916, the verses begin with a description of the persecution suffered by Lampião's family and the murder of his parents, which Lampião sets out to avenge. Deeply religious, he visits Padre Cícero in Juazeiro do Norte to beg forgiveness and ask for protection:

> Viajou pra o Ceará
> Foi até o Juazeiro
> Aonde estava o Padre Cícero
> Pregando a todo romeiro
> E disse assim -meu padrinho
> Vim pedir vosso carinho
> Pois tornei-me bandoleiro! (58)

He travelled to Ceará and went to Juazeiro, where Padre Cícero was, preaching to the pilgrims, and he said to him: "father, I come to ask for your forgiveness, because I've become a bandit!" (58)

Several *folhetos* deal with the judgement of Lampião after his death, such as *A Chegada de Lampião no Céu*, by a poet already mentioned, Rodolfo

Coelho Cavalcante. The first part of the poem sees the bandit condemned by Christ, despite his claims that the crimes of others explain his own misdeeds:

> Disse o bravo Virgulino
> Senhor não fui culpado
> Me tornei um cangaceiro
> Porque me vi obrigado
> Assassinaram meu pai
> Minha mãe quase que vai
> Inclusive eu coitado
>
> Os seus pecados são tantos
> Que nada posso fazer
> Alma desta natureza
> Aqui não pode viver
> Pois dentro do Paraíso
> É o reinado do riso
> Onde só existe prazer. (59)

Brave Virgulino said: "Lord, I was not guilty, for I became a bandit because I was obliged to. They killed my father, and nearly my mother too, and even myself, poor thing." The Lord said: "Your sins are so great that I cannot do anything. A soul of that nature cannot live here, for paradise is the kingdom of laughter, where only pleasure exists." (59)

Finally, Lampião repents of his sins and the Virgin intercedes and forgives him:

> Aglomerado de Anjos
> Todos cantando louvores
> Lampeão disse: Meu Deus
> Perdai os meus horrores
> Dos meus crimes tão cruéis
> Arrependeu-se através
> Da Virgem seus esplendores. (60)

The angels gathered together, singing songs of praise. Lampião said: "Dear God, pardon all the horrors I have committed, all my cruel crimes." Through the Virgin, in all her splendour, he expressed his remorse. (60)

In the final verses Lampião is sent to purgatory to await further judgement.

Another traditional theme within the *folheto* is the recording of *desafios* or *pelajas* fought between *cantadores*. These are poetic duels, where the poets sing alternate verses, improvising as they go along, testing their rival's skill with rhyme and metre and his knowledge of traditional themes, such as astrology, biblical material and the life of Charlemagne. When one is unable to continue, the other is declared the winner. Many such contests have been written down later in *folheto* form, either by one of the contestants who took part or by a third poet. They are obviously not accurate transcriptions of the verses improvised, but recreations of the contest as recalled later. The most celebrated *desafio* of all was one held between Ignácio da Catingueira and Francisco Romano, two of the most famous *cantadores* of their day, in Paraíba in 1870, which, according to some sources, lasted several days. Leandro Gomes de Barros later wrote a *folheto* about the event entitled *Romano e Ignácio da Catingueira*, which opens with the each of the competitors acclaiming their superior skills:

> Romano:
> Ignácio tu me conheces
> E sabes bem eu quem sou,
> Que à Catingueira inda vou,
> Vou derribar teu castello,
> Que nunca se derribou
>
> Ignácio:
> É mais facil um boi voar,
> O cúrurú ficar bello,
> Arurá jogar cacête,
> E cobra calçar chinello,
> Do que haver um barbado
> Que derribe meu castello. (61)

Romano: "Ignácio, you know me, and you know very well who I am, and that one day I'll go back home. But first I'm going to knock down your castle, which has never been knocked down before."
Ignácio: "It's easier for an ox to fly or for a toad to become beautiful, or for an alligator to juggle or for a snake to put on slippers, than for some other man to knock down my castle." (61)

Verses from the duel are included in Suassuna's *A Pedra do Reino*, with Quaderna recalling his fascination at the idea of constructing a literary castle and defending it against rivals. It inspires him to use literature to build his own realm where he can fulfil his personal ambitions, and restore the lost glory of his family, without endangering his own life. (62)

Today, *desafios* of the type mentioned rarely take place. *Cantadores* do frequently sing in pairs at markets and fairs, alternating improvised verses as before, but the element of competition has disappeared. Generally, the *cantadores* sing about members of the public listening to them, encouraging them to donate money to them, and all donations received are divided between the singers at the end. Furthermore, some of the *desafios* which appear in *folhetos* never in fact took place at all, and are pure inventions of the poet concerned.

All these traditional themes are less common in the *folhetos* produced today, in which current news items and issues tend to dominate, but verses still do appear which look back on the era of *cangaço*, or proclaim the virtues of pious behaviour. In 1989, for example, Apôlonio Alves dos Santos published *Romaria e Milagre do Padre Cícero Romero*, a *folheto* telling of the poet's recovery from ill health as a result of a promise made to Padre Cícero, and a 1992 poem by Jotabê, *A Vinda de Jesús*, warns the reader to repent in preparation for the return of Christ. It is clear, however, that for the poets and their traditional public the original sources for the verse are of secondary importance. It is the recreation of the material by the poet, reinterpreting it according to his public's world view and employing a system of language and symbols specific to them, that is the crucial process that gives the content special significance for the reader. Any subject, no matter how alien to the life of the poor in the North East it may appear, can thus be made to strike a chord of recognition and identity with that *folheto* public. It has already been seen how the chivalrous knights of traditional romances are linked to the life of the *cangaceiro*. The same process occurs with contemporary sources. Robert Rowland, for example, refers to a *folheto* based on a newspaper item about Sacco and Vanzetti, two poor Italian immigrants in the United States, who, after a considerable struggle to find work and establish themselves, became involved in the anarchist movement, were arrested by the authorities, charged with murder during a post office raid, and eventually tried and executed in 1923, despite their claims of innocence. Again, the poet presents the material in such a way as to link the theme to the fortunes of the North Eastern emigrants who travel to the south of Brazil, only to join the ranks of the unemployed and the *favelados*. The original source is refashioned in order to confirm the poet's vision of the world. (63)

Despite the vast range of subject matter covered by the *folhetos*, they are really rearrangements of a limited number of fairly set plots. These are constantly repeated in varied forms, within the conventions associated with the popular literary tradition, to deepen and strengthen the common perspectives of the poet and public. Working in such familiar patterns, the *folheto* has reinforced its role as a communal form of expression. Candace Slater, in the most detailed structural study of the *folheto*, identifies a broadly common structure which gives an essential unity to this whole body of traditional popular poetry. She demonstrates how the traditional *folheto* develops a plot in six stages, starting with a situation of harmony, passing through a period of disruption, in which trials or tests have to be overcome, until in the end judgement is passed, rewarding righteousness and condemning wrong, so that harmony is finally restored. Slater argues that this conventional framework, linked to a popular vision of how the world should ideally function, permits a shared tradition to be passed on, whilst still allowing scope for individual variations and creativity. But her research, conducted in the late 1970s, already identifies clearly the changes taking place in the *folheto*, and she suggests that the traditional structure will erode as the consumers become more diverse and new demands and expectations emerge. (64) Today, effects of that process are clearly evident. The traditional *folheto* which has here been outlined, characterised by certain thematic and structural conventions, and rooted in communal practices of production and dissemination, is now much rarer. Yet *folhetos* continue to be produced, with new characteristics corresponding to the new circumstances of its existence. This popular poetry is not a folkloric vestige of a past era, nor a once popular form now suffering a process of adulteration due to the consolidation of the mass culture industry in Brazil. Both those views are frequently proposed, but it will be argued here that the *folheto*, like other forms of popular cultural expression, can best be understood as a field of debate, where diverse elements from a wide range of sources - some from folkloric tradition, and others inspired by the mass media - are incorporated and reviewed. More importantly, it is also a field of conflict, where schemes of dominant class thought and expressions of resistance to it are in contention. There are *folhetos* which convey a deeply conservative view of the world. Others, however, challenge, criticise and seek change.

iv] The *folheto* as a field of ideological debate

Many scholars have argued that the peasant is unable to form his own coherent world view because he is tied to an individualistic and fragmented social environment, and that this lack of class consciousness is evident in the popular poetry of the North East. According to this view, the thematic content of the *folheto* shows no real awareness of a body of workers, who, despite their differences, share a collective interest that differentiates them from, and places them in conflict with, the interests of opposing social classes. It is argued that, as a consequence, there are few explicit references in *folheto* poetry to a specific socio-economic structure, and what criticism that is conveyed is only expressed as a generalised discontent with social injustice and the abuse of power in the North East. Instead of presenting a radical response to the problems of the North East poor, the *folheto* is a literature that provides the consolation of fantasy, humour or melodrama, its major themes essentially eternal and unchanging. The work of Renato Carneiro Campos, studying the ideological content of popular poetry, serves as an example of such a view:

> We cannot detect a real, well-defined political ideology in the work of the popular poets, who are generally individualists: they always deal with the situation of the individual, rarely of the collective or of humanity. They frequently record political events which have occurred in the region, or in another part of the country, but without making extensive comments of the type that might indicate what their true political tendencies are. If they criticise some government policy they hardly ever suggest an alternative. They do not show the correct policies which should replace the mistaken ones. They admire courage. Individual courage from a solitary person is highly valued, but the collective motives behind political or social heroism have little effect on them. (65)

Here the Brazilian peasant is viewed as conservative and individualistic, stoic and righteous in the face of poverty. In this light, the *folheto* comes to be praised as a worthy instrument for reinforcing the moral values and good sense of the peasant, a good means of teaching him sound standards and behaviour. He goes on to write:

> (...) the chap-books, given their intelligent, didactic orientation, could become extremely valuable instruments for instructing the worker, teaching him about problems of hygiene, giving him orientation on matters relating to his work, and exalting the sons of the region who have worked towards its greatness. (66)

Such views provide the basis for the constant repetition of the stereotyped characteristics so commonly associated with the Brazilian peasant - fatalism, conservatism, superstition, resignation, individualism - and his forms of expression are readily exploited to verify this image.

Popular poetry is therefore commonly seen as repository of traditional values, essentially acritical and non-political, as shown by the statement of one of the major scholars of the field:

> (...) In Brazil, there are no radical or rebellious popular poets. The very rare exceptions are completely artificial (67)

These views reveal more about the ideological position of the erudite scholars concerned than about Brazilian popular literature. As Mauro W.B. de Almeida observes in a study of such interpretations, it is no coincidence that such studies first emerged in the late 1950s and early 60s, at a time of peasant mobilization in the North East under the *Ligas Camponêses,* and when the effectiveness of the *folheto* as a system of communication among the rural communities of the region had long been established. (68) For decades before, rural popular poetry, or *literatura de cordel,* had been generally disdained in erudite literary circles, to the point of being defined in many Portuguese dictionaries as a literature of 'little or no value'. (69) Now, at a crucial juncture in the social history of the rural North East, such cultural phenomena could no longer be ignored. Traditional values associated with the rural poor, like acquiescence, conservatism, passivity and good sense, needed to be reaffirmed, and the image of an essentially compliant peasant was reinforced, harmonising conveniently with both the dominant structures of the rural North East and Brazil's overall pattern of development, and minimising the significance of the contradictions resulting from the conflict between the two.

The *folheto* therefore, along with other forms of popular expression, became an important arena of ideological conflict. Its importance lay not only in the fact that it represented a dynamic communications network controlled almost exclusively by the peasants themselves, but also precisely because it was not so apolitical as many erudite sources suggested. Mauro W.B. Almeida emphasises the significant role played by popular poetry in the mobilisation process of the Peasant Leagues, where it served as a means of stimulating awareness and solidarity, a role recognised by Francisco Julião, one of the leaders of the Leagues. (70) Some politically radical *folhetos* have in fact been produced, as will be seen later. Their scarcity is hardly surprising given the strict censorship imposed by the military government following the coup of 1964. Many poets recall cases of print-shops being closed, *folhetos* confiscated and poets arrested, a phenomenon verified by other researchers. (71) Almost inevitably, most poets avoided openly political themes during the years of military rule for fear of reprisal, and *folheteiros* were extremely reluctant to sell any such political poetry in public. In a newspaper interview, Edson Pinto da Silva, who sells *folhetos* in the large market of São José in Recife, stated in 1978:

> Today, if a poet publishes a chap-book criticising the government, he's had it. He's done for, he disappears. Before the 1964 revolution it wasn't like that. The poets used to criticize. They might even get themselves into trouble, but there was some protection. A deputy in the Assembly would speak in their defence, or an association would organise to help them. And there would even be people of influence who would come out in agreement with them. (72)

So external restraint helps to explain the lack of overt political content in the *folhetos,* rather than mere apathy towards the subject on the part of the poet. If such apathy really existed, why should censorship against the poets and their associates be necessary in the first place? More significant than the oppressive activities of the authorities is the self censorship that the poets impose on themselves. Antônio Arantes quotes the example of one poem that was substantially altered by the poet, with a number of highly political statements deleted an account of fear of the consequences that would arise if it were published. (73) The few *folhetos* openly criticising the authorities that do get printed are invariably under a pseudonym, or with no name at all.

Crucial to the understanding of the *folheto* therefore, with all its contradictions and limitations of expression, is the ideological dialectic at its very centre, created by the constant tension between the intervention of dominant class values and popular resistance to such intervention. It is in the context of this ideological conflict that the growing interest in popular literature shown by erudite writers will have to be considered. Certainly, there appears to be little coherence to the peasants' perception of the world about them. Their vision is fragmented, laden with concepts and attitudes passed on by other social sectors and eras. This lack of a global view of society, and consequently of a clear appreciation of their position within it, largely explains the limitations of the philosophical content of the *folhetos.*

However, if the peasants' structural position in society - the nature of their productive activities and the pattern of life resulting from it - hinders the development of a coherent world view, the poor communities scattered around the vast rural interior of the North East still share the same basic economic and social realities, and this necessarily generates broadly common patterns of thought, perception and behaviour. For Maria Ignez S. Paulilo, the most fundamental aspect of this common experience is that of dependency or *sujeição*. (74) With the traditional *latifundio* structure still prevailing in the rural North East, the vast majority of the region's population is heavily dependent upon the landowning class for their means of support, virtually forced to enter into clientelistic relationships in order to ensure their survival. They depend on the landowner or *patrão* for all their basic necessities of life: access to the land, paid work when necessary, housing, advancements of seed and money during unpaid periods, and general support during periods of need or difficulty. This situation signifies immense power for the *patrão*, and nearly total subordination from the peasant, explaining the prime desire of the latter to free himself from *sujeição* and establish an alternative pattern of life, as well as his limited capacity to transform that desire into concrete social action, or even a clear conception of a radically different, alternative structure. For many peasants the alternative is limited to the idea of owning lands and so joining the propertied classes themselves, rather than progressing to any real reordering of society. To this basic vision, Alda Britto da Motta adds other characteristics. Firstly, he notes the tendency of the peasant to fuse the natural with the supernatural through ritual, articulated by the linking of religious practice with the agricultural cycle, so that the mystical and the real are not automatically conceived of as two clearly separated universes. Secondly, the peasant's world is essentially one of use values, where activities of immediate utility are given greatest priority and appreciation. Thirdly, and largely resulting from the previous two, the peasant views his creative activities as inseparable from his daily routine of work and ritual; as an integral and necessary part of his whole rhythm of life. (75) This, of course, has given the popular poetry of those rural communities a character that distinguishes it fundamentally from erudite literature.

It has already been seen that the creation, production and dissemination of the *folheto* has traditionally been a socially derived process that has served to reinforce the collective attitudes and common experiences of the rural poor of North East Brazil, and those have naturally been embodied in the content of the work itself. In this way, many *folhetos* do exhibit a clear ideological content, by making certain affirmations about all the basic problems shared by the social class concerned, and attempting to resolve those problems metaphorically in their poetry. The concrete conditions of life of the peasant are reproduced in a symbolic language, recognised by the rural poor, and regarded as their common property, through the manipulation of which the poor agricultural labourer, generally symbolised by a popular hero, can overcome the difficulties that burden him through his qualities of courage, audacity, inventiveness or astuteness. As suggested previously, the poetry does not directly confront the socio-economic order as a whole, but rather deals with the problems it creates in a fragmentary and localised manner, concentrating on specific aspects like hunger, inflation, exploitation, injustice and social and sexual relations.

Protest, therefore, both explicit and implicit, is a common characteristic in the *folheto* poetry, directed at all aspects of life. Frequently it amounts to a simple lament; a crying out against the oppressive conditions of life. Typical is *A Dor qui mais Doi no Pobre é a Dor da Umilhação*, by Jota Rodrigues, who, writing of his move from the North East to a *favela* in Rio de Janeiro, contrasts the sense of solidarity among his fellow *favelados* with the scorn directed against him by the society outside.

> E pelos irmãos da favela
> Zé Rodrigue é estimulado
> Porem saindo na rua
> Quaze sempre é umilhado
> Nas calçadas que Zé paça
> O povo dis cheio de graça
> La vai o velho favelado
>
> Aquilo pra Zé Rodrigue
> Feria le o coração
> Vendo o povo le encarar
> Com odio e umilhação
> Desprezos por todo lado
> E a pobre Zé favelado
> Ninguem le tem afeição.
>
> So os vizinhos da favela
> E quem le da atenção
> Reconhecendo no Zé
> Homem de bom coração
> Tratando o com respeito
> Por ver seu sistema e geito
> De um sofrido cidadço. (76)

His friends and neighbours in the "favela" all respect Zé Rodrigues, but when he goes into the streets outside, he's nearly always humiliated. As he walks along the pavements, people mock him and say: "There goes the old man from the shanty-town!" That wounds the heart of Zé Rodrigues, seeing people look on him with hate, causing humiliation. Everywhere there's just disdain, and it seems that nobody feels affection for poor Zé from the shanty-town. Only the neighbours from the "favela" pay him any attention, recognising him to be a good man at heart. They treat him with respect, seeing in his manner and habits the signs of a long suffering citizen. (76)

The poet's social protest is implicit rather than explicit however, for he appears to accept the actual social division between rich and poor as the natural order of things, albeit regrettable. It is the disdainful attitude of the rich towards the poor that he protests against, as he sadly relates the humiliation he suffers in the shops and the streets, yet the final plea for change amounts only to a request that everyone should show more respect for the poor:

> E para quem le este livro
> Faço recomendação
> Lembre si qui os favelado
> Mereci voça atenção
> São pobres mais são vivente
> São jenti umildi qui senti
> A dor da umilhação. (77)

And to the person who reads this little book, I'll make a recommendation. Remember that the people from shanty-town are worthy of your attention. They are poor, but human beings nonetheless. They are humble people who feel the pain of humiliation. (77)

Another popular poet, Flávio Fernandes, does identify the suffering of the poor with the lust for profits of the rich. In *História do Feijão Preto e o Sofrimento do Pobre* he writes:

> Ganâcia de tubarão
> É quem faz esta anarquia
> Para explorar o povo
> Esconde mercadoria
> O pobre necessitando
> Enfrenta esta tirania.
>
> Todos viram que o Papa
> No Brasil pediu a paz
> Para defender o povo
> Do laço dos maiorais
> E o rico ganancioso

Com nada se satisfaz.

Em toda nossa cidade
Existe esta ingratidão
Existem muitas crianças
Que vivem em desnutrição
Por falta de vitamina
Que existe no Feijão. (78)

The racketeers make huge profits out of this madness. They hide goods away, in order to exploit the people, and those in need have to cope with this tyranny. Everyone saw that the Pope, when he came to Brazil, asked for peace and defended the people against the bonds of the rich and powerful, but the profiteering rich are never satisfied. This lack of sympathy exists throughout our city. There are many children who suffer from malnutrition, lacking the vitamins found in basic foods like beans. (78)

Again, however, no radical solution is offered. Assuring he has no interest in political activity, the poet simply pleads that the government should be more attentive to the needs of the poor:

Não faço verso agitando
Não suporto agitação
Sendo pra fazer o certo
Não me falta inspiração
Sei que muitos vão dizer
Que o poeta tem razão.

(...)

É preciso que os homens
Que estejam no poder
Olhem bem para a pobreza
E procurem entender
Que pobre também é gente
E nasceu para viver. (79)

I don't write verses to stir people up. I don't support unrest. I want to do what's right, and I won't lack inspiration. I know there will be many who'll say that the poet is correct (...) It's vital that the men who are in power pay attention to poverty, and try to understand that the poor are also human, and were also born to live. (79)

Most *folhetos* dichotomise the world in this way, into them (the rich, the foreign interests, the landowners and the bosses) against us (the poor). At times, the poet transcends the simple protest against injustice, and achieves a deeper understanding of the mechanisms of exploitation directed against his social class. In a *folheto* entitled *A Pobreza Morrendo a Fome no Golpe da Carestia*, José Costa Leite, for example, sees the poor agricultural worker as producing everything and receiving nothing, whilst the parasitical rich collect the best produce and sell it to the multinational companies, to their mutual advantage:

>   Rico não vai limpar cana
>   e nem vai fazer levada
>   não planta milho, feijão
>   e o pobre torna chegada
>   planta inhame, macaxeira
>   para a nação brasileira
>   e no fim não vale nada.
>
>   (...)
>
>   Se o pobre não plantasse
>   rico o que ia fazer?
>   tem o dinheiro no bolso
>   mas não presta pra comer
>   o homem de pé no chão
>   é quem faz a produção
>   pra ver o Brasil crescer!
>
>   Café na terra do café
>   a preço de ouro é vendido
>   o matuto bebe aguado
>   bem fraco e desenchavido
>   quem ganha com isso, leitor
>   só é o cafeicultor
>   com um lucro garantido.
>
>   Porque o cafeicultor
>   com astúcia se aproveita
>   recebe dinheiro do banco
>   muito antes da colheita
>   o governo paga bem
>   mas café bom ninguem tem
>   pois o bom ninguem enjeita.

Não paga aos apanhadores
é esta a pura verdade
escolhe o café bichado
de inferioridade
vende caro aos brasileiros
e vende a estrangeiros
o de melhor qualidade. (80)

The rich man doesn't cut sugar cane, nor does he dig irrigation ditches. He doesn't plant maize or beans. It's the poor man who sets the lesson. The poor man plants yams and cassava for the whole of the country, but in the end it's all worth nothing (...) If the poor planted nothing, what would the rich man do? The money in his pocket can't be eaten. It's the man on the land who produces in order to see Brazil grow! Coffee, in the land where coffee is grown, is sold at the price of gold. The poor man from the countryside has to drink it weak and watery, and who gains out of this, dear reader, is the coffee grower, who has his profit guaranteed. The coffee grower, shrewdly makes sure he does well. He receives money from the bank long before the harvest, and the government pays well. Everybody wants good coffee, but nobody can get it. The grower won't pay the pickers, that's absolutely true, and he chooses the worst quality coffee to sell to the Brazilians. The best is sold to foreigners. (80)

The Brazilian Government generally remains in the background in such *folhetos*, sometimes chastised for its apparent reluctance to act positively for the benefit of the poor, but only rarely openly condemned. In one such example, entitled *O Brasil Prometido aos Pobres na Epoca de Eleição ou os Amigos do Voto e Inimigos dos Eleitores*, José Saldanha Menezes makes an onslaught on the politics of the dominant classes, warning his readers of their complete untrustworthiness, and their interest in only using the poor for their own ends:

Eu como pobre poeta
Vivo no mundo esquecido
Só em época de eleição
Dos tubarões sou querido
Embora depois do voto
Por nem um sou conhecido.

Os políticos com promessas
Tem arranjado o mundo
Prometendo bom emprego
Até mesmo ao vagabundo
Depois da política ganha

Fica o pobre moribundo.

(...)

Pobre é jumento do rico
Escravo sem libertade
Cão sem dono abandonado
Cego sem sociedade
O rico surra e espanca-se
E o obriga a ter-lhe amizade
Por aí nova política
Vão novamente exerser
Já estão prometendo o mundo
Para o pobre se intreter

Vem recurso é para os ricos
Porém o pobre não vê. (81)

I, a poor poet, live forgotten in the world. Only at election time do those big fish show me any interest, but once the voting is finished, they all forget who I am. The politicians, full of promises, have organised the world. They promise good jobs, even to the vagrants, but after they've won the vote, the poor are left to starve (...) The poor man is the rich man's beast of burden, a slave without liberty. He's an unwanted dog, abandoned, a blind man alone in the world. The rich man beats him but still expects affection from him. Now there's a new policy which they are going to carry out. They're promising the world to keep the poor man happy. The resources all go to the rich. The poor man never sees them. (81)

So *folhetos* expressing a radical political message do exist. Eduardo Diatachy B. de Menezes verifies this in his own research, quoting the example of *A Sujeição dos Brejos da Parahyba do Norte,* a *folheto* written by José Camello de Mello Rezende, protesting at the exploitation of agricultural workers in the North East. The poet, like many others, starts with a series of verses describing the misery of these labourers, condemning it as a form of slavery. He goes on, however, to trace the causes of the problem to the conflict between the greed for profits of commercial agriculture and the real needs of the peasants, as represented by subsistence farming. He writes:

Porque os homens do Brejo
Tangidos pela ambição
Plantaram canas nas terras

que se plantava algodão
Cafés nas terras que se dava
Milho, arroz, fumo e feijão. (82)

Because the men in the scrublands, driven by ambition, planted sugar cane in areas where cotton used to be planted, and coffee on lands which used to produce maize, rice, tobacco and beans. (82)

He also criticises the use of religion, *falso cristianismo*, as he calls it, by the dominant classes as a means to control the exploited, calls upon the landowners to repent and improve their treatment of their workers and asks God to punish those who abuse their power by sending plagues across their properties. Yet at the same time he recognises the need for social and economic change, which he implies will be implemented by the poor themselves:

Ninguem pense qu' assim
Se acabará com certeza
Dos brejos de Parahyba
Toda fonte de riqueza:
Isto não, pois virá outra
Trazida pela pobreza. (83)

Nobody should think that every source of wealth will be totally wiped out in the scrublands of Paraíba. No, alternatives will be found, brought about by the poverty. (83)

In the new order that will be established, the peasant, free from *sujeição*, will grow staple crops like beans, rice, potatoes and cassava. The poet ends by admitting his fear of the power of the rich, but reaffirming his sympathy and sense of identity with the labourers concerned. The poet himself was a carpenter from a rural town in Pernambuco. Diatachy de Menezes claims that there are in fact many *folhetos* making equally penetrating criticisms of the dominant social and economic order. (84)

However, the new order envisaged by such *folhetos* is never precisely defined. Essentially, it appears as a distant, dreamlike utopia, vaguely glimpsed. As in the last example, freedom for the peasant and an abundance of food stuffs are its major characteristics, hardly surprising in an environment dominated by dependency and hunger. Manoel Camilo dos Santos, a popular poet from Paraíba, typifies this in a *folheto* entitled *Viagem a São Saruê*. São Saruê is a mythical paradise in which existing conditions and practices that oppress the rural poor of the North East disappear, substituted by a new vision of the world:

Tudo lá é bom e facil
não precisa se comprar
não há fome nem doença
o povo vive a gozar
tem tudo e não falta nada
sem precisar trabalhar. (85)

Everything there is good and easy. There's no need to buy anything, and there's no hunger or illness. The people just live to enjoy themselves. They have everything, lacking nothing, without the need to work. (85)

Man is freed completely from the necessity to work for a livelihood, which for the majority of the rural poor of the North East signifies either the harsh drudgery of the fields or exploitative unskilled labour in the cities. Instead, nature provides everything in São Saruê. Trees produce ready made clothes, hats and shoes. Bank notes grow in clusters on the ground, whilst gold and silver coins grow on bushes like cotton. Such imagery strikes an immediate chord of recognition with a public used to work in the fields. The whole natural environment in São Saruê is converted into food, eliminating all hunger:

Lá eu vi rios de leite
barreira de carne assada
lagoa de mel de abelhas
toleiro de coalhada
açude de vinho quinado
monte de carne guisada.

As pedras de São Saruê
são de queijo e rapadura
as cacimbas são café
já coado e com quentura
de tudo assim por diante
existe grande fartura. (86)

There I saw rivers of milk, and fences of roast meat. There were lakes of honey, and quagmires filled with curd, reservoirs of cinchonized wine and hills of stewed beef. The stones of São Saruê are of cheese and sugar, and the wells are full of coffee, already prepared and nice and hot. All these things, and others, are found in great abundance. (86)

These are all the familiar foodstuffs the peasant families are constantly struggling to obtain. So, although the new world created is magical and

61

mystical, it is composed of elements and images that form a basic and essential part of the everyday life of the rural poor in the North East, and is expressed in a language specific to that group. In this way, the poem reinforces their common values and perceptions. It is a utopia created specifically for the North East peasant, built with the objects and substances he best knows and most values, and according to his particular priorities, with work eliminated and food provided in abundance.

The poetry of the *folheto*, therefore, makes clear statements about the social structure of the rural North East, and the patterns of life generated by it, rooted in the common experience of the region's poorest social sectors. Commonly implicit in such statements is a desire for change, despite ambiguity regarding the means to achieve it, and the new order that is to result. As already seen there are numerous *folhetos* narrating stories of popular heroes who, either through acts of courage, as in the case of *cangaceiros* such as Lampião or Antônio Silvino, or through trickery, as with *pícaros* like João Grilo, avenge the abuses committed against the poor by the rich and powerful.

In one of the most perceptive studies produced on North East popular poetry, Antônio Arantes, like Candace Slater, notes that most narrative *folheto* poems share a broadly common structure. (87) Arantes, however, focuses on the wide range of *folhetos de valentia*, which deal with the daring exploits of a popular hero, usually a peasant from the interior. Essentially, there are all variations of one basic plot, which is structured on the basis of a series of transformations that unfold in the course of the poem. Typically, a landowner abuses his immense power by brutally exploiting and generally mistreating his workers. The hero arrives and obtains work on the plantation, but refuses to submit himself to the whims of the *fazendeiro*. He then demonstrates his bravery by overcoming the landowner's animals and bodyguards, and finally successfully challenges the landowner himself. In the course of the poem therefore, the power of the *fazendeiro* is gradually undermined, through the destruction of the symbols that represent it, whilst the potential force of the peasants, subservient at the beginning, is gradually realised through the action of the popular hero. So class conflict is implied in most poems of this sort, with the peasantry eventually avenging itself metaphorically through the hero's victory over the perverse landowner.

However, these transformations narrated by the poem are limited by contradictions. They obviously imply radical social change, with the existing social structure symbolically subverted through the triumph of the peasant hero over the *fazendeiro*. In the end though, no such revolutionary transformation of society is proposed, for such poems typically finish with the victorious hero paid off by the defeated landowner with land, money and his daughter's hand in marriage, thus enabling him to become a *fazendeiro* himself. So the solution to the peasants' problems is sought within the existing system of dominant class values, with private property, wealth, paid labour and social status simply rearranged slightly to favour the peasant. Individualism and private initiative still appear to dominate, for it is the strong peasant hero who reaps the reward, and though he commonly pledges to treat his newly acquired workers with greater respect, there is no suggestion that a fundamental change in their social and economic position will occur.

Within the basic thematic framework however, considerable variation of plot can be noted, corresponding to the different viewpoint of each individual poet. As Arantes argues, in some poems the transformation implied is far more radical than in others. Some examples will serve to illustrate this point. In *A Morte de Carneiro e a Vitória de Arranca Véu*, by Antônio Batista Romão, the popular hero, Arranca Véu, overpowers a ruthless landowner to win the hand of his daughter:

> Arranca Véu se achava
> com o velho subjugado
> se não quizer ser meu sogro
> me diga velho danado
> a velha gritou: minha filha
> abranda este estorpado
>
> Arranca Véu se mordendo
> gritou eu vou te dar fim
> o velho disse: meu Deus
> tenha compaisão de mim
> botou a lingua pra fora
> um pedação bem assim (88)

Arranca Véu found he had the old man overpowered. "Now tell me if you don't want to be my father-in-law, old man." And the old lady cried out: "My daughter! calm down this brute!" Arranca Véu, in a fury, shouted: "I'm going to finish you off!" And the old man said: "My god! Have pity on me," and panted with exhaustion (...) (88)

In this case, the enemy of the peasants is not seen as the landowning class as a whole, but simply certain individuals within it, seen as cruel, exploitative and perverse. Though *fazendeiros* who abuse their power can be fought and overcome by the peasants, their actual right to that power, rooted in the highly stratified social system of the North East, remains unquestioned. The differences between landowner and peasant are finally reconciled, symbolised by the marriage between the landowner's daughter and Arranca Véu. The popular hero does not challenge the dominant social stratum as a whole, and is eventually integrated into it by his marriage.

Another *folheto*, *O Heroismo de João Canguçu no Engenho Gameleira*, by a poet from Paraíba, Apolônio Alves dos Santos, presents a rather more radical view of such conflict. The hero, João Canguçu, finds work on a sugar plantation where the *fazendeiro* refuses to pay his workers the wages owed to them, and has them killed when they complain:

> Ali os trabalhadores
> não viam nunca um tostão
> tudo quanto precisavam
> compravam no barracão
> desde do calçado a roupa
> a toda alimentação
>
> Mas se um pedisse a conta
> dizendo que ia embora
> ele mandava matá-lo
> oculto fora de hora
> depois queimar o cadáver
> na caldeira sem demora (89)

There the workers never saw a cent. Everything they needed they had to buy in the plantation store, including shoes, clothes and all their food. But if one of them asked to settle his bill, saying he was leaving, the boss ordered him to be killed, in secret, late at night, and then the body to be burned in the furness without delay. (89)

Witnessing these abuses, João Canguçu avenges the workers by overpowering the landowner, *coronel* Edmundo, and forcing him to divide all his money among them. Again, the plot rests on the individual action of the hero, contrasted with the submissiveness of the majority of the rural workers, and no change in the existing order is proposed. In the end, the authorities reward João Canguçu for exposing the crimes of the *fazendeiro*, and the plantation is taken over by a new, benevolent owner, who treats his workers with fairness and respect:

> Depois as autoridades
> procuraram o Canguçu
> logo o gratificaram
> com patente e com tuto

por ter quebrado a panela
e derramado o angu

Isto apenas por ter sido
ele o denunciante
daquela grande tragédia
do Edmundo pedante
lhe deram de detetive
uma medalha importante

O novo proprietário
do Engenho Gamaleira
decretou novo regime
agindo em boa maneira
hoje os seus moradores
vivem alegre a vida inteira (90)

Afterwards, the authorities looked for Canguçu and thanked him, rewarding him with privileges and money, for having been the first to have taken action to resolve the situation. Since he had been the one to denounce the great tragedy caused by the vain Edmundo, they gave him an important medal for his police-work. The new owner of the Gamaleira plantation initiated a new regime there, operating in a correct manner, and today the plantation workers live their lives happily. (90)

Nevertheless, in this poem the conflict between landowner and peasant is more clearly drawn in class terms. João Canguçu's action is motivated not by total self interest, but by his desire to avenge the mistreated workers on the plantation. Challenging the landowner, he demands retribution for them all:

O senhor vivia aqui
oprimindo os sofredores
propondo seus obstáculos
com planos exploradores
roubando suor e sangue
dos pobres trabalhadores

Há duas coisas previstas
portanto velho decida
pague já a todos nós
para fazermos partida
das duas pode escolher

ou o dinheiro ou a vida (91)

You have lived here, making others suffer, oppressing them with your exploitative plans, cheating those poor workers with your demands for sweat and blood. You have two choices and it's up to you to decide: you can pay all of us now, and we'll go away, but you can have a choice: pay us the money, or pay with your life. (91)

The third example, referred to by Arantes himself, is a *folheto* by another poet form Paraíba, Francisco Sales Areda, entitled *O Coronel Mangangá e o Seringueiro do Norte*. This offers the most radical ending to the plot, with the perverse landowner finally killed by the peasant hero, who then seizes his daughter and marries her, thereby inheriting his lands. These he then divides up among all the workers living on it. (92) Outright victory for the peasants is therefore achieved, the power of the landlord destroyed by their force, and the division of the land at least suggests the possibility of a new order to replace the existing *latifundia*.

In fact, the death of a *fazendeiro* at the hands of a peasant is rare in the *folhetos*. Most commonly, the hero, acting as a mediator between the landowner and the peasants, uses his special attributes to reach the position of being able to negotiate with the landowner in order to improve his economic and social position. No new order of society based on an alternative system of values is coherently expressed. At best it is only glimpsed. Generally, the dominant order continues intact, and the basic contradiction between the peasants desire for change and a socio-economic system that frustrates that desire, remains unresolved.

As already stated, these contradictions in the content of the *folhetos* are understandable given the internal constraints on the peasant world view, rooted in the nature of his social existence, and the external constraints on his expression, with dominant class hostility to anything considered offensive to the prevailing political, social and moral order. Furthermore, the variations of a simple plot show that dissenting voices do exist within a broadly common set of values and a common poetic tradition. It must be repeated, however, that such limitations and contradictions do not in any way invalidate these *folhetos* as a popular means of expression. On the contrary, they are the key to its understanding, reproducing the tension that characterises the peasant relationship with the social and physical world around him. That tension provides the originality of the *folheto* expression, and at the same time demarcates its conceptual parameters. Those parameters are not static however. It has already been seen that some popular poetry does incorporate a new vision of society, and there is no denying that the *folheto* does embody a conflictive quality, questioning and challenging the

66

world about it, and, as suggested by its role during the time of the peasant leagues, that potential can be realised under specific historical circumstances.

The fact that such *folhetos* relate directly to the concrete conditions of existence of the rural poor of the North East explains the dynamism of their production and consumption during so many decades. Those conditions, and the wider historical processes that shaped them, are reduced to an abstraction of reality, with a symbolic language discussing, and attempting to overcome metaphorically, the social tensions that daily affect the North Eastern poor. All aspects of life are dealt with. The corruption of modern living, with the erosion of traditional family life, is another common theme. In a *folheto* entitled *O Povo Desembestado*, Chico Ramalho, from Paraíba, compares the old pattern of family life with the changes occurring today:

> Filhos respeitavam os pais
> Irmão respeitava irmã
> Respeitavam até os velhos
> Tomavam até a benção
> Hoje estão dando valor
> A revista e televisão
>
> Escola de caratê
> Ensina o povo a brigar
> A televisão ensina
> Até a criança a furtar
> Mulher deixa a igreja
> O marido abandona o lar
>
> Vai ouvir filmes impróprios
> Nos domingos no cinema
> Vai tomar banho na praia
> Marca o passo da ema
> Nos clubes sem respeito
> Ou no Changô da Jurema. (93)

Sons used to respect their parents, and brother respected sister. They even respected the elderly folk, and they used to ask for blessing. Today they are more interested in magazines and television. Karate Schools teach people how to fight, and television teaches even little kids how to pilfer. Women abandon the church, and men abandon their homes. They go to watch unseemly films at the cinema, on Sundays. They bathe on the beaches and get drunk, unashamedly, in clubs or in 'Jurema's bar'. (93)

There is sadness in the poet's verses as he calls upon his readers to resist moral decay, and save their souls before it is too late. The acceleration of the process of integration of the rural communities of the interior into the national economy, and the consequent dissolution of the old rhythm of rural life, has created acute social problems for the inhabitants of those communities. Traditional moral and cultural values are brought increasingly into direct confrontation with new ones emanating from modern, urban, industrial life. Many *folhetos* nostalgically retreat into earlier eras in the North East, romantically recreating a golden age, sadly lost. Others, dealing with modern life, evoke a sense of being stranded, deploring and resisting the imposition of new ways, but finding traditional patterns of organisation of life disintegrating all around. In *O Tempo Bom Foi Embora*, Francisco de Souza Campos, a poet from Pernambuco, writes:

> Há trinta anos atrás
> Se via qualquer rapaz
> Ser obediente aos pais
> Mas isto era em outrora
> Hoje o respeito acabou-se
> A bandalheira avançou-se
> O povo desmantelou-se
> O tempo bom foi embora.
>
> O mundo está em escombro
> Rapaz de cabelos ao ombro
> Servindo até de assombro
> Parecendo uma senhora
> Sai na rua de calção
> É a maior confusão
> Se isto é evolução!
> O tempo bom foi embora. (94)

Thirty years ago, any lad would be obedient to his parents, but those are past times. Today respect has ended. Shameless behaviour has spread everywhere, and people have fallen low. The good times have gone. The world is in ruins. Young men have their hair down to their shoulders, causing astonishment, looking just like women. They wander round the streets in shorts, causing the greatest confusion. Is this evolution? The good times have gone. (94)

The changes in sexual relations is another problem area dealt with frequently by the poets. In *Os Namorados de Hoje*, José João dos Santos, a poet from Paraíba better known by his pen name, Azulão, writes about young women in present day Brazil:

> Lê revista escandalosa
> Sexo, nudismo, ilusão
> Quer ser artista de rádio
> Cantar em televisão
> Ganhando em troca de honra
> Boemia e perdição.
>
> Moça pobre de favela
> Só quer ser americana
> Pinta cabelo de loiro
> Tira onda de bacana
> Ainda diz ao namorado
> Eu sou de Copacabana.
>
> Só veste calça comprida
> Querendo falar inglês
> Dar bola a qualquer pilantra
> Namora dez duma vez
> Não faz parada em emprego
> Quatro, cinco em cada mês. (95)

They read scandalous magazines, full of sex, nudity and illusion. They want to appear on radio, or sing on television, trading their honour for a life of perdition. The poor girl from the shanty town only wants to be American. She dyes her hair blonde, pretending to be what she's not, and tells her boyfriend that she's really from Copacabana. She's always dressed in trousers, and wants to speak English, and invites attention from any rogue. She has ten boyfriends at a time, and never stays long at any job, but has four or five different ones each month. (95)

Behind the humour of the verses, concerns of real significance to the *folheto* readers are being aired. Two worlds are seen in conflict: the harsh reality of the *favela*, with its daily struggle for a basic existence, and the mass, industrial culture of modern, urban Brazil, with its image of opulence and liberty. The poet recognises that image as mere illusion, and warns his readers not to be tempted:

> Cuidado com vigarismo
> Fingimento e fantasia
> (...)

Eu sou um homem vivido
Que dos vícios me governo
Não me iludo com charmes
Mulher do mundo moderno
Por mim elas morrem e vão
Se estourar no inferno. (96)

Beware of trickery, pretence and make believe (...) I'm a man with experience in life, who has learned to control vices. I don't deceive myself with the charms of these modern women today. As far as I'm concerned, they'll die and explode in the flames of hell. (96)

Most *folhetos* paint a similarly negative picture of the modern culture that is encroaching, and call upon their public to resist its false values.

The dynamism of *folheto* verse is therefore demonstrated in the way that it has constantly incorporated new themes. Throughout the 1970s, for example, as the economic policies of the military government led to increasing hardship for the poorest sectors of Brazilian society, *folhetos* decrying the high cost of living and unscrupulous profiteering of the business community abounded. Most emphasise the widening gap between rich and poor, demonstrated particularly by their different eating habits. Verses from *O Clamor da Caristia*, by João Vicente Molia, state, for example:

A caristia de hoje
Não tem jeito que dê jeito
O escândalo tomou conta
Já acabou-se o respeito
O tempo está muito ingrato
Pois o jeito é comer rato
Enfiado num espeto

O rico come churrasco
Galinha e carne de galo
E o pobre fica olhando
Chega sente aquele abalo
Dizendo o tempo ruim
Já se chegasse pra mim
Mesmo a carne de cavalo (97)

There's no way of solving the inflation of today. Shameful behaviour has taken over, and all respect has gone. These are miserable times. We're reduced to barbecuing rats to eat. The rich eat barbecued beef or roast chicken, whilst the poor can only watch, feeling such misery, lamenting the bad times that have hit them and wishing they had even horse meat to eat. (97)

The same theme is developed in a *folheto* of similar title, *Os Clamores da Carestia*, by Expedito F. Silva, originally from Pernambuco, now resident in the outskirts of Rio de Janeiro. The poet condemns the plight of the poor, among whom he includes himself, and calls for change:

> A fome já tomou conta
> Do norte sul e sertão
> Cada dia o pobre fica
> Apertando o cinturão
> Vai dormir lhe falta o sono
> Vai comer não tem feijão
>
> Se morrer vai dar trabalho
> Se viver vai passar fome
> Se não trabalhar não tem nada
> E se trabalhar não come
> Porque a mercadoria
> No estrangeiro se some
>
> Vamos cultivar lavouras
> Pra ser mais estimulada
> Dando o direito a todos
> Que trabalham na enxada
> Lhes dando terra e semente
> E uma vida adequada
>
> Nunca eu tive pretensão
> De ofender a ninguém
> Sou Expedito F. Silva
> Que escreve e nada tem
> Porque a minha barriga
> De fome ronca também (98)

Hunger has spread through the north, the south and the interior. Each day the poor have to tighten their belts. They spend sleepless nights, and don't even have beans to eat. If they die they'll create problems for others, but if they live they'll suffer hunger. If they don't work they have nothing, but if they do they still don't eat, for the produce all disappears abroad. Let's develop agriculture, and ensure the rights of all those who work with the hoe, giving them land, seeds and a decent life. It's never been my intention to offend anyone. I'm

71

Expedito F. Silva, who writes, and has nothing, because my stomach rumbles with hunger as well. (98)

All contemporary social problems affecting the lives of the poor are dealt with in *folheto* verse, the poet often writing from personal experience. In *O Brasil e o Estudante Pobre*, Jota Rodrígues, already mentioned, complains of the difficulties faced by the poor in educating their children and alludes to the problems low educational standards will create nationally:

> Hoje o Brasil somos nós
> Amanhã é nossos filhos
> Quem hoje não tem diploma
> Morre apagado sem brilhos
> E um Brasil analfabeto
> E um trem fora dos trilhos
>
> (...)
>
> O governo da escola
> Colégios e faculdades
> Mantendo os professores
> Nos municípios e cidades
> Merenda e material
> Em pequenas quantidades
>
> Porém os materiais
> Tomam rumos diferente
> Por gente inescrupulozas
> Soçaites encociente
> Qui da pra o estudante rico
> O qui e do estudante carente
>
> E o ponto bázico qui tenho
> Como a justificação
> São os meus próprios filhinhos
> Qui sofrem a umilhação
> Sem pasta livro ou caderno
> Remendado e os pês no chão (99)

Today, we form Brazil, but tomorrow it will be our children. But today they have no qualifications, and they'll die having lived in ignorance, with no skills. A Brazil without education is like a train that's derailed (...) The government provides schools, colleges and universities, and teachers in our cities and towns, paying them and giving them materials, albeit not much. But those materials end up going elsewhere, due to unscrupulous people, immoral people, who give to the rich student that which belongs to those who are needy. And the basic example I have to justify all this is the case of my own small children, who suffer the humiliation of not having books, folders or notebooks, and have patched clothes and go without shoes. (99)

The persecution of street vendors by the authorities in Recife is the theme of *O Problema do Camelô no Recife*, a poem by Bernardino de Sena, from Pernambuco. Many poets, often combining the sale of *folhetos* with that of other cheap articles, such as combs, pens and key rings, have complained of such problems:

> O vendedor ambulante
> É um sujeito sofrido
> Corre daqui, vai pra li
> Lhes chamam de atrevido
> Vendendo o que é seu
> Mas mesmo assim, perseguido
>
> (...)
>
> Devido ao tão grande número
> De homens necessitados
> Que vivem assim, pelas ruas
> Até marginalizados
> Os homens sentem o problema
> Bem sério, e complexado (100)

The street vendor is forced to suffer. He goes here, there and everywhere, but people think he's impudent, and though he simply sells what's his, he faces persecution. (...) There's a huge number of needy people who live like this, working in the streets, marginalised. The problems affect them seriously, making them feel inferior. (100)

Apolônio Alves dos Santos, another poet already referred to, has produced *folhetos* on many contemporary issues, such as *O Divórcio*, arguing in favour of divorce, *O ABC do Feijão e os Tumultos nas Filas*, describing the queues which developed when there was a shortage of beans, and *Os Nordestinos no Rio e O Nordeste Abandonado*, dealing with the theme of emigration from the North East to the big industrial centres of the Brazilian South. The poet, himself an emigrant from Paraíba living in Rio de Janeiro, laments the fact that so many North Easterners have been driven out of their native region by the need to find employment:

> Assim passa toda vida
> o pobre na quebradeira
> com fome e sacrificado
> trabalha semana inteira
> por fim o saldo que tira
> não dar para ir a feira.
>
> Eis aí qual o motivo
> que obriga o nordestino
> deixar seu torrão amado
> e sair sem ter destino
> pelo mundo foragido
> feito mesmo um peregrino. (101)

The poor man spends his whole life in misery, with hunger and sacrifice. He works all week, but the money he obtains for it isn't enough to go shopping. So that's why the North Easterner is obliged to leave his beloved native land, and set off, with no clear destination, like a fugitive, to wander the world. (101)

The poet complains of the exploitation suffered by North Easterners in factories and on building sites in Rio de Janeiro, but states that it is still preferable to agricultural labour in the North East. Highlighting the contrast between North and South, the poem ends with reference to the continual suffering of emigrants from the North East, forced by necessity to move to the South, but constantly yearning to return home:

> Enquanto o Sul do País
> de mais a mais engrandece
> nosso Nordeste coitado
> de dia a dia enfraquece
> enquanto o sulista engorda
> o nordestino emagrece.
>
> Enquanto o sulista canta
> e sorrir alegremente
> o nordestino coitado
> chora copiosamente
> por se achar desterrado
> da sua terra ausente. (102)

Whilst the south of the country becomes more and more prosperous, the poverty stricken North East grows poorer each day. Whilst the southerner gets fatter, the North Easterner grows thin. Whilst the southerner sings, and smiles with happiness, the poor North Easterner weeps endlessly, because he's exiled far from his land. (102)

As was seen earlier, there are many other themes besides social problems covered by the *folhetos*. In addition to the poetry recreating traditional materials that have already been referred to, there is a wide variety of *folheto* verse which simply aims to entertain, and which relies entirely on humour, with such titles as *O Rapaz que Casou com uma Porca no Estado de Alagoas*, by José Soares, and *A Mulher que Rasgou o Travesseiro e Mordeu o Marido Sonhando com Roberto Carlos*, by Apolônio Alves dos Santos, and there are also *folhetos* of pornographic verse, termed *folhetos de safadeza* or *folhetos de putaria*, which have at times brought the poets responsible into conflict with the authorities.

Regardless of the theme, however, all such *folheto* poetry is expressed in a language specific to the social group concerned, contrasting sharply with the more formal Portuguese employed traditionally by the erudite writer. Grammatical rules are ignored, new words invented and a rich array of colloquialisms incorporated. It is a popular language with which the rural poor in the North East immediately identify. More importantly, words can have specific meanings for the group that differ from their formal, dictionary defined meaning. The poets reappropriate the language and use it for their own purposes. For example, words and terms which formally have a pejorative sense can be given a positive value in the *folheto* poetry. This can be seen, for example, in the numerous *folhetos* about the *cangaceiros*, where terms referring to robbery and violence - such as *ladrão* and *bandido* - are often redefined in a positive light, legitimising, even eulogising, the actions of the popular bandits. Similarly, the *folhetos* employ a system of symbols with set meanings for the North Eastern poor. Mário Pontes, for example, has examined the various uses made of the images of the Devil and of Hell in popular poetry, which frequently come to symbolise the hostile natural and social forces confronted by the peasant. (103) Sometimes the symbols used embody an abstract concept for the reader. The *Casa Grande*, for example, frequently symbolises the whole power of the landowning class, and whereas the coastal plantation is commonly associated with confinement, the *sertão* often represents freedom. It is invariably the *sertão* which produces the courageous popular heroes, *valentes* or *cangaceiros*, of *folheto* poetry.

In a number of different ways therefore, the *folheto* can be seen as a product, not so much of an individual author, but of the social class to which it has traditionally belonged: the poor of the rural North East. In summary, it is a form of expression that has served to strengthen the bonds linking that class, defining it, separating it from the rest of society, which it generally regards with suspicion, sometimes even clear hostility. The activity of the poet is regarded as a legitimate trade by his traditional public, and the production, distribution, sale and reading of the *folheto* has formed part of their daily lives, inseparable from other activities in which they engage. The content of the poetry, though varying with each individual author, adheres essentially to a broad, traditional framework, which reinforces collective attitudes and concerns, emanating from common social and economic experience. Likewise, the language and symbolism used in the *folheto* is specific to that group, being part of a popular literary tradition handed down among them from generation to generation, and innovations in style are not readily accepted by the traditional public. New themes, however, have been readily incorporated. So, rooted in its own particular social context, as an integral part of the social life of a particular sector of the Brazilian population, it is important to see the *folheto* as constituting a form of literature that is significantly different from the erudite literature produced by other social sectors, in the perceptions it conveys, the way it is produced and the way it relates to the community which it has long served.

We have seen that in many ways traditional *folheto* poetry can be considered a socially integrated literature, an intimate part of the life of a large social class. Here, a clear contrast can be drawn with erudite literature, most of which has always been confined to a narrow educated elite, separate from other forms of social activity, with the idea of writing viewed as an essentially private activity, closed off from society as a whole. Obviously, this conclusion highlights the problematic nature of the approach taken by contemporary Brazilian writers such as Ariano Suassuna, based on the idea of fusing popular and erudite literature in an attempt to create some form of nationally representative literature.

v] The development of the *folheto* in recent decades

By the 1960s, the process of *folheto* production was showing clear signs of decline. The social tension embodied in the centre of popular poetry, stemming from the decay of traditional patterns of life in the rural North East as the region was steadily integrated into the broad process of national economic development, eventually came to undermine the production of the *folheto*, along with other aspects of traditional rural community life. With inflation increasing the costs of printing and reducing even further the spending power of the rural poor, the number of poets and resellers gradually declined, and print-shops closed down. One of the most famous of these, the *Tipografia José Bernado da Silva*, which in healthier times used to print around 100,000 *folhetos* a week, had by 1970 reduced its output to between 1,000 and 2,500 each week, with several machines non operational. (104) Today, production is at a far lower level still, with only a handful of these traditional print-shops specialising in the production of *folhetos* now existing in the North East. In addition, Candace Slater highlights the decline of the traditional open air markets in the North East, once vital for the dissemination and distribution of popular poetry, as another factor undermining the *folheto*. Economic and commercial development has opened up new retail outlets and changed consumer behaviour, and the local street markets no longer have the same vital social role as before. (105) The expansion of urban, industrialised society has brought with it a new life style, with the mass media penetrating the *sertão*, offering alternative sources of information to the inhabitants. One observer has even commented that the increasing consumption of American style comics in the North East has been in detriment to *folheto* sales. (106)

This process of decline has itself become a theme developed by the poet, as seen in *Literatura de Cordel (O Prenúncio do Fim)*, a *folheto* written in 1980 by Marcelo Soares, from Pernambuco, describing the problems confronting popular poetry in Brazil:

> A nossa literatura
> de cordel, tão popular
> de cantada em verso e prosa
> começa a agonizar
> por isso falo das causas
> que lhe ameaçam acabar
>
> Primeiro que tudo mostra
> que uma dessas razões
> são sem sombras de dúvida
> os meios de comunicações
> radios, TV, jornais
> e outras publicações
>
> (...)
>
> Cobram alto ao poeta
> para fazer um cordel
> reclamam que todo mês

sobe o preço do papel
e que além dos empregados
têm água, luz e aluguel

Sendo xilogravador
e poeta popular
sinto ser meu o dever
de a todos alertar:
A literatura de cordel
está para se acabar! (107)

*Our "literatura de cordel", always so popular, whether written in verse or prose,
is in a critical state, and I'll talk about the causes which threaten it with
extinction. First, everything shows that one reason, without any doubt, is the
effect of the mass media, the radio, the television, newspapers and other such
publications (...) The poet pays a lot to publish a poem. Every month the price
of paper rises, and then there's the cost of the labour, and the rising cost of
water, electricity and rents. I'm a woodcut artist and a popular poet, and I feel
it my duty to warn everybody: Our "literatura de cordel" is close to
disappearing! (107)*

This decline has been used by academic institutions, government
bodies and individuals to justify the extension of their interests in
popular literature, to the point of intervening directly in the process of
production, distribution and consumption, in an effort to protect it, and
ensure its survival. It is also true that some poets have requested such
assistance, seeing it as the only way that will permit them to continue
publishing. (108) A number of universities have taken on the task of
printing works that the poets themselves cannot afford to produce, and
have launched projects to extend research on popular poetry, and devise
other methods of supporting it. Some State Governments have played a
similar role through Departments of Education or Culture. Meanwhile,
a São Paulo publishing company, *Luzeiro*, has bought the rights to
produce new versions of popular *folheto* poems. Unable to print them
themselves, and facing increasing financial hardship, many poets have
had little alternative to sell their rights to authorship, and by 1989 *Luzeiro*
had two hundred titles under its control. (109) It has printed the poetry
in a new format; a larger, more sophisticated booklet form, with
colourful comic-book covers, which some critics inevitably see as a
further degradation of the *folheto* tradition.

A new, middle-class public has emerged for the *folheto*, with
salons putting on recitals of popular song, and bookshops and craftshops
selling *folhetos* as a curiosity. One source notes:

> The new emerging public have almost always looked for
> "literatura de cordel" because they see it as something
> folkloric, in the worst sense of the word, that's to say,
> something archaic, traditional and exotic. Very rarely do
> they want it because they see it as a living element of
> our culture, which reflects popular, contemporary views
> of reality. (110)

Most poets still selling *folhetos* in public places confirm this change in the
composition of their consumers, with students, academics and tourists
accounting for an increasing percentage of sales. Clearly, such a change
will have a profound impact on the content of the work itself, with an
increasing number of *folhetos* produced for new tastes and perceptions.

Today, it is mainly brief eight page *folhetos* that continue to be
produced. There are no longer the economic conditions nor the
readership for the thirty-two page romances printed in previous decades.
News items and current affairs now provide the most common thematic
content, continuing the well-established journalistic role of the *folheto*.
Many *folhetos* are now produced as souvenirs of events of national
importance, such as the visits made to Brazil by the Pope, in 1980 and
1991, or written in homage to popular heroes at the time of their death,
such as the singer Luiz Gonzaga (1989) and racing driver Ayrton Senna
(1994). Discussion of political developments in Brazil has long formed a
strong current in popular poetry, and the turbulent events of recent years
has provided ample new material. The election of Tancredo Neves to the
presidency in 1985, signifying Brazil's return to democracy after twenty
years of dictatorship, his death before being able formally to take office,
and the impeachment of President Collor in 1992 were dramatic events
which stimulated the publication of dozens of new poems. For many
observers, present-day *folhetos* as a whole show a reduction in quality
and scope which is symptomatic of the general decline of the form, yet
it retains sufficient vigour to respond rapidly to events, and offer the
public a critical discussion of them.

A whole new industry for popular poetry has now emerged,
with record companies recording poets and *cantadores*, radio stations
emitting broadcasts, and an array of books, magazine articles and films
appearing on the subject, all of which are well beyond the access of the
traditional *folheto* public. With this situation, a new type of popular poet
has emerged, more commercially minded, orientated towards a new,
more affluent audience, like Pedro Bandeira, *cantador* of Joazeiro, who
runs a new car, regularly signs contracts with record companies and
radio stations and only appears at highly paid concerts. (111) Examples
of such financial success are few however, and by all accounts most

poets are exploited in deals made with agencies and companies. (112) As one journalist writes:

> At the same time as our film directors, dramatists, journalists and writers transform popular literature into a succulent dish, filling entire pages with praise for it, our poets are having to abandon the profession because they cannot maintain their families (...) In crowded halls, on nights when they sign autographs and consume imported whisky, such people are shameless enough to take the poets from their own environment and bring them to these luxurious concert halls in order to exhibit them and their picturesque act of begging for some cash.(113)

There are now a significant number of *folheto* writers from the middle-class professions, who use the traditional form to create a poetry that is different in style and tone, and in the vision of the world conveyed. Created under very distinct conditions, and with an essentially middle-class writer in mind, this verse is far removed from traditional *folheto* poetry.

The production of *folhetos* is now much more complicated and divided. On the one hand, the traditional sector continues, now limited to a few poet-printers struggling to preserve independence of production and content. Some poets and *folheteiros* still seek customers in the markets and towns of North East, whilst in other areas the *folhetos*, as a popular means of expression, are adapted to meet new circumstances. Joseph M. Luyten, for example, has produced a study showing how new, highly political *folhetos* have recently circulated among workers and trade unionists in São Paulo, recounting strikes and criticising government policies. He cites the example of Rafael de Carvalho, originally from Paraíba, Toni de Lima, born in Alagoas, and Pedro Macambira, whose origins are unknown, but who has produced a considerable quantity of poetry on labour struggles in São Paulo, including *A Luta da Oposição Metalúrgica Contra a Besta-Fera da Inflação*:

> Tudo mundo bem sabe,
> Vivemos em sociedade
> Que está dividida em classes
> Com gente de toda idade.
>
> Uma coisa eu lhes garanto
> Os filósofos estão analisando,

Porém, são muito poucos,
Os que o mundo estão mudando.

Do bolo que estão comendo
Não permitem a divisão.
Se não puder viver: -MORRA!
Esta é a sua canção. (114)

Everybody knows that we live in a society where people of all ages are divided into classes. One thing I can assure you: the philosophers are analysing the world, but there are few people who are actually trying to change it. Those who have food to eat, don't want to share it out. "If you cannot live, then die!" That's what their song is. (114)

On the other hand, there is another sphere of production, where *folhetos* are sponsored by dominant class institutions and organisations. As would be expected, protest is more muted in poetry of this kind. The most blatant examples of this type of production are the *folhetos de encomenda*, poems commissioned by companies or politicians for propaganda purposes, demonstrating that the *folheto* is recognised as an extremely effective way of conveying information to large sectors of the Brazilian working class and rural masses. During state elections, for example, the poet José Francisco da Silva was commissioned to write a *folheto* for Gilberto Santana, an MDB candidate standing for election as a State Deputy for São Paulo:

Atenção Trabalhadores
Contaremos com vocês
As eleições vem aí
Força coragem altivez
E para um Brasil melhor
Agora chegou a vêz.

A união faz a força
Unidos vamos lutar
Dr. Gilberto Santana
Pronto para trabalhar
Votar em Dr. Gilberto
É garantir seu lugar. (115)

Attention all workers, we will count upon you. The elections are coming, so strength, courage and pride! The opportunity has come for a better Brazil. Unity makes strength, and united we will fight. Dr Gilberto Santana is ready to work.

Voting for Dr Gilberto will guarantee you a voice. (115)

In recent years, therefore, a widening division has appeared between a growing body of dependent, patronised and compromised poetry and a small but still vigorous sector of autonomous *folheto* poetry, still produced by the poorer sectors of the population essentially for their own consumption, and underlying these different patterns of production are the conflicting ideological approaches to popular poetry referred to earlier. As already stated, it was in the context of this conflict that writers like Ariano Suassuna developed their ideas for a fusion between popular and erudite literature.

The poet closely observes the changes and conflict occurring around him. Some, through financial need, turn to the organisations of patronage in search of support. Others complain bitterly of the exploitation and interference of outsiders. And, inevitably, they write *folhetos* on the subject. In *O Artista Injustiçado*, Azulão pours scorn on the false poets who sell themselves to patrons, and condemns the hypocrisy and paternalism of the whole patronage system:

> Os falços são preferidos
> Porque são bajuladores
> Insistentes e egoistas
> Da mentira, pregadores
> Tem astúcias de macaco
> E vivem puchando o saco
> De todos seus protetores.
>
> (...)
>
> Só querem nosso folhetos
> E gravar o cantador
> Dar parabens, bater palmas
> Porem não dão o valor
> Fazem proveito do dom
> Mas o dinheiro que é bom
> Poeta nem vêr a côr.
>
> (...)
>
> Sei que muita gente vai
> Achar ruim os versos meus
> Porque a verdade fere
> Esses pensamentos seus

Querem fazer do poeta
Uma bagagem completa
Para enfeitar os museus. (116)

Fake poets get preferential treatment, because they're good at flattery. They're persistent, and they're conceited, and they spread lies. They've as many tricks as a monkey, and they live by grovelling to all their protectors (...) People want our poetry, and to record our songs, and they congratulate us and give us applause, but they don't want to pay us. They enjoy the gifts we have, but the poet never sees any money. (...) I know that many people will think that these verses of mine are terrible, because the truth hurts and offends them. They want to convert the poet into an exhibit to adorn the museums. (116)

vi]   Conclusions

Folheto poetry must be understood first and foremost as a cultural process; a form of expression which continually responds to the changing social environment within which it is produced. It has been seen in this chapter how patterns of production, distribution and reception have changed over the years. Much argument among scholars has ensued over this issue. Arguing that the popular poetry tradition of the North East needs to be protected and preserved, some have participated in projects to support poets and their work, which, as already mentioned, are frequently sponsored by government institutions or universities. Other scholars have condemned such activities as interference which only serves to corrode the *folheto* tradition, arguing that, uprooted from its original sphere of production and separated from its traditional public, the poetry concerned will assume such radically different characteristics that it will no longer be recognisable as popular verse. One of the most outspoken of these critics is Liêdo Maranhão, who summarised his views in a newspaper interview in 1979, in which he condemned all those responsible for such interference:

> They come from all over the place. Even American and French Universities are attempting to woo our popular artists, making suggestions, putting forward themes. The danger is that our popular culture will slip from the hands of the people and gain "University Status" (...) The problem of our popular poetry is how it can return to its basic qualities, and the fact that it's disappearing from our fairs, squares and our ranches. (117)

At times however, such views also develop into arguments for the preservation of popular forms of expression; arguments which fail to give recognition to the dynamism of popular culture, and conceive of popular poetry as essentially static; a form of folklore, associated with, as the above quotation suggests, disappearing patterns of social life, focused on the old open markets and town fairs long held throughout the North East, and the traditional life of the *fazenda*. From such a viewpoint, new material and themes which the poet himself chooses to incorporate into *folheto* verse are frequently condemned as further evidence of distortion.

Ariano Suassuna has been one of the most prominent participants in this debate on popular literature in the North East. He has voiced his concern about the decline in the production of *folhetos*, and in the early 1970s, through the Universidade Federal de Pernambuco, provided production facilities to poets lacking resources to print their poetry. As Minister of Culture for Pernambuco in the 1990s he has continued that task. His objective has been to give support without undermining the poets' own control over the production of their work. He acknowledges the development of new themes within *folheto* verse, but it is noticeable that in selecting sources for his plays and novels he chooses a particular type of *folheto* poetry with which to work: that with the oldest tradition, discussed earlier in this chapter, with clear and direct links with European medieval romances and frequently religious in theme. It is through this poetry that he attempts to recreate the *sertão* of his childhood in the 1930s, and discuss within his work questions which are of personal concern to him. As mentioned in this chapter, it is the more traditional poetry that captivates Quaderna, the protagonist of *A Pedra do Reino*, helping him construct in his imagination an alternative world. Thus, a *folheto* by Leandro Gomes de Barros, *O Reino da Pedra Fina*, relating the story of an enchanted kingdom dominated by large rocks, is quoted with enthusiasm by Quaderna, who immediately relates it to his native *sertão*, and his family history within it. (118) Quaderna's alternative realm is largely built on values he detects in such traditional poetry: the confirmation of religious faith as the hope for man's salvation and the magical recreation of the world into a realm where beauty and harmony prevail, and humans are exalted, imbued with courage and pride. Quaderna is enthralled with tales of heroic deeds and strength of faith, as conveyed in the poem *A Nau Catarineta*, which he recites at one point. Of Portuguese origin, but with various Brazilian versions as well, it narrates the shipwreck suffered by a famous nobleman, Jorge de Albuquerque Coelho, in 1565, during a voyage from Brazil to Portugal. Albuquerque discovers that one of his sailors is the devil who offers to save him from drowning in exchange for his soul. Albuquerque refuses, declaring that he would rather die and give his soul to God. Casting himself into the sea, he is saved by an angel:

> - Que queres então, Gajeiro?
> Que alvíssaras hei de dar?
> - Capitão, eu sou o Diabo
> e aqui vim pra vos tentar!
> O que eu quero, é vossa Alma
> para comigo a levar!
> Só assim chegais a porto,
> Só assim vos vou salvar!
> - Renego de ti, Demônio,
> que estavas a me tentar!
> A minha Alma, eu dou a Deus,
> e o meu corpo eu dou a mar!
>
> E logo salta nas águas
> O Capitão-General!
> Um Anjo o tomou nos braços,
> nao o deixou se afogar! (119)

"So what do you want sailor? What reward do you expect from me?" "Captain, I'm the devil, and I've come here to tempt you! What I want is your soul, to take away with me. That's the only way you will arrive in port. It's the only way you can save yourself!" "I reject you, demon who's trying to tempt me. My soul I'll give to God, and my body I'll give to the sea!" And then he leapt into the water, the Captain-General. But an angel caught him in his arms, and would not let him drown. (119)

The need for faith and the hope of human redemption is the most fundamental theme running through Suassuna's work, and it is to develop that theme that many of the *folhetos* are used within it. It is, for example, a popular poem dealing with the intervention of the Virgin Mary to save a condemned soul that forms a central part of his major play, *Auto da Compadecida*. Suassuna's work shows, therefore, a very selective use of popular literature to fulfil the specific objectives of the author, as will be seen in a later chapter dealing with Suassuna's plays and novels. In the process however, the dynamism of *folheto* poetry as a form of social expression and communication, which this chapter has emphasised, is lost. Ultimately, it is not popular poetry as a cultural process that is of concern to Suassuna, but popular poetry as a repository of universal and eternal values.

NOTES

1   One of the major examples of this approach is Carlos Estevam, *A Questão da Cultura Popular*, (Editora Tempo Brasileiro, Rio de Janeiro, 1963)

2   See: R. Redfield, *Tepoztlan, a Mexican Village: A Study of Folk Life* (Chicago University Press, Chicago, 1930)

3   See, for example, Mário Margulis, 'La cultura popular' in A. Colombres (ed), *La cultura popular*, (Premià, Puebla, Mexico, 1987). Margulis summarises the point (pp. 43-44) by describing mass culture as "... a culture for mass consumption. Mass culture comes from above to those below: it is produced by professionals, skilful manipulators, with suitable ingredients. It responds to the needs of the system," whilst popular culture is "the culture of those below, produced by them themselves, lacking technical means. The producers and consumers are the same people: they both create and use their culture. It is not a culture to be sold but to be used. It responds to the needs of the popular sectors."

4   W. Rowe and V. Schelling, *Memory and Modernity: Popular Culture in Latin America* (Verso, London, 1991)

5   Ramón Menendez Pidal, *Estudios sobre el romancero* (Espasa Calpe SA, Madrid, 1973), passim

6   C.C. Smith, 'On the Ethos of the Romancero Viejo', in N.D. Shergold (ed), *Studies of the Spanish and Portuguese Ballad* (Tamesis Books, London, 1972), passim

7   J.G. Cummings, *The Spanish Traditional Lyric* (Pergamon Press, Oxford, 1977), p.1

8   Veríssimo de Melo, 'Origenes da Literatura de Cordel', in *Tempo Universitário*, Vol 1, No 1, Natal, 1976, points out German and Dutch influences, whilst Roberto Benjamim, 'Breve Notícia de Antecedentes Franceses e Ingleses da Literatura de Cordel Nordestino', *Tempo Universitário*, Vol 6, No 1, Natal, 1980, refers to the influences of French and English pamphlet literature.

9   Luis da Câmara Cascudo, *Cinco Livros do Povo* (José Olympio, Rio de Janeiro, 1953), passim

10   Leandro Gomes de Barros (1865-1918), from Pernambuco, is believed to have been one of the first fully professional *folheto* poets. His output was prolific, and though no precise figures are available, some sources claim he produced over a thousand *folhetos* during his career. João Martins de Athayde (1880-1959), born in Paraíba, was not only a well-known author of popular poetry, but also one of the first major publishers of *folhetos*,

responsible for the printing of thousands between the 1920s and the 1950s.

11   Luis da Câmara Cascudo, *Vaqueiros e Cantadores* (Ouro, Rio de Janeiro, 1968), pp.15-23

12   Luis da Câmara Cascudo, *Literatura Oral no Brasil* (Coleção Documentos Brasileiros, José Olympio, Rio de Janeiro, 1978), passim

13   Luis da Câmara Cascudo, *Cinco Livros*, p.30

14   Colin Henfrey, 'The Hungry Imagination: Social Formation, Popular Culture and Ideology in Bahia', in S. Mitchell, *The Logic of Poverty* (Routledge & Keegan Paul Ltd, London, 1981), p.77

15   Luiz Beltrão, *Folkcomunicação: a Comunicação dos Marginalizados* (Cortez Editora, São Paulo, 1980), pp.51-52

16   Luis da Câmara Cascudo, *Literatura Oral*, pp.23-24

17   Robert Rowland, Cantadores del Nordeste brasileño: estructura y cambio social en el Nordeste del Brasil', in *Aportes*, No 3, January 1967, Paris, p.133

18   Antônio Arantes, *O Trabalho e a Fala* (Editora Kairós, São Paulo, 1982), pp.15-16

19   Luis da Câmara Cascudo, *Cinco Livros*, p.30

20   Manuel Diégues Júnior, 'Ciclos Temáticos na Literatura de Cordel', in *Literatura Popular em Verso*, Tomo 1, (Casa de Rui Barbosa, Rio de Janeiro, 1973), p.15

21   Mark Curran, *A Literatura de Cordel* (Universidade Federal de Pernambuco, Recife, 1971), p.11

22   Franklin Maxado, *O que é a Literatura de Cordel?* (Editora Codecri, Rio de Janeiro, 1980), p.52

23   *Antologia da Literatura de Cordel*, Vol 1, (Secretaria de Cultura, Desporte e Promoção Social de Ceará, Fortaleza, 1978), p.35

24   Ibid, p.35

25   Roberto Benjamin, *Literatura de Cordel: Produção e Edição* (Universidade Federal Rural de Pernambuco, Recife, 1979), p.7

26   Antônio Arantes, *O Trabalho*, p.37

27   Roberto Benjamin, *Literatura de Cordel: Produção e Edição*, pp.9-10

28   Mark Curran, *A Literatura de Cordel*, p.11

29   Marlyse Meyer (ed), *Autores de Cordel* (Abril Educação, São Paulo, 1980), p.91

30   Maria Edileuza Baptista, 'A História do Poeta-Repórter que Não Foi Agricultor, Não Deu para Pedreiro e Vive Feliz Escrevendo Cordel', in *Jornal do Comércio*, Recife, February 1st, 1978, part C, p.8

31   Ricardo Noblat, 'A Literatura de Cordel', Fatos e Fotos, *Gente*, Rio de Janeiro, January 1971

32   Rodolfo Coelho Cavalcante (popular poet), quoted in Orígenes Lessa, *Getúlio Vargas na Literatura de Cordel* (Documenério, Rio de Janeiro, 1973), p.56

33   Ariano Suassuna, quoted in Ricardo Noblat, 'A Literatura de Cordel'

34   Manuel Diégues Júnior, 'Ciclos', p.25

35   Manuel Caboclo e Silva, *A Sentença de Jesus e a Morte dos Apóstolos*, folheto, Joazeiro do Norte, Ceará, undated, verses 1 and 2

36   José Pacheco, *Os Sofrimentos de Cristo*, folheto, no details, verses 1 and 2

37   Apolônio Alves dos Santos, *Nascimento, Vida e Morte do Padre Cícero Romão*, folheto, Guarabira, Paraíba, undated, verse 47

38   Ibid, verse 59

39   Enoque José de Maria, *A voz do Padre Cícero*, folheto, Joazeiro do Norte, Ceará, undated, verse 4

40   Ibid, verses 5 and 6

41   Manoel Rodrigues Tenório, *A Morte de Meu Padrinho Cícero*, folheto, Joazeiro do Norte, undated, verses 61, 62 and 64

42   Ibid, back cover

43   Antônio Caetano, *A Surra que o Padre Cícero Deu no diabo*, folheto, no details, verses 30, 31 and 32

44   Amaro Cordeiro, *Estória de um Crente que Foi Castigado por Frei Damião*, folheto, Joazeiro do Norte, undated, verses 77 and 78

45   José Costa Leite, *A Santa que Falou Profetizando*, folheto, no details, verses 22 and 23

46   João Lopes Freire, *A História de Carlos Magno e os Doze Pares de França*, folheto, Rio de Janeiro, undated, verses 25 and 26

47   Luis da Câmara Cascudo, *Cinco Livros*. On page 448, the author writes: "*A História do Imperador Carlos Magno e Os Doze Pares de França* continues to be published in Portugal and Brazil but in a summarised form, adapted for todays rapid reading. Many scenes were eliminated, the plot compressed and the language of the dialogues modernised to produce a summary acceptable to modern readers."

48   Ariano Suassuna, *Romance da Pedra do Reino* (José Olympio, Rio de Janeiro, 1976), p 56. Later, on pages 280-281, Quaderna also quotes verses from *A História de Roberto do Diabo* by the Paraíba poet João Martins de Athayde, one of the many recreations of a traditional ballad about Robert the Duke of Normandy. Quaderna notes that the verses describe the Duke as a *cangaceiro*, thus confirming his opinion that, "(...) the noblemen of Normandy were *cangaceiros,* and a *cangaceiro* is worth as much

as a medieval knight." (p.281)

49   Jerusa Pires Ferreira, *Cavalaria em Cordel* (Hucitec, São Paulo, 1979), passim

50   Luis da Câmara Cascudo, *Cinco Livros*, p.186

51   See Luis da Câmara Cascudo, *Vaqueiros*. On page 189 of the work, Câmara Cascudo writes, "Malzarte came to us from the Peninsula, weaving plots and always escaping without serious consequences (...) The Portuguese *Mala-Artes*, foolish and lazy, comes from a verbal confussion of *maas-artes*, Malasarte, meaning silly or weakminded."

52   Expedito Sebastião da Silva, *As Diabruras de Pedro Malazartes*, folheto, Joazeiro do Norte, Ceará, undated, verses 2 and 4

53   In fact, João Grilo has a counterpart in Spanish America: Juan Grillo, another typical *pícaro*, frequently appears in popular literature in Argentina and Uruguay from the late nineteenth century onwards.

54   João Martins de Athayde, *Proezas de João Grilo*, folheto, Joazeiro do Norte, undated, verses 1 and 4

55   Leandro Gomes de Barros, *A Vida de Canção de Fogo e o Seu Testamento*, folheto, no details, verse 15

56   João Martins de Athayde, *Proezas*, verses 35 and 36

57   Rodolfo Coelho Cavalcante, *Lampião - Terror do Nordeste*, folheto, Salvador, undated, verse 28

58   Antônio Teodoro dos Santos, *Lampião, o Rei do Cangaço*, folheto, Luzeiro, São Paulo, undated, verse 30

59   Rodolfo Coelho Cavalcante, *A Chegada de Lampião no Céu*, folheto, no details, verses 13 and 14

60   Ibid, verse 16

61   Leandro Gomes de Barros, *Romano e Ignácio da Catingueira*, folheto, in *Literatura Popular em Verso, Antologia, Tomo 3: Leandro Gomes de Barros 2* (Universidade Federal de Paraíba, João Pessoa, 1977), pp.216-217

62   Ariano Suassuna, *A Pedra do Reino*, p.68

63   Robert Rowland, 'Cantadores', p.144

64   Candace Slater, *Stories on a String: The Brazilian Literatura de Cordel* (University of California Press, Berkeley, 1982)

65   Renato Carneiro Campos, *Ideologia dos Poetas Populares* (Funarte, IJNPS, Recife, 1977), p.35

66   Ibid, p.67

67   Raymond Cantel, interview in *Veja*, April 7th, 1976

68   Mauro W.B. de Almeida, 'Leituras do Cordel', in *Arte em Revista*, No 3, p.35

69   From the *Dicionário de Antônio Morães e Silva*, 10th edition,

Lisbon, quoted by Dr Silveira Bueno, in 'Literatura de Cordel', in the *Jornal do Comércio*, Recife, November 9th, 1982

70   Mauro W.B. de Almeida, 'Leituras', p.38
71   See, for example, Antônio Arantes, *O Trabalho*, p.44, and Mauro W.B. de Almeida, 'Leituras', p.35
72   Edson Pinto da Silva, 'Cordel Político: Irônica, Sensível e Censurada, a Voz do Povo', interview with Luzanira Rêgo in *Diário de Pernambuco*, Recife, June 16th, 1978
73   Antônio Arantes, *O Trabalho*, p.44
74   Maria Ignez S. Paulilo, 'A Parceira no Sertão Paraibano: Uma Análise de Ideologia', in *Boletim de Ciências Sociais*, No 24, Universidade de Santa Catarina, Florianópolis, Jan-March 1982, passim
75   Alda Britto da Motta, 'Notas sobre a Visão de Mundo do Camponês Brasileiro', in *Revista de Ciências Sociais*, Vol X, Nos 1 & 2, Universidade Federal de Ceará, Fortaleza, 1979
76   Jota Rodrigues, *A Dor qui Doi no Pobre é a Dor da Umilhação*, folheto, no details, verses 13, 14 and 15
77   Ibid, verse 29
78   Flávio Fernandes Moreira, *História do Feijão Preto e o Sofrimento do Pobre*, folheto, no details, verses 9, 10 and 11
79   Ibid, verses 36 and 38
80   José Costa Leite, *A Pobreza Morrendo a Fome no Golpe da Carestia*, folheto, Casa das Crianças, Olinda, undated, verses 26, 30, 31, 32 and 33
81   José Saldanha Menezes, *O Brasil Prometido aos Pobres na Epoca de Eleição ou os Amigos do Voto e Inimigos dos Eleitores*, folheto, Universidade Federal do Rio Grande do Norte, Natal, 1981, verses 3, 4, 33 and 34
82   José Camello de Mello Rezende, *A Sujeição dos Brejos da Parahyba do Norte*, folheto, verse 27, quoted by Eduardo Diatahy B. de Menezes, 'Estrutura Agrária: Protesto e Alternativas na Poesia Popular no Nordeste', in *Revista de Ciências Sociais*, Vol XI, Nos 1 & 2, Universidade Federal de Ceará, Fortaleza, 1980, p.39
83   Ibid, verse 33
84   Eduardo Diatahy B. de Menezes, 'Estrutura Agrária', p.32
85   Manoel Camilo dos Santos, *Viagem a São Saruê*, folheto reproduced in *Antologia da Literatura de Cordel*, Vol 2, pp.329-335, verse 20
86   Ibid, verses 15 & 16
87   Antônio Arantes, *O Trabalho*, p.76
88   Antônio Batista Romão, *A Morte de Carneiro e a Vitória de Arranca Véu*, folheto reproduced in Liêdo Maranhão de Souza,

Classificação Popular da Literatura de Cordel (Vozes, Petrópolis, 1976), verses 33 & 34

89   Apolônio Alves dos Santos, *O Heroismo de João Canguçu no Engenho Gameleira*, folheto reproduced in *Antologia da Literatura de Cordel*, pp.86-96, verses 6 & 7

90   Ibid, verses 120-122

91   Ibid, verses 102 & 103

92   Francisco Sales Areda, *O Coronel Mangangá e o Sertanejo do Norte*, folheto reproduced in Antônio Arantes, *O Trabalho*, pp.127-133

93   Chico Ramalho, *O Povo Desembestado*, folheto, Universidade Federal do Rio Grande do Norte, Natal, 1980, verses 7-9

94   Francisco de Souza Campos, *O Tempo Bom Foi Embora*, folheto, Casa das Crianças, Olinda, undated, verses 6 & 7

95   José João dos Santos, (Azulão), *Os Namorados de Hoje*, folheto, no details, verses 31-33

96   Ibid, verses 36 & 39

97   João Vicente Molia, *O Clamor da Caristia*, folheto, no details, verses 2 & 3

98   Expedito F. Silva, *Os Clamores da Carestia*, folheto, Rio de Janeiro, undated, verses 29-32

99   Jota Rodrígues, *O Brasil e o Estudante Pobre*, folheto, no details, verses 2, 8, 9 & 10

100   Bernardino de Sena, *O Problema do Camelô no Recife*, folheto, Casa das Criaças, Olinda, undated, verses 7 & 22

101   Apolônio Alves dos Santos, *Os Nordestinos no Rio e o Nordeste Abandonado*, folheto, no details, verses 10 & 11

102   Ibid, verses 33 & 34

103   Mário Pontes, *Doce como O Diabo* (Editora Codercri, Rio de Janeiro, 1979), passim

104   Marlyse Meyer (ed), *Autores*, p.91

105   Candace Slater, Ibid, pp.31-32

106   Sebastião Vila Nova, in 'Professor Vê Fim da Literatura de Cordel', in the *Diário de Natal*, Natal, November 13th, 1975

107   Marcelo Soares, *Literatura de Cordel (O Prenúncio do Fim)*, folheto, Rio de Janeiro, 1980, verses 1, 2, 13 & 14

108   As an example, in 1990 poet and printer Jota Borges asked Ariano Suassuna to help seek ways of supporting the production of *folhetos*, which, he claimed, was in danger of disappearing altogether. Reported in 'Cordel Pede Socorro a Ariano Suassuna', in *Diario de Pernambuco*, Recife, April 29th 1990, p.A21

109   Reported in 'Cordel Sofisticado, uma Morte Anunciada' in *Jornal do Commércio*, Recife, October 16th 1989, p.8

110   *Antologia da Literatura de Cordel*, Vol 1, p.22

111 Vanderley Pereira, 'Cantadores: Do Alpendre das Fazendas às Agências de Turismo', in the *Jornal do Brasil*, Rio de Janeiro, September 28th, 1974

112 See Marcos Cirano and Ricardo de Almeida, *Arte Popular e Dominação* (Editora Alternativa, Recife, 1978), pp.68-69

113 Leo Ramos, 'Cultura Popular: Cordel e os Poetas Famintos', in the *Tribuna da Imprensa*, Rio de Janeiro, December 29th, 1975.

114 Pedro Macambira, *A Luta da Oposição Metalúrgica contra a Besta-Fera da Inflação*, folheto, quoted in Joseph M. Luyten, *A Literatura de Cordel em São Paulo* (Edições Loyola, São Paulo, 1981), pp.100-101

115 José Francisco da Silva, *Gilberto Santana é o Nosso Candidato*, folheto, no details, verses 1 & 2

116 José João dos Santos, *O Artista Injustiçado*, folheto, 1979, verses 15, 20 & 24

117 Liêdo Maranhão, 'Declaração de Guerra aos Invasores do Cordel', *Diário de Pernambuco*, Recife, January 21st, 1979, p.D-4

118 Ariano Suassuna, *A Pedra do Reino*, pp.256-257

119 Ariano Suassuana, *A Pedra do Reino*, p.168. An almost identical Portuguese version is included in A.C. Pires de Lima and A. Lima Carneiro, *Romanceiro Popular Português* (Domingos Barreira, Porto, 1984), pp.97-98

- Que queres tu, meu gajeiro?
Que alvíssaras te hei-de dar?
- Capitão, quero a tua alma
Para comigo a levar.
- Renego de ti, demónio,
A minha alma é só de Deus,
O corpo dou eu ao mar.

Tomou-o um anjo nos braços,
Não o deixou afogar;
Deu um estoiro o demónio,
Acalmaram vento e mar;
E à noite a nau Catarineta
Estava em terra a varar.

THE VIEW FROM ON HIGH: ERUDITE
VIEWS OF BRAZILIAN CULTURE

i]   The development of regionalism and cultural nationalism

Many North East writers before Ariano Suassuna have sought ways of reaffirming the cultural values of their region in their work. Since from its beginnings the production and consumption of erudite literature has been confined to a small and isolated sector of the North East population, a crucial part of that regionalism has been the need for those writers to contribute to bridging the social and cultural chasm separating them from the mass of the region's inhabitants. As will be seen, for many of them the popular *romanceiro* tradition discussed in the previous chapter has provided vital material to work with, in both its oral and written forms. While some of the resulting formulations presented by individual writers or groups of writers over the decades proposing ways of integrating their literary work with the lives and culture of the wider populace have long been superseded, others have survived in a modified form up to the present day. The purpose of this chapter is to sketch out the various stages of thought which North East regionalism has passed through, highlighting the different approaches towards popular culture, and particularly popular literature, which have resulted. It will be necessary to consider changing perceptions of national culture over time, since, as already mentioned in the Introduction, the exaltation of regional values has frequently emerged as an integral part of broader schemes of cultural nationalism.

The colonial exploitation of Brazil was conducted through a succession of socio-economic growth poles in different zones of the territory, essentially isolated from one another, with virtually all commercial and cultural links confined to the metropolis. Each area thus developed its own distinct social and cultural characteristics, determined by the particular process of land occupation or economic exploitation which prevailed, the racial or social groups which participated in that process and the specific articulation the area concerned had to the national and, more importantly, international economies. It is in this sense that Alfredo Bosi speaks of colonial Brazil as an *arquipélago cultural*, and emphasises the relevance this formation still has for Brazilian literature today. (1) The *Movimento Armorial* of the 1970s, to be examined later, and the popularity of novels produced more recently by writers such as João Ubaldo Ribeiro, demonstrate that regionalism remains a significant force in Brazilian art and literature; a symptom of that fragmentary pattern of development which Brazil has experienced throughout its history, and continues to experience today.

The elites of the North East prospered during the early colonial period, as Bahia, Paraíba and Pernambuco developed into the major sugar producing area in the world. The economic and political importance of the region was demonstrated in the establishment of Bahia as the colonial capital in 1549, and today, in cities such as Recife, Olinda and Salvador, some elegant colonial architecture, especially opulent churches, still stand as testimony to the great wealth generated by the sugar trade. During that period, a literary tradition became firmly established among the privileged sectors of society, initially the landowning aristocracy, and then later incorporating urban professional classes. That tradition has been earnestly cultivated by generations of intellectuals ever since, undeterred by the region's political and economic decline. Indeed, it has been suggested that the dynamism of intellectual and artistic activity in the North East has been stimulated at least in part by a desire to compensate for that decline; an attempt to highlight the region's distinct position within, and contribution to, the historical development of the nation. (2) A striking feature of the literary circles that emerged in the early development of that regionalist tradition however, was their insularity, with their intellectual work totally alienated from the lives of the illiterate masses of the region. It was a growing consciousness of that alienation and the desire to relate their work more directly to the wider social life of the North East that provided a major stimulus to writers in the region during the nineteenth century.

The political movement which finally gave formal independence to Brazil in 1822 was essentially conservative, shaped by the interests and perspectives of the traditional dominant elites. The restrictive political and economic links with Portugal had to be severed in order to permit the more advantageous integration of Brazil into the commercial system being elaborated by the industrialising capitalist nations. External capitalism channelled its interests through the Brazilian dominant classes, which, in return, saw their own interests protected by those same external powers. In this way the Brazilian elites worked in cooperation with the interests of foreign capitalism, both complementary and interdependent parts in the same economic, political and ideological system. The dominant ideology of the period had to reconcile the paradoxical position of the Brazilian ruling classes, which, externally dependent and hence externally orientated, nevertheless had to forge a national cultural complex, which would consolidate their power and integrate the rest of the population into the established order. Against the reality of a deeply divided society, where a small minority monopolised political and economic power, and relied heavily on slave labour, a national culture would need to be affirmed, emphasising independence and unity. It was into the resulting ideological framework that most literature produced in Brazil in the early nineteenth century would be integrated.

It was Romanticism, still dominating European art of the period, that provided the model for that literature. Attempting to cast aside

Portuguese models following the political break with the metropolis, Brazilian writers turned to other European nations, notably France and Britain, for alternatives. In those countries, Romanticism had developed in the late eighteenth century in response to specific historical circumstances, - the beginnings of the Industrial Revolution, the ascent of the bourgeoisie and the expansion of modern, capitalist systems of production. No such conditions existed in Brazil however. The landowning aristocracy still dominated, slave labour still prevailed and the bourgeoisie was still weak. The Brazilian writer was thus caught between the European schemes of cultural expression into which he was integrated and the distinct realities of his native land. His response was to give those romantic tendencies transplanted from Europe new forms and connotations as demanded by the particular circumstances of the national environment. Suitably adapted, romantic perceptions and aesthetic models would thereby provide the vital instruments for the task of forging a nationally representative art and literature in the wake of independence.

Inevitably, contradictions resulted. Roberto Schwarz highlights the fundamental imbalance that exists within the work of Brazil's finest Romantic novelist, José de Alencar (1829-1877), due to the irreconcilability of the European form adopted, and the local thematic content, drawn from Brazilian social life, that was incorporated. From that contradiction stems the weak points of the novels: a degree of artificiality and incongruity in plot and action. However, Schwarz argues that it was through those weaknesses that Alencar was able to make his most significant contribution to the development of the Brazilian novel, for it brought to the forefront real contradictions within Brazilian cultural life which necessarily had to be negotiated by writers if Brazilian literature was to advance. (3)

The process of recasting reality in accordance with the matrix of the dominant ideology was compounded by the writer's own isolation and alienation within nineteenth century Brazilian society. Given the rigid class divisions that existed, and the external orientation of the privileged classes to which he was associated, the writer was in no position to comprehend the reality lived by the mass of the population, but which he wanted increasingly to incorporate into his work. The result was the superficial and picturesque vision of Brazil that characterised much Romantic writing.(4)

Two of the major elements cultivated in European Romantic literature were the wild natural environment and the Indian, or noble savage, both of which epitomised the romantic resistance to a reality characterised by the growth of industrialism, materialism and competition, all associated with developing capitalism, and the desire to return to a state of complete liberty, harmony, innocence and spontaneity. It was the same elements which became the major nationalist symbols for the Brazilian Romantics. In the poetry of Gonçalves Dias and the prose of José de Alencar the idealised vision of the natural world is combined with an equally romanticised image of the Indian to present a picture of harmony between man and nature. Against the harsh national reality of poverty and inequality, a utopian vision of Brazil is elaborated. The Indian provided the Romantic writers with an ideal symbol to be incorporated into the nationalist ideology that was in the process of development, facilitating the repudiation of Brazil's colonial past and the creation of a mythical national patrimony. Perceived as the only autochthonous social element, the Indian was lauded as a hero who had resisted European colonisation. In fact, Indian culture had been virtually annihilated in the first century of Portuguese colonialism, and the Indians that still lived in contact with nineteenth century Brazilian society were for the most part destitute and subservient, bearing no resemblance to the image created by Gonçalves Dias or Alencar. This, however, perhaps explains the attraction of the Indian for some writers, for as the symbol of a defeated culture, he offered no threat to the existing order.

In Alencar's best-known Indianist works, *O Guarani* (1857) and *Iracema* (1865), the idealised Indian appears as the central element in the reconstruction of a mythical national past. In *Iracema*, the love affair between a Portuguese sailor and an Indian girl, Iracema, ends in tragedy when she dies whilst he is away fighting in Ceará, but their son, Moacir, is left as a symbol of the Brazilian *mestizo*, the core of the people of Ceará and of Brazil as a whole. Sánzio de Azevedo emphasises the regional aspect of the myth:

> We are dealing with a legend, created in
> order to narrate the origins of the people
> of Ceará, with Moacir the symbol of the
> son of our land (...) (5)

In fact, Alencar creates a myth of not just regional but national identity. Fusing history and legend, the two conflicting cultures, European and Indian, are harmoniously united, with Moacir effectively representing the new Brazilian culture that is created. In this way, *Indianismo* served to negate the reality of Brazil's colonial past and create the illusion of a distinct and original Brazilian culture, that could be traced back to the earliest period of Portuguese rule. The negro slave, a vital source of wealth and power for the landowning oligarchy, was conveniently ignored. History was thereby reconstructed within the framework of a new nationalist perspective, eradicating conflict and affirming a particular Brazilian identity and culture which, as the natural result of the blending together of the finest qualities of two races, effectively gave legitimacy to the existing socio-economic order.

Alencar argued forcefully for the elaboration of a national literature, and a crucial element within his thinking was the aim of establishing a distinct Brazilian idiom within literature, in opposition to the standard classical Portuguese which, though obviously identified with the former metropolis, was still employed by most Brazilian writers. Alencar saw that the language would necessarily undergo modifications in the new environment and these had to be incorporated into literature.

> Language is the nationality of thought
> just as the motherland is the nationality
> of the people. Just as just and rational
> institutions indicate a great and free
> people, so a pure, noble and rich
> language indicates an intelligent and
> enlightened race. (6)

Alencar used various mechanisms to Brazilianise the language of literature. Indian vocabulary and expressions were incorporated into his novels, and he experimented with sentence construction to create a more poetically Brazilian style. Certainly, a major part of the originality of *Iracema* and much of its appeal, resulted from the linguistic innovations introduced by Alencar, mainly through his lyrical prose style, employing many Indian terms, which gives the language an oral quality, evoking spoken legends and ancient epic tradition. This was a new development in Brazilian literature; the first really systematic attempt to produce a distinctly Brazilian literary language. *Iracema* is an exceptional example, however. In other works such linguistic experiments resulted in artificiality, with Indian words and popular expressions merely adding piquancy to the formal and erudite prose.

Folklore played a vital role in the programmes for a national literature developed by writers like Alencar, whose novels contain detailed description of popular beliefs, regional customs and crafts, and popular stories, songs and poems. It was through their interest in popular cultural expressions and local customs that the Romantic novelists and poets made their major contribution to specifically regionalist literary tradition. Their motivation was not only the need to seek elements able to symbolise the nation, but also the desire felt by many Romantics to escape from their present and return to a collective past. A number of North Eastern writers incorporated elements of popular verse into their poetry, such as the Bahian poet and monk, Luís José Junqueira Freire, (1832-1855), and Juvenal Galeno, (1836-1831), a poet from Ceará. Speaking of this influence in his work, Galeno alluded to the distance that separated the dominant classes from the mass of the population:

> I know I will be badly received in the salons of the aristocracy, and among some critics who, studying our people in books written by foreigners, are so unfamiliar with them that they write of the lack of popular poetry in Brazil. (7)

Such a statement exposes the problem confronting the writer utilising popular expressions, yet totally alienated from the sectors of the population from which they originate. In *O Sertanejo*, (1875), José de Alencar, portraying the backlands of his native Ceará, uses a traditional romance to develop his theme, and includes much detailed description of local customs and examples of popular verses to provide the narrative with atmosphere and colour. The following extract is typical:

> Mais longe, em frente às casas dos vaqueiros, a gente do curral fazia o serão ao relento, deitada sôbre os couros, que serviam de esteiras. Uma voz cheia cantava com sentimento as primeiras estâncias do 'Boi Espácio', trova de algum bardo sertanejo daquele tempo, já então muito propalada por toda a ribeira do São Francisco, e ainda há poucos anos tão popular nos sertões do Ceará.
> > Vinde cá meu Boi Espácio
> > Meu boi prêto caraúna
> > Por seres das pontas liso
> > Sempre vos deitei a unha.
> Os tons doces e melancólicos da cantiga sertaneja infundiram um enlêvo de saudade, sobretudo naquela hora plácida da noite. (8)

Further away, opposite the houses of the cowherds, the people who worked in the corral relaxed in the open, lying on hides which served as mats. A full voice sung, with feeling, the first stanzas of 'My wide horned ox', the ballad of some backland minstrel of that time, which had spread the length of the river São Francisco, and

which up to a few years ago was still very popular in the backlands of Ceará.
> *Come here, my wide horned ox*
> *my poor black ox*
> *your horns are so smooth*
> *you're easy to overpower.*
The sweet and melancholic tones of the song instilled a sense of nostalgia, especially at that tranquil time of night.(8)

Divorced from their true social context, isolated and refashioned according to a romantic vision and Romantic literary conventions, such popular forms of expression emerge in the erudite novel as picturesque touches blended into the fantasy world created. In this particular case, Alencar recreates the *sertão* as a medieval kingdom according to the patterns of chivalric romance, with typical heroes, heroines and feudal lords. Manuel Cavalcanti Proença provides a vivid description of the hero of the work:

> Like a medieval hero, the backlander takes part in a tournament of horsemanship. He's a masked rider, and he excels in the competition, in a pure transposition of Ivanhoe, the friend of Richard the Lion Heart, and hero of Walter Scott. (9)

It will be seen that Ariano Suassuna's vision of the North East *sertão* nearly a century later has striking similarities with that of Alencar. *O Sertanejo* highlights one of the major problems of Alencar's project to create a national literature. Aspects of popular culture are seen as vital sources for the writer, but, removed from context and transformed by the author's imagination, they lose their original significance to become little more than items of curiosity or ornamentation within the erudite work. For José Guilherme Merquior, the imitation of popular forms in an effort to nationalise literature has often imposed such severe limitations on literary works that they have ended up stranded between erudite and popular expression, without achieving the attributes of either, and this is a defect he detects in some of the work of Alencar:

> That which is exuberant and beautiful in folklore becomes something ordinary, a cliché, in the domain of erudite art. The popularity of Alencar is not an argument against the psychological simplicity of the heroes of *O Guarani*, *As Minas de Prata* or

O Sertanejo. At heart, the problem of
Alencar is that which effects all Brazilian
literature in its formative phase: that in
order to be authentic, to create roots
within the country, literature had to rid
itself of the mental sophistication of its
European models, and had to place itself
on the frontier of semi-literature of sub-
genres of literature, and, above all, had to
renounce 'criticism of life'; that capacity
to problematise human existence and
society which, ever since Romanticism,
has been at the very heart of Western
art.(10)

In the latter part of the nineteenth century, certain writers,
detecting the contradictions resulting from the attempts to fuse romantic
perceptions and literary form with documentation of rural life and popular
culture, became increasingly critical of Alencar's project for literary
nationalism. One of the most notable of these critics was Franklin Távora,
(1842-1888), a lawyer, public official and novelist from Ceará, who, under
the pseudonym *Semprônio*, contributed to a series of articles on Alencar's
novels in a Rio de Janeiro journal, *Questões do Dia*, in 1871 and 1872. For
Távora, Alencar's literary nationalism had failed because the author's
romantic imagination had prevented authenticity in his portrayal of
popular customs, cultural expressions and local environment. What was
required, Távora implied, was a more realistic interpretation of Brazil's
natural and social environment, based on more rigorous analysis and
observation.

Távora's criticism was not purely a disagreement over literary
approach, however. He also resented the decision by Alencar, a fellow
cearense, to write novels such as *O Gaúcho* (1870) and *Til* (1872), based on
Southern regions of the country, at a time when, on the basis of the
flourishing coffee economy, the Centre-South appeared to be establishing
economic, political and cultural hegemony over the rest of the nation,
including the once dominant North East. Távora argued fervently for the
elaboration of a distinctly North Eastern literature, for it was in his native
region, he believed, where authentically Brazilian traditions were best
preserved, whereas the South had become distorted by cosmopolitan
values. (11) The notion of the North East embodying most typical of Brazil,
essentially because the region's particular historical development has
produced a much slower rhythm of change of its social structures and
traditional patterns of life than in other zones of the country, has

reappeared in the work of many other North East writers right up to the present day. As will be seen in subsequent chapters, it can be detected in both the *Movimento Regionalista* of 1926 and the *Movimento Armorial* of 1970, for example. It reveals both the strong sense of regionalism that has continued in the North East, and the contradictory position of the writer, seeking to affirm regional culture, yet unable to reconcile himself to the dynamism of that culture, constantly changing and assuming new qualities.

ii]   Sílvio Romero and Euclides da Cunha

By the last few decades of the nineteenth century, Romanticism had been superseded by a whole new approach towards literature in the North East of Brazil. The roots of this change lay in the transformation undergone by Brazilian society at large during the course of the century, with the expansion of the economy, fostered chiefly by coffee exports, stimulating the modernisation of the basic socio-economic structures which had been established under the colonial regime. The expansion of commerce, accelerating urbanisation and the emergence of the first industries were reflected at the social level by the decline of the traditional plantation aristocracy, and the rise of the urban middle classes, totally divorced from the land. From those middle sectors emerged new ranks of writers and intellectuals increasingly vociferous in their challenge to aristocratic thought and values, epitomised by monarchism and slave ownership.

This changing environment provided a receptive atmosphere for the whole gamut of scientific formulations that had emerged in Europe in the course of the century, such as Positivism, Evolutionism and Naturalism, all of which were integrated into the thought of the ranks of the Brazilian intelligentsia. On the one hand such theories provided the basis for a new critical and scientific intellectual approach to the study of society and culture, more in keeping with the pattern of modernisation and economic development, whilst on the other they furnished new material for the dominant ideology. Racial and climatic determinism not only justified imperialist control over Brazil at the international level, but also the position of the Brazilian dominant classes nationally.

Nowhere in Brazil was this process of change more evident than in the North East. At the socio-economic level, the gradual replacement of the traditional sugar mills by the *usinas* was clear evidence of the decline of the old sugar aristocracy, the *senhores de engenho*, and the pattern of plantation life associated with their patriarchal dominance. This process of decline was to be documented by numerous twentieth century North Eastern writers. At the cultural level, the *Escola do Recife* emerged in the latter decades of the century as a major focus for the new scientific doctrines emanating from Europe, demanding a new critical and systematic analysis in all disciplines, through the implementation of scientific criteria. Based at the Recife Law school, the most influential figure of this group of intellectuals was Tobias Barreto (1837-1889), a lawyer, journalist and teacher from Sergipe, who argued for the complete renovation of Brazilian thought, paralysed, he believed, by stagnant, out-dated romantic perceptions. In literature, such thinking was almost inevitably reflected by the replacement of the idealist, romantic vision, dominant for so many decades, by the explicit desire to create a more authentic impression of the world; to record it with greater realism and objectivity.

The work of Sílvio Romero (1851-1914), a law student from Sergipe who became one of Barreto's main disciples, encapsulated this new outlook, and was to be a major influence on many twentieth century Brazilian intellectuals. However, for Romero, and many other Brazilian scholars still struggling to define a national identity, the realist perspective they adopted tended to engender a pervasive pessimism. The theories of racial and climatic determinism which they assimilated appeared to prove scientifically the inevitability of the superiority of some nations over others, and to condemn Brazil to perpetual underdevelopment. Romero's ambiguity regarding so many fundamental problems is symptomatic of this continuing contradiction in the position of the Brazilian intellectual, on the one hand working to affirm a national identity, yet on the other integrated into the framework of European perspectives which led to exceedingly problematical conclusions about the nature of that identity. Although the more untenable notions propagated at the time, particularly those related to race and climate, were soon discredited and discarded, others, refracted through the work of critics like Romero, have maintained a certain influence to the present day.

Romero attacked Romanticism and Indianism for distorting Brazil's historical development, and attempted to reach a more objective interpretation through the application of new scientific criteria. The fact that those criteria were as much the product of European ideology as of scientific research, explains the contradictions in the resulting work. Rejecting the Indian as a national symbol, Romero saw true Brazilian culture embodied in the *mestizo*. Miscegenation had created a new type, conditioned by the physical environment and a transplanted European culture:

> All Brazilians are mestizos, if not by
> blood, then in their ideas. Those
> responsible for that basic fact have been

the Portuguese, the blacks, the Indians,
the physical environment and imitation of
foreign patterns. (12)

However, the theories of biological determinism which Romero
was incapable of rejecting, implied the inevitable inferiority of the
Brazilian *mestizo*, and Romero was forced to try to resolve the dilemma by
advocating increased European immigration in order to whiten the
population, through the process of natural selection, and thereby enhance
its capabilities. The conclusion is inevitably pessimistic, with the *mestizo*,
the true Brazilian, perceived as inadequate and in need of transformation.
As will be seen, the idea of the emergence of a completely new racial type,
peculiarly Brazilian, was to be developed by many other intellectuals,
notably Gilberto Freyre, who attempted to rectify Romero's negative
interpretation in the process.

In accordance with his scientific approach, Romero also rejected
the literary nationalism of the Romantic era as being too concerned with
superficial, external appearances, and making no attempt to understand
the psychology of the Brazilian people. His efforts to tackle this problem
led him on a search for a spiritual quality unique to Brazilians, the *alma
brasileira* that determines national identity:

> Being Brazilian means being it in the core
> of one's spirit, with all our defects and all
> our virtues. And having within oneself
> something indefinable but real, which is
> ours alone, and which no else has. (13)

As with other intellectuals, this concept provided the basis for a systematic
classification of the psychological characteristics of the Brazilian, which
could then be used as explanations, at least partial, for virtually all aspects
of national reality, including cultural manifestations.

Alma brasileira is perceived as a quality common to all Brazilians,
transcending regional and class differences. Yet those differences, vividly
exposed by the varied forms of cultural expression throughout the
country, were too obvious to be ignored. Romero's solution to the problem
was to argue that Brazil's condition of dependency meant that some
regions and certain social sectors, namely the privileged classes, had
become imbued with alien values which acted as a barrier against an
authentically Brazilian expression. For Romero therefore, such an
expression had to found among the poorer mass of the population:

It is in popular cultural expressions that

national character can be clearly seen today. (14)

Significantly, it was this period of development of the social sciences at the end of the nineteenth century that produced the first systematic studies of popular culture in Brazil. Celso Magalhães (1849-1879), from Maranhão, another member of the *Escola do Recife*, wrote *História da Poesía Popular* in 1873, the first study of North Eastern popular poetry, and Romero himself soon followed by compiling a detailed catalogue of such material, published as *Contos Populares do Brasil* (1883) and *A Poesia Popular Nordestina* (1885). Soon, many North Eastern scholars, such as João Ribeiro Fernandes (1860-1934), a Sergipe journalist, and José Rodrigues de Carvalho (1867-1935), from Ceará, were contributing to the study of regional folklore.

The ideological implications of this interest in popular culture must not be overlooked. The dominant classes, attempting to construct an ideology of national culture which would legitimise their position, were obliged to find the necessary tools in the very classes they dominated, and this contradiction deeply marked much of the work of the many writers who, consciously or unconsciously, participated in the process. It could already be detected in the work of Romero himself. On the one hand he asserted the existence of a national character, rooted in a spirit or soul which fundamentally united all Brazilians, whilst on the other he argued that character could only be properly perceived in particular social classes.

For Romero, the contribution an author made towards distinguishing national identity in his work was regarded as a major criterion for evaluating its merit. Imitations of European tendencies were condemned, and encouragement given to writers to project that which could be regarded as most characteristic of Brazil. It was an attitude shared by many other writers and scholars of the time, clearly evident, for example, in the thinking of the two Ceará critics, Araripe Júnior (1848-1911), and João Capistrano de Abreu (1853-1927). Such a nationalist stance frequently led to distortion, encouraging writers to record in detail the appearance of things without considering the forces underlying them. The notion that some aspects of national life were more Brazilian than others could only compound this very unbalanced portrayal of national reality, with authors emphasising those particular features that appeared to serve their ends. Like Távora, Romero saw the North East as the region where national character was best revealed, and he too, conscious of the contrast between the growing dominance of the South and the decadence of his native North East, was anxious to reaffirm the cultural tradition of his region's elite. Later North Eastern writers were to feel the same necessity.

These attitudes came to predominate in intellectual circles of the North East at the end of the nineteenth century, propagated by groups such as the *Escola do Recife*, and providing the main orientation for most literary criticism of the time and a host of writers in the Naturalist-Realist vein. Academic research and literary production flourished in the region during this period, an indication of how socio-economic development, with increased urbanisation and the expansion of the reading public, had broadened the base of that production. This was demonstrated by the significant increase in the number of newspapers printed in the region in the latter decades of the century, the strengthening of educational institutions and the founding of numerous literary associations throughout the region, such as the *Academia Francesa*, which functioned between 1872 and 1875 in Ceará, and in which Capistrano de Abreu was a major participant, and the *Padaria Espiritual*, also in Ceará, founded in Fortaleza in 1892. The manifesto of the *Padaria Espiritual* typically revealed the regionalist and nationalist preoccupations of the time:

> 21: Any piece of literature which speaks of fauna and flora not native to Brazil, such as the skylark, the elm tree, the nightingale, the oak tree, etc, will be considered to be unworthy of publicising (...)
> 34: The *Padaria Espiritual* undertakes to organise, as soon as possible, a book of popular songs which are genuine creations from Ceará. (15)

The emphasis on Brazilian subject matter and the attraction towards popular culture, characteristic of so much erudite writing of the period, was to be developed further by the Modernist Movement of the 1920s.

It is necessary, however, to emphasise the social and cultural gulf that separated these nineteenth century intellectuals from the poorer sectors of the population in which they were interested. Their intellectual formation was incapable of furnishing conceptual tools and techniques which could enable them to record the life of the urban and rural poor. Many North Eastern writers of the time, however, believed that Naturalism provided the answer. Through its emphasis on the natural forces of heredity and environment as explanations for the human condition, they saw the hope of a scientific approach for dealing with regional reality, particularly its contradictions and conflicts. The efforts by Naturalist novelists such as Domingos Olímpio and Rodolfo Teófilo to document objectively the reality of their environment did add new elements to the thematic content of North East literature, and produced a detailed, historical record of many aspects of regional life. However, they were too imbued with determinist ideology to achieve the objectivity to which they aspired. The lives and culture of the poor, of whom they sought a deeper understanding, were adapted to fit into that ideological framework. Distant from their subjects they tended to relay on minutely detailed description of physical appearance to suggest the personality of the character being portrayed, and, typical of their fundamentally pessimistic view, such characters are frequently depraved or pathological. Characters frequently lack animation, but are presented as mere types at the mercy of hostile forces, like the persecuted negro, the plantation worker crushed by poverty or the *sertanejo* dehumanised by the drought. Helpless against such forces, the characters seem at times fatalistic, stoic in their acceptance of misfortune, and at others the tragic victims of adversity. When included, popular poetry and song is either presented as a lament to suffering, or simply used in an attempt to increase accuracy in the representation of regional life. Comparing this with the approach towards popular culture of earlier Romantic writers, one critic writes:

> The element of folklore, unlike that in the earlier regional novel, was not an inherent central interest in the naturalistic novel of Brazil. On the contrary, one has the feeling that this note is injected artificially by some novelists in an attempt to add to the authenticity of their documentation. (16)

In the absence of objective conditions similar to those which had engendered the movement in France, Naturalism was unable to establish itself as a dominant, pioneering force in Brazilian literature as a whole, and the Naturalist novel steadily degenerated into pompous verbalism and florid phraseology, with far greater importance conferred upon style than on content and ideas. The early years of the Old Republic (1889-1930) were fraught with political strife and severe economic difficulties, and the series of internal divisions, between the modern and the antiquated, the city and the country, the prosperous and the impoverished, appeared to be sharper than ever. It was a period of conservative government, with the oligarchies of the most powerful states ruling through a system of mutual accord, concerned only with attaining a degree of stability and the protection of their own economic interests, and incapable of tackling the major problems of national integration or of recognising the need for a more viable and democratic system of national government. So strong was the pessimism and determinism among the Brazilian intelligentsia that most writers could only respond to such conditions by either retreating into pure aestheticism, seeking refuge from the discord in the society around them behind the maxim of art for art's sake, or by producing a conservative, pro-establishment literature which avoided political and social problems.

Only a few writers managed to escape this cultural paralysis afflicting the Brazilian literature of the time, and confront crucial national issues. Such critical thinking is most clearly demonstrated in *Os Sertões*, by Euclides da Cunha (1866-1909), a work that was to have a profound impact on Brazilian literature, above all in the North East, for, although da Cunha was born in the state of Rio de Janeiro, it was the backlands of Bahia that provided the material for the book. The messianic movement at Canudos, and the military conflict that ensued, were symptomatic of the chronic disorders afflicting the region, at a time when the newly formed Republic was emphasising the need for accelerated modernisation and development. Most members of the educated classes, concentrated in the expanding urban centres strung out along the coast, remained largely oblivious to the appalling social conditions which prevailed in the interior of the North East, where periods of drought merely aggravated the poverty generated by an unjust social system. It was a major achievement of *Os Sertões* to stir the consciousness of those middle classes, by ruthlessly confronting them with a hitherto disregarded dimension of Brazil, and forcing them to face the magnitude of national problems. The book was instantly acclaimed by critics upon publication, and its rapid sales testify to the impact it had on the reading public. Certainly, more than any other work published in the first two decades of the century, *Os Sertões* ruptured the established literary culture, characterised by the writers social detachment and consequent tendency to evade social problems.

The dramatic force of the language and style adopted by da Cunha certainly helps to account for the book's success, but, as will be seen, Skidmore makes a valid point by suggesting that the absence of any radical propositions within the work may have been another significant reason:

> Most of the answer probably lies in the fact that Euclides was able to touch the raw nerve of the elite's guilt about the gap between their ideal of nationality and the actual conditions of their country without making his readers uncomfortable by questioning all their basic social assumptions. (17)

The fact is that *Os Sertões* reveals the same ambivalent attitude towards the mass of the Brazilian populace and to the problem of defining the nation as that which characterised the work of many other thinkers at the turn of the century. Though sensing the social causes underlying the tragedy, and anxious for greater social justice, da Cunha is unable to extricate himself from the web of determinist philosophy, and this contradiction explains the ambiguity of so many of his reflections and conclusions. Not surprisingly, as Dante Moreira Leite clearly shows in his perceptive study of the thought of da Cunha, his reaction towards the problem of racial composition is particularly confused, on the one hand attempting to perceive the possibility of future national development, whilst on the other still accepting the notion of progress governed by biologically determined racial aptitude. (18) So, although he asserts that no racial unity exists in Brazil, and possibly never will, he argues that as social development carries the country towards national integration, so a *raça histórica* will emerge, a people fused together by national development to affirm a true Brazilian nationality:

> We are predestined to form a historic race
> in the distant future, if an extensive
> period of autonomous national life is
> allowed to pass. In this respect, we will
> invert the natural order of things. Our
> biological evolution requires the
> guarantee of social evolution. (19)

The notion of continual process of miscegenation gradually producing an authentic nationhood was a common one at the time, explaining the inadequacies of the present whilst offering hope for the future. Olavo Bilac even employed the theory to account for the difficulties in affirming a national literature, arguing through Darwinian concepts that diverse racial elements were still struggling against one another in Brazil, and only when the final racial type had emerged from the process could an authentically Brazilian literature be produced. (20)

Euclides da Cunha accepts the precept of superior and inferior races, and therefore sees miscegenation as having produced a mass of degenerated *mestizos*, with the attributes of the strongest races degraded by inferior blood. This would appear to undermine his hopes for an historic race in the future:

> And the mestizo (...), rather than an
> intermediary, is a decadent being, without
> the physical energy of his primitive

ancestors, nor the intellectual capacity of
superior forefathers. Far from productive
and creative, he reveals signs of
extraordinary moral hybridity: a spirit
which flares inconsistently, lighting up
one moment and then quickly
extinguishing itself, damaged by the
fatality of biological laws, brought down
to the inferior level of the least favoured
race. (21)

However, he sees the inhabitants of the North East interior, the *sertanejos*
or *jagunços*, as an exception, arguing that, unlike the *mestizo* of the coastal
regions, they have evolved in the isolation of the *sertão*, free from the
distorting pressure of having to adapt to an alien way of life:

The backlander is, above all, a strong
character. He does not have the
debilitating sickness of the mestizos on
the coast. (22)

The author goes on to describe with enthusiasm some of the traditions of
the *sertanejo*, including popular poetry and song. Yet there is inconsistency
in his arguments. Having negated the possibility of racial unity, da Cunha
then suggests that the *sertanejo* is the basis of true Brazilian nationality,
describing him as:

The heart of our nationality (...) the
bedrock of our race. (23)

The contradictions produced by determinist philosophy are clearly evident.
Like other intellectuals of the time, da Cunha was unable to make a
distinction between race and nationality, to break through the conceptual
framework of European ideology in order to develop a more
autochthonous perception of Brazil. The conflict persisted between the
need to affirm a national identity on one hand, and the credence given to
racial and environmental determinism on the other.

The sympathy da Cunha holds for the *sertanejos* increases as the
military campaign against them continues, and their ingenuity, courage
and dignity become increasingly evident. His doubts about biological
factors as a satisfactory explanation for their primitiveness leads him to
consider socio-historical factors as well, thereby indicating a critical social
consciousness unusual for the time. He recognises, for example, the

problems caused by patterns of land ownership in the North East *Sertão*:

> (...) The plantation owner of the
> backlands lives on the coast, far from his
> extensive properties, and at times he's
> never ever seen. They have inherited an
> old historic vice. Like the old landholders
> of the colonial period, they parasitically
> use up the profits from their lands. Their
> cowherds are submissive serfs. (24)

With determinist philosophy superseded, the North East novelists of the 1930s would develop this critical social analysis of regional and national problems. Yet if da Cunha was able to at least glimpse the real significance of the maladies besetting the *sertão*, he also recognised the alienation of the intellectual, and the abyss that separated him from the mass of the population:

> We are caught up in the current of
> modern ideas, but in the heart of our
> country we have a third of our people left
> in darkness. We are beguiled by a culture
> lent to us, disseminating, through blind
> copying, all that we consider best of the
> culture of other nations, and we sharpen
> the contrast between our way of life and
> that of our simple countrymen, who are
> more like foreigners in this land than the
> immigrants from Europe. For we are
> separated from them not by a sea, but by
> three centuries. (25)

The real originality of *Os Sertões* lay in the fact that it presented a penetrating critical analysis of Brazilian society, probing the deep seated contradictions of the nation's historical development that underlay such phenomena as the messianism of Canudos. The baseness of Brazil's dominant society came to disturb da Cunha more than the understandable deficiencies of the *sertanejos*, and it is with increasing irony that he records the fortunes of the civilising mission conducted by the nation's armed forces. Blaming society as a whole for having failed the *sertanejos* and thereby provoking the tragedy, he comes to view the entire campaign as virtually a criminal act. The situation must be remedied, he believes, through a positive effort to integrate such marginalised sectors of the population into society:

> That whole campaign would be a useless
> and barbaric crime if we did not take
> advantage of the paths opened by the
> artillery with a strong campaign,
> continuous and persistent, to bring those
> rough and archaic compatriots of ours
> into our time and incorporate them into
> our pattern of existence. (26)

So, despite da Cunha's penetrating social criticism, the fundamental values of Brazil's dominant culture remained essentially unchallenged. Instead, the social problems afflicting the backlands of the North East are explained by society's neglect of the region's inhabitants. Euclides da Cunha still views the lives and perceptions of the *sertanejos* as an anomaly that must be corrected by the more advanced dominant society. He looks upon them with paternalism, delegating to society the duty of absorbing them and reeducating them. True to the positivist philosophy of the time, the best course for Brazilian development is seen to rest upon the extension of the hegemony of the dominant classes and the further imposition of dominant class values.

Nevertheless, da Cunha's commitment to a critical analysis of Brazil's social contradictions clearly differentiated his work from most of the products of the dominant cultural matrix of the period, and presaged a new attitude on the part of the writer, which would be consolidated by the Modernist Movement of the 1920s. Few other writers at the beginning of the century were able to attain the same level of penetrating criticism. Their work generally remained confined to imprecise condemnation of the stagnation of the existing cultural environment. In the North East, for example, various groups worked to stimulate greater interest in, and production of, literature. (27) Cecília de Lara has documented the work of the *Nova Cruzada*, a literary association of middle-class professionals in Bahia that functioned between 1901 and 1910, and concludes that, though lacking any clear and cohesive ideological identity, and generally producing rather banal and conventional poetry and prose, the unifying factor of the group was the common desire of its participants to combat local indifference and invigorate the artistic life of Salvador, and this enabled it to make a significant contribution to literary tradition in Bahia. Emphasis was given to the rich artistic past of the state and the desire expressed to restore some of its lost prestige. (28)

All these critical tendencies, despite their contradictions and widely varying viewpoints, were indicative of growing strain on the narrow and restrictive political and cultural framework serving the interests of the traditional landowning oligarchy, as increasingly vociferous middle and working classes applied more and more pressure in an effort to see their demands represented. The stimulus given to national industrial development by the First World War simply acted as a catalyst for this process, with political organisation and industrial strikes increasing appreciably, until a critical stage was reached by the 1920s. The *Tenente* Movement, a rebellion of young military officers in alliance with dissident politicians in all states, demonstrated how the political monopoly held by the traditional landowning classes, with the São Paulo coffee bourgeoisie in the forefront, was beginning to crack. Dissension among those classes themselves, upon whose consensus the functioning of the oligarchical political system depended, eventually led to the complete collapse of the Old Republic in 1930, and the consequent fragmentation of political power. An industrialising, urban bourgeoisie seized its opportunity to challenge for political leadership and work for a national reorientation towards the development of industry, centralization and the overall modernisation of its social, political and economic structures.

Correlative developments took place at a cultural level. The ascending urban sectors required new forms of expression to articulate their particular perception of a modern Brazil, with reshaped national economic and social structures; a modernising vision aiming to close the gap between Brazil and the industrialised nations of the West. Before Modernism, writers had only been capable of expressing a vague, unarticulated unease about the established cultural complex and its specific approach towards artistic activity, but the Modernists of the 1920s presented a head-on challenge, as new European tendencies were assimilated by Brazilian intellectuals, providing them with the conceptual tools and formalistic innovations necessary for a thorough renovation of existing cultural patterns. Viewed as central to that process was the need to break the isolation of the erudite artist, and to establish a more intimate relationship between his work and the life and culture of the mass of the Brazilian population.

iii] Modernism

Brazilian Modernism was too heterogeneous and eclectic in character to bear any coherent and consistent philosophy. Nevertheless, the *Semana de Arte Moderna*, launched in São Paulo by a group of young artists in February 1922, provided a forum for the concretion of the diffuse ideas that had evolved during the preceding years, and initiated another vital phase in the debate on the issue of national identity. An onslaught was made on what they regarded as the narrow, alienated academicism of the

Parnassian literature still prevailing in Brazil. It was this offensive, the overriding desire to negate virtually all the values lauded by the traditional literary establishment, that united writers of diverse political and aesthetic tendencies behind the Modernist cause in the early phase of the movement, and thereby provided much of its initial dynamism. (29) A new artistic vision was called for, rejecting anachronistic poetic abstraction in favour of a more realistic transcription of contemporary Brazilian society. The modernisation of literature was to accompany the modernisation of national structures. Clearly implied was a new attitude on the part of the writer, abandoning his insularity to immerse himself in the social world around him and register the lives of all the Brazilian populace. Through the development of this consciousness on the part of the writer, the Modernists made the long running problem of affirmation of national identity a major objective of their programme. Sérgio Buarque de Holanda emphasised this idea, stressing the need for the writer to base his work in the realities and needs of the Brazilian people:

> Brazil must have a national literature, and
> it must, sooner or later, attain literary
> originality. Inspiration from national
> issues, respect for our traditions and
> submission to the deep voices of our
> people will accelerate the final result. (30)

For Mário de Andrade, the onus was on the writer to develop an intimate sense of identity with his native land, and with its population as a whole, in order to overcome the perennial problem of disinterest and alienation which, he believed, had long hindered the emergence of a distinctly national literature. Only with this type of national creative consciousness could the Brazilian writer achieve the artistic originality necessary to make a truly valid contribution to universal literature:

> Only being Brazilian, that is to say by
> acquiring a patriotic Brazilian personality,
> will we become universal, because that is
> how we will contribute something new,
> which enriches human culture. (31)

This nationalistic approach was concretely expressed in the broad thematic content of the Modernist poetry that emerged in the years following 1922. A positive effort was made to include those aspects of Brazilian social life shunned as unpoetic by the Parnassians, who had tended to regard classical, academic themes as the exclusive content for erudite verse. Much of the work of the São Paulo poets, Oswald de Andrade, Ribeiro Couto and Menotti del Picchia, for example, shows a clear desire to capture the everyday life of the expanding urban environment that was such a striking feature of the Centre-South of Brazil, whilst, as will be seen, other writers frequently turned to regional traditions, folklore and dialect as the sources for their work. Manuel Bandeira (1896-1968) summarises the movement in the following terms:

> The Modernists introduced free verse into Brazil; they sought to express themselves in language free of both Parnassian rhetoric and Symbolist vagueness, less bound by the dictates of logic, adhering less closely to classic Portuguese standards of vocabulary and syntax. They boldly broadened the field of poetry, taking in the most prosaic aspects of life. In its beginnings, their movement was destructive in nature and characterised by novelty of form. Later it took on a decidedly nationalistic tone, seeking to provide an artistic interpretation of Brazil's present and past. (32)

The desire of the Modernists to produce a poetic expression that was more representative of the nation as a whole, with all its variety, contradictions and social complexity, forced them to look increasingly towards the rural and urban masses comprising the majority of the Brazilian population. This implied the recognition that the symbols which needed to be assimilated into creative literature in order to make it a distinctly national expression had to be located within the culture of those working masses. For many of the Modernists, breaking down the barriers between erudite and popular cultural expression offered the hope of creating a truly national art. (33) For Mário de Andrade it also offered a personal solution to his sense of alienation. He carried out extensive studies on Brazilian popular culture between 1925 and 1929, especially that of the North East, where he collected popular songs, poems and legends and watched dances and festivals, noting how such expressions were integrated into the daily social life of the communities concerned. He regarded this work as being of considerable importance for his development as a writer, and he published several studies on folklore and later founded the Brazilian Society of Ethnography and Folklore. During a visit to Pernambuco in the late 1920s, he listened to a violinist from a peasant community and afterwards wrote his impression of the music:

> There were the oxen going out into the
> countryside; there were the cowherds
> gathering the animals together; and the
> trotting of hooves on the roadway; the
> sound of the stampede; the call of the
> cowherd calming the frightened beasts
> (...) of course, the piece was terribly
> crude, badly played and naive. But it still
> had some useful sections and ingenious
> descriptive inventions. And above all it
> was moving. When you have your heart
> in the right place, capable of seriously
> facing up to the abuses against the
> people, then something like this moves
> you greatly, and you never forget it.
> Beyond the imperfections of what the
> people create there comes a force, a
> necessity which, in art, is equivalent to
> what faith is in religion. That is what can
> move mountains. (34)

The popular legends and myths he heard provided vital sources for some
of his poetry, as seen in the collection *Clã do Jabuti*, published in 1927. One
example is the poem *Toada do Pai-do-Mato* (Father of the Woods), where he
adopts a popular ballad form, a *toada*, to present a figure of folklore from
Alagoas, the *Pai-do-Mato*, an enormous beast, devourer of humans, taller
than all the trees of the forest, whose roaring and laughter can be heard
at night:

> A môça Camalalô
> Foi no mato colhêr fruta.
> A manhã fresca de orvalho
> Era quase noturna.
> -Ah ...
> Era quase noturna ...
>
> Num galho de tarumã
> Estava um homem cantando.
> A moça sai do caminho
> Pra escutar o canto.
> -Ah ...

Ela escuta o canto ...

(...)

O homen rindo secundou:
-Zuimaalúti se engana,
Pensa de que sou ariti?
Eu sou Pai-do-Mato.

Era o Pai-do-mato! (35)

The girl Camalalô went into the woods to gather fruit. The morning was fresh with dew. It was almost dark as night. Ah ... it was almost dark as night. On the branch of a tree there was a man singing. The girl wandered off the path to listen to the song. Ah ... she listened to the song. (...) Laughing, the man said: "Young girl, you are mistaken. Do you think I'm from your tribe? I'm the father of the woods." It was the father of the woods! (35)

For many of the Modernist poets, it was such popular myths and legends, which they saw as the distinct creation of the Brazilian imagination, that provided the raw material for a national self-expression. Such an emphasis on images regarded as unmistakably Brazilian often produced a strong element of the picturesque and the exotic in the resulting poetry, seen in some of the work of Mário de Andrade and a major Modernist poet of the North East, Jorge de Lima (1895-1953), from Alagoas, who employed aspects of the negro popular culture of his region in his verse. To some extent, however, this exoticism was counterbalanced by the genuine attempt made by the Modernists to reach a deep understanding of popular cultural forms and of their social significance, as in the detailed studies carried out by Mário de Andrade in the North East. This contrasted sharply with the Romantic writers of the previous century who were also attracted to folkloric forms, but who could only view them from afar, idealising them so as to blend them into their romantic world view. Jorge de Lima, for example, was well acquainted with the Afro-Brazilian songs, poems and religious rituals of the North East, and directly employed the idiom and rhythms associated with them to produce his so-called *negrista* poetry. The use of such sources creates a very distinct and original atmosphere and some very vivid verse. However, though some of Jorge de Lima's poetry protests against white attitudes towards the negro, other verses tend towards a colourful exoticism which detracts from the real problems experienced by the black population.

Although the nationalist current in Brazilian Modernism is rightly emphasised, its most memorable products result not from attempts to cast aside Western literary tradition and return to what is perceived as a pristine, primitive Brazilian culture, but rather from the utilisation of Surrealist, Dadaist, Futurist and other European vanguard influences to recreate popular cultural and folkloric sources. The clearest example is *Macunaíma*, published by Mário de Andrade in 1927, an extraordinary fusion of Indian legends, folk-tales and popular beliefs in a unique prose form, often poetic, which combines phrases and vocabulary from varied regions of Brazil. In terms of the conception of the development of a national culture, the vision embodied in the work contrasts significantly with that of the earlier Romantics who elaborated a mythical national past with the Indian at its centre. Instead of harmony, *Macunaíma* presents a vision of cultural discord and conflict within Brazil. Having left his tribe in the jungle and experienced life in the contrasting world of São Paulo, the hero, Macunaíma, finally destroyed, ascends to the sky, and the last images in the work show the culture from which he originated in ruins. In the novel popular culture is employed to produce a critical view of Brazil's cultural past, present and future which shatters the idealistic vision of a harmonious national culture produced by other writers. The work also demonstrates how Modernism had consolidated a change in the writer's attitude towards popular culture, leaving behind the detached observation and documentation of the nineteenth century writers, to adopt a position of more active involvement, actually using popular cultural manifestations as the essential substance for literary creation.

Through his work with popular culture, Mário de Andrade confronted the major problem of bridging the social divisions that sharply split the nation, where the contrasts between capitalist modernisation and underdevelopment appeared ever more acute. Some of his poetry laments such divisions, and expresses a longing for greater social unification. One Modernist solution to this problem was to attempt an amalgamation of the numerous and disparate cultural manifestations they encountered, producing a loose cultural synthesis that more accurately reflected the intense diversity within the nation. It was this type of fusion that was attempted by Mário de Andrade in *Macunaíma*.

Even more striking than the new thematic material that emerged in Modernist poetry were the innovations pertaining to form and technique that were developed. Free verse, unorthodox syntax and lexical experimentation became common devices, breaking down the rigid grammatical code and phraseology the Parnassians had decreed for poetry. A major motivation for these linguistic experiments was the desire to affirm a distinctly Brazilian language in literature. Brazilian Portuguese clearly had its own diversity, with numerous variations according to region, ethnic group and social class. The Modernists believed that capturing that diversity, and evolving a literary idiom that was based on the colloquial speech of the masses rather than on the formal grammar of academics, which they saw as restrictive, even suffocating, was an obvious method of developing a more nationally representative literature. Manuel Bandeira, for example, argued that the writer had lost contact with the language of the streets that could give vitality to his work and *Brazilianise* it, and had become imprisoned within a web of formal, linguistic conventions.

The broadening of literary language was certainly a vital achievement, conquering greater liberty of expression for writers in the future. The North Eastern novelists of the 1930s, such as Lins do Rego and Amado, were to take full advantage of this when they came to write their social novels centred on regional life. Yet these linguistic experiments had clear limitations when considered within the context of the Modernist project for cultural nationalism. Mário de Andrade, one of the most active Modernists in this direction, recognised this:

> The Modernist spirit recognised that if we were now living on the basis of our particular Brazilian reality, we needed to revise our instrument of work so that we could express ourselves with a distinct identity. Almost overnight a fabulous 'Brazilian language' was invented, but it was still too early (...) the lack of an adequate scientific framework, reduced everything to individual manifestations. (36)

At times the language used by the Modernists appears artificial, with the original popular expressions and vocabulary divorced from their wider social context and welded together in the poem to form a new, colourful idiom expressing the personal vision of the writer. Some of the poems of Jorge de Lima, for example, place such strong emphasis on cadence and musicality that the content tends to evaporate into exoticism, and it is when he injects a note of social criticism into his *negrista* poetry that the most memorable work results.

As has been seen, the problem of national identity was a major force of motivation for the Modernist writers, and it was to provide a wide variety of intellectual responses. The common desire to renovate Brazilian literature and establish a new role for the writer tended to mask the essential heterogeneity of the movement during the early years, but once the broad aims had been presented, and the attack against the literary establishment launched, the sharp divergences of thought within the Modernist ranks quickly became apparent. The question of cultural identity steadily led the movement away from its initial concentration on purely artistic problems, and on to a broader philosophical plane. A number of sub-groups formed throughout the 1920s, each issuing its particular perception of Brazilian culture, and the role the artist was to play in its construction.

Oswald de Andrade was the main motivating force behind the so-called primitivist groups, *Pau-Brasil* (1924) and *Antropofagia* (1928), which called on the artist to free himself from the traditional, elitist erudition, which had only served to stifle natural, spontaneous creativity, and seek inspiration instead through direct contact with indigenous subject matter. (37) Brazil wood, *Pau-Brasil*, the country's first export as a colony in the sixteenth century, and which gave the nation its name, symbolised the national culture Oswald de Andrade envisaged, where the artist would return to the native roots of Brazilian civilisation for inspiration. That native, popular culture would reshape imported Western values to produce a new Brazilian cultural identity. *Antropofagia* carried these ideas further. It provided another metaphor for the new culture, a cannibalistic culture in the sense that it would devour cosmopolitan influences, rather than be destroyed by them. Again, those influences would be recreated in a manner that was uniquely Brazilian. Although some critics have considered it to be escapist, Mário da Silva Brito indicates how *Antropofagia* rose in opposition to the extremely conservative movements of cultural nationalism, *Verde-e-Amarelo* and *Anta*, to present a more radical and rebellious notion of Brazilian culture:

> Now, in 1928, Oswald de Andrade launched the *Antropofagia* movement, with Tarsila do Amaral at his side, both opponents of *Verde-e-amarelo* and *Anta*. Like those movements, *Antropofagia* preached a return to the primitive, but to the primitive in a pure state, if one can call it that, or rather, without any obligations to the established social order, whether religious, political or economic. It's a return to the primitive before it became linked to society and to Western, European culture. *Antropofagia* values natural man. It's antiliberal and anti-Christian. (38)

In contrast, *Verde-e-Amarelo* (1926) and *Anta* (1929), the latter essentially an extension of the former, represented the position of the extreme right. Typically, they stressed national unity as the vital factor, conceived of in deeply subjective terms; the familiar inner spirit that unites all Brazilians. The manifesto of *verdamarelismo* declared:

> It is the very physiognomy of the Brazilian people, not categorised by philosophical or political definitions, but manifest in common tendencies. (39)

A warning is given against questioning this concept of national unity by making distinctions among the population. Instead, the artist is called upon to reject all theories and preconceived ideas and simply produce, without questioning, in order that cultural identity may evolve naturally, from the inherent spirit of the Brazilian people, free from ideological constraint:

> We invite our generation to produce without debate. Whether it be good or bad, to simply produce (...) We seek to write without preconceptions, not to experiment with styles or to advance certain theories, whatever they may be, but with intuition, free from prejudices.(40)

However, inconsistencies within the group's manifesto soon betray the deeply reactionary and authoritarian nature of their approach. Having claimed to be fighting the tyranny of ideological systematisation in the name of freedom of thought, they state:

> We accept all the conservative institutions, for it is within them that we will carry out the inevitable renovation of Brazil, as has always been the case. (41)

The text of the manifesto therefore appears to invert completely the fundamental objectives of the group. Behind the call to the artist to cast aside all ideological preconceptions in order to express himself freely, is the clear desire for intellectuals to cease thinking for themselves in order to accept mindlessly the rigidly conservative ideology espoused by the group itself.

By the late 1920s, the intensity and pertinacity of the nationalist debate was bringing a negative reaction from some writers, such as those associated with the *Festa* group (1927). Retreating into intense subjectivity, they advocated that poetry should return to the. spiritual, the mysterious and the sublime. (42) None of these groups were capable of undertaking the deeper analysis of Brazilian society that was required if an understanding of its underlying dynamics was to be reached. Instead, they expended their energies devising impressive sounding formulas that too often offered a diversion from fundamental problems rather than a constructive contribution towards their exposure and examination. Nevertheless, it will be seen that the delineation of basic ideological lines that emerged with the various Modernist groups affirmed a number of concepts and positions on the question of cultural identity that are still discernible in much contemporary Brazilian literature.

In conclusion, bringing the writer into more direct interaction with forms of popular culture, which were studied and assimilated into erudite works, and breaking down many restrictive conventions of literary forms and style in order to create space for a freer expression, were major achievements of the Modernists. However, some of the key problems they set out to tackle remained unresolved, notably those arising from the issue of cultural nationalism. Though the discussion on national culture produced many original ideas, the concept itself was viewed as essentially unproblematical by many Modernists of the 1920s, so that its political and social connotations remained unchallenged. The result was revealed in a tendency towards the exotic in some Modernist art. In attempting to nationalise Brazilian literature by refashioning manifestations of popular culture, the writer carried the risk of producing a picturesque abstraction of the reality underlying that culture, a process that could reinforce rather than question the ideology of a harmonious national culture. (43)

Few Modernist writers showed such sensitivity towards the contradictions within Brazilian society as Mário de Andrade. In 1942 he looked back on the work produced by himself and his fellow Modernists twenty years before in a remarkable essay of self criticism, which Carlos Guilherme Mota considers to be "um dos limites mais avançados de conciência política do momento" *"One of the most advanced boundaries of political consciousness of the time"*. (44) The poet criticised himself for being too blinded as a young writer by his privileged social position, his *aristocracismo*, to recognise the ideological dimensions of his work, and saw now that the discussions on cultural nationalism in which the Modernists became embroiled were never able to provide a penetrating analysis of the nature of Brazilian society, nor of the social and political roots of that cultural nationalism. He wrote:

Sincere, and keen, many of us were not combative enough in our work. The approach was right at the beginning. The error was that we began to fight against phantoms. We should have filled our discourse with more anguish, and more rebellion against life. Instead we broke windows and discussed fashions, and eternal values, or satisfied our curiosity about culture. And if I look over my numerous works, which represent an entire career, I do not see myself once grasp the problems of the moment and attack them as I ought to have done. (45)

The Modernist Movement nevertheless constituted a vital phase in the whole debate on erudite and popular culture and many of the ideas that resulted, radical and conservative, would be developed by others in the following decades.

iv]   Gilberto Freyre and the *Movimento Regionalista* of 1926

As Mário da Silva Brito has indicated, the initial phase of Brazilian Modernism was very much a São Paulo and Rio de Janeiro phenomenon. (46) It was only in the atmosphere of those two rapidly developing and cosmopolitan cities that middle-class intellectuals were in a position to launch a concerted attack on the cultural establishment and propose alternative ideas. However, the movement rapidly radiated out to other urban centres, including those of the North East. Despite attempts by Gilberto Freyre and others to minimise the Modernist influence in Recife in the 1920s, the subsequent writings of Joaquim Inojosa have convincingly demonstrated that the Modernist presence in the city was in fact of considerable strength during the period. (47) The active Modernist group founded in Recife in October 1922 by Austo-Costa, Durán Miranda, Raul Machado, Ascenso Ferreira and Inojosa himself undoubtedly had a significant influence on artistic circles throughout the North East through their dissemination of Modernist trends and innovations.

Parallel to these developments, Gilberto Freyre launched his Regionalist Movement at a specially organised congress in Recife in February 1926, with the objective of affirming and promoting the cultural values of the North East. There has been much heated discussion on the relative dependence or relative autonomy of Freyre's movement *vis-à-vis* the wider Modernist Movement. Whereas some critics have stressed its strong Modernist influence, Freyre himself always strongly denied this. (48) Hardly anything constructive has emerged from this debate, too often concerned with matters of personal prestige rather than objective analysis. In fact, throughout the 1920s and 1930s, there was a close interaction between Modernist and regionalist ideas in Pernambuco. Both tendencies emerged in response to the growing pressure for artistic renovation and, as such, searched for an expression that could contribute to a more nationally representative art and literature, often intertwining in the process. Indeed, much of the creative force of the North Eastern writers who developed their work in the subsequent years, such as Manuel Bandeira, Jorge de Lima and the social novelists of the so-called *Geração de Trinta* derived from the ability to fuse the two trends, combining the formalistic innovations of the Modernist with the regionalist impulse for sociological inquiry into North Eastern life and values.

However, significant ideological differences over the question of national culture and popular culture are evident when a comparison is made of statements by some of the leading Modernists and others made by Freyre. Mário de Andrade recognised the dynamism of popular culture, constantly transforming in interaction with Western cultural practices and models, whilst for Freyre the popular culture of the North East represented a way of life that was under threat from the corrosive influence of cosmopolitan values. It was the cosmopolitanism of Modernism that Freyre most objected to, whereas Mário de Andrade criticised regionalism for being too restrictive and insular. (49) Freyre's Regionalist Movement may be seen as part by-product of, and part reaction to, the Modernism of the Centre-South. The active participation of the regionalists in the general movement demanding cultural reassessment and artistic renovation meant that certain affinities were inevitable. Yet, at a time when the regional oligarchies who had long monopolised political power were facing increasing pressure from the centralising, industrial bourgeoisie based in the Centre-South, a process that culminated in 1930, when the latter would assume power and begin to establish a centralised state apparatus, the emphasis that the North Eastern intellectual elite placed on regional traditions is easily explained. For the likes of Freyre, Lins do Rego and José Américo de Almeida, major figures in the *Movimento Regionalista*, Modernism also represented an affirmation of the hegemony of the dynamic Rio-São Paulo axis over the formal cultural life of the nation. Hence Freyre's constant references to the need to protect regional traditions against the surge of modernisation and cosmopolitanism, and his description of the Regionalist Movement in its manifesto:

It is concerned with all those elements of

regional culture which need to be
defended and developed. (50)

The retrograde nature of the Regionalist Movement is thus clearly
revealed. Freyre saw the popular culture of the North East, embracing
living conditions, diet and art forms, as being in a state of steady decline,
even extinction, suffocated by a relentless process of cultural massification,
and thus in need of protection by those with the necessary intellectual and
financial resources. For this purpose, Freyre proposed regional museums,
craft shops and folkloric festivals. His elitist paternalism reaches the point
of absurdity when he deals with the disappearing culinary tradition of the
North East, of which he states:

> This whole tradition is in decline, or at
> least in crisis, in the North East. And a
> cuisine in crisis means an entire
> civilisation in danger: the danger of
> losing its distinctive character. (51)

His answer is to establish a restaurant in Recife specialising in local dishes
and complete with appropriate regional *décor*; including palm trees and
parrots in cages. (52) When it is remembered that the North East has one
of the highest rates of malnutrition in the whole of Latin America, the true
depth of Freyre's conservatism is clearly exposed.

Despite such evident detachment from the underprivileged mass
of the population, Freyre reiterates the by now well-established view that
it is precisely with those sectors that authentic Brazilian culture rests, and
that to affirm a national cultural identity, artists and intellectuals must
work for greater approximation to them. This, he believes, constitutes the
greatest motivating force for artistic and intellectual creativity in Brazil:

> In the North East, whoever gets close to
> the people delves down to the roots and
> origins of life, and of regional art and
> culture. If you reach out to the people
> you will be among masters and can
> become an apprentice, even if you are a
> Bachelor of Arts or a doctor of medicine.
> The power of Joaquim Nabuco, Sílvio
> Romero, José de Alencar, Floriano, Padre
> Ibiapina, Telles Júnior, Capistrano,
> Augusto do Anjos, Rosalvo Ribeiro,
> Augusto Severo, Anto de Sousa and other

> great representatives of North East
> culture came principally from contact
> they had, when children in the
> countryside or in the city, with popular
> traditions, and the poor people of our
> region. (53)

In many ways, Freyre's regionalist philosophy highlights the contradictions plaguing the alienated Brazilian intellectual. Striving desperately to elaborate a national cultural identity, and recognising the poverty stricken masses as the only possible supplier of the necessary materials, Freyre remains incapable of extricating himself from the restrictive ideology of his social class in order to come to a deeper understanding of the conditions of life experienced by those masses. The result is a detached, patronising vision of the people, whom he views as ingenuous and compliant.

Dante Moreira Leite and Carlos Guilherme Mota have shown how Freyre's conservatism is equally discernible in his major work, *Casa Grande e Senzala*, published in 1933. Freyre's objective was to reinterpret Brazil's social and cultural formation, ostensibly through a detailed study of social history, highlighting the vital and positive role miscegenation played in the process. Brazil is shown to have benefited considerably from the contribution of the three formative races, whose attributes have blended together to form a distinct, and favourable, Brazilian character. It was this optimistic interpretation, involving the rejection of any notion of the inferiority of certain races on the one hand, and the appreciation of the contribution of the previously denigrated negro on the other, that led to the book being hailed as innovative, and even radical, in the 1930s, a period when fascist doctrine was extremely influential. More recent criticism has undermined such appraisals. Carlos Guilherme Mota points out that Freyre's apparently benevolent view of the negro is decidedly one-dimensional, concentrated on a figure of subservience and acquiescence, and that, more significantly, each race is still perceived as having distinct, innate psychological traits, that help explain its pattern of behaviour. (54) This means that Freyre, who, like other intellectuals before him, made no distinction between race and nationality, conceived national identity to be formed essentially by psychological characteristics which he himself distinguished by his own intuition, but which were scientifically unverifiable. Dante Moreira Leite has further shown how, around this intensely subjective interpretation, Freyre attempted to mould his documentary evidence, employing it in such a way as to completely undermine its objective value. (55)

Freyre's assertion that the cultural behaviour of Brazilians is determined fundamentally by inherent psychological qualities, rather than by socio-economic realities, permitted him to mask the question of class divisions within Brazil, and to perpetuate and reinforce the mythology of an all inclusive national culture. The theme of a common psyche, developing through the process of miscegenation, to unify the race, and hence the nation, is constantly repeated throughout *Casa Grande e Senzala*:

> Predisposed through hereditary factors to life in the tropics, due to long experience of tropical conditions, the Jewish element, mobile and adaptable, gave to the Portuguese Coloniser some of the principal physical and psychological conditions for his resilience and his success. (56)

> Every Brazilian, even when white with blond hair, carries in his soul, if not in his body, the shadow, or at least a dash, of the Indian or the negro. (57)

For Freyre, this basic psychological unity has been reinforced by certain objective factors that have further contributed to cultural homogeneity, namely the Catholic church and the patriarchal family. (58) It is this overall vision of unity, the harmonious formation of a national culture, that enabled Freyre to universalise his interpretation of Brazilian development, and present it, not as the perception one particular social class has of its own history, but as an objective study of the Brazilian population as a whole.

Carlos Guilherme Mota has lucidly explained the precise social roots of Freyre's ideological approach, which he describes as the *visão senhorial*. (59) Attached to the old rural aristocracy being edged from power by new social forces, Freyre's work can be interpreted as a reaction to the decline of his social class, and an attempt to redeem it through a favourable reinterpretation of Brazil's social history. It is in this context that Freyre exalted the role of the traditional rural oligarchy in the process of national development, stating at one point:

> It has been in the great houses of the landowners where, right up to the present, the Brazilian character has best been expressed. (60)

Freyre saw the old patriarchal plantation regime, based on slave labour, as having been an essentially positive force in Brazil's socio-economic history, laying down the foundation for national identity and the development of a unique racial democracy, by creating an atmosphere that encouraged miscegenation rather racial segregation. The contribution of the rural elites is thereby projected into the future, linking them positively to the modernising capitalist development that was then, in the 1920s and 1930s, reshaping the social and economic structures of the nation. Historical evidence that is incompatible with this vision of harmonious social evolution, such as social uprisings, class antagonism and the brutality of the slave system, is either ignored or incorporated in an appropriately attenuated form. As already stated, Freyre's interpretation, embodying the world-view of a particular privileged social class, is presented as universal and objective, the evidence being manipulated for the purpose, in the manner indicated by Dante Moreira Leite.

Freyre's interests always focused on the North East, with the bulk of his research and published work based on that region. Yet he and other regionalists could not simply isolate themselves from national political realities, particularly with the process of centralisation exposing ever more clearly the decline and dependence of the North East. Ultimately, they had to express themselves within a national context, and it is not surprising that Freyre, having so strongly emphasised the distinctive characteristics of his native region, should still refer to a national character and national culture. The apparent paradox is explained in terms of the dilemma facing a social class whose regionally based power was being eroded by national political centralisation. Freyre however, was unable to reach any understanding of the process of articulation between the regional and the national, tending simply to extend his conclusions on the North East to the national level. Moreira Leite observes that Freyre

> Accused of employing almost exclusively material relating to the sugar producing area of the North East, and afterwards generalising his conclusions for the whole of Brazil, he replies that his travels through other regions confirm his interpretations. (61)

This tendency to generalise inevitably resulted in contradictions in Freyre's work. Having, for example, argued that different regions produce different psychological types, he still tried to define the typical national character. The problem is that the ideological restrictions of his class prevented Freyre from understanding the significance of the socio-economic development of North East Brazil within a more global context. His vision remained essentially parochial.

Nevertheless, Freyre's pioneering role cannot be denied. His main achievement was that, through the application of new theories in the social sciences, he presented a radical reassessment of Brazilian history, which countered the determinist philosophies that were still influential at the time, and offered a positive vision of the nation's cultural formation. His work, especially *Casa Grande e Senzala*, consolidated the shift to culture as the centre of analysis, rather than race, highlighting the role of cultural rather than racial syncretism. (62) Freyre's ideas and his Regionalist Movement established a firm basis for the sociological study of North East life and culture in the following years. His regionalism was symptomatic of the developing consciousness of local intellectuals of the accelerating decline of the North East within the context of overall national development. The disintegration of traditional regional structures was accompanied by little compensatory modernisation or development, and the continuing stagnancy and poverty of the region was increasingly highlighted by the rapid expansion of the industrialising centres of the South. Against such a background, local writers and artists felt an increasing inclination to regenerate the deep-rooted regionalist tradition, now provided with a new rationale by Freyre's regionalist doctrine. This sharpened social consciousness with regard to regional problems was reinforced by the gains now consolidated by Modernism: the propensity for national introspection, presaged in the North East by Euclides da Cunha, and the new aesthetic values established, which would open up new possibilities for literary expression. (63)

v]   Social Realism and the work of Jorge Amado

In the 1930s and 1940s, the North East proved to be one of the most richly productive regions for the Brazilian novel. A whole series of social realist works appeared in various North Eastern states. Their authors became known collectively as the *Geração de Trinta*, though in truth, the only common factor that linked them together was their overriding preoccupation with living conditions and social relations within the North East, viewed with a varying degree of criticism. Although the works produced early in this period tended to be starkly realist sociological studies of local life, some of the authors, most notably Jorge Amado, would later develop their regionalist writing through the incorporation of many elements of North East popular culture.

Some of these writers, namely José Américo de Almeida and José Lins do Rego, eulogised the most traditional cultural values of the rural interior, threatened perhaps, but surviving still, and their work clearly reveals the influence of the regionalist thought of the time, with its sense of nostalgic longing for a past era. Nostalgia particularly marks the novels of Lins do Rego, and he himself emphasised the impact that Freyre's ideas had on his literary career. (64) There was clearly a strong philosophical affinity between the two. Lins do Rego was also the descendant of a traditional, plantation owning family, and had to face the same reality of social and economic decline in the North East, with the disintegration of the traditional patterns of life which revolved around the *casa grande* of the plantation owner. Lins do Rego's response to the decadence of his social class, and of the whole way of life it determined, is to retreat into a past era, reconstructing with consuming nostalgia the semi-feudal rural society of the family-owned mill and tenant farmers. His early novels, written between 1932 and 1936, and referred to collectively as the *ciclo da cana de açucar*, are therefore strongly autobiographical, broadly tracing his own childhood and adolescence against the background of the profound transformations that were occurring in the sugar zone of the North East in the early part of the twentieth century. (65) The mechanised production of the factory mills, controlled by large corporations, steadily eroded the social relations associated with traditional sugar production, dominated by long established families, thereby leading to the establishment of new patterns of life, and new values.

Lins do Rego links his own lost childhood with the disappearing world around him in novels such as *Menino de Engenho* (1932) and *Banguê*(1934), both pervaded by a sense of melancholy, of time remorselessly destroying everything. From this perspective, the past is idealised. In *Fogo Morto* (1944), for example, admiration is expressed for the traditional landed aristocracy, vigorously upholding their code of honour and justice against the increasing corruption and violence of the world around them, and sympathy conveyed for the poor rural workers, abused and wretched, but still retaining their creativity and intuitive wisdom, revealed, for example, in the ballads constantly sung by the negro, José Passarinho, which, by narrating traditional stories, captivate and move the others on the plantation. It is a deeply romantic vision of the past, with the harsher aspects of the family plantation and slavery eradicated to present an overall picture of tranquillity and harmony, now seen as being destroyed by the encroaching modernised forms of agricultural production. The poor in his novels appear as the hapless victims of their environment, and humanitarian paternalism on the part of the benevolent property owner is seen as the most viable solution to their situation.

Lins do Rego's own contact with the masses of the rural North East led him to appreciate the popular culture of the region, and like Freyre, advocate it as a major source of material for Brazilian artists. He claimed that his approach to writing, instinctive rather than rationalised, and based largely on the spontaneous recollection of events from memory, was influenced above all by the blind popular poets he had seen in fairs throughout the North East. In *Poesia e Vida* he writes:

> (...) when I imagine my novels, I am always guided by the way things are said as they come to my memory, like the simple methods used by the popular poets. The Brazilian novel does not need to find a Charles Morgan or a Joyce to give it real existence. The poets in the market places will serve the writer better, just as the wandering minstrels of France served Rabelais. (66)

Certainly his prose style frequently reveals this influence, seemingly written in haste without revision, so that refined literary style is sacrificed in an effort to achieve a greater sense of spontaneity. Nevertheless, the type of empathy to which Lins do Rego alludes was obviously impossible, and the results were limited to a stylistic imitation of popular forms, used to recreate his own highly personal vision of the rural North East.

Where his colloquial narrative style is arguably most effective is in his works based more directly on regional popular culture, such as *Pedra Bonita* (1938), focusing on the theme of messianism, and characterised by the simplicity and directness of its narrative, a mixture of chronicle and folk tale. The novel reworks real events that took place in 1837 in the Serra Talhada in the *sertão* of Pernambuco, where, at a site dominated by large, towering rocks - Pedra Bonita - a large messianic community carried out ceremonies of human sacrifice in order to release Dom Sebastião from his state of enchantment so that he could lead them to redemption. The community was eventually massacred by a locally raised army. It is these same events which feature, in a strikingly different form, in Suassuna's *A Pedra do Reino*. In *Pedra Bonita*, Lins do Rego develops the theme in a modern fictitious context, which centres on the deep-rooted hatred existing between the inhabitants of the traditional backlands communities in the vicinity of Pedra Bonita, and those of the small town of Assu, who dream of modernisation and development. The two communities fought in 1837, and the conflict between them has continued ever since. The novel's central character, Antônio Bento, is caught between them, having his roots in the backlands, where he was born and brought up, and where his family still lives, but then, following a drought, having been taken in and looked after by Padre Amâncio in the town, despite opposition from all the other townsfolk. The tension finally breaks into violence again, when another messiah appears at Pedra Bonita, organising another religious community and promising redemption. The response of the townsfolk, as in the previous century, is to call for armed action, and an army is duly sent. In the last pages of the book, as the army sets off on its mission to destroy Pedra Bonita, Antônio is faced with a decision. Padre Amâncio is dying and sends him to fetch a priest to hear his final confession. Antônio can either fulfil the dying wish of the priest, his *padrino*, to whom he owes so much, or go to Pedra Bonita to warn his people of the approaching army. He chooses the latter course of action. His *padrino* is too pure and honourable to require the blessing from anyone in a society that is so corrupt and debased. The theme of opposition between civilisation and barbarism is raised once again, with Antônio deciding that it is modern society, represented by the authorities, the army and the townsfolk, that is the true embodiment of barbarity.

The novel therefore reworks some of the key issues raised by da Cunha in *Os Sertões*, over thirty years before, emphasising the continued tension in the North East between traditional patterns of life and the forces of modernisation, once again seen as essentially dehumanising by Lins do Rego. Banditry, popular poetry and above all messianism are all employed by the author to reinforce that central theme, emphasising the distinct traits of life in the *sertão* and the distinct world view of its inhabitants, for whom, starving and sickly, fanatical Sebastianism offers the only hope of change. In a later work, *Cangaceiros*, published in 1953, when Ariano Suassuna was producing his early plays also composed from popular sources, Lins do Rego uses features of popular poetry to the full, employing colloquialisms, refrains and extracts from popular songs to create an oral, lyrical style, indicative of an increasing inclination among North East writers to assimilate the actual forms, styles and techniques of popular literature into their work.

This interest in assimilating constituent elements of popular culture into the erudite novel is also evident in the work of Raquel de Queiroz (born in 1910), from Ceará. Her initial preoccupation with documenting the life of the poorest sectors of North East society, in her social realist novels of the 1930s, gradually gave way to an increasing attraction towards the colourful and folkloric manifestations of regional culture, which overlay the harsher realities that had provided early inspiration. The novels which she wrote between 1930 and 1937 - *O Quinze* (1930), *João Miguel* (1934) and *Caminho de Pedras* (1937) - very clearly embody the influential literary tendencies prevalent in Brazil at the time, synthesising the propensity for a declared social and political commitment, the preference for a freer and more colloquial language, as advocated by the Modernists, and the interest in regional life and culture. The resulting focus on the struggle of the underprivileged social sectors of Ceará gained her a reputation for political radicalism, but in fact, from the very beginning her attitude towards the poor of the North East was essentially paternalistic and philanthropic. The hero and heroine of *O Quinze*, Vicente and Conceição, both from progressive landowning families, respond to the suffering of the poor with acts of charity, and it is their love affair, and their personal dilemmas in the face of the problems posed by the environment around them, which become dominant in the novel, tending to limit the dramatic potential of the tragic deprivation of the poor, which becomes increasingly subordinated as a backcloth to the personal predicament of the main characters. Overall, the human tragedy of the North East is attributed more to fate than to objective, human-made conditions, and in seeking a solution to the problem, the emphasis is placed, not so much on social and political change, as on the need for change within the individual's own philosophy towards life, so that each may find his or her own way of confronting its problems and conflicts.

In the 1950s Raquel de Queiroz wrote two plays based on aspects of North East popular culture, *Lampião* (1953), dealing with social banditry, and *A Beata Maria do Egito* (1958), on messianism. In both cases, these tragic and romantic themes are developed to considerable dramatic effect through a terse, colloquial language, yet her main concern is not so much to reach an understanding of the popular material she employs, but to reconstruct it into an erudite form in order to convey her own perspectives and preoccupations, seen in her use of the main female protagonists of the two plays, Maria Bonita and the Beata respectively, in order to study the particular psychological conflicts affecting women in North East society. Part of the tension in *Lampião*, for example, derives from Maria Bonita's conflict between her desires for a new life, free from the danger and bloodshed of *cangaço*, and her love and loyalty for Lampião, which in the end costs her her life. As Adonias Filho shows, on the one hand the work examines the strict code of honour, liberty and justice which binds the *cangaceiros* together, and on the other, highlights the problems of Maria Bonita in adapting to that code. (67) From the original sources Raquel de Queiroz extracts aspects which afford her the opportunity of developing and dramatising her own areas of concern.

Of the *Geração de Trinta*, it is the Bahian novelist, Jorge Amado (born 1912) who has made greatest use of popular culture in his work. He established his career in the 1930s, with the development of his so-called proletarian novel, dealing essentially with the development of political consciousness among the poorest working sectors of Bahian society, rural in the case of *Cacau* (1933), and urban in *Suor* (1934). In these novels, Amado, armed with extremely simplified breakdown of Communist Party ideology of the time, employs a very stark, simple documentary style in an attempt to convey the misery and exploitation of the working poor and their struggle to free themselves from those circumstances. In its compilations of snippets of descriptive detail, this realist style does succeed in providing some earthy images of the squalid living conditions of the poor. Yet even here there are signs of the sentimentality and romanticism that would become so prevalent in Amado's later works. In *Suor*, for example, the austere description of the impoverished lives of the inhabitants of a slum dwelling in Salvador occasionally lapses into sentimental digression, with the dreams and ambitions of the characters contrasted with the sordid reality of the objective conditions around them. Thus, an unemployed violinist is made to escape into a fantasy world of famous concerts and world tours, whilst an ex-circus clown locks himself in his room at night, dons his costume and performs his act to an imaginary audience, only to weep afterwards as realisation of reality returns.

Similar tendencies can be detected in *Cacau*, which is given a romantic, almost fairy-tale ending when the hero, a young plantation worker who gradually develops his sense of solidarity with fellow workers, finally renounces the opportunity of marrying the landowners daugther and becoming a plantation owner himself, and sets off to join the class struggle in Rio. Amado does attempt to avoid the sense of fatalism detectable in other social novelists of the North East, and lend a more optimistic note to the class struggle in Brazil. Yet his tendency to reduce his social criticism to a framework of simplistic dogmatic formulas tends to dissipate the potential power of the content of his work.

Escaping from those restrictions enabled him to write his best work, notably *Terras do Sem Fim* (1942), documenting the struggle that developed between rival planters in Bahia in an effort to secure themselves a privileged position in the increasingly prosperous cacao trade. Cacao determines the life of everybody in the region, and they are all dehumanised by the values and conflicts it generates. Popular songs are occasionally incorporated into the work to give the struggle taking place an epic, legendary quality, and to emphasise the suffering of the poor, exploited workers, who, with no practical possibility of changing their condition, are shown to lament their anguish through song and retain vague hopes for an alternative existence in their dreams:

> -Minha sina é esperança ...
> É trabalhar noite e dia ...
> (...)
> -Minha vida é de penado
> Cheguei e fui amarrado
> nas grilhetas do cacau ... (68)

My fate is to retain hope, to work night and day ... My life is one of suffering. I came here and was fastened to the shackles of the cacao plantation. (68)

In earlier works of the 1930s, however, Amado had already developed the use of regional popular culture. *Jubiabá*, for example, published in 1935, examines the Afro-Brazilian culture of Bahia, focusing on the character of Antônio Balduíno, a negro whose aimless life of debauchery is finally given new purpose when he obtains work and organises his fellow labourers to fight for their rights, an effort which culminates in a successful strike. Popular poetry and stories play a crucial part in Balduíno's development of political consciousness, as, through them, he learns about the rebellious heroes, such as Lucas de Feira, the *cangaceiro*, and Zumbi, leader of Palmares, the community of escaped slaves who resisted all attempts to recapture them. Balduíno even dreams of a popular poem, an ABC, a biographical form of poem detailing the adventures and deeds of popular heroes, being composed by the people in his honour, eulogising his own contribution to their struggle. Recalling the *cantador* who composes such verses, he thinks:

> (...) um dia aquêle homem iria escrever o
> ABC de Antônio Balduíno, um ABC
> heróico, onde cantaria as aventuras de um
> negro livre, alegre, brigão, valente como
> sete. (69)

One day that man would write an ABC of Antônio Balduíno, a heroic ABC, in which he would sing of the adventures of a free black man, happy, pugnacious, and extremely strong. (69)

At the end of the work, Balduíno realises that the strike has served as his ABC, linking him to his people and their continual struggle, and affirming the positive part he has played in it:

> Agora sabe lutar. A greve foi o seu ABC. (70)

Now he knew how to struggle. The strike was his ABC. (70)

However, the tension generated by the political theme, continued from Amado's earlier proletarian novels, tends to be diluted by sentimentality in the way that the lives of the poor, especially that of Balduíno, are narrated, and by the manner in which popular cultural expressions are frequently described, which, although attempting to demonstrate the creativity and rebelliousness of the poor, often result in exoticism, seen, for example, in the vivid and colourful depiction of *candomblé* ritual:

Catavam em côro outra canção de macumba:
-Ê ôlô biri ô b'ajá gbá kó
a péhindá
e estavam dizendo "o cachorro quando anda mostra o rabo". Também Oxossi, o deus da caça, veio para a festa da macumba do pai Jubiabá. Vestia de branco, verde e um pouco de vermelho, um arco distendido com a sua flecha pendurado de um lado do cinto. Do outro lado conduzia uma aljava. Trazia daquela vez, além do capacete de metal com casco de pano verde, um espanador de fios grossos.

Os pés descalços das mulheres batiam no chão de barro, dançando. Requebravam o corpo ritualmente, mas êsse requêbro era sensual e dengoso como corpo quente de negra, como música dengosa de negro. O suor corria e todos estavam tomados pela música e pela dança. O Gordo tremia e não via mais nada senão figuras confusas de mulheres e santos, deuses caprichosos da floresta distante. (71)

In chorus, they sang a macumba song - Ê ôlô biri ô b'ajá gbá kó a péhindá - and they were saying, "When the dog walks it shows its tail". Oxossi, God of hunting, also came to the macumba festival of Father Jubiabá. He was dressed in white, green and a little red, and hanging on one side of his waist he had a bow and arrow. On the other side was a quiver. He brought with him, in addition to the metal helmet covered in cloth, a brush with thick fibres. The bare feet of the women beat on the earth floor, dancing. They moved their bodies languidly, in ritual, but this movement was sensual and coquettish, like the hot body of the black woman and the sensual music of the blacks. Sweat poured from them and everyone was taken over by the music and the dance. The fat man trembled and saw nothing other than confused figures of women and saints, and capricious Gods of the distant forest. (71)

Furthermore, a certain ambivalence towards popular religious ritual is detectable in the work, stemming from the contradiction between, on the one hand, Amado's attraction for such forms of popular expression, and his recognition of their fundamental role in the lives of the Brazilian poor, and on the other, his strict adherence to Communist Party ideology, which allowed no serious role for religious beliefs and rituals. Towards the end of the novel, Balduíno comes to question the reliance of the poor masses on religious practices and argues that they can only truly change the condition of their lives through political struggle. Despite all he learns from *candomblé*, it is his political involvement that gives him a sense of fulfilment.

Amado's next work, *Mar Morto* (1936), lyrically narrates the lives of Guma, one of the poor Bahian sailors who eeks out a living from the sea, only eventually to be drowned, and his wife, Lívia, left to continue the daily fight to survival. Again, the poor fishing community articulates that struggle through traditional songs, picturesquely presented by the author:

> (...) Depois Maria Clara cantou. A sua voz penetrou pela noite, como voz do mar, harmoniosa e profunda. Cantava:
> "A noite que êle não veio
> foi de tristeza pra mim..."
> Sua voz era doce. Vinha do mais profundo do mar, tinha como seu corpo um cheiro de beira de cais, de peixe salgado. Agora a sala ouvia atenta. A canção que ela cantava era bem dêles, era do mar.
> "Êle ficou nas ondas
> êle se foi a afogar".
> Velha *moda do mar*. Porque só falam em morte, em tristeza essas canções? No entanto o mar é belo, a água é azul e a lua é amarela. Mas as cantigas, as modas do mar são assim tristes, dão vontade de chorar, matam a alegria de todos. (72)

(...) Afterwards Maria Clara sang. Her voice penetrated the night, like the voice of the sea, harmonious and deep. She sang: "The night he didn't come was a night of sadness for me". Her voice was sweet. It came from the depths of the sea, and carried with it the smell of the quay and of salted fish. Now the room listened to her attentively. The song she was singing belonged to them. It was a song of the sea. "He was caught in the waves, carried away and drowned". An old custom of the sea. Why did they only speak of death, and of sadness in these songs? And yet the sea is beautiful. The water is blue and the moon is yellow. But the songs,

the customs of the sea, are sad, and they make one want to cry, killing everyone's happiness. (72)

The spirits from the Afro-Brazilian cults worshipped by the members of the community are frequently referred to throughout the novel. Lívia is afraid of the Goddess of the sea, Janaína, but after the death of Guma she expresses her defiance, symbolically the defiance of the whole community, by venturing out into the sea, merging herself with the Goddess of popular belief:

> (...) E o velho Francisco grita para os
> outros no cais:
> -Vejam! Vejam! É Janaína.
> Olharam e viram. Dona Dulce olhou
> também da janela da escola. Viu uma
> mulher forte que lutava. A luta era seu
> milagre. Começava a se realizar. (73)

And old Francisco shouted to the others on the quay: "Look! Look! It's Janaína". They looked and they saw her. Dona Dulce also saw her from the window of the school. She saw a strong woman who was a fighter. Her struggle was her miracle. She was beginning to fulfil her potential. (73)

This sentimentalised view of the struggle of the poor finds its extreme expression in *Capitães de Areia*, where the narration of the lives of a group of poor, homeless boys, led by Pedro Bala, who live on the beach and exist through stealing, at times resorts to pathos, and the ending, where again the boys discover purpose in life through participation in a strike, is highly romanticised:

> (...) Agora o destino dêles mudou. A voz
> do negro no mar canta o samba de Boa-
> Vida:
> Companheiros, vamos
> pra luta ...
> De punhos levantados, as crianças
> saúdam Pedro Bala, que parte para
> mudar o destino de outras crianças.
> Barandão grita na frente de todos, êle
> agora é o novo chefe. De longe, Pedra
> Bala ainda vê os Capitães da Areia. Sob a
> lua, num velho trapiche abandonado, êles

levantam os braços. Estão em pé, o
destino mudou. (74)

*(...) Now their destiny changed. The voice of the black man in the sea sang the
samba of welcome: "Comrades, let's go and join the struggle ..." With their
clenched fists raised, the children saluted Pedro Bala, who was setting off to
change the destiny of other children. Barandão shouted in front of them all. He
was now the new chief. Far away, Pedro Bala could still see the captains of the
sand. Under the moon, in an old abandoned warehouse, they raised their arms.
They were standing up. Their destiny had changed. (74)*

Once again, the familiar elements of popular culture used by Amado -
candomblé ritual and popular song - are employed to reinforce this
idealised, sentimental vision. In this subsequent novels, the overt social
content virtually disappears, resulting in works such as *Gabriela, Cravo e
Canela* (1958) and *Dona Flor e seus Dois Maridos* (1967), picturesque tales
and anecdotes of regional life, lacking the clear ideological orientation of
his earlier writing. This emphasis on regional colour and the sentimental
view of the poor that runs through most of Amado's work leads Alfredo
Bosi to describe it as a form of literary populism (75).

Amado developed his work with popular culture even further in
the 1960s and 1970s, publishing novels that made much more direct use
of the thematic and stylistic conventions of North East popular literature.
Through such works he aimed to express his solidarity with the struggle
of the poor and oppressed by highlighting the strength, defiance and
creativity embodied in their various forms of cultural expression. Amado
has continually declared that his sympathy for the poor has always been
the major motivation for his work (76). He claims that his whole approach
to writing, and the forms that he has developed on the basis of popular
sources, have resulted form his ability to identify with the poor and share
their experiences and aspirations (77).

Amado argues that his increasing use of popular literature has
enabled him to achieve a greater insight into Brazil's social problems and
a closer identification with the struggle of the oppressed, since recreating
popular literary forms that recount the experience of the poor permits him
to analyse that experience from the inside, rather than observing and
documenting it from afar and making his own condemnations, as in his
earlier political novels. In all the resulting works, however, Amado's own
idealised vision of a pure and gallant people heroically battling against
adverse social conditions is strongly conveyed. In the romanticised
atmosphere created in the novels, the creativity of the people is
ingenuously, and at times, sentimentally, extolled.

In *Os Pastores da Noite* (1964), for example, he adopts some of the tone of popular poetry, attempting to capture in his prose the simple, oral style employed by the poets, by avoiding formal literary devices and language and following a colloquial, conversational method of narration. At the very beginning, the narrator introduces himself as a simple story-teller, whose style contrasts sharply with that of the professional novel writer:

> Abram a garrafa de cachaça e me dêem
> um trago para compor a voz. (...) Quem
> não quiser ouvir pode ir embora, minha
> fala é simples e sem pretensão. (78)

Open the bottle of cachaça and give me a drink to compose my voice (...) Anyone who doesn't want to hear can go now. What I've got to say is simple and unpretentious. (78)

Through the central theme of the novel, a land invasion and the establishment of a *favela* by the homeless of Salvador, Amado conveys his condemnation of the squalor and poverty experienced by the poor, though again, the social criticism is undermined by romantic or comic subplots and a tendency towards the picturesque:

> Foi uma animação, todo mundo a
> construir barracos nos terrenos do Mata
> Gato, colina bonita, de onde se tinha vista
> magnífica do mar, e a brisa constante,
> jamais se sentia calor. (79)

It was very lively, everyone building shacks on the lands of the Mata Gato, an attractive hill, from where one had a magnificent view of the sea, and with a constant breeze so that one never felt hot. (79)

Two novels written by Amado in the early 1970s - *Tenda dos Milagres* (1970) and *Tereza Batista Cansada de Guerra* (1972) - follow a similar pattern. The small workshop referred to in *Tenda dos Milagres* is the focal point for a wide range of popular arts and cultural practices, including the printing of pamphlets or *folhetos* of popular verse. Within this setting, amid vivid description of popular music, dance and ritual, Amado attempts to trace the struggle of the people of Bahia through the life of the main character, Pedro Arcanjo, who begins writing popular poetry and then progresses to erudite literature, but always uses his literary skills and intellectual abilities to defend the rights of the poor against the oppressive authorities, and to extol their culture. He becomes a popular hero, about whom songs and poems are composed by *cantadores*. The result is a romantic view of the writer at one with the people, sharing their vision of the world and serving their interests.

In *Tereza Batista Cansada de Guerra*, the structure, tone and characterisation are all drawn from popular poetry. The five sections of the work are presented as *folhetos*, each of which adapts common themes of popular verse to detail episodes in the life of the heroine, Tereza, a prostitute, in her battle to overcome hardship, exploitation and adversity. Her character is based on a well-known figure in popular literary tradition, the *Donzela de Guerra*, a young woman of strength and courage, who temporarily casts aside the conventional female patterns of behaviour of the day to assume the male role of fighting to defend family honour. Tereza's strategies for overcoming the various abuses she faces, mixing courage with cunning, echo those employed by the popular heroes of pamphlet poetry, and other elements of North East folklore - festivals, popular music, and popular religion - are woven into the plot. Tereza's victory over adversity symbolises the courage and unbreakable resolution of the people, but again it is expressed in highly romanticised terms, with her marriage to an ideal partner in the final part of the novel. Popular material is adapted to convey the author's personal vision of Bahian society and culture, in which the poor and oppressed preserve dignity and moral virtue through resistance, expressed daily through their own dynamic cultural expressions and practices. Significantly, in both *Tenda dos Milagres* and *Tereza Batista Cansada de Guerra* the successes of the poor in their struggle are not achieved through their own political organisation, as was the case in the earlier novels, but through the intervention of sympathetic supernatural forces. The *candomblé* deities intervene to assist both Pedro Arcangel and Tereza Batista in their fight against the oppressive authorities. Amado had long since abandoned Communist Party ideology. From a fixed scheme of class struggle mechanically leading to a new revolutionary order, he moved to a broader, populist vision of the virtuous, indefatigable Brazilian people, class divisions now more blurred, continuing their heroic fight for an alternative order.

Tereza Batista Cansada de Guerra is a novel characterised by idealisation and sentimentality. The assimilation of popular culture enables Amado to maintain his broad theme of popular resistence, whilst also providing much of the regional colour, humour and exoticism which have made his novels so popular with a large reading public. He has consolidated his position as Brazil's best-selling novelist whilst continuing to classify himself as an *engagé* writer, although his political criticism has become increasingly diluted in his novels of the last three decades. Despite his claims of identification with the poor and their forms of expression, popular materials are reworked to convey Amado's own ideology. A year following the publication of *Tereza Batista* a popular poet adapted the story to write a *folheto,* and in comparing the two, Candace Slater notes significant differences in the vision conveyed. Whereas Amado's novel centers on action, the *folheto* story is more a reflection on Tereza's sufferings, which symbolise those of the poet and his readers and the positive character of Amado's heroine differs from the prostitute of the popular poem, who is presented as both victim and sinner. (80) In the 1970s, the interaction between popular and erudite literature in the North East was more intense than ever before. Jorge Amado and Ariano Suassuna produced works whose entire construction depended on the assimilation of forms and themes of popular culture, though, as will be seen, their underlying motives differed considerably.

Finally, mention must be made of João Ubaldo Ribeiro's highly acclaimed *Viva o Povo Brasileiro,* published in 1984, which took up once again the question of national identity, at the time when Brazil was preparing itself for a return to civilian government after twenty-five years of military dictatorship. For Ribeiro, the essential characteristic of Brazilian history is the continual struggle between diverging social forces, and the novel follows that struggle through various historical stages: slaves against slave-owners, idealist revolutionaries against conservative oligarchies, and, in the 1970s, the forces of the left against the military authorities and dominant elites. Parallel to the socio-political contest, the work examines the corresponding ideological conflict. Two perspectives of Brazilian history are juxtaposed: on the one hand, the official history developed by the dominant classes, with their ideology of national culture, constructed to serve their own interests and justify the continuation of neo-colonialism, and on the other, the efforts of the poor and oppressed to reappropriate their own history and identity. National myths have reached absurd proportions, Ribeiro suggests, because of the extraordinary efforts that have had to be made in order to conceal the deep contradictions of Brazilian life and culture. A major objective of the work is therefore to demythologise the official history of Brazil, with satire and parody as the main tools. The myth of national unity and homogeneity, for example, is constantly exposed, to reveal the deep social and racial divisions concealed underneath. The process of capitalist modernisation traced by the novel is shown not to have diminished those divisions. The present-day bourgeoisie is presented as alientated, and the state machinery, especially the military, continues to play an oppressive role, and the final pages of the work carry an apocalyptic vision of the future, characterised by increasing hunger, violence and brutal exploitation. That vision is counterbalanced by an element of hope: the reaffirmation of the strength, energy and creativity of the Brazilian people, whose spirit is indomitable, and whose resistance will therefore continue.

Popular resistance is expressed in the novel through the familiar forms of cultural expressions employed by other North East regionalist writers - messianism, the Afro-Brazilian religious rituals of *candomblé*, and popular oral literature which evokes the exemplary rebels and revolutionaries of the past. These forms are presented in the novel as channels through which dominant class myths can be challenged, and the people can rediscover their own identity and a sense of their own power. In many ways, Ribeiro's use of popular culture follows that of Amado. It is a novel which uses humour to powerful effect in critically examining the debate around the issue of national culture, but which still resorts to a colourful, stereotypical presentation of well-known figures and forms of North East folklore. Idealised backland bandits and messianic worshippers play familiar roles as popular rebels, whose actions are inspired by a highly developed political consciousness. For some critics, the novel is another example of literary populism. It demonstrates, however, that in the 1980s, the question of national identity remained central to Brazilian literature, and regional popular culture was at the heart of its discussion.

vi] Conclusions

The socially committed novel of the 1930s and 40s was an important phase in the development of Brazilian literature. It signified the consolidation of, on the one hand, the desire on the part of the writer to look inwards and examine and analyse national problems, and, on the other, the formal innovations established by the Modernists. To this extent at least, the basis for a more nationally orientated literature was laid, with the narrow isolation of the erudite writer sufficiently broken to allow him or her a far greater understanding of other sectors of the population. This whole process, a constant interplay between national and cosmopolitan perspectives, was made possible by objective social and economic changes which altered the position of the writer, and his own conception of his role. The breaking down of colonial structures, the expansion and modernisation of economic production and the increasing social complexity of the nation, all contributed to the opening up of new possibilities for the writer.

However, the entire issue has been confused by the frequent attempts to conceive this process of literary development as simply an integral part of the steady evolution of a distinctly Brazilian cultural identity, stimulated by the gradual emergence of national consciousness among the mass of the population. To this day, Brazil remains a country of acute social, and hence cultural, divisions. The notion of the development of a national culture has been a cornerstone of the ideological system constructed by the hegemonic classes in order to conceal those divisions under a fraçade of unity, and hence justify the socio-economic status quo that privileges them. The affirmation of a national identity must therefore be seen in ideological terms and not as the natural, cohesive process it is frequently claimed to be.

Many writers who have sought to contribute to shaping Brazilian identity through the development of national literature, have often unwittingly merely reinforced that dominant ideology. Attempts to enhance the national flavour of literary work by selecting symbols that can be identified as distinctly Brazilian, has often resulted in artificiality and distortion. Popular culture is one of those elements that has been most abused, with numerous of its manifestations recast to suit the tastes of other classes. At worst, this has led to literary populism, a colourful abstraction which claims to truly reflect the lives and aspirations of the exploited masses, and defend their interests, when in fact paternalism frequently predominates. Many critics have unfortunately reinforced this deception by exaggerating the proximation that has developed between the writer and the masses, like José Osório de Oliveira, who writes of the Modernists:

> The Brazilian writer (who has liberated himself from European intellectual preconceptions) is, to some extent, on an equal footing with the people; he shares, very often, the same tastes, feelings and ideas, and he has, or adopts, many of their habits and customs. This is simply because social culture is stronger in Brazil than what we call intellectual culture, distinguishing it from the living culture of the people. (81)

Such interpretations naively imply that, in a highly stratified society, the writer has completely broken through class barriers and been able to accurately capture and convey the lived experience of the poor masses. Yet even the most sincere and dedicated writer can never document social reality with total objectivity, as observed by Rubén Bareiro Saguier, commenting on the socially committed novel in Latin America:

> In short, the search for literary identity via the development of a social and politically committed novel represents an important stage in the process of identification of social reality. But in some ways it was a false search. The very criteria of 'documentary authenticity' which was adopted was misleading, because it presented a superficial reality which was deformed by

143

the utopian intentions each author had for his work. In this sense, the classification of 'sociological literature' which was attributed to such work is also dubious. (82)

This point is clearly illustrated by the many twentieth century novelists of North East Brazil who have attempted to document the lives and struggles of the underprivileged masses of the region. Courageous and fearful in Euclides da Cunha, helpless victims in Raquel de Queiroz, picturesque and inventive in Jorge Amado, the poor of the North East have appeared in the erudite novel in a variety of guises.

As has been seen, a crucial part of the development of the ideology of national identity has been the interpretation and assimilation of popular culture by the intelligentsia of the dominant class. Over the decades, new concepts and viewpoints have contributed to this process, constantly providing new interpretations of popular culture. Many of the attitudes involved have been discredited and superseded in the course of time, as with the ambiguous racial theory so evident in the work of Euclides da Cunha. Other notions, however, have lingered on to influence contemporary writers. It will be seen that all the basic ideas underlying Ariano Suassuna's *Movimento Armorial* can be traced back through that developing process which aims to assert national identity through the promotion and manipulation of popular culture.

NOTES FOR CHAPTER 2

1   Alfredo Bossi, *História Concisa da Literatura Brasileira* (Editôra Cultrix, São Paulo, 1970), pp.13-14

2   See Maria Elisa Collier Pragana, *Literatura do Nordeste em Torno de sua Expressão Social* (José Olympio, Rio de Janeiro, 1983). On page 18 the author writes that, for the North East, the arts and literature of the region constitute "(...) one of the most significant forms of compensation for the loss of leadership and decline of activity in other sectors, which, in socio-economic terms, are of greater practical value."

3   Roberto Schwarz, 'The Importing of the Novel to Brazil and its Contradictions in the Work of Alencar', in *Misplaced Ideas*, pp.41-77 On page 45 Schwarz writes "... everyday life in Brazil was regulated by the mechanics of favour, which were incompatible (...) with the melodramatic plots of a Realism that had been heavily influenced by Romanticism."

4   Nelson Werneck Sodré, among others, emphasises this point with the following comment on Brazilian Romantic writing: "That

superficiality, the tendency to imitate, the absence of original thought, revealed the underlying transplantation, and the formidable effort made to substitute profound truth with superficial truth, dressing literary manifestations, both in prose and in verse, with a patriotic spirit, involving linguistic differentiation, the exaltation, of the picturesque and the tireless search for the banal, the everyday and the ordinary." Nelson Werneck Sodré, *História*, p.197

5 Sánzio de Azevedo, *Literatura Cearense* (Academia Cearense de Letra, Fortaleza, 1976), p.52

6 José de Alencar, in the postscript of *Diva*, in *Obra Completa*, Vol 1 (Editôra José Aguilar, Rio de Janeiro, 1959), p.559

7 Juvenal Galeno, in Sánzio de Azevedo, Literatura Cearense, p.41

8 José de Alencar, *O Sertanejo*, in *Obra*, Vol 3, p.1123

9 M. Cavalcanti Proença, *Estudos Literários* (José Olympio, Rio de Janeiro, 1974), p.105

10 José Guilherme Merquior, *De Anchieta*, p.83

11 Franklin Távora, preface to *O Cabeleira* (Editôra Ática, São Paulo, 3rd edition, 1977), p.10

12 Sílvio Romero, *História*, Vol 1, p.54

13 Ibid, Vol 2, p.383

14 Ibid, Vol 2, p.384

15 Extracts from the manifesto of the *Padaria Espiritual*, which is reproduced in Leonardo Mota, *Padaria Espiritual* (Edésio, Fortaleza, 1938)

16 Dorothy Scott Loos, *The Naturalist Novel of Brazil* (Hispanic Institute in the United States, New York, 1963), p.109

17 Thomas Skidmore, *Black into White: Race and Nationality in Brazilian Thought* (Oxford University Press, New York, 1974), p.109

18 See Dante Moreira Leite, *O Caráter*, pp.203-211, for a critique of da Cunha's thoughts regarding race and nationality.

19 Euclides da Cunha, *Os Sertões*, in *Obras Completas*, Vol 2 (José Aguilar Editora, Rio de Janeiro, 1966), p.141 A

20 Olavo Bilac quoted in Thomas Skidmore, *Black into White*, p.97

21 Euclides da Cunha, *Os Sertões*, p.167

22 Ibid, p.170

23 Ibid, p.479

24 Ibid, p.175

25 Ibid, p.231

26 Ibid, p.431

27 See, for example, Sánzio de Azevedo, *Literatura Cearense*, pp.365-377, and *Apontamentos de Literatura Maranhense*, by various authors (Edições Sioge, São Luís, 1977), pp.163-166

28   Cecília de Lara, *Nova Cruzada: Contribuição para o Estudo do Pré-Modernismo* (Instituto de Estudos Brasileiros, São Paulo, 1971), passim

29   Mário de Andrade, 'O Movimento Modernista' in *Obras Completas*, Vol X (Livraria Martins Editora, Brasília, 1972), p.235

30   Sérgio Buarque de Holanda, quoted in Mário da Silva Brito, *História do Modernismo Brasileiro* (Editora Civilização Brasileira, Rio de Janeiro, 1964), p.176

31   Mário de Andrade, in Manuel Bandeira, *A Presentação da Poesia Brasileira* (Casa do Estudante do Brasil, Rio de Janeiro, 1972), p.17

32   Manuel Bandeira, *Brief History of Brazilian Literature*, translated by Ralph Edward Dimmick (Pan American Union, Washington, 1958), p.144

33   Telê Porto Anacona Lopez notes how the work of Mário de Andrade developed in precisely such a way: "(...) The nationalist endeavour of our writer gradually broadened, as he came to understand that the frontiers between erudite art and popular art are in reality frontiers between social classes which have developed in the course of history. He came to believe that erudite art, privileged in its development, could, or rather had to, draw on the resources of popular creation in order to free itself from the weight of an imported culture and become a national art, and, in the future, a universal art." Telê Porto Ancona Lopez, 'Um Projeto de Mário de Andrade', in *Arte em Revista*, Ano 2, Número 3, (Kairós, São Paulo, March 1980), p.52

34   Mário de Andrade, 'Na Pancada do Ganzá', (prefácio), in *Arte em Revista*, Ano 2, Número 3, p.56

35   Mário de Andrade, 'Toada do Pai-do-Mato', (extract), from *Clã do Jabuti*, in *Poesias Completas* (Martins, São Paulo, 1955), p.177

36   Mário de Andrade, *Obras Completas*, Vol 10, pp.244-245

37   Summarising this position, Peregrino Júnior writes: "The *Primitivists* turned towards our innocent origins, moved by a nationalistic sympathy for the autochthonous people of the country, and they rejected all alien influences, leaving aside even the most ancient and illustrious, in a deliberate act of liberation, attempting to take inspiration from the native environment, take the pulse of the land." Peregrino Júnior, 'Modernismo', in *Tres Ensaios*, (Livraria São José, Rio de Janeiro, 1969), p.48

38   Mário da Silva Brito, 'Metamorfoses de Oswald de Andrade', in *Revista Civilização Brasileira*, Ano IV, Número 17, (Jan-Feb 1968, Rio de Janeiro), p.210

39   'Manifesto do Verde-Amarelismo ou da Escola da Anta', in Gilberto Mendonça Teles, *Vanguardia Européia e Modernismo*

Brasileiro (Editora Vozes, Rio de Janeiro, 1972), pp.233-240

40 Ibid

41 Ibid

42 Manifesto of 'Festa', in Gilberto Mendonça Teles, *Vanguardia*, pp.219-222

43 Antônio Cândido has warned against such nativism, which: "(...) reduce human problems to a picturesque element, transforming the passion and suffering of the rural population into a colourful tropical dish. Such an attitude not only amounts to a servile imitation of styles, but also provides the urban European reader, or the Europeanised Latin American reader, with the type of tourist view of Latin America that he or she likes to see. Without being conscious of it, the most sincere nativism runs the risk of becoming an ideological manifestation of the same old cultural colonialism (...)" Antônio Cândido, 'Literatura y subdesarrollo', p.181.

44 Carlos Guilherme Mota, *Ideologia*, p.109

45 Mário de Andrade, in Carlos Guilherme Mota, *Ideologia*, pp.107-108, from the original *Testamento de uma Geração* (Globo, Porto Alegre, 1944)

46 Mário da Silva Brito, *História do Modernismo Brasileiro* (Editora Civilização Brasileira, Rio de Janeiro, 1964), p.178

47 See Joaquim Inojosa, *O Movimento Modernista en Pernambuco* (Tupy, Rio de Janeiro, 1972). On page 32 Inojosa asserts that "Without doubt, it was in Pernambuco, after São Paulo and Rio, where the clamour for renovation had greatest repercussion."

48 See Gilberto Freyre, *Região e Tradição* (José Olympio, Rio de Janeiro, 1943). On page 61 Freyre states that "The Regionalist and Traditionalist Movement of Recife must in no way be confused with the Modernism of Rio or São Paulo."

49 Examples of this discord can be found in John Nist, *The Modernist Movement in Brazil* (University of Texas Press, Austin, 1967), which records that Mário de Andrade once wrote, "Regionalism is poverty without humility (...) It is a poverty that comes from so few means of expression and from narrow concepts", (p.104) whilst Gilberto Freyre stated that Modernism "(...) sacrificed regionalism and traditionalism for the sake of cosmopolitanism." (p.110).

50 Gilberto Freyre, *Manifesto Regionalista* (Instituto Joaquim Nabuco, Recife, 3rd edition, 1979), p.17

51 Ibid, p.12

52 Ibid, p.12

53 Ibid, p.15

54   Carlos Guilherme Mota, *Ideologia*, pp.69-72
55   Dante Moreira Leite, *O Caráter*, pp.270-275. There the author states
      that *Casa Grande e Senzala* "(...) ostensibly presented as history or
      as a general interpretation of Brazil, is better considered as a
      literary construction," and goes on to affirm that "The studies of
      Gilberto Freyre appear to use the historical method, that is to say,
      the reconstruction of an era via primary documents: letters, books,
      personal records, newspaper announcements, etc. However, the
      work of Gilberto Freyre has a fundamental deficiency: the total
      disdain for the chronology and the geographical space of the facts
      described."
56   Gilberto Freyre, *Casa Grande e Senzala* (José Olympio, Rio de
      Janeiro, 1943), p.85
57   Ibid, p.486
58   Ibid, p.67 and 69 respectively.
59   Carlos Guilherme Mota, *Ideologia*, pp.58-59
60   Gilberto Freyre, *Casa Grande*, p.62
61   Dante Moreira Leite, *O Caráter*, p.275
62   Central to Freyre's thesis was the work of the anthropologist,
      Franz Boas, under whom he studied in the United States. Boas
      argued that the differences between peoples were not to be
      explained by innate racial characteristics, but rather by cultural
      factors.
63   See Souza Barros, *A Década 20 em Pernambuco* (Gráfica Editora
      Académica, Rio de Janeiro, 1972) for details of the impact of
      Modernist and regionalist ideas in Pernambuco in the 1920s.
64   See the preface of Gilberto Freyre, *Região e Tradição* (José Olympio,
      Rio de Janeiro, 1943), page 16, where José Lins do Rego, writing
      about Freyre, states: "I write about him, and I almost speak of
      myself, so much do I feel myself to be his creation, and such
      influence did he exercise on my character."
65   The *Ciclo de Açucar* comprises five novels: *Menino de Engenho*
      (1932), *Doidinho* (1933), *Banguê* (1934), *O Moleque Ricardo* (1935),
      and *Usina* (1936).
66   José Lins do Rego, *Poesia e Vida* (Editora Universal, Rio de Janeiro,
      1945), pp.54-55
67   Adonias Filho, *O Romance Brasileiro de 30* (Edições Bloch, São
      Paulo, 1969).
68   Jorge Amado, *Terras do Sem Fim* (Martins, São Paulo, 1961), pp.223
      and 224
69   Jorge Amado, *Jubiabá* (Martins, São Paulo, 1961), p.108
70   Ibid, p.318
71   Ibid, p.103

72   Jorge Amado, *Mar Morto* (Martins, São Paulo, 12th, edition, undated), p.149
73   Ibid, p.262
74   Jorge Amado, *Capitães da Areia* (Martins, São Paulo, 1967), p.299
75   Alfredo Bosi, *História Concisa*, p.457
76   In an interview with *Index on Censorship,* Vol 10, No 6, December 1981, p.61, Amado states that: "All my work, from the first book to the most recent, deals with this theme, with the life of the ordinary people. The only hero of my books is the people of Brazil, and in particular the people of Bahia, whom I know best, because I have lived there most of my life. Whatever changes have occurred in style, my work has always been marked, above all, by its stance together with the people against their enemies."
77   See Jorge Amado, *Documentos* (Publicações Europa-Americana, Lisboa, 1964). On page 36, .i.Amado, Jorge;Amado comments that: "(...) If there is one virtue that I have possessed, it is that of being close to the people, mixing with them, living their life, integrating myself into their reality."
78   Jorge Amado, *Os Pastores da Noite* (Martins, São Paulo, 1965), introduction.
79   Ibid, p.208
80   Candace Slater, *Stories on a String,* p.148
81   José Osorio de Oliveira, *História Breve da Literatura Brasileira* (Editôra Cultrix, São Paulo, 1945), p.113
82   Ruben Bareiro Saguier, 'La literatura Latinoamericana, crisol de culturas', in *El correo,* March 1972, Año XXV, p.31

4

OUT OF THE SCHOLAR'S CHAIR: SUASSUNA
AND THE SEARCH FOR A MEETING POINT

i] **The early years of Ariano Suassuna and his vision of *sertão*
culture**

Ariano Suassuna has now established himself as one of the most
prominent figures of contemporary Brazilian literature, and no other
Brazilian writer has done more to explore popular culture and assimilate
its forms of expression into his own work. Since the late 1940s he has
gradually clarified and developed his theories on art, and in particular
on literature, formulating his thoughts in movements in which he has
participated and attempting to put them into practice in all the poems,
plays and novels which he has written. This process culminated with the
crystallisation of his ideas in the *Movimento Armorial*, which he launched
in Recife in 1970. He has constantly argued for the further development
of distinctly North Eastern erudite art forms based on the utilisation of
the popular artistic expressions of the region. He sees his work as part
of a long tradition of regionalist art movements, and even claims to have
timed the inauguration of the *Movimento Armorial* to coincide with the
centenary of the *Escola de Recife* in recognition of this relationship. (1) His
work represents the most important recent attempt to fuse erudite and
popular literary expression in North East Brazil, and a significant phase
in the continuing debate over the issue of national culture.

His fundamental ideas on art are not original, but rather
developments of the broad arguments and objectives expressed by earlier
North Eastern writers and intellectuals already mentioned, such as Freyre
and Lins do Rego. However, Suassuna has given those basic ideas a new
interpretation, and argues for a different approach and method in
putting them into practice in artistic production. He is therefore keen to
differentiate his writing from that of earlier poets and novelists, to the
point of giving it a distinct title: *arte Armorial*.

> My plays and my novels are not modernist, like
> *Macunaíma*, and Mário de Andrade's short stories, nor
> are they regionalist like the novels of José Lins do Rego:
> they are Armorial works; that's to say, they owe
> something to all those writers, but are not to be
> confused with any of them. (2)

Ariano Suassuna was born in the capital of the state of Paraíba,
then called Cidade de Nossa Senhora das Neves, on June 16th, 1927. The
Suassunas were one of the powerful traditional families which comprised
the landowning oligarchy that for decades had dominated regional

political life, and at the time of Ariano's birth his father, João, was Governor of the State of Paraíba. It was a period of mounting political tension and violence in the North East, as in other regions of the nation, and it is important to outline the developments that took place, since these would deeply mark the work later produced by Ariano Suassuna.

Until the 1930s Brazilian political life was characterised by the predominance of locally based political power and decision making, with the central authority relatively weak and detached. As elsewhere in Latin America, a small number of powerful families dominated social and political life in the North East of Brazil, to such a degree that the central government was obliged to negotiate with them in order to reach agreement about political control at the local level.

The Empire (1822-1889) maintained a precarious balance between provincial interests and those of central government, and when it did attempt to centralise authority to a greater degree, it met with strong resistance from the regional elites. The Republic, established in 1889, attempted to decentralise power with a new constitution in 1891, and the problems arising from a low level of national integration and weak central government remained unresolved. Political power at local, state and national level was decided by arrangement, through a system of patron-client relationships, the basis of which was a network of kinship ties in each region - the extended family and the *compadrio* system - which established a chain of loyalties through all levels of the political machinery. These were the politics of the elite and involved the participation of only a small percentage of the national population. The land tenure system ensured the dependence of the mass of the rural populace on the large landowning families, and, as already noted, the problems of that dependence have been constantly expressed in the popular poetry of the peasant communities concerned. At times the local landowning families feuded in order to settle rivalries; at others, they formed alliances and organised even broader power blocks to extend their influence. These regional elites negotiated between themselves to determine the nature of national government, with those of the economically dominant states inevitably fulfilling the deciding role. For years the oligarchies of São Paulo, based on coffee production, and of Minas Gerais, based on cattle, alternated the Presidency, an arrangement popularly known as the politics of *café com leite*. North Eastern states were among those which complained about these monopolistic politics of the Centre-South interests, which excluded them from the central control of the system.

The delicate and uneasy balance between the regional oligarchies finally split altogether in 1930. The outgoing President, Washington Luis, broke agreed convention by choosing a fellow *paulista* to succeed him, instead of a candidate from Minas Gerais, in the hope of perpetuating his policies and style of government. Various states launched a successful uprising against the São Paulo faction led by Washington Luis, and, backed by the military high command, managed to get their appointed leader, Getulio Vargas, from Rio Grande do Sul, installed as President.(3)

This conflict at the national level was paralleled by provincial conflicts. In Paraíba in the North East, the landowning elite, the Suassuna family among them, had been facing increasing pressure from other social groups, especially the urban bourgeoisie, in the early part of the present century. Large rival power blocks formed and the conflict between them grew increasingly bitter. João Suassuna gave up the office of Governor in 1928 to be replaced by João Pessoa, who represented rival, essentially urban based interests, and was soon invited to be Vargas' Vice-President in the new Administration to be established once the national power struggle had been resolved. However, the struggle at the national level further compounded the local tensions and strife within Paraíba, where family feuds became fused with political conflict. Finally, violence erupted. In July 1930 a relative of the Suassuna family assassinated João Pessoa, essentially to avenge a personal affront, and a few months later, on October 9th, João Suassuna was killed in revenge by Pessoa supporters. Barely a week before his death, on October 3rd, the forces led by Vargas launched their Revolution against the Old Republic.

This history of political strife, with national conflict interweaving with regional conflict in the North East, and which led to the death of his father, had a profound and lasting impact on Ariano Suassuna, and, as will be seen, it has played its part in shaping his view of the world and in the construction of his novels published in the 1970s. Broadly, the violence, the 1930 Revolution and the gradual construction of a centralised bourgeois state apparatus that followed, with new economic and political objectives, more orientated towards industrialisation and accelerated capital accumulation, signified another phase, perhaps the vital, final phase, in the decline of the traditional landowning aristocracy, their regional power and the traditional, patriarchal patterns of life they determined. This sense of fragmentation of a whole way of life, and the loss of the security and framework of reference it seemed to provide, was compounded for Suassuna by the death of his father, inevitably giving the whole historical process outlined here a deep, personal significance for him. As in the work of Freyre and Lins do Rego before him, his novels register a profound sense of loss and of nostalgia.

His attachment to the life of the rural interior of the North East can be traced to his childhood there, for, though born in the town, he was still at an early age when his family decided to leave Nossa Senhora das Neves and move to the family estates in the *sertão*. The effects of the political hostility and turbulence of the late 1920s were in a large part responsible for that decision. In the *sertão*, Ariano would have first-hand experience of the patterns of life and cultural expressions that he would later recall in his work. The songs, poetry, puppet shows (*mamulengo*) and popular festivals of his childhood years were to provide the raw material of his writing, interwoven into his own particular reconstruction of *sertão* history and legend, to form what he describes as:

> (...) my mythical world of the sertão. (4)

This childhood experience underlies his personal affiliation to regional popular art forms, for he considers them to be integral parts of his own philosophical development and formation. Explaining the principles behind his approach to literature, he will invariably turn to popular art and artists as examples to illustrate and support his arguments. This is the basis of his mission to bridge cultural divisions and develop what he perceives as

> (...) a national, erudite art and literature, with its base in
> the roots of popular North Eastern culture. (5)

He has grown up with and assimilated the basic elements of popular culture which his formal literary training and experience is to refashion into an erudite art form, and he urges his fellow artists to embark on the same course and thereby consolidate an authentically Brazilian literature. The practical problems which this process of assimilation entails are never expounded by Suassuna, who generally confines himself to the same abstract notion of the artist developing a spiritual empathy for popular expressions to which other North Eastern writers already mentioned have alluded. For Suassuna, it is that empathy that opens the way for outstanding North Eastern literature. A purely rational, intellectual response to popular culture, he believes, leads the writer into sterile academicalism and erudition. (6) With regard to his own work, the question of assimilation appears to be almost irrelevant for Suassuna, for he sees his own linkage with popular culture in terms of an intuitive understanding and empathy forged during his childhood.

Within such a perspective, the relationship between cultural expression and social class becomes extremely tenuous, and Suassuna's allusions to the question are ambiguous. He does frequently employ the term *povo* when referring to the popular culture of the North East, and appears to reaffirm it as an expression of the poorest sectors of the population. It is in this sense that he views it as an authentically

Brazilian expression, which contrasts with the more cosmopolitan, imitative cultural patterns discernible among other social groups. (7) At other times however, he emphasises the unity of traditional North East rural culture, under such terms as *civilização de couro*, embodying the notion of a large cultural block in which the different social sectors appear congealed into a whole, integrated way of life. (8) The cultural divisions which he perceives in Brazil are usually expressed as contrasts between these ways of life which transcend class differences. He starts with the conflicting cultures of the Europeans, native Indians and Africans who constituted the basic ethnic elements of Brazilian society, stating that:

> Brazil suffers from a division, a cultural split which has
> resulted from the conditions within which the country's
> formation took place. On the one hand, we were born in
> the seventeenth century, the fruit of Mediterranean,
> Iberian culture, inheriting the cultural patrimony which
> came to us with the language and customs of the
> Portuguese. On the other hand, we inherited strong
> elements of African and Indian culture, and their
> "mestizo" descendants soon began to recreate and
> reinterpret the Iberian cultural elements which were
> brought here by the colonisers. (9)

The Portuguese brought a cultural tradition, he argues, composed of both erudite and popular elements. These coexisted, often intermingled, in the European forms of expression transplanted in Brazil:

> (...) we are the heirs of Mediterranean tradition, with its
> erudite, renascent and aristocratic roots on one side and
> its popular roots on the other. The latter are just as
> vigorous and as important as the former. (10)

So, although Suassuna does make a distinction between erudite and popular forms of expression, he continually shifts from that premise of cultural division to the notion of one monolithic cultural block where the two become merged, suggesting homogeneity rather than heterogeneity. This tendency is particularly evident when he contrasts the traditions of the North East *sertão* with cultural forms emanating from elsewhere. In this way, he conceives of the conflict between *sertanejo* interests headed by his father and urban interests led by João Pessoa as to a large extent a clash between two different ways of life, referring to it as:

(...) the inevitable confrontation between two different cultures. (11)

He sees that conflict culminating in the Revolution of 1930, which he clarifies as a struggle between rival elites within Brazil. (12) This view is not particularly controversial, for many political scientists and historians have interpreted the 1930 Revolution as essentially a power struggle for hegemony within the ranks of the dominant classes. It shows, however, Suassuna's inclination to conceive of *sertão* culture as a way of life fusing together diverse social sectors, a tendency which blurs the significance of class conflict in the North East. Instead, he prefers to stress the idea of alliance between peasant and landowner. An example can be seen in the way he vigorously rejects the claim by Rui Facó that the revolutionary army organised by Luis Carlos Prestes in the early 1920s was not only supported by sections of urban middle classes and working classes, but by the peasantry of the *sertão* as well, who identified Prestes as an ally in their fight against the latifundistas. Instead, Suassuna argues:

> (...) that the backlanders, rich or poor, have a dislike for the communists, and whenever the Marxists, or others on the left, go there to help with what they consider to be a struggle on behalf of the people, they are surprised to find that their love is not returned: the poor backlanders ally themselves with the so-called *feudal landowners*, and fight the communists, despite their talk of the class struggle and the like. (13)

Later in the same article he summarises what he sees as the main flaw in Facó's argument:

> It happens that these abstract theories, ideologically obliged to give exclusive pre-eminence to the economic element in human relationships, persist in ignoring the importance of other factors, such as human affection or love of the land. It was for that reason that the Prestes column experienced the disappointment of seeing the backlanders, the peasants, ally themselves to the landowners; the very landowners whom, according to those theories, they ought to hate, but who were in fact their godfathers, friends or perhaps godfathers of their children, and who shared with them the same culture and the same hard struggle on the land which was, for

155

all of them, their motherland, the sertão (...) (14)

Ideological dogma has blinded Facó from reality, Suassuna concludes. Obviously, it is not the purpose of this study to debate the degree of support Prestes received from the peasantry. The irony, however, is that Suassuna's own ideological bias makes him overlook the not infrequent clashes between landowners and peasants in the history of the North East. Suassuna wrote the quoted passages in 1973, when the military authorities made any type of organised rebellion extremely difficult, but it had been little more than ten years before, for example, that large-scale peasant mobilisation had taken place in the region, through the already mentioned *Ligas Camponeses*, in an effort to impress peasant demands on the landowners. About that process, Josué de Castro writes:

> The leagues arose spontaneously from the peasant mass,
> a natural consequence to the unequal struggle to realise
> minimum aspirations against maximum resistance on the
> part of feudal oppressors. (15)

This differs sharply from Suassuna's picture of social relations in the *sertão*. It is true that the relationship between landowner and peasant has traditionally been highly personalised, almost semi-feudal in nature, in contrast to the far more impersonalised relations between employer and employee in more modern sectors of the economy, but this cannot disguise the social, economic and political gulf between those who own the land and those who own nothing, which is necessarily paralleled by a marked contrast in world views and hence in cultural expression.

Referring to Brazil's present stage of development, Suassuna frequently speaks of the danger posed by the influx of mass culture through powerful mass media such as television, radio, cinema and the Portuguese translations of North American popular comics, all of which have spread steadily throughout the North East in recent decades. Whereas the middle and dominant classes of the country have simply aped those models, he sees the poorer social classes, particularly the peasantry, as having preserved their own particular cultural identity. He writes, for example, that:

> The foreign and cosmopolitan cultural currents try to
> make Brazilians feel ashamed of their particular
> attributes, and their idiosyncrasies. It's only the common
> folk who still retain those Brazilian characteristics, which
> we now seek to defend and recreate, against the
> Europeanising, cosmopolitan currents. We do it by

attempting to link our work as creative writers and artists to popular literature, art and festivals. (16)

Such statements, however, reveal but a vague linkage between class and cultural expression, recognised in passing and viewed as a mere detail rather than a dynamic relationship central to the understanding of the forms of expression that result. His refusal to give full consideration to the social and economic bases of cultural behaviour leads him to speak of the assimilation of the principles underlying popular art in the North East by the region's erudite artists, relegating to a secondary plane the fundamental difference in production, distribution and reception inherent in the distinct social bases of popular and erudite art. In this way, Suassuna can separate the roots of popular culture from the environment which created them, nurture them elsewhere, reshape them to meet the needs of a different milieu, a different public and a different vision, and, above all, blend them into the hegemonic cultural system - national culture or *cultura brasileira* - in an effort to reinforce its defining characteristics, and safeguard its distinct identity against what he sees as

> (...) The deformation imposed, not by foreign culture,
> but by the mass culture which is a caricature of foreign
> culture, reduced to a low level by the media. (17)

Preferring to concentrate on the formal aspects of cultural expression rather than its social dimension, Suassuna argues against a rigorous separation of popular and erudite literature. He believes that this type of separation has led to a general disdain for popular forms among erudite artists and critics, who consider them to be crude, primitive and plainly inferior. Such an attitude has, he argues, led too many Brazilian artists to copy European models, instead of seeking inspiration in the creativity of the Brazilian people. Instead, Suassuna continually emphasises the idea of fluidity between erudite and popular forms, the on-going process of interchange between them, showing that much of what is commonly regarded as great literary work has its origins in popular creation, and that much popular literature shows the clear influence of erudite work. He argues that:

> (...) the popular poets and cantadores of the North East
> have their own form of culture, which certainly includes
> primitive elements, but also elements inherited from
> European culture, including what we might describe as
> aristocratic, erudite European culture. (18)

It is important to recognise the dangers of a rigid division between the erudite and the popular, which hierarchies cultural forms in the way Suassuna suggests, and which tends to diminish the significance of interaction between different forms of expression. However, such a preoccupation with formal aspects tends to distract Suassuna from the fundamental issues that underlie them: the particular social conditions of origin, production and consumption of cultural expression, and the specific world view it embodies. Yet it is the contrasts in those conditions which provide the foundation for the differentiation between the erudite and the popular. A tendency to disregard those differences is a necessary part of Suassuna's aim of fusing the erudite with the popular to create national art. He frequently stresses the universality of popular art. The most popular art is the most universal, he argues, since it is rooted in profound and eternal human problems and emotions. He states that:

> (...) the most popular stories, and those which are most
> representatively national, are really the most universal
> and the most dynamic, because they express exactly the
> most primordial and deepest elements of the ordinary
> folk, wherever they maybe; those elements which most
> characterise humans everywhere. (19)

More contradictions arise here however, for Suassuna makes clear his rejection of most modern popular art forms, such as the internationally popular music produced by British pop groups in the 1960s and 70s. He ridicules the suggestion that such music might also embody certain universal values, and argues that the young musicians concerned were so lacking in originality that they finally had to turn to popular Indian music in the 1960s for inspiration. Contemptuously, he describes how British popular music of the period:

> (...) was causing such a clamour in the world, even
> among long-haired Brazilians with their guitars, who
> described such British music as 'universal', and wanted
> us to imitate it here. Finally I said to such people: "You
> should note that European culture is so worn out, that
> young British musicians had to imitate exotic music
> from Asia in their effort to produce something new."
> (20)

ii]   The development of a dramatist

The basic attitudes outlined above would gradually be elaborated and substantiated over many years to form Suassuna's concept of *arte Armorial*. In the 1940s, 50s and 60s he attempted to put them into practice in a series of literary works. In 1942 the Suassuna family moved to Recife, where Ariano, then aged fifteen, studied at the *Ginásio Pernambucano*. He entered Law School in 1946, and soon published his first poems in Recife literary supplements. These poems are notable for their use of rhythms and metres traditional to the popular oral poetry of the *sertão*, as shown in their titles, such as *Galope à Beira-Mar* and *A Morte do Touro Mão-de-Pau*. However, relatively few of the poems Suassuna wrote were published. By 1947 he was already writing plays, and it would be as a dramatist and novelist that he would become best known. He has never abandoned poetry however, but sees it as a basic constituent of all his writing, as he confirmed in an interview with José Augusto Guerra:

> Really, my work began with poetry. I still write poetry
> today, and I consider my poetry to be the basic source
> of everything which I write. (21)

He sees poetry as the most spontaneous and primordial of literary genres, and the vital link between his work and the popular culture of the *sertão*. Poetry is therefore fundamental to all his writing. One of the main attractions he sees in the novel is that it permits the interweaving of elements of various different genres. (22) For Suassuna, poetry is the form that enables him to return to the realm of imagination and spontaneity that he believes was neglected by the literature of the 1930s and 40s. When he started writing in the mid 1940s, the social documentary literature of regionalist novelists such as Ramos and Lins do Rego still predominated in the North East. Concerned as they were with the particular life and culture of the region, these writers undoubtedly had some influence on Suassuna, but he rejected their approach to content and form, which he describes as neo-naturalism, essentially a development of the naturalism that dominated North East literary circles in the late nineteenth century. (23) Suassuna sees naturalist writing as closely linked to sociology, and dislikes them both. In their attempt to identify with and document the concrete, everyday social world, such writers stifled their imagination and limited their creative possibilities, according to Suassuna. It is in this sense that he speaks of their work as revealing the limitations imposed by sociological thought. Of the *Geração de Trinta*, the writers he most appreciates are Lins do Rego and Amado:

> (...) precisely because they are the two who give free
> reign to the imagination ... (24)

In opposition to the social realist approach to literature, Suassuna speaks of returning to what he perceives of as a freer, more imaginative recreation of reality, using popular poetry, myth and legend to find:

> (...) a magical spirit ... a theatre of greater poetic
> invention ... a greater recreation of reality ... (25)

He argues that most great playwrights, like Shakespeare, Gil Vicente and Federico García Lorca have used popular or folkloric forms to create a theatre of rich poetic invention, which stresses imaginative recreation rather than the realist documentation found in naturalism. (26) Also of special interest to Suassuna is the long tradition of popular poetry of religious content, discussed in chapter 2. Born a Protestant, but converted to catholicism in 1951, at the age of 24, religion has played a decisive role in his life and his literary career. (27) It is the problems of religious faith - the role of Christian values in an increasingly materialistic and competitive society, for example, and the retention of faith in a world he perceives to be pervaded with tragedy and anguish - that form the most fundamental themes of his work. In a newspaper interview in 1972 he stated:

> (...) I think the fundamental problem of life is that
> concerning God, and whether or not one accepts the
> existence of God. All other problems are dependent
> upon that. (28)

He employs many *folhetos* of religious content to discuss such problems within his work, as clearly seen in the series of plays he wrote between 1948 and 1960.

His interest in the theatre really developed as a result of contacts he established whilst a law student in the mid 1940s. Most influential of all was Hermilo Borba Filho, who, along with Suassuna and other students founded the *Teatro do Estudante de Pernambuco* in 1946. As well as staging plays, the group provided a forum for discussion on philosophy and art, especially drama. Borba Filho was the dominant figure of the group, being the member with most experience in the theatre and the clearest ideas on the type of drama required in the North East. His two basic tenets were the need to redemocratise Brazilian theatre, and the need to recognise its political implications. He argued these points in a conference paper given at the Law Faculty in April 1946 to launch the new theatre group, and it is interesting to note the difference in emphasis between his view of the popular theatre and that later developed by Ariano Suassuna:

> What the *Teatro do Estudante* seeks to do is to redemocratise Brazilian theatre, based on the principle that, since the theatre is an art belonging to the people, it must get closer to those who live in the working-class districts, those who cannot afford to pay the high prices demanded by most theatres, and who therefore feel indifferent towards them. It follows that the dramatic arts will draw more benefit from taking theatre to the people than by trying to bring the people to the theatre. (29)

The theatre was popular in origin, Borba Filho argued, and had to be relinked with its popular roots. The group therefore avoided traditional theatres and salons at the beginning, and chose to perform in squares, parks, working-class *bairros* and workers' centres, in an attempt to break out of the confinements of elitist art and reintegrate drama into the lives, problems and aspirations of the wider population. The theatre, Borba Filho claimed, had become too narrow, confined and self indulgent. In his opinion it was:

> (...) drama which does not reflect the thought of the people, but which persists in ignoring their wishes, and does not try to seek solutions to their problems. Instead it presents sentimental, bourgeois stories; anti-social works which fail to represent the aspirations of the people. (30)

Perhaps most significant was Borba Filho's recognition of the political implications of breaking out of the traditional mould:

> The *Teatro do Estudante* will have a revolutionary role, fighting against the commercialisation and bourgeois nature of art (...) (31)

A popular theatre therefore necessarily meant a politically committed theatre:

We are no longer in the age of the ivory tower, when
the conception of art for art's sake prevailed. The artist
cannot remain indifferent to the aspirations of the rest of
humanity, their struggles and their suffering. He or she
cannot remain apathetic, isolated in their art, polishing
words and publishing erudite works which have no
objective. The function of the artist now is to stir up
national consciousness, struggle on behalf of the
oppressed, and soften the suffering, exposing it without
evasion so that solutions can be found more easily. (32)

Borba Filho announced the *Teatro do Estudante* was to democratise
content as well as the process of production, by moving away from
traditional, erudite themes and basing its plays on popular concerns, to
be expressed in appropriate popular form:

Brazilian theatre must make an impact on the public
with the passion of carnival and of football. We must
fight to make theatre truly popular. (33)

Borba Filho could be criticized for being too idealistic, simplistic and
even patronising in his perception of the *povo*, but his ideas are
interesting for the political terms in which they are couched, and the
basic assertion that any attempt to link erudite expression with popular
expression is in effect a political act. This concept of a politically
committed theatre has been developed in different directions by other
Brazilian directors, including Augusto Boal, in recent decades. (34)

The *Teatro do Estudante* operated for six years. Although it did
attempt to put into practice the ideas advocated by Borba Filho, there
was not a consensus of opinion within the group. As financial problems
mounted, the radical proposals became increasingly diluted, and they
did eventually stage plays in the Santa Isabel Theatre in Recife, often
reverting to erudite material, and charging for admission. Joel Pontes has
commented on the predominantly transitory and fluid nature of the
group's activities, partly due to practical problems like finance, but also
because of the differing lines of thought of the participants:

Ideologies crossed and mixed together in the strangest
of ways, and it was only on the basis of action, of
various types, that the students organised themselves,
working in groups which existed precariously ... The
Teatro do Estudante did not have a guiding principle; a
doctrinal point of departure capable of providing a

162

common base for all its members. (35)

Suassuna was among the most active participants of the group throughout its existence, though his later writings would show significant differences of thought from Borba Filho. In launching the theatre group in 1946, the latter had stressed the idea of the end of the war and the defeat of fascism signifying the beginning of a new era, with the arts fully participating in the next phase of the struggle for social change. Pontes has also commented on the effect the end of the war had on the students of the group, suggesting that all of them, despite their ideological differences and the general lack of clarity of their ideas, were at least united in their desire to debate possible new directions for artistic activity and to find a role in the new developments that would occur in the arts in the coming years. (36)

In the late 1940s the group staged some plays written by its own members, namely José de Morães Pinho and Suassuna himself, who thus began his career as a playwright producing work specifically for the group. His first play, *Uma Mulher Vestida de Sol*, written in 1947, earned him the Nicolau Carlos Magno prize of 4,000 cruzeiros, and was followed by a series of others in the following years - *O Desertor de Princesa* (1948), *Os Homens de Barro* (1949), *Auto de João da Cruz* (1950) and *O Arco Desolado* (1954) - all based on a reconstruction of elements of North East popular culture, fused with influences from the classic works of Iberian theatrical tradition. José Laurêncio de Melo, another member of the group, writes of these plays:

> At the artistic level, this period was characterised by the
> preoccupation with bringing together the influence of
> the Iberian classics, especially Lope de Vega, Calderón
> de la Barca and Gil Vicente, and the themes and forms
> integral to the popular North Eastern *romanceiro*. (37)

For Suassuna, this fusion of the erudite and the popular to create new plays is not problematic, for he stresses the connections between classic Iberian drama and popular forms of drama and literature in North East Brazil. He argues that the same influences - such as *autos*, morality plays and various religious rituals - can be seen in both, testifying to their common origins and to the constant interaction of erudite and popular forms over many centuries, as seen in the work of classic playwrights like Gil Vicente and Lope de Vega, and in the poetry of the *cantadores* of North East Brazil. It is in this sense that he sees a regionally based literature and drama - that is, incorporating locations, situations, representative types and action characteristic of the North East - as

163

having a universal quality, for many of its themes, arguments and dramatic forms go back to fundamental emotions, dilemmas and concerns that are basic to all humans, transcending time and space. In this way he establishes the links between the regional, the national and the universal, and emphasises the relationship between North East popular literature and other literary forms, constantly speaking in terms of common origins, common bonds and common emotions:

> All literature has its beginning in the oral, the mythical, and the rhapsodic, loaded with hidden meanings, symbols, signs and emblems. It has a beginning of well-defined extremes and clear boundries where everything appeared clear and sharp, where blood was blood and laughter was laughter, with the epic, the satire, morality, tragedy and comedy, all clearly defined. Such was the beginning of Mediterranean literature, be it Greek or North African, and of Medieval Iberian literature, and also of the literature of so called "primitive" cultures. And such was the beginning of our own popular North Eastern literature. (38)

In his plays, Suassuna emphasises these links between classical Iberian theatre and the popular dramatic representations of the North East by drawing upon many formal similarities which they share. The figure of the Virgin Mary which appears in some of his early plays, for example, is taken from the Marian tradition - *tradição mariana* - the cult of the Virgin Mary found in both classic Iberian drama and in popular plays in the North East. Yet the perception of such elements and symbols must necessarily differ from one social group to another. It is not the particular perception which the poor of the rural North East have of those symbols which is of major concern to Suassuna, however, but rather the value he considers them holding as embodiments of universal concerns, needs and aspirations.

Suassuna himself emphasised this point in an interview given to a Recife newspaper, *Folha da Manhã*, in 1948, when commenting on his first play, *A Mulher Vestida de Sol*:

> In my play, I tried to preserve that which is eternal, universal and poetic in our rich "romanceiro" tradition (...) (39)

Not completely satisfied with the original version of the play, Suassuna rewrote it in 1958. The work centres on the tragic feud between families that results from a land dispute fought by the two landowners, Joaquim Maranhão and Antônio Rodrigues. The son of Rodrigues, Francisco, and the daughter of Maranhão, Rosa, fall in love, and their relationship heightens the tension between their fathers. For a while an uneasy peace reigns, with both landowners giving their word not to set foot on their rivals' land. Maranhão breaks his oath however, in order to have Francisco killed. The play ends with Maranhão being caught and killed in turn for his treachery, and Rosa, heartbroken at the death of Francisco, committing suicide. The fundamental themes of the work - the attachment of the *sertanejos* to their land, honour betrayed and then avenged, the role of fate and the importance of religious faith - are all common to traditional popular poetry of the North East. The centre of interest of the work, however, is not the peasants but the landowners, and the land on which they fight serves as a microcosm for a world in which human pride and greed constantly lead to tragedy. At one point the judge who visits the scene of the dispute to investigate the case comments:

> Pobreza, fome, sêca, fadiga, o amor e o sangue, a possessão das terras, as lutas pelas cabras e carneiros, a guerra e a morte, tudo o que é elementar ao homem está presente nesta terra perdida. (40)

Poverty, hunger, drought, exhaution, love and blood, possession of the land. The struggle to rear goats and sheep, war and death, everything that is most elementary to man is present in this lost land. (40)

A Mulher Vestida de Sol shows that from the beginning of his writing career Suassuna was concerned with highlighting the traditional Christian values conveyed in much North East popular culture, though it is considered by many critics to be an 'embryonic work', testing certain forms which were then abandoned or radically changed in his later plays. Suassuna himself has stated that it was only in 1955, with *Auto da Compadecida*, which would prove to be his most successful play, that he felt that he had really succeeded in capturing the essential qualities of North East popular culture in his work. (41) It is in effect a type of collage, drawing together the content of three popular *folhetos* which are fused together into one basic plot. To unify the diverse elements, Suassuna uses a clown to present each piece of action of the play and comment upon it, partly in the style of a circus ringmaster, and partly like the popular poet reading his work, stopping periodically to comment and test audience reaction. In his opening stage instructions, Suassuna states:

(...) o autor gostaria de deixar claro que seu teatro é
mais aproximado dos espetáculos de circo e da tradição
popular do que do teatro moderno. (42)

*(...) the author would like to make it clear that his theatre is closer to the circus
show and to popular tradition than to the modern theatre. (42)*

As in Suassuna's other plays, the atmosphere of the *sertão*, which
provides the setting for the work, the language and songs used and the
characterisation - employing types typical of the North East *romanceiro*
tradition - all help to reinforce the regionalist character of the work.

Mark Curran has identified the three *folhetos* employed by
Suassuna in the play. (43) The first, *O Entêrro do Cachorro*, of which
various versions have been produced by different poets in the *sertão*,
satirises the mercenary attitudes of certain sectors of the church by
relating the tale of a priest who refuses to give a Englishman's dog a
church burial until hearing that he will benefit from the dog's will,
which brings about a sudden change of heart. Suassuna uses this plot in
the first main action of his play, which centres on a baker, rich and
mean, and his attractive wife, who is regularly unfaithful to him. When
her beloved dog dies she asks the priest to give it an orthodox Catholic
burial, but the priest rejects the request as preposterous. The popular
hero, João Grilo, then appears, modelled on the *pícaro* typical of much
folheto literature, a poor, weak and downtrodden character who survives
through wit and cunning. He tricks the priest, verger and the bishop into
giving the dog the burial requested, mentioning that it has left a large
sum of money to the church in its will, from which each of them will
benefit. The basic plot of the original *folheto* is thus developed, expanded
through the addition of details, to create a popular farce, employing
characterisation and language conventional to regional popular literary
tradition.

For the central part of the play, Suassuna draws upon another
popular poem, *História do Cavalo que Defecava Dinheiro*, which, according
to Enrique Martínez-López, has a long tradition, with at least 105
different versions existing, 27 of which are Hispanic, 62 from other
European countries and 16 Oriental or African. (44) It deals with a
peasant who tricks the landowner by selling him a horse which he claims
is capable of defecating money. In the play, João Grilo gains revenge on
the baker and his wife, who have frequently abused him, by selling them
a cat with the same miraculous ability. Finally, the last action of the
work is based on a *folheto* entitled *O Castigo da Soberba*, in which a
condemned soul is saved by the compassionate intervention of the Virgin
Mary. All the characters in Suassuna's play, including João Grilo, are

killed by *cangaceiros* and then reappear in the afterlife for judgement, with Christ as judge and the Devil prosecuting them. One by one they are all found guilty - the baker of greed, the wife of adultery, the members of the church of hypocrisy and dishonesty, and João Grilo for all the tricks he has used to deceive others. Suddenly however, João Grilo invokes the *Compadecida*, the Virgin Mary, full of pity and compassion, whom he describes as:

> Gente como eu, pobre, filha de Joaquim e de Ana,
> casada com um carpinteiro, tudo gente boa. (45)

Someone just like me, poor, daughter of Joachim and Ann, married to a carpenter; all good people. (45)

The Virgin duly argues the defence of all the condemned characters, declaring that their actions are to be explained and excused by their fear of suffering, hunger, solitude and of death itself. All are then sent to purgatory, with the exception of João Grilo. He attempts to persuade the Virgin to grant him direct salvation instead, and she reaches the compromise of returning him to earth to allow him another chance to live a righteous life. The same broad development of events as in the original *folheto* is used, the same arguments and the same style of language, though the verse of the *folheto* is converted into prose by Suassuna. He still uses the last verse of the *folheto* to close the play however, with the clown returning once more to say:

> A história da compadecida termina aqui. Para encerrá-la,
> nada melhor do que o verso com que acaba um dos
> romances populares em que ela se baseou:
> > Meu verso acabou-se agora,
> > Minha história verdadeira.
> > Toda vez que eu canto ele,
> > Vêm dez mil-réis pra a algibeira.
> > Hoje estou dando por cinco,
> > Talvez não ache quem queira. (46)

The story of the mother of compassion ends here. To close it, there is nothing better than the verse which ends one of the popular poems on which it is based: "My poem is finished now, this true story. Each time I recite it, I get 10 "mil-reais" in my pocket. Today I'm selling them for five. Perhaps I won't find anyone who wants them." (46)

In both form and content, the play appears strongly regionalist, but as

Angel Rama and Ligia Vassallo have both pointed out, Suassuna uses the popular material concerned to return to the medieval farce and early Latin drama. (47) The most basic themes of the play can in fact be traced back many centuries through Iberian dramatic and literary tradition. In an article on *O Auto da Compadecida*, Enrique Martínez López highlights the two most striking of these traditional elements. The first is the Marian tradition already mentioned. *Autos* narrating acts of mercy and compassion by the Virgin Mary were performed in the Iberian peninsula as far back as the twelfth century. The second is the trickery of the central character, João Grilo, which is rooted very firmly in the Iberian picaresque tradition, typified by *Lazarillo de Tormes*. Many well-known *pícaros*, often popularly referred to as *amarelinhos* in the North East, are found in the popular poetry of the region. João Grilo is one of the most popular, with numerous *folhetos* narrating his cunning exploits composed by many different poets. Martínez-López describes this fusion of ancient forms with current popular Brazilian forms as *neopopularismo*:

> Suassuna, is a similar way to Gil Vicente, Lope de Vega and García Lorca with his farces, bases himself on a neopopularist dramatic formula, the results of which entertain rich and poor alike. For him, neopopularism does not consist of an imitation or transposition of popular culture, but rather a higher phase of recreation of that culture, where the dangers of a picturesque and jingoistic parochialism will be carefully avoided, along with the dangers of an art which lacks humanity and the spirit of the people. (48)

Martínez-López goes on to speak of the moralising and satirical tone of *Auto da Compadecida*. Just as in popular literature, he argues, João Grilo, the *pícaro*, redeems and avenges the poor, exploited classes he represents from the more powerful sectors of society. This leads him to speak of the subversive quality of the play, in which the poor and downtrodden are the real heroes:

> (...) they are the only ones who, in a world of liars, represent the essential truth rather than the apparent truth. This means nothing less than demolishing the truth and virtue of those in high, official office. It's not the powerful, the learned or those dignitaries who watch over morality who posses the truth, Suassuna tells us, but rather the weak, the foolish and the despised. (49)

It is true that Suassuna has developed a typical popular theme that is in essence a metaphorical expression of the poor avenging themselves against the rich and powerful, but this is incidental to Suassuna's work, rather than a major concern within it. It is quite clear from Suassuna's statements elsewhere on politics and culture that his views are far from radical. His major concern in the work is to convey a basic Christian message: the need to recognise one's sins, consider those of others with tolerance and always retain faith. Ultimately, faith will be rewarded with compassion in the final judgement. However, though João Grilo is in the end returned to earth, he is at first condemned by Christ, for showing racial prejudice, deceiving others and, above all, expressing class hatred by cursing his bosses who have exploited him, the baker and his wife, and attempting to avenge himself against them, which, Christ reminds him, is a grave sin:

> O caso é duro. Compreendo as circunstâncias em que João viveu, mas isso também tem um limite. Afinal das contas, o mandamento existe e foi transgredido. Acho que não posso salvá-lo. (50)

This case is serious. I understand the circumstances in which João lived, but that too has its limits. In the end, the commandment exists and it was transgressed. I do not think I can save him. (50)

The emphasis of the play is on forbearance and forgiveness, rather than the subversion which Martínez-López highlights.

Although Suassuna appears to be incorporating the peasant world view into this and other plays, he is filtering the popular materials he employs, refocusing them according to his own vision of the *sertão* and its culture, to end up with a recreation of the popular, or what Martínez-López terms a *neopopularismo*, that is significantly different from the real peasant world and culture where the original material was created. Suassuna has selected specific elements and themes of popular culture, and reconstructed them in a particular way, so as to compose his own, personal mythical world of the *sertão*. It is a vision that emphasises Christian morality, and is essentially nostalgic, deliberately seeking to reconstruct a mythical past of the *sertão*, rather than dealing with the contemporary problems of tension and transformation affecting life throughout the North East in the 1950s, 60s and 70s, when Suassuna was producing most of his writing. (51) Hence his predilection for the traditional themes of popular religious belief, *catolicismo sertanejo* as he calls it, and of *cangaço*, the popular banditry rife in the *sertão* until the late 1930s. These are indeed two major themes of *folheto* literature, on the one hand recording a collective history and on the other often making certain statements about present conditions and the desire for change. In the work of Suassuna, however, it is their legendary, folkloric qualities that are developed, to recreate the past and express the particular concerns of the playwright himself.

Suassuna appears to recognise this process of refocusing of perspective, referring to the *sertão* as his mythical world and speaking of the need for other writers to recreate elements of popular culture according to their own individual temperament and skills. Yet he then appears to contradict himself by declaring that the erudite literature which results is popular, somehow created and nurtured within the spirit and vision of the North East peasantry. *Auto da Compadecida* received considerable acclaim in the 1950s and is still widely read today. Its popularity is largely explained by the way it skilfully blends satire, farce and moral teaching in a form that is both inventive and entertaining. This is what Suassuna sees as a return to a more magical, poetical theatre, which emphasises the imaginative recreation of reality rather than the attempt to document that reality as accurately as possible. However, it is illogical to then proceed to rationalise this form of writing in terms of an attempt to produce a literature that is truly national in the sense of emanating from the collective vision and experience of the rural poor.

In another play, *O Santo e a Porca*, written in 1957, Suassuna uses elements of popular farce, commonly found in *folhetos*, to give voice to his concerns. The major character is Euricão Arábe, intensely avaricious and miserly, who jealously guards his life savings in a wooden pig, which he worships and calls upon his patron saint, Santo Antônio, to guard. Throughout the play he wrestles with the problem of dividing his devotions between the pig and the saint; a conflict between material and spiritual values. At one point, believing the pig to be stolen, he fears Santo Antônio has become jealous of his divided loyalties and has abandoned him, but then, finding the money safe, feels reassured that he can have both money and saint, without having to choose between them. He praises Santo Antônio for helping him, only to discover that all the money in the pig is old currency that is no longer valid. He concludes that Santo Antônio has taught him a lesson:

> Foi uma cilada de Santo Antônio, para eu ficar novamente com ele. Vou então ficar aqui: Trancarei a porta e não a abrirei mais para ninguém. Porque não quero mais ficar num mundo em que acontecem estas coisas impossíveis de prever. (52)

It was a trap set by Saint Anthony, to get me to go back to him. So I'll stay here: I'll bolt the door and won't open it again for anyone, because I no longer want to be in a world where such unforeseeable things occur. (52)

The plays action, characterisation and humour, again making use of the *pícaro* tradition, are based on North East popular poetic tradition, but Suassuna, in the introduction to the play, emphasises its universal dimension. Again, he is preoccupied above all with the question of religious faith. If man, through his obsession with material concerns, abandons God, his world will become absurd, devoid of all meaning. Only by returning to faith in God will he find the strength to face the chaos of life. In the words of Suassuna:

> (...) o que Euricão descobre, de repente, esmagado, é que, se Deus não existe, tudo é absurdo. E, com esta descoberta, volta-se novamente para a única saída existente em seu impasse, a humilde crença de sua mocidade, o caminho do santo, Deus, que ele seguira num primeiro impulso, mas do qual fora desviado aos poucos, inteiramente pela idolatria do dinheiro, da segurança, do poder, do mundo. (53)

(...) what Euricão suddenly discovers, completely overwhelmed, is that if God does not exist, then everything is absurd. And with that discovery he returns to the only way out to his impasse that exists: the humble faith of his youth, the path of the saint, of God, which on first impulse he had followed, but from which he was gradually deflected, entirely through the idolisation of money, security, power and worldliness. (53)

The same basic message, the corrupting effect of worldly concerns and the need to turn to faith in God, is repeated in *O Casamento Suspeitoso*, also written in 1957. Another farce, the action of the play relies heavily of the character of Canção, based on Canção de Fogo, the *pícaro* of *folheto* literature referred to earlier. Lúcia, encouraged by her mother and her lover, attempts to trick a wealthy young man, Geraldo, into marrying her in order to gain access to his inheritance. Geraldo is fooled and agrees, but the trickery of Canção, who disguises himself as a priest and conducts a sham ceremony, saves him from disaster. The tricksters are exposed, and leave defeated. All the characters return to the stage at the end however, to summarise the moral of the work. One by one they confess their sins, including Canção, who admits that he lusted after both Geraldo's money and Lúcia. All humans are sinners, and the only hope is God. Geraldo brings the play to a close:

GERALDO- Por isso lanço um olhar melancólico a nosso conjunto e convido todos a um apelo. É uma invocação humilde e confiante, a única que pode brotar sem hipocrisia desse pobre rebanho que é o nosso. E assim, juntando-me aos outros atores e ao autor, peço que digam comigo:
TODOS- Que o Cordeiro de Deus, que tira o pecado do mundo, tenha misericórdia de todos nós. (54)

GERALDO- And so I cast a sad eye over our group and I invite everyone to join me in an appeal. It's a humble confident invocation, the only one which can come without hypocrisy from a poor flock like ours. And so, joining in with the other actors and the author, I ask you to say with me : EVERYONE- May the holy lamb of God, who cleanses the world of sin, take pity on us all. (54)

A Pena e a Lei, (1959), introduces further elements of popular culture into Suassuna's work, most notably *mamulengo*, the popular theatre tradition of the North East. The puppeteer, Cheiroso, fulfils a similar function to that of the clown in *Auto da Compadecida*, introducing and commenting upon the action of the play, reminiscent of the popular poet reciting his verses in the market place. The character Benedito is another *pícaro*, using tricks and deception to rectify injustices and humiliate those who abuse their wealth and power. The final message of the work, however, echoes that of the previous plays. In the final act, all the characters meet up again after death and await judgement. When Christ appears, they cast blame on God for creating a world and a race that are so defective. Finally, however, under questioning from Christ, they all admit that, despite the anguish and suffering that life entails, they would accept God's world and live again if they had the choice. Their faith redeems them, and Christ, acted by Cheiroso, emphasises the moral:

Pois, uma vez que julgaram favoravelmente a Deus, assim também ele julga vocês. Erros, cegueiras, embustes enganos, traições, mesquinharias, tudo o que foi a trama de suas vidas, perde a importância de repente, diante do fato de que vocês acreditaram finalmente em mim e diante da esperança que acabam de manifestar. (55)

So, once you judge God favourably, he will judge you likewise. Errors, stupidity, fraud, deceit, betrayal and pettiness: all the things that made up the plot of your lives suddenly lose importance when placed alongside the fact that you finally believed in me, and the hope that you have just shown. (55)

In 1960 Suassuna completed another play, *Farça da Boa Preguiça*. As he explains in the work, the three acts are modelled on a traditional plot from *mamulengo*, a popular poem and a traditional story. The play contrasts a hard-working and wealthy businessman, Aderaldo Catacão, and a poverty stricken, indolent popular poet, Joaquim Simão. Despite his prestige and power on earth, Aderaldo is condemned to purgatory at the end of the play, on account of his greed and profanity. He has been totally corrupted by worldly concerns. Joaquim Simão, however, though criticised, is saved, because his faith remained unbroken throughout his life. Though laziness is sinful, the poet has at least used his time to fulfil himself spiritually, creating beauty and expressing the enjoyment of life when supported by faith in God. Suassuna states in the introduction:

Pode haver nobreza e criação na preguiça, pode haver
feíura e roubalheira no trabalho. (56)

There can be nobility and creation in idleness, and there can be vileness and dishonesty in work. (56)

It can be seen that the same vision of Christian morality is repeated throughout Suassuna's plays, and all the popular materials he employs are used to serve that end. It is religion that is seen to provide the only real solution to man's existential anguish. It is true that some popular poets discuss such questions in their work, but many others concern themselves with different issues, and seek answers outside religious belief, analysing the social conditions within which they live and work. Suassuna selects those *folhetos* which can be most readily adapted to his own view of the world.

It is not only through the content and form that Suassuna attempted to link his plays with popular culture. He also experimented with the actual process of theatrical production. With other members of the *Teatro do Estudante* in the late 1940s, he took productions into working-class urban districts and workers' centres, following Borba Filho's aim of taking art to the people. The group was eventually presented with a truck to assist them. Significantly, they called it the *barraca*, after Lorca's travelling theatre, and which they inaugurated with a work in homage to the murdered Spanish playwright. Lorca, writer of poems and plays based in the folkloric traditions of Southern Spain, organiser of a travelling theatre and the victim of fascism, seemed to symbolise many of the ideals motivating the group. Even after the group disbanded, overwhelmed by financial problems, and its leader Borba Filho had left for the South, Suassuna continued to try to organise similar activities. In the mid 1950s he formed theatrical groups of workers and students to present plays by Sophocles, Plato and Molière, supported by two local academics interested in the notion of democratising cultural activity, Murilo Guimarães and Paulo Freire. Workers and students also composed the audiences for those works.

Suassuna's participation in such radical artistic experiments with clear political implications at first seems incongruous in the light of the conservative statements about culture and art which he would later make, but it is important to bear in mind the cultural atmosphere in the North East at the time. Popular organisation - of students, workers and peasants - was gaining momentum steadily throughout the 1950s, and artists and intellectuals were obliged to respond to the situation. (57) Much artistic activity in the North East in the fifties and early sixties reflected the highly charged political atmosphere. Corresponding to the growth of popular forces at the national level, Miguel Arraes was elected State Governor of Pernambuco in 1960, signifying the establishment of one of the most radical governments seen in the North East for many years. Within its programme of substantial reform, cultural development played a key role. A broad educational and artistic movement was founded, the *Movimento de Cultura Popular* (MCP), promoted and funded by the State Government, in order to carry out a broad programme of cultural and artistic activities. The ideological basis of the movement was largely formed by the educational theories of Paulo Freire, according to which educational and cultural activity at all levels was to be conducted with the expressed aim of stimulating the social consciousness of the masses, in order to politicise them and enable them to develop their own political options in the struggle for change. A series of education programmes, from basic literacy upwards, was established on this basis, and 'educate for liberty' became one of the main slogans of the movement. A wide range of artistic activities was also promoted, including music, crafts and theatre groups, with middle-class artists participating alongside workers and peasants. It was to be a process of mutual learning. At one level the activities aimed to break the alienation of many intellectuals and artists, their condition of being isolated from the sectors of the population that most interested them, essentially the urban working classes and the peasantry, and at another it was hoped that it would help integrate poorer sectors of the population into mainstream cultural activity, giving them the means to organise themselves and engage in new areas of cultural production. In this way it was hoped to develop confidence in the belief in self determination and in the respect for the popular cultural traditions of the North East. Although it denied being a political movement, the MCP clearly emerged in response to the growing organisation of peasants, workers and students already in progress, and was essentially an attempt to link the work of radical artists and intellectuals to that broad process.

Four theatre groups were created under the auspices of the MCP, the *Teatro de Cultura Popular* being the most productive. Through a process of gradual experiment, performing in working-class urban districts and among rural communities, it encouraged those living in such areas to participate actively in the productions. From the beginning, a process of dialogue was established between the artists and the audience of workers and peasants, so that responses and suggestions could be incorporated into future works, and gradually the composition of the group was altered to actively incorporate workers and peasants as actors or assistants. There was a deliberate attempt therefore to move away from the concept of individual creativity, and develop instead the notion of collective creativity, so that forms of dramatic representation might eventually evolve that were to a large extent the creation of the people themselves. The group put on a series of successful productions, until the military coup of March 1964 abruptly ended the whole MCP programme. Years later, Luís Mendonça, director of the *Teatro de Cultura Popular*, wrote about the whole experience, concluding that for a truly popular theatre to succeed official support from a sympathetic government organisation was necessary, that theatre had to be taken out to the people, and that it must respond to the needs of the popular audience:

> The themes which have greatest effect on the people are those based on their own circumstances. One must use the concrete reality which they live as a starting point, not in the sense of showing them their own experiences on stage, but in the sense that the characters convey something capable of convincing them; that's to say, they carry the spectators along with them. (...) The important thing to point out is that it's vital to use the people's experiences as a starting point, to get down to meet the people and gradually bring them along until they can assimilate what you want to give them. And give them theatre, entertainment, a show. Otherwise, no matter how committed to their cause you might be, and no matter whether you speak of things that really concern them, the people will not accept it. (58)

The MCP brought together many intellectuals and artists, including Suassuna, who declared his broad support for it and participated in some of its events. By maintaining a wide range of activities, free from rigid doctrines, the movement was able to attract participants of differing political persuasions who were nonetheless stimulated by the atmosphere of inquiry and experimentation being generated. Thus the late fifties and early sixties created the conditions that brought together many contrasting attitudes, enabling them to work together and interrelate. The coup and its aftermath dispersed the participants in different directions and clearly exposed the differences in their thinking and political persuasions.

Even during the years of MCP activity however, there was evidence of Suassuna's differences with other participants. In 1959 he and Hermilo Borba Filho founded another theatre group, *O Teatro Popular do Nordeste*, and Suassuna eventually wrote its manifesto, the emphasis of which contrasts in significant ways from Borba Filho's earlier writing on drama, and from the declarations from other supporters of the MCP, such as Paulo Freire, Germano Coelho and Luis Mendonça. The manifesto also sketches out the basic ideas that Suassuna would repeat when launching the *Movimento Armorial* in 1971. Firstly, Suassuna demands a complete break with academic art, which he sees as essentially sterile and imitative. Popular sources must provide artistic inspiration, he argues:

> (...) breaking, once and for all, in the North East, the
> bonds between our art and academics of every kind. (59)

More significant is his refutation of the notion of popular theatre as necessarily a political activity. The commitment of the artist using popular forms is not essentially political, he argues. In fact, work that is clearly shaped by a particular political ideology is a degraded form of art:

> We also reject demagogic art, enlisted for a political
> cause, and which only concerns itself with one element
> of the problems faced by humankind; an art distorted by
> political motives, an art of propaganda, which
> introduces into the creative work an alien body, the
> thesis, and so converts the theatrical performance into a
> petition serving political ends. We believe that art must
> be neither gratuitous nor politically compromised (...)
> Therefore, our commitment is not an adopted position,
> concerned only with the political dimension of reality.
> On the contrary, we are committed to the totality of
> existence, from its ordinary, daily aspects to its most
> sacred and transcendental. (60)

For Suassuna, political and social questions are not the most striking aspects of popular cultural expression. Instead he emphasises what he perceives as its more eternal, universal themes:

> (...) Unlike "engagé" artists, we do not refuse to recognise that the whole tradition of Brazilian and North Eastern popular art is religious, tragic, comic, and concerned with morality, mystery, metamorphosis and the miraculous. (61)

This view implies a rejection of the argument that religious, moral and mystical aspects of popular art are all interrelating components of a world view that is shaped by social existence, and which therefore cannot be considered independently of crucial political questions concerning class relations and the role of ideology. Instead, Suassuna implies that religious, tragic, moral and mystical aspects of popular art are not so much socially formed, but emanate from a deeper, spiritual realm within humankind. Politics are to be transcended for that realm to be reached; a realm which he perceives as the essence of human emotions and responses, but which can only be referred to in obscure, abstract terms such as *espírito* and *sangue*:

> (...) art must not be gratuitous nor politically compromised: it must be committed in the sense of maintaining a productive interchange with reality, speaking on behalf of the collectivity and of the individual, and keeping in harmony with the deep spirit of our people. Producing popular theatre does not mean imposing a predetermined vision of the world upon the people, but making one's work move to the rhythm of their heart beat, so that, imperceptibly, and naturally, what our theatre transfigures, and expresses in its mysterious way, is what is felt and expressed in the spirit of the people (...) (62)

Other problems arise here. Firstly, although he rejects the approach of others on the grounds that they work with popular art on the basis of preestablished formulas, his own work and writings on popular culture are clearly determined by conceptions of that culture, and of those who give it expression, which are established a priori. Secondly, although he sees the vital link between the erudite artist and popular culture being forged by emotional empathy, Suassuna never elucidates this point in order to explain how the process might work, preferring instead to refer to it in a language that is almost mystical.

In the end, Suassuna's concept of the popular theatre appears extremely vague, as he attempts in his manifesto to fuse together contradictory notions - that of individual creativity with an expression of collective experience and vision; that of an essentially non-political theatre with an expression of the collective aspirations of the rural poor of the North East; that of a theatre that is distinctly popular and North Eastern yet which still performs the works of Greek tragedy, Shakespeare or Ibsen. The term popular is stretched by Suassuna to cover a vast array of drama of extremely varied nature:

> Our theatre is popular. But for us *popular* does not in any way mean simple, or merely political. We include Greek tragedy, Latin comedy, medieval religious theatre, the Italian Renaissance, Elizabethan theatre, French tragedy, the world of Molière and Gil Vicente, the Golden Age of Spain, the theatre of Goldoni, the French romantic drama, Goethe, Schiller, Anchieta, Antônio José, Martins Pena and all those who, in Brazil, and especially in the North East, seek to produce a theatre in harmony with the popular collective spirit (...) (63)

It is clear therefore that whilst Suassuna agrees with many other Brazilian artists on the need to develop popular drama, and though the aims of his work appear at times to coincide with those of others, like Borba Filho or Mendonça, his conception of popular culture and how it can and should be assimilated by the erudite artist is different in significant ways.

As a result, Suassuna's work in the theatre diverged considerably from that of the many radical drama groups that emerged in Brazil from the late 1950s onwards; groups which formed part of a Latin American wide movement to develop a new popular theatre that would revolutionise drama with the objective of using theatre as an instrument for transforming society. A crucial influence for that movement were the theories of Brecht, which sought to break with the conventions of bourgeois drama, and, through a dialectical approach, create a revolutionary theatre that presented a world that was changeable rather than immutable, and which transformed passive spectators into active participants, and thus prepared them for wider social and political action. Whilst Suassuna rejected the Brechtian theatre, arguing that it destroyed the illusion and enchantment he believed to be essential to the art form, (64) other dramatists and drama theoreticians sought to develop those theories to create a new political theatre in Latin America. In

Brazil, Augusto Boal would undoubtedly become the best-known representative of the latter position. For Boal, the first step for creating a theatre for political change is to democratise the means of artistic production, removing it from the control of those dominant classes which had appropriated it and reshaped it as an instrument to suit their own needs, and returning theatre to the mass of the population for its own use. (65) All Boal's techniques, brought together in his *Teatro do Oprimido*, were developed with the aim of breaking down the barriers he saw as restricting drama production, and changing passive spectators into active participants in the creative process. Formal theatres were rejected in favour of the streets and squares, and a popular dramatic language developed, involving admonition, bold, simple characterisation, simplified plots and Manichaean techniques presenting the conflicts between the forces of good and the forces of evil. Above all, it was a theatre that sought to eliminate the division between actor and spectator, converting all into protagonists in the transformation of society, and, by breaking down passivity and experimenting with alternative courses of action, serving as a rehearsal for social change. (66) For Boal, the popular theatre can only be a politically committed theatre. It must address itself first and foremost to Brazilian reality, which for Boal is characterised above all else by a conflict of opposing social forces which is too stark to be blurred or ignored. The popular theatre has to adopt a clear position with regard to that conflict if it is to become a truly popular form of expression with real capacity to stimulate change. (67)

Boal's views stand in stark contrast to Suassuna's rejection of a purely political theatre, his emphasis on a spiritual universe rather than the social, and his vision of an all-embracing theatre which attempts to bring together different tendencies, options and attitudes, rather than choosing between them. Such ideas would be rejected as mystification by Boal. It is interesting to note that whilst for Boal art is only popular in the sense that it evolves in direct interaction with the peasants, workers and *favela* dwellers who comprise the mass of the Brazilian population, stimulating their participation until they can take control of the whole productive process themselves, Suassuna moved away from attempts to establish direct contact with a popular audience in the years which followed his theatrical experiments of the early 1960s, and went on to produce work directed almost exclusively towards an educated middle-class public. For him therefore, popular refers essentially to the assimilation of material of popular origin into the erudite work concerned, rather than to the way the creative process is organised or to the audience for which it is intended - questions which are of vital concern for Boal, and the other dramatists of the New Latin American Popular Theatre.

iii]   The *Movimento Armorial*

The 1964 coup and the installation of a military dictatorship dramatically changed the conditions for artistic production in Brazil. The radical cultural programmes which had achieved considerable dynamism in the preceding years, such as that of the MCP, were rapidly suppressed, and artistic activity in most fields strictly circumscribed. (68) The whole question of popular culture was regarded with suspicion by the new authorities, and it became impossible in the 1960s to follow the radical direction proposed by the likes of Freire or Boal. In fact, both men were among the many artists and intellectuals eventually forced into exile. Those who remained to continue working in the field of popular culture could only do so within certain defined parameters.

Suassuna's work, however, had already begun to move in a different direction, simply reflecting the development of his own artistic interests and ideas. In 1960 he had completed his last major play, *Farça da Boa Preguiça*, and then concentrated on his plan to write a trilogy of novels, on which he had begun to work two years earlier. More and more of his time was spent on this project and his activities in the theatre virtually ceased. However, he did continue his efforts to increase recognition of, and support for, the popular artistic expression which he saw as the foundation for a truly national art. Although no sympathiser of the military regime, he did work with state institutions which he believed could help promote that basic aim. In 1967 he became a founder member of the *Conselho Federal de Cultura*, leaving in 1973, and in 1975 became Secretary of Education and Culture for Recife. His collaboration with these bodies met with criticism from many quarters, the issue made even more sensitive by the fact that the last years of the 1960s and early 1970s saw repression on the part of the military regime reach an unprecedented level, heightening the problem of the relationship between intellectuals and the state or state-related institutions.

Suassuna also worked closely with the Federal University of Pernambuco in Recife during this time, serving as Director of the *Departamento de Extensão Cultural* from 1969 to 1974, which provided him with the necessary platform for promoting traditional North East art. He brought together a large number of local artists - musicians, painters, sculptors, writers - all of whom were strongly influenced by North East popular art forms, in order to coordinate their activities. A quintet and an orchestra were formed to develop a programme of music based on popular North East traditions, an exhibition of regional art organised and the writers encouraged to produce works recreating the local *romanceiro*. Though Suassuna also arranged finance for the publication of a number of *folhetos* by popular poets unable to print their work themselves, virtually all the activities he organised in his capacity of Director of the Department fell very definitely into the category of erudite or high art, intended for a middle-class audience. The work produced was collectively named *arte Armorial* by Suassuna, and in Recife on October 18th, 1970, with a concert entitled *Tres Séculos de Música Nordestina - do Barroco ao Armorial*, by the *Orquestra Armorial de Câmara*, together with an exhibition of North East art, the programme officially became a movement, the *Movimento Armorial*, representing the culmination for Suassuna of over twenty years work with popular art of the North East. When Suassuna relinquished the Directorship of the university department in 1974, new support for his movement came from the State Government of Pernambuco when he became its Secretary of Education and Culture.

During the course of its development through the 1970s therefore, the *Movimento Armorial* received significant assistance from official institutions. In reply to criticism made of this, Suassuna rejected the argument that political implications were involved, arguing that his interest in promoting Brazilian Culture did not necessarily demand any political options, but was rather a question of opening up as many avenues for cultural activity as possible:

> First of all, none of the people who supported me demanded any particular political position or choice on my part, and that refers especially to professor Murilo Guimarães and the mayor Antônio Farias. Secondly, the proposals of the *Movimento Armorial* are far broader than exclusively political issues. Most of those who judge everything according to political criteria are narrow-minded dogmatists who see everything in simplistic, black and white terms, and their opinion doesn't interest me. Thirdly, the public posts I hold or have held are not of a·political nature (...) I am public spirited. I would like to do more for Brazilian culture than I'm already doing because, without believing that everyone ought to be like me, I think I have an obligation to mark out Brazilian paths forward in as many areas of artistic and literary activity as I can. (69)

Though already dealt with, the problem of separation between cultural activity and political options is clearly exposed here. There is the assumption that simply through an intuitive sympathy for popular art, the artist can capture and reproduce a spiritual essence embodied in that art - an essence which expresses Brazilian nationality. The artist, therefore, simply has to create intuitively, without need to consider how exactly his work relates to society at large or to the popular culture he is seeking to assimilate.

Suassuna never indicated any approval of the regime's cultural policy of the 1970s. Indeed, in 1981 he withdrew from public life, announcing that he had been mistaken to have worked in collaboration with the governmental institutions of the time, and that he was totally disillusioned with their approach towards national culture. This will be dealt with later. However, in the 1970s Suassuna detected no major conflict of perspective or ideas, and this broad common ground helps to explain how he was able to launch a movement promoting popular cultural expression, with official backing, at a time of strict censorship and considerable oppression in Brazil, whilst others dealing with similar questions had left for exile. A document published by the Ministry of Education and Culture in 1975 outlining cultural policy presents a number of concepts, arguments and propositions which overlap in certain respects with those of Suassuna, and since such ideas are vital for an understanding of Suassuna's movement, his own work and, indeed, a lot of other art inspired by popular artistic expression, they need to be examined in greater detail. Sections of that 1975 cultural policy document were reproduced in a Brazilian periodical in 1980, together with a perceptive criticism of it by Renato de Silveira. The document defines national culture in the following way:

> National Policy on Culture seeks to understand Brazilian culture in terms of its own particular characteristics, especially those which have resulted from the syncretism attained in Brazil on the basis of the principal sources of our civilisation - the Indian, the European and the African (...) we understand Brazilian culture to be that which has been created, or has resulted, from acculturation, shared out and diffused by the national community. (70)

National Culture has evolved from a unique process of syncretism and acculturation between the different cultural systems of the major ethnic groupings in Brazil. Once again, the emphasis is placed on the notion of harmonisation between the different cultures to form a unified whole - the *comunidade nacional* - unified by a common essence:

> (...) The first action to be taken must seek to reveal what constitutes the kernel of the Brazilian man and woman and the content of their life. Before anything else, we

need to ascertain what is the very essence of our culture. (71)

It is the duty of the state, the document continues, to formulate cultural objectives on the basis of interpretation of national aspirations, and to maintain levels of quality of cultural production and protect it from excessive innovation, which might threaten its specifically national characteristics:

> (...) In order to maintain quality, it is necessary to take precautions against certain dangers, such as the cult of novelty, which is a characteristic of a developing nation, due to the mass media and the imitation of developed societies. The desire to innovate frequently undermines quality. (72)

The dangers of a State under the control of military authoritarianism assuming the right and the duty to define national aspirations, the quality of artistic production and the authenticity of national art are clear. As Renato de Silveira argues, such statements simply function to justify the government's aim of centralising control over artistic production, ensuring that it conforms to preestablished criteria, and necessarily restricting free artistic creation as a result. (73)

The policy document also raises once again the problematic question of preservation of culture, which, as has already been seen, is a central idea in much thinking on popular culture and national culture:

> The preservation of goods of cultural value has as its goal that of conserving the riches which have emerged, and of keeping alive the national memory, thus ensuring the perpetuity of Brazilian culture. (74)

The paper ends with a series of propositions for government action for supporting cultural activity in Brazil for the rest of the 1970s. This involves support not only for the erudite or mainstream art forms, such as literature, theatre, cinema, music and dance, but also for folkloric manifestations, including popular dance, music, customs and *folheto* literature. In general terms, these practical objectives do not differ greatly from those which Suassuna was already attempting to realise through the *Movimento Armorial* in Recife.

Indeed, perhaps the most significant point made by Renato de Silveira is that the basic concepts underlying the document are by no means specific to the government of 1975. They are simply variations of deeply engrained notions of culture which have recurred time and time again throughout the present century among Brazilian artists and intellectuals of the most diverse political persuasions. Suassuna is certainly a case in point: the same basic ideas can be seen in all his explanations of the thinking behind the *Movimento Armorial*, even though they are naturally expressed in his own particular form and language.

To begin with, he frequently employs the same abstract notion of national unity. The term *povo* is often used to convey this, used on the one hand as a synonym for nation, and on the other to allude to the poorest sectors of society, workers and peasants, which he sees as forming the basis of that unified nation, thereby echoing da Cunha's vision of the poor *sertanejos* of the North East as the bedrock of the Brazilian race, referred to in the previous chapter. Launching the *Movimento Armorial*, Suassuna writes:

> The national unity of Brazil stems from the people (...) (75)

In similar vein, he writes of one of the artists involved in the movement, Fernando Lopes da Paz, a sculptor:

> Fernando Lopes da Paz is a man of the people, and he carries in his veins that strong sap of national Brazilian blood. (76)

It is significant that this sense of the nation is only referred to in abstract terms, as can be seen in the way he describes the naming of the Armorial orchestra, the *Orquestra Romançal Brasileira*, emphasising that the word *romançal* should not suggest an essentially European basis to its music:

> (...) if the orchestra is called *romançal*, it's also called Brazilian - and in that we must include the Moorish-African element, and the Indian, all forming a new chestnut brown race: the brown puma Brazilian people (...) (77)

Concomitant with the idea of the nation, therefore, is that of a basic Brazilian Culture which has resulted from a syncretism of inputs from different sources; roots which have merged together to form new, distinctly Brazilian forms of expression and behaviour. In another reference to Armorial music he writes:

> In some of the pieces we play, like the *Romance de Bela*

> *Infanta*, for example, the Iberian roots of our culture
> prevail. In others, such as *Toré*, it's the Indian roots.
> Finally, in pieces like *Lancinante, Aralume* and *Guerreiro*,
> one can no longer clearly separate Iberian, African and
> Indian roots, for they are entirely Brazilian *mestizo*
> pieces. (78)

If the *povo* form the basis of the Brazilian nation, so their culture forms
the basis of national culture. That is the basic argument for using its
varied manifestations - popular literature, tapestry, engraving and music
- as the foundation for a truly national artistic expression, as opposed to
art that is simply a poor imitation of foreign forms. Popular culture
therefore is to be valued because it embodies the essence of Brazilian
nationality, another concept which can only be expressed through
abstract terms, with, as has already be seen, metaphors like *blood, spirit*
and *sap* being used interchangeably.

> What we seek to do is to immerse ourselves in that
> inexhaustible spring, in search of roots, so as to unite
> our work with the desires and spirit of our people, and
> make our pulse beat in harmony with theirs. (79)

For Suassuna, the major contribution of Armorial art lies in its ability to
capture and reproduce this essential Brazilian quality - *espírito mágico* -
embodied in popular art of the North East, such as the *folheto*.

> (...) I can give a general definition of our art by saying
> that Brazilian Armorial art is that which has as its
> principal common feature the bond it has with the
> magical spirit of the popular chap-book poetry of the
> North East, with the woodcuts which illustrate the
> covers, and with the spirit and forms of the popular art
> and festivals which are related to that poetry. (80)

Just as the Ministry of Education and Culture assumed the government's
ability to interpret the aspirations of the population as a whole, so
Suassuna assumes the artist's ability to interpret accurately the magic
spirit of North East popular art - in other words, the world view and
aspirations of the *sertão* peasantry - and then assimilate it into his or her
work. Clearly, what this magic spirit really refers to is Suassuna's own
preconceived notions of the nature of the popular culture of the *sertão*,
and of the *sertanejos* themselves, whose perception of the world he
typically describes in such terms as:

> (...) the tragically fatalistic, cruelly happy and mythically truthful vision which the Brazilian people have of reality. (81)

Adjectives such as epic, magic and picaresque are consistently used by Suassuna to describe *sertão* popular art, terms which would mean little to the *sertanejos* themselves. They simply denote his particular reading of the form and symbolic language of the popular arts which provide the sources for Armorial work, and which express, above all for Suassuna, the dreams of the *sertanejos*. His is a highly romanticised view of the rural population, creative and imaginative in spite of their poverty, and it is noticeable that his descriptions of popular expression tend to emphasise the colourful, the fantastic, the flamboyant; in other words, the formal aspects of that expression. Referring to one of the painters involved in the movement he writes:

> Lourdes Magalhães has always been attracted by that greatness of the people of the North East, who, in all their poverty, organise pageants and festivals in which the banners and costumes of popular princes conjure up in one's mind elaborate oriental temples (...) (82)

This raises the basic problem of the relationship between form and content. Suassuna gives vivid descriptions of popular forms and techniques, but, as has been seen, no real interpretation of the content of popular art is ever offered, beyond the abstractions mentioned. He concentrates on the formal attributes which characterise Armorial painting, for example, such as lack of orthodox perspective and relief, rough, striking design and preference for pure colours, all identified as major features of popular *sertão* painting. Likewise, he explains Armorial music as that which uses traditional instruments, played with traditional techniques to recreate the simple, unpolished rhythms and melodies that typify amateur bands of the rural interior. They are the forms, representing the most authentic expression of national culture, that Armorial artists are to use as raw material, refashioning it into an erudite form:

> (...) We are aware that Armorial art, using the popular roots of our culture as a starting point, cannot and must not limit itself to repeating those popular cultural expressions. We have to recreate them and transform them in accordance with the temperament and particular universe of each one of us. (83)

A contradiction arises here. Suassuna suggests that popular North East art is one of the few authentic expressions of national culture left, and then speaks of the need to redevelop it to create an equally authentically national erudite art. Any refashioning of the original forms under entirely different conditions of production and reception must necessarily result in an entirely new artistic expression. As has been seen, a vital part of popular art is the interaction between the artist and his community in the process of production, but all Armorial art has been created in virtual separation from the rural communities that produced the original material, and has been produced for a totally different audience with very different responses and perceptions. Improvisation, another important aspect in popular art, with musicians and poets frequently changing and developing their performance in response to audience reaction, is precluded in the case of Armorial art, where musicians present a preestablished repertoire and poets prepare work for publication rather than performance, to be read in silence rather than declaimed aloud. The crucial attributes which distinguished those popular forms - the dynamism, popular participation and improvisation, in other words, the social process that explains the particular nature of those forms - are lost, and only the formal trappings are left, frozen in the form of folkloric artefacts. Suassuna writes in a newspaper article:

> Art is the song which comes from the people and
> returns to them better than it was when it came. (84)

He apparently sees no contradiction in speaking of the authenticity of popular art on the one hand, and of refining it on the other. The implication is that popular forms can be projected into the sphere of high art without any significant transmutation taking place; the forms may be refined a little, but the essential spirit remains in tact. The quality of the work produced by the Armorial Movement is a separate issue. As will be seen, it did in fact produce some highly imaginative and original art. The essential point here is that the rationale behind the movement is fraught with contradictions, largely because the concepts around which it has developed are so problematic.

The difficult question of authenticity of national art highlights those problems. In his attacks on Brazilian artists who utilise foreign models - the Europeanising, cosmopolitan current, as he calls it - and who thereby fail to conserve and strengthen the peculiarities of Brazilian culture, Suassuna comes close to the warning against excessive innovation contained in the government's cultural policy for the 1970s:

> (...) we ought to do the opposite to all that so-called

"modern" and "functional" work which is being produced, which is really the result of a lack of creative imagination, of a mania for imitating that which comes from abroad, and from a lack of courage in fighting against established ideas. (85)

He opposes any experiment or innovation that appears to be introduced from abroad. In music, for example, he argues vehemently against the use of electronic instruments and vanguard forms which some Brazilian musicians have employed in their work. There was even some disagreement between himself and some members of the *Quinteto Armorial* over this question, when he wanted them to revert to old-style instruments of the *sertão*, such as the *pífano* and the *rabeca*, instead of their modern equivalents, the flute and the violin. Though he argued that this would produce a harsher, stronger, more authentically regional sound, the musicians declined, arguing that the quality of sound of the modern instruments was far preferable. Later, one member of the original quintet, Cussy de Almeida, proposed that the movement should form an orchestra to help promote Armorial music. Suassuna had strong reservations, principally because the orchestra was not a traditional formation in *sertão* music:

> (...) In the case of the orchestra, I had another misgiving: it was that, with the foundation of a traditional European-style orchestra, Armorial music might lose that particular Brazilian vigour and intensity (*garra brasileira*) which had cost me so much effort, including trying to convince musicians of European musical training that it really was important. (86)

In the end, Suassuna compromised, agreeing to the establishment of the orchestra on the understanding that the instruments used in the quintet, such as the flutes and the percussion, should be incorporated into it, in order to help maintain some of the traditional character of the music. These disagreements were minor incidents, and there is no indication of real conflict between members of the movement, but they do highlight the problems resulting from the contradiction between preservation of traditional, popular forms on one hand, and refinement into erudite forms on the other.

It has been argued in this work that culture can only be understood as a constantly changing process, where innovation is consistently producing new forms. This obviously makes the concept of cultural authenticity very problematical. In his view of the historical development of Brazilian culture, Suassuna appears to accept this basic idea of culture as a process, recognising the inputs from outside that have contributed to the popular arts of the *sertão*, for example. It has already been seen how he detects a wide variety of influences in popular music of the region, describing it as:

> (...) the popular music of the *sertão*, which I link to indigenous music (half Asiatic), to Iberian-Moorish music and to Gregorian music, all of which have helped to give "sertão" music what we might call the popular spirit of medieval motets or less aristocratic renaissance music. (87)

The importance of European influence in the past is duly recognised, so that the objectives of the *Quinteto Armorial* are described as:

> (...) searching for a North Eastern composition, an erudite Brazilian music based on popular roots, a distinctly Brazilian sound, within a chamber orchestra capable of playing European music (principally the earliest types, so important for us Brazilians), but also able to express all the non-European qualities of Brazilian culture. (88)

However, though he accepts the process of assimilation of European forms in the past, and expresses, for example, a particular liking for *folhetos* based on European romance themes, such as the adventures of Charlemagne and Roland, he then appears to argue for the process to be frozen and further European cultural influences resisted. Therefore, a major aim of returning to traditional forms, techniques and instruments is to:

> (...) re-educate our musicians, and guide them through a process where they cast aside conventions, and reach a purity and a distinctly Brazilian musical structure which distances them from standard European patterns. (89)

This is a fundamental aspect in Suassuna's thinking. He appears to argue for a cut-off point in the cultural process, a point where acculturation has enabled the development of authentic national art, but where further acculturation will distort and corrupt that art, making it standardised, uniform and cosmopolitan. That cut-off point represents his personal conception of an ideal, authentically Brazilian cultural expression. Objectively, it makes little sense to explain the differences between traditional music of the *sertão* and modern popular music of other contemporary Brazilian musicians in terms of one being more Brazilian than the other. Clearly, those differences can only be explained by the fact that they are products of different social conditions, different perceptions and differences in production and consumption. Just as it was seen in chapter 2 how the content and presentation of the *folheto* has developed, with medieval heroes gradually giving way to modern equivalents, so erudite art will continue to assimilate themes, techniques and forms from abroad.

In his writing on Armorial art, however, Suasssuna persistently attempts to argue that what distinguishes it from other art is that it manages to break free from foreign models and suggestions, by rooting itself in the pure cultural expression of the *sertão*. He therefore makes a distinction between great artists from Brazil and great producers of Brazilian art, and of the composer Villa-Lobos and painter Portinari writes:

> Villa-Lobos always worked within European orchestral concepts and even when he composed "Brazilian music", he did so with his eyes firmly set on European models, like Debussy and Stravinsky. Furthermore, Villa-Lobos was a city man and knew virtually nothing about *sertão* music, for example. Most of his work consists of European musical pieces, into which he introduced Afro-Brazilian or romantic elements, superimposed onto the European structures. One can say the same about Portinari, with painting: he was a great painter from Brazil, but not a great Brazilian painter. Here and there in his work one notes the desire and the intention of achieving a Brazilian expression, but almost always that's as far as he goes, attempting to Brazilianise Picasso. (90)

In fact, Armorial art itself reveals a mixture of influences, including European, as will be seen in the techniques employed by Suassuna in his own novels. All Brazilian artistic expression has been shaped by the interaction between local and cosmopolitan concerns and interests, and in that sense there are no autonomous, purely Brazilian cultural structures. What Armorial art essentially expresses is an idealised vision on the part of a group of North East artists, most with personal links with the *sertão*, of the cultural expression of their region. It is a vision rooted in the past, in terms of time, and in the North East *sertão*, in terms of space. Suassuna and the other participants in the movement deny that their work reveals a nostalgia for the past, yet there is a clear tendency to link the concept of authenticity to a notion of the traditional, the antique, thereby evoking a bygone era, before patriarchal, semi-feudal structures and patterns of life were radically changed by the expansion of the capitalist economy. Cussy de Almeida says of Armorial music, for example:

> It's a new cultural expression marked by a passionate search for some firm musical qualities, which are more authentically Brazilian and which therefore tend to be older. This search has led the movement directly to the sources of European renaissance music from the era of Brazil's discovery. (91)

Suassuna often echoes these sentiments. Popular art of the *sertão* may have developed through the decades, but its value lies in the fact that it has developed within the clearly marked parameters of local tradition. Patterns and forms that have disappeared elsewhere have been preserved in the specific conditions of the North East interior. It is this that gives the region its unique cultural manifestations. Although they recognised the popular arts of other regions, and encouraged, with limited success, movements similar to their own to develop elsewhere in the country, Armorial artists never completely escaped from the notion of the North East *sertão* culture as somehow special, more authentic because its traditions have been less disfigured by the expansion of mass society, as shown in these words of Suassuna:

> Nos centros mais populosos do litoral, é difícil observar os requícios da música primitiva. É importante este fato, porque essa música primitiva será o futuro ponto de partida para uma música erudita nordestina (...) No sertão é fácil, porém, estudá-la, pois ali a tradição é mais severamente conservada. A música sertaneja se desenvolve em torno dos ritmos que a tradição guardou. Não é ela penetrada de influências externas posteriores ao período do pastoreiro, continuando como uma sobrevivência arcaica coletiva que o povo mantém heroicamente. (92)

In the densely populated urban centres on the coast it is difficult to find the vestiges of early, primitive music. That fact is important, because that is the music which will be the future basis for North Eastern music (...) In the "sertão", however, it is easy to study such popular expression because the tradition has been more strongly preserved there. "Sertão" music develops round the rhythms conserved by tradition. It has not really been penetrated by external influences since the period of the "pastoreiro", but has continued as a collective, archaic relic defended heroically by the people. (92)

It is true that the popular forms used by Armorial artists are not dead folklore, but manifestations that still endure in parts of the *sertão*. The *folheto* is an obvious example. However, as was seen in the second chapter, such expressions do not endure in a static form, but undergo constant change and development, corresponding to new circumstances at all levels of life, and that sense of movement is not conveyed in Armorial art. The artists have been selective in deciding exactly what examples of popular expression to use, and they show a marked predilection for the more archaic forms and the traditional themes of rural life in the backlands, such as messianism, *cangaço*, family feuds and traditional codes of honour, all recalling an earlier period of *sertão* history rather than more recent decades. The more contemporary themes increasingly dealt with by the *folhetos* of the present day, referred to in chapter 2, are generally ignored.

It is significant, for example, that many Armorial artists make frequent mention of Brazilian baroque art, which flourished between 1650 and 1800 approximately. Suassuna himself regards it as the most creative and imaginative art yet produced in the country. It is not difficult to see why the attitudes it embodies and techniques and forms it employs should appeal to him. The emphasis it places on intuition rather than reason, its strong elements of myth and mysticism, its flamboyant and exuberant style and free use and adaptation of a whole variety of artistic sources all find their echo in Suassuna's own writing, and in his conception of Armorial art. As already mentioned, Suassuna distinguishes between the contribution the baroque has made to the popular art of the *sertão*, and the present day external influences on Brazilian culture, which, he argues, propagated by the powerful machinery of the mass media, threaten to swamp Brazilian cultural expression, destroy its distinguishing characteristics and peculiarities, and lead to a standardised, uniform culture. The baroque, he states, came from Europe and was reformed, recreated within the new environment to become a distinctly new form, a national form, which Suassuna describes as:

> (...) not the Europeanised baroque, but that which was
> worked upon, turned primitive, by the vigour and spirit

of our brown puma race, the Brazilian people. (93)

This quotation raises once again the problem of Suassuna's differentiation between positive cultural interaction in the past and what he perceives as the negative cultural interaction of the present. It also demonstrates his almost mystical view of the Brazilian people.

The *Movimento Armorial* began with nineteen artists in 1970, and this expanded quite rapidly in the following years, reaching approximately eighty by the latter years of the decade. Music, literature and the plastic and graphic arts were the major activities of the group, though other areas, such as tapestry and dance were soon incorporated as well. The support from official institutions already mentioned was vital for the movement's dynamism, ensuring that performances and exhibitions could be organised and literature and works of art produced. The name Armorial was selected by Suassuna himself, very much the inspiration behind the whole movement. The choice of the word, which refers to the book used to register the coat of arms of noble families, may seem inapt for a movement working so closely with popular culture, but it is in fact a further indication of Suassuna's own perception of that culture. It emphasises the links with the feudal past, recalling the traditional rural world of great landowning families and peasant masses. For Suassuna, heraldry symbolises the unity of that world, representing the aristocracy on one hand, but also the masses on the other, for it evokes all the emblems and insignia created by the popular artists of the *sertão*, comprising not just the coat of arms of the nobility, but also extended to include church carving, carnival decorations and football club emblems. It thus becomes an all-embracing term, linking the popular with the aristocratic and the past with the present. He stated:

> The term *Armorial* refers to the emblems, crests,
> standards and flags of a people, and in Brazil heraldry
> is more of a popular art form than anything else. (94)

The movement never produced a formal manifesto detailing the theories that underlie it. For Suassuna, that would imply a restriction of individual creativity, by suggesting that all artists involved should work according to a recipe or programme. In an interview he stated:

> I don't want the *Movimento Armorial* to be a sort of
> prescription or programme which hinders the creative
> liberty of each of its members. Everyone must take the
> shared patrimony of popular Brazilian culture and
> recreate it in his or her own way, to express their own

particular universe. (95)

What united the movement were broadly common attitudes: an interest in the popular culture of the *sertão*; an understanding of that culture as the expression of deeply-rooted beliefs and aspirations of the mass of the population, and therefore as an authentic national expression; a belief in the need of erudite art to assimilate that popular culture in order to create a truly national art, able to resist the degrading and standardising effect of mass culture. Certainly, free interpretation of popular sources produced some very imaginative music, literature and art work, but the lack of theoretical clarity means that certain problems basic to the group's work remained unresolved. Suassuna's references to the empathy that the Armorial artist had for the popular culture of the *sertão* is inadequate for explaining exactly how - by what means or mechanisms - that artist, living in a very different social environment and working in a very different sphere of artistic production, was able to assimilate *sertão* popular expressions into his or her own work whilst still preserving its fundamental significance and form. The concepts of national expression and authentic expression which were persistently used are extremely problematical. *Sertão* popular culture was considered to be an authentic national expression by the Armorial artists precisely because it was rooted in the daily life of the mass of the North East population, but how that authenticity can be retained when the material concerned was refined or reconstituted, with the objective of creating a truly national erudite art, remained unexplained.

The differences between Armorial art and the popular art upon which it is based are generally immediately obvious. More refined and polished, the work of the Armorial artists does not aim simply to reproduce popular art forms, but recreate them for a different public. The Armorial musicians, for example, remodelled traditional rhythms of the *sertão*, such as a *galope* or a *dobrado*, into more sophisticated melodies. Much of the primitive, raucous sound Suassuna so much admires is necessarily eliminated. This process will be examined later in the analysis of Armorial literature, but for now an interesting example concerning woodcuts, studied by Candace Slater in one of the few articles written on the *Movimento Armorial*, will suffice as an example. Woodcuts, or *xilogravuras* are a traditional art form in the North East *sertão*, often used to decorate the covers of *folhetos*, and they too have been used as a source for some Armorial artists. Slater compares one woodcut by a popular artist, Dila, with another by Armorial artist Gilvan Samico. Both works are similar in depicting a rider on a rearing horse, and in utilising similar formal techniques, but, Slater points out, the perceptions and intentions underlying each are different, and those differences are reflected in differences in details of style. Dila's woodcut was ordered by a poet as a cover for his latest *folheto*. It was produced quickly, in the simple and stark design conventional to such work, with the prime objective of attracting the attention of potential customers to the theme of the *folheto* in order to encourage sales. Samico, on the other hand, spent much longer producing a more polished, stylish design with added detail, which attempts to convey the atmosphere of mystery and magic identified with an age-old rural culture. Slater comments:

> While for Dila the portrait of horse and rider is first and foremost the illustration of a particualr story, for Samico it is a symbol of a whole, magic universe (...) At heart, Samico is less concerned with the protagonist than with a culture capable of producing virtuous heroes and Birds of Fire (...) Playing up the static quality already present in his model, Samico freezes his subject in an attempt to draw the viewer with him into another, more timeless universe (...) Shying away from those humorous and journalistic elements common in contemporary *folhetos*, he devotes himself to older, fairy-tale-like themes inviting a more meditative treatment which lends itself to allegory. (96)

As has been seen, Suassuna sees such differences as a necessary part of the process of recreation of raw popular material into erudite art. The important point, he argues, is that the artist retains the atmosphere and the quintessence of *sertão* popular culture, what he generally refers to as its spirit. The problem is defining exactly what that spirit is, and how it should be interpreted. Deliberate concentration on the reproduction of magical or fairy-tale elements and the attempt to create an atmosphere of mystery and timelessness carries with it the danger of producing an exoticism which reinforces the stereotyped vision other social sectors have of traditional rural culture as quaint and naive. A major problem with Armorial art is that it interprets and utilises the magical and metaphorical symbols employed in popular cultural expression in such a way that the vital relationship between those symbols and the concrete social existence of the communities which create them is obscured. It was seen in the first chapter how the magical figures of the *folhetos*, for example, often have metaphorical value, being instruments for conceptualising the community's interaction with the wider world, and thereby for understanding and seeking solutions to basic problems faced. In their attempts to capture the spirit of popular culture - what they see as magical, mystical and eternal values above all else - Armorial artists are in danger of neutralising that crucial dynamism of popular expression, which, instead of being presented as a means for understanding the lives and struggles of the rural masses, appears more mysterious and distant than ever.

In her article, Candace Slater concludes that the *Movimento Armorial* represented a form of pastoralism, but one of unusual force and dynamism, which she explains mainly through the social background of its members. Firstly, she argues that though all the artists concerned lived in the city, the fact that the vast majority of them had close family links with the *sertão* gave them a particular capacity to support their vision of a more wholesome, creative rural culture with works of concrete force, rooted in a living culture, as opposed to the romantic abstractions associated with much pastoral art. Secondly, Slater suggests that the fact that the movement essentially comprised a mixture of artists from wealthy landowning families on the one hand, and from poor family backgrounds on the other, all from the same rural environment, helps to explain both the contradictions within it, and its particular variety and dynamism, which resulted in good measure from the unity of purpose of those different artists in reaffirming the value of popular *sertão* culture.

Despite their rejection of the qualification of pastoral artists, there is no doubt that characteristics of arcadianism are strongly present in their work. They exalt the simplicity of traditional rural life, and the code of values it embodies, whilst cultivating allegorical associations to give it greater moral, even religious, significance. Using elements of *sertão* culture, they create a fictitious world, a mythical world in Suassuna's own words, and the elements they choose are more often than not associated with patterns of life which, whilst not dead, are certainly undergoing radical transformation in the wake of economic and social development. Many of those elements may therefore be seen as vestiges of an old social order, the patriarchal, semi-feudal society of the *sertão*, so that Armorial art never completely sheds itself of the air of nostalgia traditionally associated with pastoralism. Suassuna's public statements give evidence of this. Berating what he sees as the degrading materialism and pettiness of modern urban life, he frequently confesses his attraction for the traditional *sertão* life of his boyhood. Of patriarchal society, he says, for example:

> (...) algumas das melhores coisas que eu tenho são herdadas do patriarcalismo (...) Eu fui criado numa casa, com uma mesa bem grande onde os trabalhadores comiam com a gente. E talvez essa convivência fraternal tenha me dado condições para resistir a tragicidade da

vida. (97)

(...) some of the best things I have have been inherited from patriarchal society (...) I was brought up in a house with a huge table at which the workers ate with us. Perhaps it's that fraternity, that togetherness, that has given me the conditions which enable me to resist the tragic side of life. (97)

The magical, mythical world recreated by Suassuna and the other Armorial artists on the basis of popular beliefs is one which seeks an essential harmony, unity and sense of purpose to life, which contrasts to what is perceived as the divisive aggression and cheap commercial values of modern urban living. For Suassuna, modern life is pervaded with tragedy and sadness. He claims, however, that Armorial art does not represent an escape into an idyllic past, but rather a positive response to the problems of modern life. Firstly, he states that his work, by converting the *sertão* into a microcosm of the world, debates not just local problems, as earlier regionalist fiction tended to do, but rather the major universal problems of oppression, justice, war, love, hate and jealousy, still as vital today as ever. Secondly, the mythical world he creates is a way of facing the world, he maintains, confronting its problems by building a dream to counterpoise against present reality in order to show alternative possibilities for humankind. In this regard, the comments he makes on the comparisons which many critics have made between his major work, *A Pedra do Reino*, and *Don Quixote*, are revealing. Whilst he admits the influence of Cervantes in his writing, Suassuna claims that the central protagonists of the two works are significantly different in the way in which they confront the world. *Don Quixote* loses his reason and tries to live out the values of a code of chivalry in an age where they are increasingly anachronistic, whilst Suassuna's protagonist, Quaderna, reads *folhetos* from the Brazilian North East as a way of avoiding madness and facing the sad, debased world he finds around him. Suassuna writes:

> Today, I can only understand those poets who dream of the past, or about the future. I can't accept those who resign themselves to the present. Don Quixote went mad reading chivalric romances. He got lost in all those struggles and adventures and believed them to be true, for he lived partly blinded by his insanity. Quaderna reads chap-books of popular poetry, and that is why, on a minor level, he has been compared with Don Quixote. But Quaderna, unlike Quixote, knows that reality is ugly, sad, unjust, cruel and petty. Reading popular

poetry doesn't turn him mad. Far from making him lose his reason, it gives him a sense of moral well-being, of equilibrium, recovery of good sense, and the possibility of accepting reality through dreams. In my opinion, we must either stop at least to some extent this mania for business, wealth and industry, and return to a more simple way of life, poorer perhaps, living in harmony with the animals and the land, the rocks and the pastures, or we'll go mad and lose ourselves once and for all - that's what I'm trying to say in my novel. I don't mean that we should return nostalgically to the past, but that we should have a dream for the future which is purer and higher than the sad and terrible present that we're living through. (98)

Whereas Cervantes ridiculed dreams, Suassuna states, his own novel values them as a way of envisaging a better future and building hope in a world of frustration and despair. One obvious difficulty here is that the poets who dream of the past or the future, lauded by Suassuna, could be interpreted as avoiding engagement with the present and its immediate problems. Such emphasis on dream invites criticism, for it could be argued that it is an approach which, rather than exposing concrete problems and injustices and demanding solutions for them, mystifies them, and rather than confrontation suggests interior retreat.

The composition of the *Movimento Armorial* was undoubtedly significant. Slater suggests that the fact that so many of the artists had roots in the traditional culture of the *sertão*, now changing so rapidly, yet lived distant from it, in the city, free from its constraints, enabled them to 'reflect constructively' on it, but it might also be argued that distance stimulated a tendency to romanticise, imbuing the *sertão* with mystery and excitement, which detracts attention from the chronic human problems of the region. (99) It is also interesting that the vast majority of the artists came from either privileged landowning families or poor families of the *sertão*. This certainly helps explain contrasts in the work of its members, though not necessarily the fundamental contradictions of the movement, as Slater suggests. Rather, such contradictions were inherent in the concepts underlying the movement's work, the problems of which this chapter has attempted to highlight; the concepts of a national culture and authentic national expression, and the notion of apprehending the quintessential spirit of popular culture and transferring it into erudite art.

iv]   **Armorial literature**

Having looked at the *Movimento Armorial* in general terms, we can now examine more closely some of the literature it produced, in order to, firstly, illustrate some of the points made so far in this chapter, and, secondly, to serve as an introduction for the analysis of Suassuna's own novels. Initially, the movement comprised seven writers: four poets, one short story writer and two novelists, including Suassuna himself. Between them they produced a wide range of work, some of it via commercial publishers, and some published by the Federal University of Pernambuco whilst Suassuna was Director of the *Departamento de Extensão Cultural* in the early 70s.

Obviously, all these writers have their own individual styles, but what links their work together is its employment of the thematic and formal conventions of the *romanceiro* tradition of the North East *sertão*. This can be seen most strikingly in the work of the poets, which, as Suassuna points out, relies heavily on imagery, rhyming schemes and rhythmical patterns traditional to popular *sertão* poetry. Marcus Accioly, for example, employs forms like the *quadrão* and the *martelo*, and devices such as patterns of enumeration, which are all commonly used by the *cantadores*:

> Um revólver-parabelo
> dois rifles papo amarelo
> três jagunços no duelo
> quatro disparos do cão
> cinco soldados no chão
> seis punhais desembainhados
> sete pescoços sangrados
> oito mortos no quadrão. (100)

One automatic revolver, two 44 calibre rifles, three gun-men in a duel, four shots from the gun, five soilders on the ground, six daggers unsheathed, seven throats bathed in blood, eight dead men in these verses. (100)

Emphasis is on creating an atmosphere of mystery, at times of almost cloak-and-dagger romance, with many Armorial poems describing action which recalls the tales of adventure and heroic deeds typical of much popular narrative poetry. In *Poema*, for example, Janice Japiassu describes a knife fight in the *sertão* in the six line form, the *sextilha*, which is that most commonly used today in *folheto* verse:

> A terra gemeu com o trote

secaram-se os olhos-d'agua
cantou a rasga-mortalha
grito de coruja amarga
o cavalo rompe o tempo
atrás da hora aprazada.

Às oito horas da noite
a hora encontra o local
dois dragões silenciosos
regem a dança do punhal
e o ferro encontrou o sangue
que esperava -principal.

A aurora estendeu os corpos
lavou-os com os dedos frios
molhou-os com o olhar de relva
guardou o eco de seu brio
- diamantes da madrugada
que não hei de repeti-los. (101)

The earth groaned with the trotting of horses, the springs dried up, the snipe sang, and the owl screeched bitterly and the horse speeds through time, after the appointed hour.
At eight o'clock at night at the fixed time and place, two silent dragons lead the dance of the daggers, and the metal met with blood, the blood which it had been awaiting.
The dawn laid out the bodies, washed them with its cold fingers, and moistened them with sparkling dew, retained the echo of their courage - the diamonds of the day break, which I will never have the opportunity to repeat. (101)

The build-up of tension as the story is narrated through the verse is very common in popular poetry. In fact, the above verses contain most of Suassuna's classic ingredients for Armorial poetry. The narrative form and the tone echo that of certain *folhetos*. An aura of mystery is retained throughout, which on the one hand embodies a sense of fate, with the repetition of *hora*, and the references to the *rasga-mortalha* and the *coruja*, two birds which, according to popular belief, bring warning of death, (102) and on the other a notion of power and mystery with regard to the natural world, with the references to the land, the night and the dawn. Typically, the action itself remains enigmatic, with few details given regarding its cause or the precise course it took. *Dois dragões silenciosos*, and the *dedos frios, olhar de relva* and *diamantes* attached to the dawn give the poem a magical air, and there is a sense of tragedy in the final verse.

All these elements are found in popular North East poetry, and the resemblance is reinforced by the use of *sextilhas* and the absence of punctuation. The selection of such elements is significant. Popular poetry dealing with present-day themes and problems is ignored in favour of more traditional romances created around such universal themes as love, hate, honour, betrayal and vengeance.

If there are many Armorial poems narrating dramatic action, most commonly a life and death struggle, there are others which, devoid of action altogether, aim to convey the atmosphere of the *sertão* through simple but striking images. The overall vision conveyed by the descriptive poems of Janice Japiassu is that of a harsh, forgotten land, pervaded with sadness and a sense of desolation, where heat, dust and barren soil condemns animals and humans alike, wretched and sickly, to a never-ending struggle for survival, and where death always haunts. Again, the air of lament commonly running through these poems evokes the mournful verses of many popular songs and poems of the *romanceiro* tradition. At times the *sertão* stimulates an almost religious contemplation of life in the poet:

> Tempo de tempo despido
> Punhais luzentes de prata
> Terra de terra sòmente
> Sem largos acontecidos
> Pérolas, sonhos sem data.
>
> Pedras fechadas, enigma
> Que se propõe ao poeta
> Canto de rio contente
> E essa estrada consumida
> No rumo da tarde quieta.
>
> Sereno de chão aguado
> E essa flor, rosa sangrenta
> Suspiro de amor doente
> E êssas amanhãs minguadas
> Nas cordas da noite tensa. (103)

Time which has been used, gleaming daggers of silver, earth of nothing more than earth, without great events, pearls, dreams with no date.
Sealed stones, an enigma which presents itself to the poet, and the song of contentment of the river, and the road that's been travelled, in the course of the tranquil afternoon.
The serenity of the land; and that flower, a blood-coloured rose; the sigh of an

ailing love; and those short tomorrows; following a tense night. (103)

Though in its melancholic tone, its simplicity and imagery such as *Punhais luzentes de prata*, the poem resembles certain traditional popular ballads of the North East, it could certainly not be mistaken for the work of a poet of the peasant communities of the *sertão*. Written to be read and meditated upon, it does not have the same oral quality demanding immediate response that is common to most of the region's popular verse, and phrases such as *enigma que se propõe ao poeta* and *E êsses amanhãs minguados / Nas cordas da noite tensa* clearly reveal the language of the erudite writer rather than that of the popular poet. For Suassuna, what this Armorial poetry embodies is, above all, the unbreakable spiritual bond between the poet and the *sertão* and its culture, which enables Japiassu and the other Armorial writers to capture the essential qualities of both. Speaking of Japiassu's birthplace, the *sertão* of Paraíba, he writes:

> An enchanted land which she carries with her in her blood wherever she goes, and which will not die with her because it will remain alive forever, immune to time and to devastation in the verses of fire which she creates. (104)

It is as if the *sertão* imbues all who live or have lived there with a common spirit. Little consideration is given to differences in perception according to social class, enabling Armorial art and popular *sertão* art to be linked together, united by that common spirit, the one essentially an exalted variety of the other.

The emblematic quality of Armorial writing is conveyed very clearly in these descriptive poems of the *sertão*. Allegorical images, frequently taken from popular literary tradition, are strung together to create the familiar atmosphere of mystery, almost reverence, as seen in *Poema do Sertão* by Deborah Brennand:

> Quando a serpente de ouro agonizar nas pedras e o cardo do tempo agreste, longe, muito longe florir para ninguem seu único coração, guarda o punhal e deixa no escuro a cruz de estrelas santificar os brutos carrascos da noite.
>
> Escuta o silêncio bicado por uma garça selvagem ou o vento que arranha nos espinhos do sonho. Escuta tudo, até o sino ordenar um sangrento levante e o profecia

cigana ler o destino do verão.

Então, não lamentes o amanhã. Ajaeza teu cavalo e segue, entre o cheiro das juremas, nos ramos da terra clara. Nos rios mortos, apanha o teu brasão, as três medalhas. O gavião da luz devora um vôo de sombras frágeis. Segue e rasga o lenço vermelho: está acesa a batalha! (105)

When the golden snake dies among the stones; and the thistle of the harsh season, very faraway, produces its only flower, in the form of a single heart, for no one to see; put away your dagger and let the cross of stars in the darkness consecrate the cruel executioners of the night.
Listen to the silence pieced by a wild heron or to the wind which scratches the thorns of the dream. Listen to it all, until the bell calls the blood-red dawn, and the gypsy prophesy reads the destiny of the summer.
Then, do not lament tomorrow. Harness your horse and carry on, among the scent of the acacias, and the branches of the clear earth. In the dead rivers, grasp your coat of arms, and the three medals. The hawk of light devours a flight of fragile shadows. Carry on and destroy the red banner: the battle is raging! (105)

Again, the language and refined lyricism of the poem clearly distinguishes it from genuine popular verse. The aim has been to capture the spirit of the most traditional elements of that verse. The use of *cruz de estrelas, santificar* and *profecia cigana ler o destino* creates an air of mysticism and recalls the religious imagery and references found in much traditional popular poetry, whilst mention of the *brasão, três medalhas, cavalo* and *batalha* give the poem an almost medieval aura towards the end. It is an evocative poem, relying on sharp visual images. However, though it uses elements culled from popular literary tradition, they have been selected and utilised in such a way as to convey the writer's particular vision of the *sertão*, which, as in much Armorial literature, is romanticised and mythical. This is not to deny that romance and myth are also significant elements of popular literature in the North East. As has been seen however, there are also popular poems on the daily problems of access to the land, hunger and insecurity and exploitation in employment. These aspects are not ignored altogether in Armorial writing, but the mystical view of the *sertão* which prevails in most of it does not allow them any prominence. In marked contrast to earlier North East literature, social criticism is minimal.

In *O Bordado, a Pantera Negra*, published in 1974, Raimundo Carrero reworks popular legend and superstition to create a short story which reads like a fairy tale. The use of extremely short sentences and simple but vivid language, narrating the story in the present tense, attempts to capture some of the oral quality and improvisation of a popular narrative. Simão Bugre, a demonic figure, is said to have emerged from a bottle. A woman, Conceição, was washing clothes at a weir when she discovered the bottle, which broke, exploding to reveal Simão Bugre. Conceição's husband, Elesbão, saw them together and in a fit of jealousy dragged his wife away by the hair. Bugre hunts and kills Elesbão and then, whilst Conceição is finishing a tapestry, enters her house and kills her too. A dragon on the tapestry comes to life - her never to be born son - and fights Bugre, joined by the horse of the dead Elesbão. The house trembles with the fighting, and the story ends enigmatically:

> A noite esconde esses mistérios no seu ventre escuro -a
> pantera negra. (106)

The night hides those mysteries within its dark belly - the black panther. (106)

The jealous rage punished by tragedy echoes the moralising narratives of some *folhetos*, particularly the *folhetos de exemplos* referred to in chapter 2, where examples are given of the suffering of individuals, seen as Divine punishment for sins committed. In the story, the forces of fate directing events are mentioned several times. More striking, however, is the atmosphere built up throughout the story. Bugre stalks at night through wild undergrowth in a desolate, isolated land, the traditional territory of an ancient Indian tribe of Pernambuco, the Umãs:

> Perdido entre o silêncio e as trevas está o Mundo Santo
> dos Umãs. (107)

Lost within the silence and darkness is the sacred world of the "Umãs". (107)

It is a night of rain and thunder, populated by mythical beings: the ghosts of horses of warriors killed in ambush, souls in torment and the Devil in various assumed forms, all taken from folkloric tradition. Simple, strong descriptive phrases are used to create a powerful visual impact, with striking metaphors and emphasis on colour and the contrast between light and dark. Numerous verbs of motion maintain the pace of the action throughout, aided by the brevity of the sentences, with words frequently combined in poetic style, as in the description of the fight at the end:

Feras. Força na força. Fogo. Fumaça saindo das ventas
do animal bordado. Lutam. (108)

Wild beasts. Power and yet more power. Fire. Steam rising from the nostrils of
the adorned animal. They fight. (108)

The story is striking and vivid, with its bright images and mysterious
action. Technically simple and presenting a naive vision of an enchanted
world, it clearly shows the primitivist traits of much Armorial art.
Popular North East mythology and lore are employed to create a world
of pure fantasy, far removed from the social reality of the region. The
dynamic relationship between popular beliefs and that social reality, with
legends and fantasy explained largely as ways of conceptualising and
confronting that reality, is lost as a result. Severed from their context,
there is always the danger of such mythological expressions becoming
static emblems, picturesque folklore which captivates the reader rather
than stimulating him or her to think critically about the real world.

Suassuna has at times used the term magical realism to refer to
Armorial literature. He argues that the Realist writing of the 1930s was
too limited, concerning itself only with documenting and denouncing
immediately visible social reality, and ignoring the myths, dreams and
fantasies which constitute an equally valid dimension of human reality
and experience. He therefore sees Armorial literature as offering a more
poetic, epic writing which supersedes the mimetic Realism of earlier
North East work. In contrast to the Realism of Graciliano Ramos, for
example, he extols the writing of Guimarães Rosa, with its employment
of poetic language, the language of myth. (109) Suassuna denies that his
magical realism is influenced by that of French or Spanish American
literature. Any similarities are coincidental, he argues, for the magical
elements in his work come partly from what he perceives as the *espírito*
mágico of Brazilian popular poetry, and partly from early Iberian
literature. The problem with Spanish American magical realism, he
claims, is that it is always in danger of becoming pure fantasy, a fairy
story. It is more magical than real, while Armorial writing attempts to be
more real than magical, paying attention to dreams and myths but not
being so absorbed into the realm of fantasy that reality is lost sight of
altogether. One significant indication of this, he continues, is the
preference of many Brazilian writers, like Guimarães Rosa, for using a
character as narrator, rather than narrating events themselves, as García
Márquez does in *Cien años de soledad*. For Suassuna, this permits the
author to assume greater distance from the magical events within the
novel:

If it is the author who narrates the story, he or she takes responsibility for the magical events suggested in the book, as if they were real. If, however, the narration is given by a character, the novel always keeps one foot on the ground: the magic elements which appear could be hallucinations or dreams of that character. (110)

This discussion of magical realism by Suassuna in his weekly newspaper column was prompted by a disagreement over a work by another Armorial writer. Maximiano Campos published *As Sentenças do Tempo*, a collection of short stories, in 1973. One of the stories, entitled *O Grande Pássaro*, deals with the vision of a young man, Felipe, whilst at the old sugar plantation of his family. Once prosperous, the property of his grandparents, it is now decayed, almost in ruins. Whilst there, Felipe has a vision. He imagines a tranquil day at the plantation during the height of its prosperity, an idyllic scene. Suddenly however, it is shattered by a strong wind. The fields are reduced to waste and animals and humans to corpses, picked at by the birds. It is, however, a brief vision, for Felipe rapidly recovers his senses and returns to the everyday world of the present:

> Depois, ele acordaria e talvez não se lembrasse mais do avô que aparecera naquele cavalo negro, nem da prima que, há tantos anos, fora alguns das melhores instantes da sua passada meninice. (111)

Afterwards, he would wake up and perhaps remember nothing about his grandfather who had appeared on a black horse, nor about his cousin who, many years ago, had given him some of the best moments of his long-gone boyhood.(111)

It is a well-written story, showing the nostalgia for the peace and harmony of a rural past common to much Armorial literature, the longing for something irretrievably lost. It can be read as a lament for the passing of a whole way of life. Hermilo Borba Filho praised the story, but criticised the ending, where, in his opinion, the dreamlike atmosphere is brusquely shattered by a too rapid return to reality, thereby undermining the beauty of the poetic vision, the impact of which is diminished by being shown to be a simple daydream. Suassuna disagreed, arguing that this was precisely the strength of Armorial magical realism:

It is precisely the ending of Maximiano Campos' story

which shows us how the author keeps his feet on the ground. His head and heart can roam among the stars, like Don Quixote does, but his feet and vision remain on the ground, alert like Sancho, and able to see that the armies carrying flags sighted by the nobleman are in reality flocks of sheep. (112)

The difficulty with this approach is that if the elements of fantasy are strictly ascribed to individual characters they simply become private dreams and fantasies, thereby undermining their broader significance as the collective expression of a whole community, integral parts of a shared world view which helps that community interact in unity with the world around. If, furthermore, the author establishes such a rigorous division between the fantastic and the real, divorcing the one from the other, he is in danger of presenting the elements of fantasy as little more than tricks of the imagination, or temporary release. It is interesting to contrast this with one of the major works of Spanish American magical realism, *El reino de este mundo*, where Alejo Carpentier attempts to show how myth and voodoo practices have a vital social function for the exploited negro masses of Haiti, serving to confirm their common identity and organise them for the struggle against oppression. Likewise, Miguel Angel Asturias shows in his Indianist stories, *Leyendas de Guatemala*, how, in the world view of the Mayan Indians, myth and reality are fused, inseparable, to form a unified vision of the world. What appears to be magical to the outsider is completely logical and rational within the terms of Indian perception and social practice. This is one of the senses in which the two opposing terms of magical and realism are linked together. Suassuna does speak of the imaginative, mythical perception of reality of the *sertanejos*, and the way it is embodied in popular literature of the North East, but when referring to erudite literature he argues for a much greater degree of separation between the real and the fantastic. The problem remains as to how the writer can assimilate the magical perceptions of the *sertão* population in his work and yet still retain a distance from them, *com os pés no chão*, as he terms it. There is the danger in Suassuna's approach that myth or dream become either the property of the inner world of the individual or simply irrational flights of fantasy, beautiful perhaps, but more of an escape from, rather than confrontation of, reality. Maximiano Campos published his first novel, *Sem Lei nem Rei* in 1968, shortly before the formal foundation of the *Movimento Armorial*, but it nonetheless contains many of the broad characteristics common to the group, and is a work much admired by Ariano Suassuna. The plot develops many themes found in *folheto* poetry. It centres on the feud between two landowners in the *sertão*, Coronel Juvêncio Teixeira, ruthlessly oppressive, who hails from the *sertão* itself, and Coronel Joaquim Wanderley, benevolent and honourable, who has moved into the backlands from the coast. They struggle for local political power, the whole area divided between them. The major character, however, is the *cangaceiro*, Antônio Braúna, out to avenge the death of his brother, killed by Coronel Teixeira. Allying himself to Coronel Wanderley, he joins in the struggle against Teixeira. Wanderley and many of his men are eventually killed by the opposing faction, but the novel ends with Antônio Braúna and his band avenging all the past crimes by killing Teixeira and his gunmen, and the last scene is of Braúna disappearing into the *sertão* with Rita, god-daughter of his former protector Wanderley, whose love he has won and who decides to marry him and share his destiny.

The language is simple and direct, imitating in some measure the style of the popular storyteller. Verses of popular ballads are included in parts as well. Describing Campos' style, Suassuna writes of:

> (...) his sober narrative prose, and his pure, powerful
> dialogue imbibed from the language of the people and
> artistically recreated (...) (113)

Avoiding pedantry, the Armorial writer is to seek inspiration in the forms of language used by the rural communities of the North East. Again however, the problem arises as to how such language may be incorporated into the erudite work and refined at the same time. Armorial prose does show the influence of popular language in its dialogue, vocabulary and colloquial phraseology, but, as has been seen in the case of poetry, it could not be mistaken for that naturally employed by the popular poet himself. The production of an erudite novel necessitates considerable restructuring and refinement of the language used.

The characterisation used in the novel also recalls that found in popular literature. The contrast drawn between the two opposing landowners, for example, one cruel and ruthless and the other considerate and honest, a man of the people, is similar to that found in many *folhetos*, and Suassuna himself has remarked how another of the novel's characters, Negro Tibiu, has many traits of the popular *pícaro*, remaining loyal to his master, Coronel Wanderley, while using trickery to ensure his own safety amid the increasing violence. Above all, however, it is the depiction of the *cangaceiro*, Antônio Braúna, embodying all the attributes of the popular hero, which emphasises the influence of *folheto* tradition. He commits innumerable crimes of violence, but justifies them on the grounds that in such an unjust society the poor have no recourse other than violence to retain their self-respect as human beings. His crimes simply attempt to redress those committed everyday by the rich and powerful, and to speak in terms of legality is meaningless to him, for the law only functions to serve the interests of the wealthy and privileged. Broadly the same attitude is found in many *folhetos* on *cangaceiros* and *valentes*, who frequently emerge victorious at the end to win the hand of a landowner's daughter, as occurs in the novel when Rita, Wanderley's god-daughter, pledges herself to Braúna. The *cangaceiro* is not presented as a common outlaw, but as a man with a destiny: that of avenging the poor and oppressed, and dying at least in freedom and dignity. At one point Braúna echoes the words of countless *folhetos* when he calls to his men:

> Vamos minha gente ... vamos que nós temos um destino,
> o destino de morrer como homem, morrer em campo
> aberto, lavando as afrontas do mundo. (114)

Let's go, men ... let's go, for we have a destiny, the destiny of dying like men, dying in open country, cleansing the abuses of the world. (114)

The book also reveals much about rural life in the North East, with its rigorous code of honour, battles for power by local landowners apparently beyond the control of any central authorities, the political and legal corruption that results and the almost feudal relationships existing between rich and poor. Some social criticism is made through this content. The rich jealously and ruthlessly protect their privileges, manipulating all institutions to that end, so that no matter which faction of the elite holds power, the wretched position of the poor remains the same. Braúna likes and admires Coronel Wanderley, but deep down he feels that all wealthy landowners are essentially the same:

> Era tudo uma cambada só, pensando sòmente em
> esmagar os pobres de Deus. (115)

They all belong to the same pack, thinking only about crushing God's poor folk.(115)

This is the same rudimentary awareness of class differentiation that is frequently expressed in *folheto* poetry. Such a perspective is not commonly conveyed in the literature of the Armorial writers, however. As has been seen, Suassuna tends to speak of conflict in the *sertão* in terms of individual or family rivalry, with traditional, feudal-type bonds of loyalty transcending class divisions. What characterises *sertão* culture, he argues, is the lack of a notable bourgeoisie, so that the major cultural expressions emanate either from the landed aristocracy or the rural poor, or sometimes as a fusion from both. It is interesting that, speaking of Campos' work, Suassuna makes a distinction between the *romance* (novel), of bourgeois origin, and the much older *novela* (short, more traditional prose narrative), which he identifies with traditional, rural societies, as found in the North East:

> (...) in Brazil, the novel is much more characteristic of urban, bourgeois circles, and the *novela*, epic or satirical, is linked to the people and the more traditional communities, in the interior, on the coastal belt or in the scrublands; communities where there is only a rudimentary bourgeoisie and the dominant elements are the people and the landowners, sharing a direct relationship, as was the case with European medieval communities. For that reason, the spirit of the novel is not so evident in the work of Maximiano Campos as the spirit of the *novela*. (116)

Particularly noticeable is Suassuna's emphasis on ancient and traditional forms of expression, and the notion of a common rural culture forged between the landowning elite and the peasantry in a patriarchal society. Although he speaks constantly in terms of popular culture, associated essentially with the rural masses, he sees this as being intimately bound to the culture of the aristocracy, both bonded together in a common, mutually dependent way of life. Hence the fusion of heraldry and popular art in his *arte Armorial-Popular*.

For Suassuna, Campos' novel has the merit of avoiding the generalised, stereotyped characterisation that he finds in much North East fiction, particularly that of overt social criticism, which, he claims, simplistically depicts the poor as angelic and the rich as villainous. Morality and immorality are found at all levels of society, and have little to do with class divisions. He admires the portrayal of Antônio Braúna, therefore, because the *cangaceiro* is shown to be a contradictory mixture of honour, loyalty and consideration on one hand, and violence and sadism on the other. Likewise, if Coronel Teixeira is shown to be brutal and totally self-interested, Coronel Wanderley is portrayed as a sympathetic and popular local figure, with strong bonds of loyalty to his people:

> A common and irritating defect in writers of social commitment, whether in novels or in essays about the

North East, is the tendency to generalise, to typify to excess, which is caused, most of the time, by ideological preconceptions. Unlike such writers, Maximiano Campos shows in one scene, for example, elements belonging to various and diverse sections of the people, all separated by as many prejudices as could be found in a Florentine court (...) in the some way, one of the landowners who appears in *Sem Lei nem Rei* is kindly and noble. The priest, always badly treated in those North Eastern novels of excessive generalisation, puts himself on the side of that chivalrous landowner, and on the side of the people. (117)

In fact, as has been seen, there are allusions in the novel to class divisions, with the suggestion that formal politics are little more than the self-interested feuds between dominant landowners. It is striking how sharply Suassuna's view contrasts with that of Boal, who identified Manichaean processes as a vital characteristic of popular art which needed to be developed by artists as a way of stimulating the political consciousness of the masses, sharpening their awareness of their relationship with other classes. Suassuna regards such a vision as too simplistic, and claims that because Campos avoids this:

(...) his social thought is much more effective than that found in those novels and plays which follow the same old, worn path of crudely outlining Good and Evil through poor characters and rich characters, bringing together literature about the sinister with literature about the innocent, full of poor angels and rich villains, which lead the reader, tired of seeing cruel landowners who murder, rob and rape, to lose all sympathy with the social thought which gave rise to such poor characterisation, and to end up sympathising with the reactionary, medieval injustices described in the work. At least the medieval era produced literature of quality in the form of the chivalric romance. (118)

Tired of simple, archetypal characters, the reader will seek quality literature regardless of the political ideology it appears to embody. Nonetheless, simplified characterisation in the form of generalised representative types is a common trait of popular *folheto* literature, as was seen in chapter 2. Again, Suassuna appears to be adapting his sources to suit his own particular vision of the *sertão*.

211

There are two other striking features of *Sem Lei nem Rei* that need to be mentioned. The first is the sadness that pervades the whole book, the feeling of *saudade* - yearning or longing - that afflicts many of the characters. Lamparina, one of the *cangaceiros* in Braúna's band, constantly recalls the green coastal region from where he originates, yearning to return, which he finally does at the end of the work. Antônio Braúna himself is continually remembering his childhood, his dead parents and murdered brother, and, above all, the elderly Coronel Wanderley can never free himself from the memories that haunt him of prosperous and peaceful days lost forever:

> De repente veio-lhe uma tristeza imensa. Onde estavam as antigas carruagens paradas na porta? Onde estavam as damas vestidas de renda? E foi-lhe chegando uma imensa frustração, frustração de quem representava mal a sua alegria, esforço para esconder uma grande tristeza.(119)

Suddenly he was filled with an immense sadness. Where were the old carriages waiting at the door? Where were the ladies dressed in lace? And he felt an immense frustration; the frustration of a man whose appearance of happiness was unconvincing. It was an effort he made to conceal his deep sadness. (119)

It is the need to escape the grief which the irretrievable past causes him that, as much as anything else, explains his political feuding:

> Sentia que tinha que acabar com aquela tristeza. Não podia admitir esmorecimentos. Por isso, tal vez se dedicasse tanto à política, era uma maneira de se atordoar. Não se desejava aumentar as riquezas, comprar mais terras, desenvolver a criação. Pouco gastava. Com êle próprio, gastava pouquíssimo. Tentou afastar a saudade que o vinha perseguindo. (120)

He felt that he had to put and end to that sadness. He could not accept despondency. Perhaps that was why he had dedicated himself so much to politics, as a way of forgetting his anguish. He had no desire to add to his wealth, buy more land or increase his livestock. He spent little. On himself, he spent very little indeed. He just tried to dispel that yearning which constantly persued him. (120)

Two rural societies are thus presented in the novel - the coastal sugar producing zone and the cattle producing *sertão*. Contrasts are drawn between them, but both are characterised by decline. It is significant that the sense of yearning for a whole way of life now lost is conveyed in so much Armorial writing, which, against the background of industrialisation, increasing urbanisation and an expanding mass culture, deliberately seeks out the alternative values and patterns of conduct identified with the traditional communities of the rural backlands.

A second notable feature of the novel is the idea of an individual being bound to his or her region of origin with strong psychological and emotional bonds. Wanderley likens his homesickness to that of the *sertanejos* who, though driven out of the backlands at time of drought, invariably return afterwards, despite the suffering and anguish endured there:

> Sentiu que o homem, além do ventre, é parido pelas primeiras coisas que vê e sente, com os olhos do menino. Assim como êle não esquece a mãe que o trouxe à vida, também não esquece a paisagem que em criança pensava ser o mundo. (121)

He felt that man, born of the womb, is also born of the first things he feels and sees with the eyes of a child. Thus, just as he did not forget the mother who gave him life, nor did he forget the countryside which, in childhood, he believed to be the entire world. (121)

Again, this sense of empathy with the rural North East is a vital feature of Armorial art, echoing sentiments of many earlier regionalist writers and artists.

Some absorbing literature was produced by the *Movimento Armorial*. Its use of rich, popular material endows it with originality and vibrancy, but also creates certain contradictions which, though most clearly evident in the attempts made by the participants to rationalise the fusion of the popular and the erudite in order to create a national art, can also be detected in many of the works themselves. Despite the writer's protestations that they are working with cultural values and expressions which still exist in the North East, and which still retain considerable dynamism, the nature of their work makes it difficult to avoid a tendency towards the picturesque and the mystical, and a strong air of nostalgia for a whole way of life felt to be under threat of extinction. Seeking to extol that way of life and the cultural expressions it generates, the writers selected elements from it in order to elaborate their own particular vision of the rural North East, not necessarily a purely idyllic vision, but certainly one which attempts to offer an alternative to what are perceived as the superficial, transitory and demeaning values of modern urban living. The notion of a popular and national literature, which Suassuna claimed to be the prime objective of Armorial writing, is therefore extremely problematical, for the vast gamut of popular themes, forms and symbols reworked by the writer clearly reveal far more about the personal vision and world of the writer himself than about the communities and culture which produced the original material.

v] The emergence of a novelist

In 1958, Ariano Suassuna began work on his ambitious project to produce a trilogy of novels, to be collectively entitled *A Maravilhosa Desaventura de Quaderna, O Decifrador*. The first volume, *O Romance d'A Pedra do Reino e o Príncipe do Sangue do Vai-e-Volta*, was published in 1971, a mammoth work of over six hundred pages, divided into five books and subdivided into eighty-five chapters. *Ao Sol da Onça Caetana*, the first part, or book, of the second volume, to be called *História d'O Rei Degolado nas Caatingas do Sertão*, was published in 1976, though it had already been produced in weekly instalments in the *Diário de Pernambuco*, reviving the *folhetim* tradition - the practice of publishing literary works in serial form in newspapers - common in the nineteenth century.

Work on the project was interrupted in the 1980s, after, in 1981, Suassuna publicly announced that, disillusioned, he was abandoning his writing and his efforts to promote North East culture. As will be seen, this decision and Suassuna's explanation for it, further highlight the intransigent problems inherent in his theory of the development of a national, popular art, and in his attempts to give that theory tangible artistic expression. Nevertheless, by the end of the decade, with a new political and cultural climate in Brazil, he had resumed writing, with the objective of eventually publishing the final part of his trilogy.

Before looking at the novels themselves, two general points should be made. Firstly, although these novels can be read as independent, individual works, and an analysis of them can provide a good understanding of Suassuna's ideas and style, it is important to bear in mind that they were originally conceived of as component parts of a greater work, a trilogy. The fact that little over a third of that complete work is currently available for study makes it more difficult to come to firm conclusions about certain aspects of structure, plot and technique, aspects which would doubtless have assumed greater clarity and validation had they been fully developed in the context of the complete trilogy. The second point, much more complex, concerns Suassuna's decision to turn his attention from drama to the novel. His own explanation is straightforward. In interviews he has emphasised his involvement for many years with a variety of literary forms, including poetry, drama and the essay, and has argued that the novel is the only genre that permits a synthesis of all those forms within a single work. Poetry, essay and fiction are all incorporated in *A Pedra do Reino* in a way that was impossible in his plays:

> The novel of the modern period is perhaps the literary genre which most easily permits the fusion of poetry, essay and fiction. So you can see that in *A Pedra do Reino* poetry is very strongly present, for that is, and always has been, a major concern of mine, but also the essay is present too. There is the attempt to interpret certain things, as you find in the essay. And fiction is there too. So that was what I felt I was lacking in the theatre, and what the novel gave me the opportunity of trying to express, as well as I could. (122)

The critical acclaim achieved by *A Pedra do Reino* upon its publication in 1971, the national prize for fiction conferred upon it the following year by the *Instituto Nacional do Livro* and the fact that by 1976 it was in its fourth edition, all testify to the impact the work made on the Brazilian reading public. Yet it is interesting, and significant, that Suassuna should turn to the novel just as his ideas on a national, popular art were crystallising, and he began to formulate them into a programme of action. Many other Latin American writers, including Brazilians, some of them mentioned earlier, had of course struggled with the problem of a national, popular literature, but when the debate on the issue of popular culture reached such intensity in the Brazilian North East in the late 50s and early 60s, the novel was not in the forefront of the discussion. The political circumstances of the time favoured practical cultural activity which combined the participation of intellectuals and rural and urban workers. The MCP, as already mentioned, selected as the arena of those activities education classes teaching basic literacy and a wide range of domestic and professional skills, art and handicraft courses and various forms of theatre.

Such activities were clearly impossible after the 1964 coup, but beyond the question of practical circumstances there remains the more complex problem of the novel itself as a form, and in what way it can really be developed as an instrument for forging a national, popular art. The popular dramatist, for example, finds in the Brazilian North East a wealth of expressive forms and symbolic language readily at his disposal. The *sertão* population has a strong tradition of theatrical forms, such as religious Autos, puppet theatre (*mamulengo*) and *bumba-meu-boi*, a fantasy drama often performed throughout the night, not to mention popular dance and carnival, which provide playwrights with rich raw materials, constituent elements which require little modification for the development of popular drama, serving as links of communication between artist and audience. Added to this are the obvious advantages in production which the theatre has as a popular form, being highly mobile, adaptable and participatory, as discovered by Suassuna himself, and other participants of the *Teatro do Estudante de Pernambuco* with the *barraca* which aimed to carry theatre to new sectors of the population.

In the case of verse, the tradition of popular poetry in the North East has produced a wide range of rhythmic, metric and linguistic schemes to which the erudite poet can relate directly, employing them as the basic structures of his work if he so wishes. The adaptability of poetic form and language, and the practicability of the act of composition, appear to give poetry possibilities for expansion among different social sectors when the circumstances are favourable, as seen in Nicaragua in the 1980s, with the *Talleres de Poesía*, poetry workshops organised for peasants, children, workers and others, largely under the direction of Ernesto Cardenal.

The novel presents more difficult problems. An alien art form to the mass of the *sertão* population, it marks more clearly than any other literary genre the divide between popular and erudite expression. Though the exact details concerning the emergence of the novel form may still be disputed, a general consensus has long accepted the broad arguments of Ian Watt, linking the genre to the development of bourgeois consciousness, particularly its emphasis on individualism, which accompanied the rise of new middle classes as the market economy expanded. (123) If it is the classic bourgeois art form, as Watt has termed it, can the novel really be adapted to assimilate the perceptions and experience of other classes? This is a particularly problematical question for the Latin American writer, aware that the region's uneven, contradictory pattern of development has exacerbated the divisions between himself and the rural and urban masses.

Suassuna's response to the problem, like that of other writers, is to attempt to construct a new type of novel, formally and stylistically distinct. His method, however, is unusual. As has been seen, he rejects the experimentalism of other writers as simply Europeanisation. For him, European innovations offer no hope of affirming a distinctly Brazilian literature. Even more controversial is his rejection of the notion of a politically committed literature as being necessary to link the writer to the lived experience of the masses. Instead, he persists in his arguments for a literature based upon popular forms of artistic expression in the *sertão*, above all the *folheto* tradition. He terms his novels popular, not in

216

the sense of a widening of readership, for the public for his work remains essentially the urban, middle classes, the traditional novel reading public in Brazil, but in the sense that it embodies the vision and experience of the rural communities of the *sertão*, rather than the particular concerns of the cosmopolitan, urban intellectual. For Suassuna, employing popular cultural expression of the *sertão* means, above all, returning to traditional, ancient forms of literature and drama; forms that can be traced back into antiquity, but which have been perpetuated, with modifications, by the specific historical conditions of the North East interior. Such forms provide him with the basis for his distinct form of novel. He classifies *A Pedra do Reino* as a *romance armorial-popular brasileiro*, and his planned second volume, *História do Rei Degolado*, as a *romance armorial e novela romançal brasileira*, with both classifications appearing prominently on the title page of each work. Suassuna has spent much time explaining the significance of such terms. Basically, they demonstrate his preference for seeing his work as being closer to the old epic and romance forms, than to the modern novel, an approximation permitted by his assimilation of popular North East literature. On his use of *romance armorial* and *novela romançal*, Idelette Muzart Fonseca Dos Santos comments:

> O duplo rótulo permite lembrar que, para o autor, a palavra 'romance' conserva seu perfume e sentido primitivo, designando a obra escrita em língua popular e vulgar, opondo-se, de tal modo, ao latim, língua dos intelectuais. Mas significa também que Suassuna recusa de antemão as classificações atuais, colocando-se voluntariamente no terreno da novela hispânica, de Dom Quixote e das novelas de cavalaria, formas diversas da epopéia moderna. (124)

The double label reminds us that, for the author, the word "romance" retains a primitive sense and feel, used to designate work written in popular, common language, and therefore standing in opposition to Latin, the language of the intellectuals. But it also means that Suassuna refuses in advance present day classifications, placing himself willingly in the terrain of the hispanic "novela", Don Quixote and the chivalric romances, all diverse forms of the modern epic. (124)

Suassuna's emphasis on the traditional aspects of North East rural culture, seen as conserving old forms of artistic expression sadly extinct elsewhere, comes through clearly in his novels. Avoiding recent economic and social changes which have significantly affected patterns of life in the *sertão*, they constantly look back, evoking the *sertão* life of the author's childhood, creating a literary universe which relies heavily on memories and vestiges of the past.

The result of Suassuna's approach is a unique and highly original work. Yet in creating his own vision of the *sertão*, his *mundo mítico*, he also debates questions of crucial personal interest: questions of art, history, religious faith and intimate dilemmas and conflicts. He states:

> Literature is also a way of solving my own conflict with
> the world, because, in my view, that is another thing
> which the writer is fundamentally seeking. (125)

Such a wide range of objectives in one work requires a complexity of structure that perhaps only the novel can provide, and, as has already been seen, it is the novel's all-encompassing quality that particularly attracts Suassuna. The contradictions, however, are plain. Firstly, in order to accommodate so many aims and interests, Suassuna has created a work of vast scope and considerable structural and technical complexity which, in the end, is far closer to the modern novels from which it attempts to distance itself than to the popular literary forms which provided much of its inspiration. Secondly, there is the question as to what extent a novel can embody both the world view of the rural masses and the private vision of the author at the same time. If the writer is to attempt to solve his existential problems through his writing, can this be reconciled with the objective of developing a national and popular literature? Suassuna's decision to turn to the novel highlights in itself the problems which his project for fusing popular and erudite art entails.

vi] The structure of Suassuna's novels

Several critics have already studied the structure employed in *A Pedra do Reino*, which, it would appear, establishes the fundamental structure for the whole projected trilogy, since the first section or book of the second novel, *Ao Sol da Onça Caetana*, follows the broad model of the first. As mentioned, *A Pedra do Reino* is divided into five parts or *livros*, each of which is subdivided into numbered chapters, designated *folhetos* by Suassuna. Totalling eighty-five in all, the titles of these *folhetos*, such as *A Aventura de Rosa e a Condessa*, *As Desaventuras de um Corno Desambicioso* and *A Cachorra Cantadeira e o Angel Misterioso* typically recall the titles of the *folhetos* of popular poetry sold in the streets and markets. This resemblance is reinforced by the themes and episodes contained in each *folheto*, the illustrations in the style of traditional woodcuts which are scattered throughout the work and the narrative style of the narrator, Quaderna, who, in the manner of the popular poet, calls to the muse for inspiration, addresses himself directly to his readers, encouraging their attention and sympathy, and employs some of the antiquated phraseology conventional to traditional *sertão* poetry. In this way, the immediate presentation and style of the work consciously seeks to capture the tone and atmosphere of popular *folheto* verse.

Looking at the work's structure at the broad, superficial level, George Rudolf Lind first divides it into two basic parts: firstly, *folhetos 1-36*, which correspond essentially to autobiographical details of the narrator and main protagonist, Quaderna, and secondly, *folhetos 37-85*, dealing with events building up to and connected with Quaderna's testimony before the *Corregedor*, visiting the town, Taperoá, to investigate certain criminal events that have occurred in the area in recent years. Lind detects a disparity between the two parts, with notable differences in the composition of the narrative, which he explains largely by the length of time - nearly twelve years - over which the work was written. Within this framework, Lind breaks up the novel into eleven basic macro-units which correspond to essential elements of the content. (126) They are worth detailing here because, although the scheme only provides a superficial analysis of the work's structure, it affords the opportunity of sketching out the plot and, consequently, the development of the narrative.

Lind's division details the work's content in the following way: [1] *Folheto 1*: the narrator introduces himself as Dom Pedro Dinis Ferreira-Quaderna, king, prophet and poet, aged 41. It is October 9th, 1938, and Quaderna is in prison in Taperoá, Paraíba. He announces to his readers that he is composing his literary work in order to make his story public and affirm his innocence. [2] *Folhetos 2-3*: Quaderna describes the entrance of a cavalcade into Taperoá three years earlier, on June 1st, 1935, headed by a mysterious boy on a white horse. [3] *Folhetos 5-10*: Quaderna relates the story of his paternal ancestors, who, between 1835 and 1838, established a number of messianic communities in the *sertão*, eventually destroyed in military conflict with the authorities, in the so called *Guerra do Reino*. [4] *Folhetos 11-15*: Quaderna gives details of his childhood in the *sertão*, and especially his developing fascination for the popular cultural expressions of the region, particularly the poetry and stories of the *romanceiro* tradition. [5] *Folhetos 16-22*: Quaderna resolves to visit Pedra Bonita, scene of the messianic movements of his ancestors a century before. After various adventures, he reaches the two stones which marked the centre of the sacred kingdom, and secretly crowns himself king of the *sertão*, thereby reviving the family dynasty. [6] *Folheto 23*: Quaderna gives details of his maternal family, the Garcia

Barretos, culminating with the mysterious murder of his stepfather, Dom Pedro Sebastião Garcia Barreto in 1930. [7] *Folhetos 24 and 25*: Quaderna introduces the two scholars who were employed by his stepfather to educate him, Clemente Hará de Ravasco Anvérsio, linked to the Communist Party, and Samuel Wandernes, involved with the *Integralistas*, the Brazilian fascist movement. [8] *Folhetos 26-36*: Quaderna relates how he and his two mentors founded their literary society, the *Academia de Letras dos Emparedados do Sertão de Paraíba*, and records his discussions on literary theory with them, secretly planning to write the ultimate masterpiece of Brazilian literature that will crown him as *Gênio da Raça Brasileira*. [9] *Folhetos 37-48*: the events leading up to Quaderna's appearance before the *Corregedor* in Taperoá are described, in particular the denunciation made against him by enemies in the town, the culmination of the ideological differences of his two mentors in the form of a duel fought between them, the growing political violence in the region in the 1930s and Quaderna's vision of Moça Caetana, symbol of death, shortly before he leaves to appear before the *Corregedor*. [10] *Folhetos 49-84*: Quaderna recalls his interview with the *Corregedor* on April 13th, 1938, part of the latter's investigation into the political uprisings of recent years and the still unsolved murder of Dom Pedro Sebastião Garcia Barreto in 1930, during which Quaderna gives details of various events that took place in Taperoá during those years. He announces that the notes taken of his evidence will form part of his planned literary masterpiece, the *Obra da Raça*, a work which will be the most complete embodiment of the spirit of the Brazilian people yet produced. This leads him to talk about matters of literary style with the *Corregedor*. [11] *Folheto 85*: The inquiry finishes for the day, and Quaderna goes home. At night, under the influence of wine, he dreams that his masterpiece is complete and that, in a special ceremony organised by the Brazilian Academy of Letters, amid the great figures of North East literature, such as Euclides da Cunha, José de Alencar and Joaquim Nabuco, he is finally crowned *Gênio da Raça Brasileira*.

Ao Sol da Onça Caetana, (1977), continues the style and basic structure of *A Pedra do Reino*. Constituting Book 1 of the five books of the second volume of the trilogy, it consists of twenty-three *folhetos*, and can be divided into three broad parts in accordance with Lind's scheme: [1] *Folhetos 1-7*: Quaderna recalls the day of December 8th, 1911, when, in a climate of growing political conflict, the major families of Paraíba, formed into two main rival groups, gathered together at one of his stepfather's *fazendas*, mainly in an attempt to negotiate a political settlement. The attempt is shown to be doomed to failure, with the Villar family ambushed by gunmen on their way to the gathering. [2] *Folhetos 8-11*: Quaderna returns to April 13th, 1938, and gives details of the victory celebrations of Clemente after his triumph in the duel over his rival, Samuel Wandernes. [3] *Folhetos 12-23*: Quaderna narrates how on April 14th, 1938, he returned to appear before the *Corregedor* for the second day. At the *Corregedor's* insistence, Quaderna fills in details of his upbringing with his father, stepfather and brothers.

The major unifying element within the structure of both works is the narrator and main protagonist, Quaderna. Through his personal experiences, family connections and his own thoughts and aspirations, diffuse historical events, characters and intellectual arguments are linked up into a coherent whole. Lots of loose ends remain, with mysterious events unexplained and problems unresolved, a deliberate technique for establishing themes to be developed in the succeeding volumes, and thereby providing continuity between them, but the use of the first person narrator, serving as a focal point for all the events and ideas as he develops a literary work that will recount his and his family's life in the *sertão*, and hopefully be the most complete Brazilian work of fiction of all time, enables a vast range of themes and arguments to be dealt with without the narrative becoming too fragmentary. This is really a development of the technique used by Suassuna in many of his plays, referred to earlier, where a character not only plays a role in the dramatic action but also comments on it, addressing himself to the audience to clarify points and summarise ideas and provide cohesion to the whole work. Quaderna plays essentially the same role in Suassuna's novels.

Looking in greater depth at the structure of the work, Maria-Odilia Leal McBride detects the characteristics of the following five narrative structures, all interrelated and pieced together in the form of a collage to construct a multidimensional novel: (I) that of the formation novel, or *bildungsroman*, focusing on the development of the protagonist, Quaderna, and composed of both a realist side, influenced by aspects of the picaresque novel, and an idealised side, with strong influence from the chivalric romance; (II) that of the detective or crime novel, with murders, abductions and political intrigue creating an atmosphere of mystery and suspense; (III) that of a narrative of discussion, to which McBride refers under the classification of anatomy, as used by Northrop Frye to refer to a form of fiction where ideas are debated in order to present a satirical study of human beliefs and behaviour. Long sections in *A Pedra do Reino* are devoted to theoretical discussions between characters on aesthetics, literature and politics. (IV) That of metafiction, with Quaderna constantly discussing with the reader the process of composition of his own planned masterpiece of Brazilian literature, his *Obra Nacional da Raça Brasileira*. (V) That of a mythical-symbolic narrative, with Quaderna using popular beliefs and myths of the *sertão* to transform reality and create an idealised vision of the world. These different substructures are united into a coherent totality by Quaderna's autobiography, for McBride shows how his life and ambitions provide the focal point for all of them, and the motivation for their development. (127)

McBride's work shows the vast array of influences that Suassuna has assimilated into his work and, in particular, the importance of old Iberian forms like the picaresque and the chivalric romance, and of traditional popular beliefs and myths, all of which still find expression in the *sertão* today, in the poetry of the *folheto* and the *cantador*. The employment of all these sources, recreated and interwoven through the life of the complex figure of Quaderna, give the work its formal originality and its vast thematic range, discussing not only issues of North East history, but also numerous broader political, social, cultural and metaphysical problems.

Few would disagree with McBride's extolment of the novel's originality and dynamism. More controversial, however, is the conclusion she draws concerning the way the work relates to popular culture, for she ends her study by stating that, through the interweaving of different narrative structures and the employment of popular expressions and beliefs,

> (...) Suassuna creates a work in harmony with the spirit
> of the Brazilian people (...) (128)

Once again, the notion of a national spirit is taken for granted, but McBride also fails to give due consideration to the changes the popular material concerned has undergone as it has been reworked by the author. Suassuna is attracted to the traditional rural culture of the *sertão*, but he does not, and cannot, share the perceptions and assumptions that it embodies. Instead, he looks upon them from a distance, sometimes with admiration, sometimes with humour, and at others with irony. Quaderna, the main narrator, is never entirely integrated into the peasant world. He has points of contact with it, but always stands slightly apart, assessing and appraising its system of beliefs and values, but never able to accept them completely. It is clearly not the peasant world view that is presented to the reader, but Suassuna's critical interpretation of it, and the difference is crucial for an understanding of the novel.

The manner in which Pedro Dinis Ferreira-Quaderna carries out his function of narrator mimics the style of the popular poet in many ways, as he constantly addresses himself directly to his readers, inserting his own comments on the events he is narrating, and encouraging the reader's sympathy and attention. His introduction to his story in the very first *folheto* of *A Pedra do Reino* echoes the call of the poet in the market place as he attempts to gather an audience for the narrative poem he is about to declaim:

> Escutem, pois, nobres Senhores e belas Damas de peitos brandos, minha terrível história de amor e de culpa; de sangue e de justiça; de sensualidade e violência; de enigma, de morte e disparate; de lutas nas estradas e combates nas Catingas (...) (129)

Listen, noble gentlemen and beautiful ladies with tender hearts to my frightening story of love and guilt; of blood and justice; of sensuality and violence; of enigmas, death and absurdity; of fights along the road and battles in the scrublands (...) (129)

These direct references to the readers, often respectfully addressed as *Vossas Excelências*, the narrator's oratorical style and his inclusion of numerous poems and popular songs, all attempt to create a strong impression of oral narration, which is reinforced by long sections of dialogue and Quaderna's interviews with the *Corregedor* which occupy approximately fifty percent of both novels. The same technique is repeated in *Ao Sol da Onça Caetana*, with Quaderna often emphasising his role as storyteller and explaining to his readers, or listeners, as he prefers to call them, the method of his narrative. At one point in this second novel, for example, he interrupts the narration of the ambush of the Villar family in the *sertão* in 1911 to recall other events in Taperoá in 1938, with the explanation that:

> (...) uma das características principais dos Romances aventurescos, bandeirosos e cavalarianos como este meu Castelo da Raça Brasileira, é deixar uma cena assim interrompida, com as belas Damas, que me ouvem, de peito opresso e coração suspenso esperando o resultado. Por isso, só depois é que retomarei, ao som da Viola, o fio desse rouco e castanho Cantar que é meu. Assim, perdoem-me esta pequena astúcia retórica. Tenham paciência, entrem com gana e garra nos meandros labirínticos do meu Castelo subterrâneo e vamos adiante porque, neste século de eficientes, eu sou apenas um Cantador arcaico que, em seu novelário de malassombros, tem mil e uma histórias para contar. (130)

(...) one of the principal characteristics of the romances of adventure, chivalry

and valour, like this one, my "Castle of the Brazilian race", is the device of leaving a scene interrupted like this, with the beautiful ladies who are listening to me left in suspense, with their hearts pounding waiting for the outcome. So a bit later, to the accompaniment of the guitar, I'll pick up again the thread of this rough, hoarse song of mine. Please pardon me for this rhetorical device. Be patient, and, with spirit and valour, enter the winding labyrinth inside my subterranean castle. Let's go forward, because, in this century of efficiency, I am just a minstrel from a bygone age who, with my songs of spirits and ghosts, has a thousand and one tales to tell. (130)

The result is a meandering narrative style, constantly breaking off from one plot to pick up another, and thereby reinforcing the atmosphere of mystery and suspense, or to discuss the various alternatives available in narrative style and technique, or the merits of different political options. As already stated, this complex structure of interrelated subplots and the debate on literary style and practice within it, clearly differentiates the form of Suassuna's work from that employed by the popular poets themselves, though by adopting the guise of the *cantador* or popular poet, parodying traditional aspects of his mode of expression, Quaderna gives that form some of the tone, atmosphere and oral quality of *folheto* literature. He is active throughout the two novels, participating in the events being narrated or discussing the development of the literary texts themselves, recreating the almost theatrical performance carried out by the *cantador* in the declamation of his work. It is essentially an illusion created by Suassuna to help conceal some of the obvious contrasts between the form of the *folheto* and that of his novels, in particular between poetic form and prose form, and between oral and written literary tradition. Quaderna, a *cantador* and a prisoner writing memoirs that he hopes will both prove his innocence and confirm him as the *Gênio da Raça*, is seen attempting to adapt the traditional poetry of the *folheto* to the prose conventional to the novel. In effect, this is a projection into the work of fiction of the role of Suassuna himself.

vii] The popular poet in Suassuna's novels

Examples of *folheto* verse, with their strict metrical and rhythmical conventions, are scattered liberally throughout the novels. This, Quaderna explains, is all part of the development of his poetic prose style, rooted in the influence of the popular *romanceiro* tradition which has engrossed his imagination since childhood. It is his identification with popular verse, and with the muses who, according to popular belief, infuse inspiration into the *cantadores*, that makes him adopt the same style for his own work:

> Assim, Vossas Excelências já entendem porque segui
> esse mesmo estilo, no meu Memorial: pretendia e
> pretendo, com isso, predispor favoravelmente a mim não
> só os ânimos de Vossas Excelências como "o Povo em
> geral" e até as divinidades divino-diabólicas que
> protegem os Poetas nascidos e criados no sertão de
> Paraíba. (131)

So, Your Excellencies now understand why I followed that same style in these
Memoirs of mine: I intend in this way to dispose everyone favourably towards
me, not only Your Excellencies, but also the "people in general" and even the
half divine-half diabolical deities which protect the poets born and brought up
in the backlands of Paraíba. (131)

Through Quaderna, Suassuna really produces a parody of the style of the
popular poet, seen in the employment the narrator makes of antiquated
turns of speech still found in some *folhetos*, as when he describes the
arrival of the cavalcade into Taperoá:

> Era, talvez, a mais estranha Cavalgada que já foi vista no
> Sertão por homem nascido de mulher. (132)

It was, perhaps, the strangest cavalcade ever seen in the backlands by any man
born of woman. (132)

and even in the grandiose title which Quaderna gives himself:

> (...) o modesto Cronista-Fidalgo, Rapsodo-Acadêmico e
> Poeta-Escrivão (...) (133)

(...) modest nobleman-chronicler, rhapsodical scholar and poet-notary. (133)

There is considerable humour in the way Suassuna exposes
Quaderna's delusions about his literary abilities. Feeling himself to be
weak, cowardly and mediocre, he is tormented by the problem of how
to live up to what he perceives as the glorious past of his ancestors: on
the paternal side, the Ferreira-Quadernas, who a century earlier
established the messianic communities which ended in bloodshed, and
on the maternal side, the aristocratic García-Barrettos, with their own
heroic but tragic history, deeply marked by the political strife between
rival families of the oligarchy. Quaderna has witnessed the decline of his

family's fortunes, but is himself completely devoid of the courage or skills that would be required to restore its power and prestige, and his conscience is afflicted by a sense of failure. As a result, literature becomes a substitute for political or military action. Having been introduced as a child to popular poetry and song by his father and Tia Felipa, both knowledgeable enthusiasts of the tradition, Quaderna learns the skills of the *cantador* from João Melchíades, his godfather and himself a famous *cantador*. (134) Melchíades tells Quaderna's father that the stars indicate that his son is destined to become a fine poet if he dedicates himself to the art. Quaderna is not only genuinely enthused by the *sertão* ballads, but also by the explanations Melchíades gives of poetic practice. Referring particularly to the *desafios* between *cantadores*, Melchíades describes how the poet builds himself a literary fortress which rivals have to challenge and overcome:

> (...) os cantadores, assim como faziam Fortalezas para os Cangaceiros, construíam também, com palavras e a golpe de versos, Castelos para eles próprios, uns lugares pedregosos, belos, inacessíveis, amuralhados, onde os donos se isolavam orgulhosamente, coroando-se reis, e que outros Cantadores, nos "desafios", tinham obrigação de assediar, tentando destruí-los palmo a palmo, à força de audácia e de fogo poético. (135)

> (...) *the songsters, just as they constructed fortresses for the bandits, also used words and verses to build castles for themselves; rocky, beautiful, inaccessible places, surrounded by walls, where the owners proudly isolated themselves, crowning themselves kings, and which other singers, in contests of poetry, were obliged to besiege, and try to destroy, inch by inch, through boldness and poetic fire. (135)*

Such ideas provide Quaderna with the solution to his dilemma. Through literary creation he can fulfil the responsibilities his family lineage entails, and even overcome his mediocrity by being consecrated as the *Gênio da Raça* or even the *Gênio Máximo da Humanidade*:

> Foi um grande momento em minha vida. Era a solução para o beco sem saída em que me via! Era me tornando Cantador que eu poderia reerguer, na pedra do Verso, o Castelo do meu Reino, reinstalando os Quadernas no Trono do Brasil, sem arriscar a garganta e sem me meter em cavalarias, para as quais não tinha nem tempo nem disposição, montando mal como monto e atirando pior

ainda! (136)

It was a great moment in my life. It was the way out of the blind alley in which I found myself! By becoming a popular poet I could rebuild, in the stone of verses, the castle of my kingdom, reinstalling the Quadernas on the throne of Brazil, without risking my neck and without having to get involved with knight-errantry, for which I had neither the time nor the disposition, given that I'm a bad horseman and an even worse soldier! (136)

A major part of the irony in Suassuna's novels derives from the contrast between Quaderna's boundless ambitions and his limited abilities. He, like all the other characters with intellectual pretensions, frequently appears ridiculous when confidently asserting his beliefs, for the author shows how sharply such beliefs contrast with reality. Quaderna, a man of very modest literary ability, who earns his living working in a minor public position, as a clerk running a small library in Tapeorá, convinces himself that he can become the supreme genius of the Brazilian race. He accepts the assertion by one of his mentors, Samuel Wandernes, that:

> O Gênio da Raça é um escritor que
> escreve uma Obra considerada decisiva
> para a consciência da sua Raça! (137)

The genius of the Brazilian race is a writer who writes a work considered to be decisive for the consciousness of the race! (137)

Yet, confessing that he lacks creative imagination, Quaderna decides that he must borrow ideas from others, and even passages from other writers' work, modified as necessary, in order to create the *Obra Nacional da Raça Brasileira* that will confirm his genius. For the popular poet, Melchíades has informed him, plagiarism does not exist. Rather, it is a question of skilful adaptation, another crucial element in the poet's art. The two novels therefore, supposedly written by Quaderna himself, are full of quotations from other writers, some popular and some erudite, some inventions of Suassuna's imagination and others real, including Antônio Gonçalves Dias, Raymundo Corrêa and the popular poet Leandro Gomes de Barros, all providing additional material of varied style which is employed to reinforce the themes and arguments of the work. Quaderna believes that, as an amalgamation of contributions by many of Brazil's finest writers, the novel will epitomise the national creative imagination. At times, however, delusions of grandeur make him lose sight of his limitations, a major source of humour in the novels. Explaining to the *Corregedor* at one point how popular poets are traditionally classified into six categories, he states that he is really exceptional because he has the qualities of all six types:

> (...) somente os maiores de todos, os grandes, os "raros do Povo" pertenecem, ao mesmo tempo, às seis categorias! Meu Pai, que Deus guarde, era Poeta de sangue e de ciência. Mas eu, modéstia à parte, sou dos poucos, dos raros, dos grandes, porque sou, ao mesmo tempo, poeta de cavalgação, a reinaço, Poeta de sangue, Poeta de ciência, Poeta de pacto, de estradas e encruzilhadas, Poeta de memória e Poeta de planeta! (138)

(...) only the greatest of all, the really great ones, the exceptionally gifted, belong to all six categories at the same time! My father, may God rest his soul, was a poet of blood and science. But myself, modesty apart, am one of the few, one of the exceptional ones, the great ones, because I am, at the same time, a poet of knight-errantry, of creativity, poet of blood, poet of science, poet of consensus, poet of roads and crossroads, poet of reminiscence, and poet of the planets! (138)

The humour of Quaderna's pomposity is reinforced by the contrast drawn between his passionate promotion of such ideas and the scathing derision which the *Corregedor* shows towards them, frequently replying in a mocking tone. If on the one hand this humour and irony makes a crucial contribution to the novels' quality and originality, on the other it distances them further from the original *folhetos*. Comic themes certainly are abundant in popular poetry, but the role of the poet himself is not treated humorously, being seen, as was shown in chapter 2, as a serious profession within the community, with a definite social function. Suassuna develops much of his humour from the contrast between the popular and erudite, and, more specifically, between the magical, mystical world view of the popular poet and the rational, scientific outlook of the intelligentsia and the *Corregedor*. Quaderna is caught between those two contrasting visions, his education having been provided in part by the two egotistical professors, Clemente and Samuel, who become his mentors, and in part by popular poets and mystics like João Melchíades. In formation and outlook therefore, Quaderna is significantly different from the poor poets with whom he associates and sympathises so much, and he constantly steps back to view them from a critical distance, within the light of the alternative set of criteria and values provided by his more formal education and reading.

Trying to live in both the world of the popular poets and in that of the more privileged classes, represented by his maternal family, the

Garcia Barretos, and his two mentors, proves to be exceedingly problematical for Quaderna. He is captivated by the creative imagination of the *cantador* and the world of popular myth and legend he represents, but does not find it easy to reconcile that with the more formal scholarship he learns from other associates, particularly the influential professors, Samuel and Clemente. For the right-wing Samuel, the *cantadores* represent the barbarous, rebellious plebs and to the communist Clemente they embody the superstitious, reactionary mentality which for so long has been perpetuated by the position of servitude and exploitation of their class, and served as an obstacle to their liberation. From their different ideological positions, therefore, both professors deride Quaderna's fascination for popular poetry. Moreover, such fascination proves to be politically dangerous. During their interview, the *Corregedor* reveals to Quaderna that certain unknown testifiers from the town have reported their suspicions about his political and moral behaviour, based on his association with undesirable social elements:

> Consta que o senhor, um funcionário, um homem de certa categoria, vive na mais vergonhosa promiscuidade com as mulheres de má-vida e com o que existe de pior na ralé daqui - os bêbedos, os doidos, os ladrões de cavalo, os contrabandistas de cachaça, os cantadores, cavalarianos e vagabundos de toda espécie! (139)

It is said that you, a public official, a man of a certain rank, live in the most shameful state of promiscuity with women of the streets, alongside the worst elements of the rabble found here - the drunkards, the madmen, the horse thieves, liquor smugglers and vagrants of every type! (139)

Quaderna decides to resolve the contradiction of his position by fusing together the two vastly different sets of perceptions and values in his literary work, to be based therefore on both formal, scholarly writing and popular poetry, blended together to form the most complete and representative work of Brazilian literature ever written. Not only will the work restore some of his family's past glory and fulfil his major personal ambitions, but also, through it Quaderna will recover some of the harmony which for so long has been missing in the strife torn *sertão* society within which he has spent his life. These wildly ambitious aims, and the seriousness with which Quaderna undertakes them, produce further comedy, but through them Suassuna also appears to mock the whole process of literary criticism, particularly the establishment of value judgements. In accordance with his dislike of the separate classifications used for erudite and popular literature, which he sees as invariably resulting from a patronising and disparaging view of the popular, Suassuna mocks such distinctions between the two in his novels. Samuel and Clemente appear ridiculous in their conceit and the adulation which they pour on their preferred scholars and writers. Dogmatic in their opinions, they vastly exaggerate their own academic and creative abilities at the same time as they arrogantly dismiss the poetry of the *cantadores* as puerile.

Quaderna himself makes little real distinction between the popular and erudite sources of his own literary work. Instead, he extols the virtues and reliability of both in grandiloquent terms, describing some of the erudite writers who have influenced him as men so noble, learned and distinguished that their word cannot possibly be doubted, whilst arguing that much of the wisdom of the popular poets is beyond question too, for it is ultimately the product of divine or mysterious astrological forces. He considers himself to be both a *cantador*, who has studied and trained in the craft, and also a disciple of the great figures who have contributed to erudite literature of the North East, such as Alencar and da Cunha. His dream which ends *A Pedra do Reino* finally sees him crowned genius of the Brazilian race in a bizarre ceremony, a mixture of popular ritual and official pageantry, with the participation of popular poets and some of the consecrated writers of North East literary history.

As will be seen, however, part of Quaderna's tragedy is that he is never able to fully accept at face value the *cantador*'s magical vision of the world. He is particularly attracted to it because it enables him to transform at the level of his imagination the harsh and hostile environment around him. He learns early on the power of the popular imagination in recreating reality. In *Folheto XIV* of *A Pedra do Reino*, Quaderna asks João Melchíades to write a *folheto* in dedication to his relatives, the Ferreira-Quadernas, and the founding of their messianic kingdom. He likes the verses which result, but points out to Melchíades that certain details differ from the official historical accounts of the events produced earlier by learned scholars. Embellishments have been added. In reply, Melchíades informs him that:

> (...) a rima e a Poesia obrigavam a gente a fazer essas mundanças de glória filosófica e beleza litúrgica. (140)

(...) rhyme and poetry oblige us to make certain changes for the sake of philosophical splendour and liturgical beauty. (140)

Poetry, Quaderna decides, can enable him to recreate the *sertão* into a glorious, heroic realm where humans are redeemed from the squalor and fragmentation of their real existences. He spends part of his life living in this dream world of his imagination, created with the myths and the images of popular literature, which is why so many critics have commented on the similarities between *A Pedra do Reino* and *Don Quixote*, and like *Don Quixote*, Quaderna appears a tragicomical figure at the end, for his illusions are constantly shattered. Much as he is attracted to the magical transformation of the world, a more rational perception constantly breaks through. Quaderna, therefore, is never a real *cantador*. Both his position within *sertão* society and his world view are significantly different.

The major popular poets who participate in *A Pedra do Reino* are Melchíades and Lino Pedra Verde, and both are viewed critically from the outside. Just as Quaderna's attempts to magically recreate the *sertão* are contrasted with the cold, derisive rationality of the *Corregedor*, so the perceptions of the two poets are constantly contrasted with those of the two scholars, Clemente and Samuel. In *Folheto XXX* of *A Pedra do Reino*, Quaderna, Clemente and Samuel lose their way whilst riding, but meet Melchíades who guides them back to the main road. Quaderna takes the opportunity to ask him his opinion on certain literary ideas, regarding him as a master of the craft of poetry. Melchíades draws contemptuous laughter from Clemente and Samuel as he explains:

> (...) Eu, Dinis, considero-me um "raro do Povo!" O Povo me considera um filho das Musas, e, por isso, me entende, me crê, me aplaude, me escuta e me atende, desde que comecei a escrever, no ano em que você nasceu, 1897. Meus versos são terrenos explorados nos campos dos Sonhos, eu versejo por guia de Deus e por inspiração do Altro, por influxo do sol e de Vênus!
>
> Clemente e Samuel estouraram na gargalhada. João Melchíades riu também, e eu nunca sabia, ao certo, se ele notava ou não a zombaria dos dois grandes homens (...) (141)

(...) I, Dinis consider myself to be a rarity among the people! The people consider me to be a son of the muse, and they therefore understand me, believe me, applaud me, listen and pay attention to me, ever since I began to write, in the year you were born, 1897. My verses are areas explored within the field of dreams. I compose poems under the guidance of God and with inspiration from above, and with influence from the sun and from Venus! Clemente and Samuel burst into laughter. João Melchíades laughed as well, and I never knew for certain whether he was aware or not of the derision from the two great men (...)(141)

Later, in *Folheto LXXXII* of the same work, Lino Pedra Verde's vision of the world is similarly contrasted with that of Samuel, to considerable comic effect. Explaining a song he has just composed, Lino confuses historical figures and events. The result is that São Sebastião, Dom Sebastião, São Jorge and Dom Pedro Sebastião Garcia Barretto, Quaderna's murdered godfather, are merged into one single person, essentially that of Sinésio, Quaderna's half-brother who, having been abducted many years before, has now returned to redeem his people, and disparate historical episodes are fused together in time and space, all concentrated into the recent struggles of the *sertão*:

> (...) no Sertão é que está enterrada a Monarquia do Brasil! É por isso que eu estava dizendo: tudo isso é uma coisa só, é a Monarquia de Dom Sebastião, do Brasil, do Sertão, de Portugal, da Africa e do Império da Pedra do Reino! (142)

It's in the sertão where the Brazilian monarchy lies hidden! That's why I was saying that it's all just one thing: it's the monarchy of Dom Sebastião, and of Brazil, of the sertão, of Portugal, of Africa and of the Empire of the Stone of the Kingdom! (142)

In this way, past events and names from varied places are converted into the present day *sertão*. For Lind, this destruction of the divisions of time and space to form one unified vision is the major artistic achievement of Suassuna's work, recreating the timelessness of the *sertão*, where past traditions long extinct elsewhere are perpetuated, and showing how the eternal hope for change and justice continues to live on in the region to the present day. (143) This is a significant point, but also significant is the way in which Lino's explanations are comically contrasted with the scholarly reasoning of Samuel, who, exasperated by such total confusion, exclaims:

> Olhe, Lino, tudo isso que você está dizendo é uma confusão terrível, que so podia partir, mesmo, da cabeça de um Cantador sertanejo instruído por Quaderna, como você! Não nego que, de certa forma, até simpatizo, em bloco, com o que você diz, mas é preciso esclarecer tudo bem direitinho, senão o resultado é péssimo! (144)

Look, Lino, everything you're saying is a terrible jumble, which could only come from the head of a sertão minstrel who's received instruction from Quaderna, like you! I admit I have some sympathy for what you say, but it's important to

232

clarify everything, completely and correctly, because otherwise what results is just awful! (144)

The comedy develops as Samuel vainly remonstrates against Lino's arguments, his counter explanations only being instantly reinterpreted by the poet in further support of his own view. For Lino, formal education can be a barrier to true, intuitive understanding, and he says to Samuel:

> O Senhor é homem formado e fica com vergonha de acreditar em certas coisas. Mas eu, que sou homem ignaro, tenho direito de não ter vergonha de acreditar na verdade. (145)

You are an educated man and you are ashamed about believing certain things. But me, I'm uneducated, and so it's all right for me not to feel ashamed about believing in the truth. (145)

Suassuna therefore plays with the two different perceptions of the world, the intuition of the popular poet as opposed to the formal erudition of the scholar, with Quaderna caught between the two, attempting to establish some sort of balance between them. The emphasis of Suassuna's novels is not so much on the vision of the popular poet itself, seen within its own terms and within the specific conditions that have produced it, but rather on a critical comparison between popular and erudite art and the different perceptions that underlie each. The reader views the *cantador* and his work from outside, evaluating at a distance, in the light of other criteria and values. This is a crucial point, emphasised by Angel Rama in a short article on the work of Suassuna, where he argues that although the novelist appears to have incorporated elements of the peasant world view into his work, he has in fact filtered them through his own humorous, critical perspective which distances him from the universe within which those elements were created. (146)

Suassuna has built his own, highly personal vision of the *sertão*, and indeed of life itself, into his novels, and uses Quaderna to give it expression. It is a vision which sees humans as tragic but heroic, as, alone, they struggle against the suffering and anguish of life, never giving up but always doomed to defeat. Quaderna seeks a solution through the popular myths and legends of the *sertão*, which seem able to recreate the world in a new light, restoring harmony, dignity and purpose. Although, therefore, he is a writer attempting to interpret the popular imagination, which partly explains his self-proclaimed title of *O Decifrador*, for he believes he has the capacity to understand and express the desires and vision of his people, Quaderna, like Suassuna himself, is really attempting to adapt popular materials to give concrete form to his own view of the world and debate his own problems. It is significant that a first person narrative, with Quaderna speaking, dominates large sections of *A Pedra do Reino*, whereas *folheto* narrative verse, apart from the frequent use of lines of introduction by the poet, conventionally use the third person. In her comprehensive study of the structure of *A Pedra do Reino*, McBride argues that the first-person narrative of Quaderna is counterbalanced by other narrators offering others points of view. In the interview between the *Corregedor* and Quaderna, the *Corregedor* effectively becomes another narrator as he confronts Quaderna with the testimonies obtained from other witnesses and with his own theories, whilst Quaderna, pressurised to give as much information about life in Taperoá as possible, tells of events which he did not witness himself, but which were described to him by other characters, and thereby converts himself into a spokesman for many other points of view. This is compounded by the inclusion of the numerous extracts of other writers which Quaderna quotes. McBride concludes that the role Quaderna plays in mediating other, at times contradictory, voices and points of view, makes his own point of view virtually neutral, what she describes as the camera point of view as conceptualised by Friedman, one which registers what occurs in front of it without selection or arrangement in order to record and transmit, without thinking, the slice of life passing before it. This neutrality enables Quaderna to reveal other aspects of *sertão* life, above all collective desires and myths, and thereby counterbalances the distance created by his own individual vision. (147)

It is true that the multi-dimensional structure of the work, operating at different narrative levels, provides various angles of vision, so that Suassuna's novels are far from conventional first-person narratives, with the limitations in point of view which that entails. At times Quaderna is in the foreground narrating to the reader directly; at others he recedes into the background, allowing other narrative voices to take over. Nonetheless, there is nothing that occurs in the book that is not ultimately channelled through him, and, as already indicated, it is he who gives overall coherence to the work, for it is his construction, his testimony, which will in the end constitute his literary masterpiece. He wants to include as many different styles and views as possible, but he has the crucial task of deciding how to arrange those different materials into one single composition. We only ever see the popular cultural expressions, collective myths and aspirations that appear in the novels through Quaderna's eyes, so they can never be separated from his own private vision on the world, and viewed through his eyes, those expressions of the popular imagination acquire new, significantly different connotations.

If Quaderna is caught between the worlds of popular and erudite literature, he is also stranded between the realms of reality and fantasy. His apparent mediocrity depresses him, for he sees himself as cowardly and devoid of talent. He was initially sent by his family to a seminary to train as a priest, but failed miserably and was expelled. Now he has a minor public office, obtained for him through his family connections, running a small library in Taperoá, and spends the rest of his time writing trivia for a local paper, studying astrology and the art of poetry and running a consultancy to advise people on their romantic affairs and a club for gentlemen, which is essentially a gambling den and brothel. His imagination exaggerates the importance of all these pursuits, so that there seems no limit to his egocentricity. In introducing himself to the *Corregedor* at the beginning of their interview in *A Pedra do Reino*, Quaderna confirms his name and the states:

> (...) sou ainda redator da Gazeta de Tapeorá, jornal conservador e noticioso no qual me encarrego da página literária, enigmática, charadística e zodiacal. Posso dizer, assim, que além de Poeta-escrivão e bibliotecário, sou jornalista, Astrólogo, literato oficial de banca aberta, consultor sentimental, Rapsodo de diascevasta do Brasil! (148)

> (...) *I'm also editor of the Taperoá Gazette, a conservative and informative journal, where I'm in charge of the page of literature, puzzles, conundrums and information about star signs. So I can say that, in addition to being a poet-notary and librarian, I'm also a journalist, astrologist, professional man of letters, consultant on matters of love and Brazilian rhapsodist and literary critic! (148)*

The disdainful reaction of the *Corregedor* sets the pattern for the comic contrast between the two characters, with the *Corregedor* continually deflating Quaderna's pompous claims. Imagination alone is not enough for Quaderna, however, for in this hard, macho environment, where the values of physical toughness and bravado are extolled, he feels himself to be pitifully unable to compete:

> Eu, que nascera e me criara admirando as caçadas, as cavalgadas, os tiroteios, as brigas de faca e outras cavalarias e heroísmos sertanejos, tinha a desgraça de ser mau cavaleiro, mau caçador e mau brigador. (149)

I myself, who grew up captivated by hunting, horseriding, gun fights and knife fights, and other acts of daring and heroism here in the "sertão", had the misfortune to be a bad horseman, bad hunter and bad fighter. (149)

He learns to survive, and even prosper at times, in such an environment by using his cunning, imitating the *pícaros* that he has learnt to admire through his reading of *folhetos*. Thus, in *A Pedra do Reino*, when he and his brother, Malaquias, are out riding and hunting with members of another local family, the Pereiras, Quaderna covers up for his lack of skill in such pursuits, and preserves his and his family's honour in the face of the old macho rivalry between the Garcia Barrettos and the Pereiras, through a series of tricks and by manipulating language in order to ingratiate himself with others. Finally, in *Folheto XX*, he even claims the ultimate trophy of huntsmanship when he shoots a puma, completely by accident. Later in the novel, during his interview with the *Corregedor*, he attempts to use the same conversational skills, albeit with little success, to evade the questions and accusations of the *Corregedor*. For Suassuna, this element of the picaresque is a crucial ingredient of his work, and Raquel de Queiroz recalls how at one point he described the book on which he was working to her - *A Pedra do Reino* - as a picaresque novel, though, after reading the book later, she herself rejected such a classification, stating that it was so complex and revealed so many influences that it defied categorisation. (150) Wilson Martins notes that *A Pedra do Reino* has many of the characteristics which typify picaresque writing, such as its tone, its intrigue and its episodic composition, with each episode reinforcing the works overall unity, but he notes that Suassuna's work breaks with many of the rigid and restrictive conventions of the picaresque. It is not the picaresque elements themselves that are significant, he concludes, but rather the way in which the work fuses the material and form of the picaresque novel with the material and form of the conventional novel. (151)

The picaresque aspects, strong as they are, are subsumed into the framework of a modern novel, into which are also incorporated sophisticated techniques and themes of vast scope, such as debates on political ideology and artistic creation, all of which are far beyond the range of the traditional picaresque novel. Quaderna is far from the conventional *pícaro* of *folheto* literature, for we see many other dimensions of his character, including his feeling of guilt, his struggle against weakness and mediocrity, his dreams and his metaphysical anguish. He is a complex character, painfully aware of his failings and full of massive dreams that far exceed mere strategies for survival. His cunning enables him to survive certain difficult situations, but it is shown to be fundamentally inadequate in dealing with the deeper afflictions that trouble him. The picaresque is thus presented in a new context, viewed in a new critical light created by the other dimensions of the novel. The result is essentially a parody of picaresque literature.

Perhaps above all Quaderna is a dreamer. He dreams about the great mission he has embarked upon: to become King of Brazil, restoring the messianic dynasty of his ancestors and leading the country into a new glorious phase of its history, and to establish himself as the genius of the Brazilian race by writing the work that most embodies the spirit of the Brazilian people. It is not simply a question of egocentricity however, for his dreams function at various levels. Quaderna is deeply saddened by the decline of traditional patterns of life in the *sertão*, and the old social relations they embodied, which is epitomised for him by the decline in fortunes of his own family, the Garcia Barrettos, once among the most powerful landowners of the region. He is proud, for example, that he and all his brothers work in traditional activities, as cowhands, popular poets or artisans, partly because the family must not be besmirched by its members selling themselves on the labour market, but also because of a deeper belief that such crafts are genuinely superior to the degrading and exploitative wage labour offered by the bourgeoisie. Thus he explains to the *Corregedor* during their interview in *A Pedra do Reino*:

> (...) nenhum Quaderna trabalha para filho-da-puta nenhum! Proibidos pelo consuetudinário-fidalgo da família, nenhum Quaderna tem patrão nenhum que exija de nós obrigações e os trabalhos que têm os industriais, os comerciantes e outros degraçados e danados Burgueses com vocação de burro de carga! Todos nós só profissões livres, ociosas e marginais de Fidalgos! (152)

> (...) *no Quaderna ever works for some other son of a bitch! It's prohibited by the traditional rights of the nobleman that any Quaderna has any kind of boss who demands duties from us, or the kind of work done by industrialists, businessmen and other wretched and cursed members of the bourgeoisie who have a vocation for being work animals! All of us only have the free, leisurely and marginal professions followed by noblemen! (152)*

This point extends beyond the confines of the *sertão*, for it seems to Quaderna that human existence as a whole has lost its spirituality, dignity and nobility. Cold, calculating rationalism has stifled the creative imagination and utilitarianism dictates behaviour, and, through his dreams, Quaderna struggles to find the values lost in the process. As has already been seen, this follows very closely Suassuna's own theories on art as embodied in the *Movimento Armorial*.

Essentially, Suassuna turns to popular culture to find those values, but it is above all the popular cultural expression of a past era. Stories and memories relayed in both novels, and especially the myths and legends that have been passed down through the years, recall distant periods of *sertão* history, helping to link the past with the present. It is this recreation of the popular memory and of a perception of the world which breaks down orthodox temporal divisions, which creates the sense of timelessness to which critics like Lind refer. Yet the main plot of the novels is focused on the early part of the present century. In *A Pedra do Reino*, the 1930s dominate. Quaderna, writing his work in prison in 1938, is concerned above all with recalling events from the previous eight years, particularly the mysterious murder of his godfather, Dom Pedro Sebastião Garcia Barretto in 1930, the abduction of the latter's youngest son, Sinésio, on the same day, and the return to Taperoá of Sinésio five years later, like a new Dom Sebastião, a saviour come to redeem his people. Those events occur exactly one hundred years after the messianic movement of Quaderna's ancestors, the Ferreira-Quadernas, in the *sertão da pedra do reino*, between 1835 and 1838, which involved human sacrifice and led to armed conflict with the forces of the authorities. A baby which miraculously survived the massacre, and was then brought up by a priest, went on to become Quaderna's grandfather. The timing of the events in the 1930s is seen as of particular significance by Quaderna, reinforcing his belief in the power of astrological forces and the forces of destiny. As a child, his initial sense of shame at the atrocities committed by his ancestors gradually gave way to a feeling of pride, a feeling that his family was marked out for a glorious destiny, and he goes on to dedicate himself to the study of the family's past:

> Tudo isso ia sendo pacientemente estudado e entendido
> por mim que, á medida que me punha adulto, ia
> guardando tudo isso em meu coração, para quando se
> completasse, de 1935 a 1938, a Século da Pedra do Reino,
> abrindo-se caminho para que um Ferreira-Quaderna se
> sentasse novamente no Trono de Sertão do Brasil. (153)

Bit by bit, with patience, I studied and understood all this, and as I grew into
adulthood, I kept all this in my heart, ready for when, between 1935 and 1938,
the century of the stone of the kingdom was complete, so opening up the way
for a Ferreira-Quaderna to once again install himself on the throne of the
backlands of Brazil. (153)

The 1930s was a period when feudal, or semi-feudal patterns of life still dominated large areas of the *sertão,* and the great struggle between the landowning oligarchy and the new, urban based bourgeoisie was reaching its apogee. Popular poetry flourished without significant competition from the mass media, then in its infancy, and bands of *cangaceiros* roamed the region. Communications and transport systems in the backlands were still very primitive. This was the period in which Suassuna spent his childhood, and which, in his novels, he recalls with nostalgia. As Angel Rama remarks, for Suassuna the seduction of the past is more powerful than the mediation of the present. (154) Now himself living in the city, Suassuna, like other Armorial artists, evokes a way of life that has already undergone significant transformation. Chapter 2 of this study attempted to show how the *folhetos* of the market place cover all aspects of contemporary life, constantly incorporating new themes and issues. Such themes are notably absent from Suassuna's novels, however. The more traditional poetry, recreating old European romances, the adventures of *cangaceiros* and miraculous and mythical subjects, are chosen instead. This clearly demonstrated by Suassuna's choice of *folheto* verses to quote in his work, *A Pedra do Reino.* In a fine study of the novel, Candace Slater identifies 24 genuine *folheto* poems cited in the work, the vast majority of them dealing with the adventures of popular heroes, religious or moral subjects or traditional satirical or picaresque themes, and eleven other ballads, presumably created by Suassuna himself, but attributed to characters in the novel, which deal mainly with mythical or mystical themes. (155) This presents a picture of the popular poet as generally conservative, essentially a conserver of tradition. In *Folheto XXXVI* of *A Pedra do Reino,* João Melchíades describes his art as a *cantador* in the following terms:

> Gosto, também, de combater o Protestantismo e os novas-seitas, porque querem se afastar dos tracejados da luz da antigüidade católica! As coisas e histórias velhas influem muito para e progresso da Poesia: as histórias passadas recordam a memória imortal dos antístites e antepassados, revivendo na memória do Poeta, que depois faz chegar ao ouvido do mais rude o toque da Memória dos tempos idos! (156)

I also like to combat Protestantism and the new sects, because they want to move away from the path of light of catholic antiquity! Ancient stories and things greatly influence the development of poetry: past stories recall the immortal memory of the ancient religious leaders and of our forefathers, coming back to life in the memory of the poet, who afterwards carries the echo of past times to the ears of even the most uneducated! (156)

There is no denying that popular poets do preserve age-old stories and myths, constantly developing them and presenting them in modified forms, but also striking is the capacity of popular poetry to adapt and address itself to new circumstances, problems and themes. That dynamism is nullified in Suassuna's novels.

viii]   Quaderna's vision of the world

To a large extent the conservative view of popular culture presented in the novels can be explained by Quaderna's, and Suassuna's, strong nostalgia for past days in the *sertão*. As has already been argued, the mythical vision of the *sertão* created in the works is composed, above all, of elements, materials and symbols from the past. Quaderna seems to fear losing touch with that past. In *Folheto XLV* of *A Pedra do Reino*, Pedro Beato, an old mystic, tells Quaderna that part of his trouble is that he is constantly struggling to recuperate the power and prestige of his family, the Garcia-Barrettos, and, in particular, *As Maravilhas*, one of their former estates, on which Quaderna grew up. Quaderna replies that that land has special significance for him, embodying the innocence and happiness of his childhood. His struggle to recuperate it therefore symbolises his broader struggle for peace of mind, dignity and contentment:

> Ali foi o começo da minha vida, Pedro, um começo
> puro, talvez o único tempo de inocência e felicidade que
> eu gozei, o tempo em que meu Pai, minha Mãe e meu
> Padrinho eram vivos e me apareciam como três imagens,
> aquelas imagens de São José, Nossa Senhora e São
> Joaquim que existem na capela da "Onça Malhada"! (157)

It was there that my life began, Pedro, a pure beginning, perhaps the only time of innocence and happiness which I have enjoyed, the time when my father, my mother and my godfather were alive, and appeared to me to be like the three images of Saint Joseph, Our Lady and Saint Joachim which are in the chapel of the "Onça Malhada" estate! (157)

Here one of the fundamental themes of Suassuna's novels emerges: the time old notion of humans doomed to betray God and fall from grace. Quaderna can never shed himself of his feelings of guilt, and an overwhelming sadness over the fate of all humans, born to suffer, separate from God, with death as the only certainty. Such feelings are reinforced in Quaderna by visions which he has, which he explains as partly Divine revelations and partly the product of his own prophetic and poetic powers. In *Folheto LXXI* of *A Pedra do Reino* he describes to the *Corregedor* a vision he had of a huge puma, vile and mangy, which for him becomes the symbol of the whole cursed world on which man is condemned to live:

> Era uma Onça enorme e mal definida, leprosa, desdentada, sarnenta e escarninha (...) Por entre os pelos e as chagas sarnentas dessa Onça-Parda, eu não via agora, mas sabia, com certeza, que errava a Raça piolhosa dos homens, raça também sarnenta e sem grandeza, coçando-se idiotamente como um bando de macacos diante da Ventania Crestadora, enquanto espera a Morte à qual está, de véspera, condenada! (158)

It was an enormous puma, but blurred, and it was sickly, toothless, mangy and sneering (...) I knew for certain, though I couldn't see anything, that among the mangy coat and the sores of that puma, the human race roamed, also mangy, and so small, scratching themselves idiotically like a troop of monkeys in the midst of the hot wind, whilst waiting to die, as they've always been condemned to do! (158)

It is a vision which never leaves him. He continues:

> (...) foi um acontecimento decisivo para mim, porque, a partir daí, nunca mais a imagem da Onça-Parda se desligou, para mim, da imagem do mundo (...) aquela visagem me jogou, de uma vez para sempre, no buraco cheio de cinza, na descoberta de que o mundo era um Bicho sarnento e os homens os piolhos e carrapatos chupasangue que erram por entre seus pelos pardos, sobre seu couro chagado, escarificado e feridento, marcado de cicatrizes e peladuras, e queimado a fogo lento pelo Sol calcinante e pela ventania abrasadora do Sertão. (159)

(...) It was a decisive event for me, because, from that moment, the image of the brown puma never separated itself from the image I had of the world (...) It was a vision which threw me, once and for all, into the ash filled pit, for I had discovered that the world was a mange ridden beast and we humans were the lice and blood sucking ticks which wandered through its brown fur, on its hide full of sores, cuts and wounds, and marked with scars and peeling skin, and

burnt slowly by the scorching sun and the hot wind of the backlands. (159)

Though some of the imagery employed resembles that found in some *folheto* verse, the concentration on the metaphysical anguish of the protagonist distances the work from the thematic content commonly found in popular poetry. There are many *folhetos* which deal with religious and moralising themes, but they are never expressed in the deeply personal manner of Quaderna.

Haunted by his thoughts of humankind condemned to suffering and death, Quaderna takes refuge in religious worship. Dissatisfied with the severe, traditional Catholicism with which he grew up, and anguished by his inability to live up to its dictates and strict moral code, Quaderna invents his own religion, which he calls *catolicismo-sertanejo*, a fusion of certain catholic beliefs and rites and others from the messianic traditions of his ancestors. Alone, he carries out his own rituals, in which he appeals to God for support, understanding and forgiveness, for his life of promiscuity and drunkenness fills him with guilt, and even fear. Thoughts of death torment him, and he begs God that he might be allowed to enjoy himself whilst he is still alive. In *Folheto LXXII* of *A Pedra do Reino* he describes one of his rituals to the *Corregedor*, in which he addresses God before he eats:

> Minha cara, minha boca, meus cabelos, hão de cair aos pedaços. Meus olhos vão ser comidos pelos Gaviões! Meu corpo se tornará um esqueleto, a princípio fétido e medonho: depois, embranquecidos pelo Sol, meus ossos hão de separar-se um dos outros! (...) Assim, já que vou ser comido pelos Gaviões e Carcarás, pelos Urubus e Cachorros-do-Mato errantes no Sertão, o Senhor, não leveis a mal que agora, enquanto estou vivo, eu me deleite comendo a carne dos bichos que cacei e matei (...)(160)

My face, my mouth, my hair will all disintegrate. My eyes will be eaten by the hawks! My body will turn into a skeleton, first ghastly and fetid, and then, bleached by the sun, my bones will separate themselves from one another! (...) So, since I'm to be eaten by the hawks and falcons, and the vultures and wild dogs that wander the "sertão", don't get offended, dear Lord, if now, whilst I'm alive, I enjoy eating the meat of the animals which I've hunted and killed (...)(160)

He fears that all sensual pleasure might be a betrayal of God, and he is haunted by his tragic vision of all humans, wretched, weak and pathetic, condemned to death in a hostile, miserable world. His religion, however, provides some solace, and conveniently enables him to enjoy life without losing his soul:

> Era, em suma, uma religião que me salvava a alma e, ao mesmo tempo, permitia que eu mantivesse meu bom comer, meu bom beber e meu bom fuder, coisas com as quais afastava a tentação da visagem da Onça e da Cinza. (161)

It was, in short, a religion which saved my soul and at the same time allowed me to carry on eating, drinking and screwing, just as I liked, all of which helped me to keep away the temptation of that vision of the puma and the ash. (161)

His personal *catolicismo-sertanejo*, however, relies in part on thought traditional to Brazilian messianism, calling on God to avenge the poor and punish the rich, for example, a notion which appears frequently in allegorical form in the *folhetos*. In his ritual, Quaderna calls out:

> Cantemos ao Deus de Fogo do Sertão, porque ele manifestou gloriosamente seu poder, precipitando no mar as máquinas e as empresas, os engenhos infernais dos Estrangeiros e traidores, castigando a força e o opróbrio dos Poderosos que nos oprimiam e exaltando o Sertão, com sua coragem, suas pedras, seus espinhos, seus cavalos e seus Cavaleiros! (162)

Let us sing to the God of Fire of the "sertão", because he has gloriously shown his power, by hurling businesses and machines into the sea, along with the sugar mills belonging to the foreigners and the traitors, and by punishing the brute force and infamy of the powerful men who oppress us, and by glorifying the "sertão", with its bravery, its stones and thorns, and its horses and horsemen! (162)

Stronger than the appeal for help for the poor and oppressed, however, is Quaderna's concern for personal redemption. He asks God to give him the faith and strength that will give his own life meaning and enable him to accept his own mortality:

> Só assim meu Reino será verdade, só assim meu sangue e meus ossos serão verdade, só assim será verdade a Furna do Mundo e a Furna sagrada para onde todos nós caminhamos e que sagra a Onça da Vida pela Onça da

243

Morte, realizando sua união final com a Onça Sagrada
do Senhor de Fogo! (163)

*Only in that way will my Kingdom be true, and my blood and bones be true as
well. Only then will the cavern of the world be true, and the sacred cavern to
which we are heading and where the puma of life is consecrated by the puma of
death, through its final union with the sacred puma of the Lord of Fire! (163)*

In this way, Quaderna borrows and adapts figures and images
from North East mythology in order to express his own personal vision
of the world, his anguish and his hopes. In *Folheto LVI* of *A Pedra do
Reino*, for example, he describes the Bicha Bruzacã to the *Corregedor*. It is
a huge, malicious monster, said to be responsible for the natural disasters
inflicted on the inhabitants of the North East, such as drought and
storms at sea. For Quaderna, it embodies all evil on earth, and one of his
major aims is to find it, kill it and drink its blood, which will bring him
redemption and make him immortal. In both novels the figure of Moça
Caetana appears, the spirit of death according to popular belief. At the
beginning of *Ao Sol da Onça Caetana*, set in 1911, she stalks through the
sertão in the form of a puma, watching the leading members of the major
families of the Paraíba oligarchy making their way to the Onça Malhada
ranch for a meeting aiming to settle their differences and reach a political
agreement. She is the omen of death and destruction, and as she lies in
wait one of the families, the Villars, is ambushed, signifying the
frustration of attempts to end the political conflicts and violence that
would deeply mark Quaderna's life. The Bicha Bruzacã and Moça
Caetana are the creations of the popular imagination, but for Quaderna
they come to serve as deeply personal symbols, through which he
conceptualises the tragic view of life, which, as will be seen, has largely
resulted from his own experience.

At times however, his creative imagination and Divine vision
combine to create an alternative, idealised view of the *sertão* and of life
itself, which gives him some sense of inner peace and hope. In *Folheto
LXXIII* of *A Pedra do Reino* he describes another of his visions to the
Corregedor, one in which his feelings of guilt, corruption and despair are
overcome, temporarily at least, by a sense of redemption. Lost in the
scrubland of the *sertão* one day, Quaderna fell asleep and saw an image
of himself, repulsive and leprous, at the foot of a rock. Morte Caetana
suddenly appeared before him and made him climb the rock, on the top
of which he felt, briefly, cleansed, redeemed and unified with the Divine
Spirit:

(...) conseguia chegar ao cimo. E aí, milagre dos

milagres! eu descobria, afinal, ou melhor, eu sentia com meu sangue, que *tudo* era divino: a Vida e a Morte, o sexo e a secura desértica, a podridão e o sangue. O Lajedo parecia com a Pedra do Reino, a do chuvisco prateado, e eu sabia, com o sangue, que se conseguisse escalá-lo, experimentaria, no alto, de uma vez só, o gozo do Amor, o poder do Reino, a fruição da Beleza e a união com a Divinidade (...) (164)

(...) I was reaching the top. And there, miracle of miracles! I finally discovered, or rather I felt in my blood, that "everything" was divine: Life and Death, sex and the dryness of the desert, decay and blood. The rock resembled the stone of the kingdom, made of silver rain, and I knew, in my blood that if I managed to get to the top, there, from up high, I would experience, for the only time in my life, the pleasure of love, the power of the Kingdom, the enjoyment of beauty and union with the Divine (...) (164)

Quaderna's search for redemption and dreams of an alternative, more fulfilling existence are intimately linked to the theme of Sebastianism that is a central part of *A Pedra do Reino*. In *Folhetos XXXIV* and *XXXV* of the novel, Samuel Wandernes tells the story of the disappearance of the Portuguese prince, Dom Sebastião, at the battle of Alcácer-Quibir in 1578, the event which provided the basis for the development of the myth of the Prince's eventual return in order to lead the poor and oppressed into a new age of freedom and prosperity. This popular belief took root in Brazil, and has played a significant role throughout Quaderna's family history. It was his ancestors who established the series of messianic communities at Pedra Bonita in the 1830s, and another of his relatives, Sinésio, who, having disappeared in 1930, apparently abducted and believed by many to have been killed, returns to Taperoá in 1935, partly to lay claim to the inheritance of his murdered father, Dom Pedro Sebastião, but also to revive the same dreams of a new, more just society that inspired the Pedra Bonita movement a hundred years earlier. Sinésio thus appears as the latest Redeemer of the *sertão* poor, given the title of *O Alumiado* by Quaderna. In introducing him in *Folheto II* of *A Pedra do Reino*, Quaderna states:

(...) para evocá-lo aqui talvez seja ainda mais necessário que eu me socorra das Musas (...) Cercava-o, efetivamente, uma atmosfera sobrenatural, uma espécie de "aura" que só mesmo o fogo da Poesia pode descrever e que, mesmo depois de sua chegada, ainda podia ser entrevista em torno da sua cabeça, pelo menos "por aqueles que tinham olhos para ver". (165)

(...) in order to invoke him here it will perhaps be even more necessary for me to seek help from the muse (...) He was surrounded by a supernatural atmosphere, a type of aura which only the fire of poetry can describe and which, even after his arrival, could be discerned around his head, at least by those who had eyes to see. (165)

Sinésio remains a mystical, almost supernatural figure throughout the novel. Much of the description associated with him, such as that of his entry into Taperoá with a cavalcade of imposing horsemen bearing flags with heraldic insignias, attempts to evoke the atmosphere of the old romances of chivalry.

   The specific interests of Quaderna and his family are inseparable from the broader aims of establishing a realm of liberty and justice which underlie *sertão* Sebastianism. Sinésio's crusade, the *Demanda Novelosa* as Quaderna terms it, not only promises to bring justice for the poor, but also the restoration of some of the power and prestige of the Garcia-Barretto family. In the process, Quaderna will have new possibilities for achieving some of his own lofty ambitions. He thus links up all the major moments in his family's history - the 1830s messianic movement, the Princesa rebellion undertaken by some of his relatives against the authorities in 1930 and the *Demanda Novelosa* - presenting them as proof of his glorious family background, and as the basis of his own claims to greatness. He says to the *Corregedor* in *Folheto LXV* of *A Pedra do Reino*:

> Sr. Corregedor, o que eu queria mesmo, confesso, era ser Imperador do Sertão e do Brasil, para me tornar Gênio da Raça Brasileira. Agora, que para isso eu queria unir o movimento da Pedra do Reino com a Revolução de Princesa e a Demanda Novelosa que empreendemos com Sinésio, isso eu queria! (166)

Sr. Corregedor, what I really wanted, I must confess, was to be Emperor of the Sertão and of Brazil, in order to become the genius of the Brazilian race. And to do that, I wanted to unite the movement of the stone of the kingdom with the Revolution of the princess and the crusade which we undertook with Sinésio, that's what I wanted! (166)

Sinésio and his army will overthrow the Bourgeois Republic, Quaderna hopes, and establish a popular monarchy to govern Brazil. That monarchy will ensure the well-being of the Brazilian people, whilst also offering Quaderna the opportunity of self-fulfilment, for he sees his own family as the natural heirs to the throne. It is true that, ultimately, it is not the dream of power or prestige that attracts him to Sebastianism, but rather its vision of a different society where harmony and justice reign, and where he will be morally regenerated, free at last from the feelings of guilt and corruption that torment him. In the end, however, it is the personal affliction of the protagonist that is emphasised by the theme of Sebastianism in *A Pedra do Reino*, rather than the collective aspirations of the mass of *sertanejos*.

Although, therefore, the tone and the atmosphere of the popular *romanceiro* are retained throughout Suassuna's novels, it is the individual perceptions and concerns of the protagonist Quaderna, and of the author himself, which always prevail. The autobiographical element of the novels has been well documented, emphasised by Wilson Martins in his article on *A Pedra do Reino*, for example, and examined in more detail by Candace Slater in her study of the same work. (167) As will be seen, some significant aspects of Quaderna's life and experiences coincide with those of Suassuna, and the protagonist clearly expresses many of the author's own views and concerns, as voiced in numerous articles and interviews, and in his writings on the *Movimento Armorial* to which reference has already been made. Significantly, Suassuna himself has stated that he considers a poem of deep personal significance to be the central part of *A Pedra do Reino*. (168) It was a prose poem which he said he dreamt, and then adapted for inclusion in the novel. There, in *Folheto XLIV*, Quaderna sleeps whilst waiting for his interview with the *Corregedor*, and dreams that the Moça Caetana writes him a message in letters of fire, which, half asleep and half awake, he writes down, understanding it to be of fundamental importance for him. It is, in effect, the sentence that awaits Quaderna. It is a poem haunted by death, where Quaderna is presented as struggling bravely, but ultimately vainly, to make sense of his life, and of the turmoil of the world around him.

Many autobiographical details can be found in *A Pedra do Reino*, but they are even more evident in *Ao Sol da Onça Caetana*, for in this second novel Quaderna faces another interrogation from the *Corregedor*, during which he is asked to give information about his past life. As a result, he reveals his personal anguish and fears, and speaks of his attempts to confront them. His recollections of childhood are almost idyllic, evoking a time of peace and purity. The colours, sounds and aromas of those days are engraved in his mind, but the sweetness of the memories is intermingled with a powerful sadness. He recalls waking up alone in a hammock, and feeling for the first time the sense of abandonment and isolation that would frequently return to him in later life, but it is above all the violent deaths of his father and godfather that have marked him, shattering his world. All his activities since then, political, religious and literary, have in one way or another represented an attempt to reconstruct that broken world and recover some of the lost peace and harmony. In *Folheto XVII* of *Ao Sol da Onça Caetana*, he sadly tells the *Corregedor* of the strange force, again conceived of as a puma, which destroyed his happiness:

> (...) aquela Onça amarela e sangrenta que destroçou
> minha vida, criando em mim, ditada não sei por qual lei,
> Sina ou divinidade cruel, a minha maldição, a obrigação
> inútil e desesperada de tentar refazer, com os escombros
> e destroços do mundo, um novo Reino, reluzente e
> sagrado como o que existia "antes". (169)

(...) that cowardly and bloodthirsty puma which destroyed my life, creating within me, dictated by what law, destiny or cruel divinity I do not know, my curse, the useless and desperate necessity to take the rubble and debris of the world and remake it into a new kingdom, gleaming and sacred like that which existed "before". (169)

Here is the strong sense of loss that pervades so much Armorial art.

As he talks, Quaderna clearly links the tragic history of his family with what he perceives to be the tragic history of the *sertão* as a whole, the decline of one matching the decline of the other. Gradually coming to accept anguish as an inherent part of human existence, Quaderna searched for ways of confronting it and decided that the creativity of his imagination offered the best solution, capable of producing an alternative world through visions, dreams and literary work. He was particularly inspired by the creations of *sertão* popular culture, which seemed to him to be more intuitive and spontaneous than erudite literature. Thus, he suggests to the *Corregedor* during their second interview that his dreams, fantasies and writings might above all be an attempt at self-understanding, and an effort to come to terms with the tragic and violent world he finds around him:

> Talvez, aliás, Sr. Corregedor, meu depoimento se dirija
> somente a mim mesmo e à minha família, àqueles que
> foram atingidos, como eu, pela morte de meu Pai e pela
> degolação de meu Padrinho. E mais ainda, Sr.
> Corregedor: talvez tudo o que eu diga, tudo o que estou
> procurando alinhar aqui aos poucos, tenha validade
> somente para mim mesmo. Talvez tudo isso seja
> somente uma busca desesperada que eu empreendo

sobre minha identidade, tentando dar algum sentido à
sangrenta desordem que, desde minha infância,
envolveu e despedaçou minha vida. (170)

*Furthermore, your honour, my testimony is perhaps only directed towards
myself and my family, those whom were affected, like myself, by the death of my
father, and the murder of my godfather, whose throat was cut. And what's more,
your honour, perhaps everything I say, everything I'm trying to outline here,
bit by bit, only has validity for myself. Perhaps it's all just a desperate search
for my own identity which I've undertaken, in an attempt to give some sense
to the bloody turmoil which, since my infancy, has overwhelmed by life, and
torn it to pieces. (170)*

Like all human beings, Quaderna is wretched, and, like all others, his
fundamental problem is his daily betrayal of God:

> (...) eu, mesquinho Decifrador de charadas, e funcionário
> público semelhante àqueles a quem desprezo; eu, cujo
> único problema, cujo único assunto é a traição contínua
> e dilaceradora que faço cotidianamente a Deus e a seu
> Reino. (171)

*(...) me, wretched little solver of puzzles, and public clerk similar to those whom
I despise; me, whose only problem, whose only action of note is the continual
and tormenting treachery which I commit every day against God and his
Kingdom. (171)*

However, through the power of his imagination he can at least confront
the sadness of life, if not actually change it. He denies that he is merely
a romantic dreamer or a clown, for his imagination offers a positive
response to the ugliness and sordidness of the real world. Laughter and
fantasy not only help him survive and preserve his sanity, he claims, but
also express his rebellion against the corruption of that world:

> E o riso-a-cavalo, grosseiro e macho, que permite reunir
> corajosamente as injustiças, as feiúras e os destroços da
> vida real para, com eles, empreender o galope do Sonho,
> e manter, assim, a chama da minha Epopéia, da minha
> insurreição permanente, contra as feiúras e injustiças do
> real. (172)

*It's roaring laughter, coarse and virile, which allows one to courageously gather
together all the injustices, the wreckage and the ugliness of real life, and with*

them gallop off into the world of dream, and so keep alive the flame of my epic, of my permanent insurrection against the ugly and unjust things of this world.(172)

Quaderna's dreams are beautiful precisely because they contrast with the ugliness of the world about him, and they are given concrete expression through his poetry and religious practices. He regularly retreats to a high rock on the outskirts of Taperoá to carry out his rituals and induce visions with the help of a powerful and sacred wine whose secret recipe was concocted by his ancestors during the messianic movement at Pedra Bonita the previous century. In *Folheto X* of *Ao Sol da Onça Caetana*, he describes one of his visions in which the *sertão* is transformed into a magical kingdom, again evoking the world of the ancient chivalric romances:

> Uma sensação deliciosa me invadia. Abri os olhos, e o Sertão me apareceu, todo, como o Reino que era para mim, desde que eu passara a entender melhor os fascínios e encantações que ele me dirigia por trás de sua aspereza, de sua pobreza dura, cruel e despedaçadora. O Sol dourava muralhas e castelos de pedra, (...) Povoavam-no astrosos desfiles de Cavaleiros e batalhas, de vinditas e emboscadas. Galopavam, em suas estradas e caatingas, Cangaceiros e Vaqueiros vestidos de couro castanho e empoeirado, trazendo aguilhadas ou compridos punhais na mão. (173)

I was filled with a wonderful sensation. I opened my eyes, and the sertão appeared before me like the kingdom which it had always been to me, ever since I had been able to understand better the fascination and enchantment which it conveyed to me beyond its harshness, its hard, cruel and destructive poverty. The sun lit up stone walls and castles with golden light (...) The sertão was alive with sad, mournful processions of horsemen, battles, acts of vengeance and ambushes. Along its roads and through its scrubland there galloped bandits and cowhands dressed in dusty brown leather, carrying goads or long daggers in their hands. (173)

Quaderna argues that such dreams and visions enable him to confront reality and visualise new possibilities, an attitude which simply follows the example of his people, the *sertanejos*, who relate to the world through myths and magic.

Quaderna's views echo statements by Suassuna himself. As has been seen, he has constantly stated that literature should allow as free a rein as possible to the imagination, and be aesthetically pleasing, rather than attempt to document or record the world according to sociological formulae, and he has strongly denied that his approach to writing is a form of escape or an avoidance of social questions, arguing that it merely attempts to address those questions in a different way. He has also emphasised the role of humour in literature, saying of *Don Quixote*, for example:

> I think that that victory through laughter over the tragedy of life is an act of courage. It's already been called tragic optimism by some, and it's a category I'd use to refer to myself. (174)

Laughter is a vital way of confronting what Suassuna perceives as the essentially tragic nature of life. In the same interview he states:

> I'm perfectly aware that the real human condition contains an element of tragedy. Death is enough to confirm that. You can see that, basically, life is a blind alley, because, no matter what you do, you're condemned to die. (175)

In the novels, therefore, Quaderna, in addition to the role of popular poet interpreting the collective perceptions and myths of the rural poor of the *sertão*, also wrestles with these major personal dilemmas of the author himself. In an interview with José Augusto Guerra, Suassuna confirms that another of the attractions which he saw in the novel was the opportunity it afforded him to deal with aspects of his personal experience, something he was not able to do as a dramatist:

> I turned to the novel precisely because some of the things I had within my inner world did not fit into plays for the theatre. The experiences I had in my childhood, for example, the struggles of my family, all those things were not material for the theatre, but the theme for a novel. (176)

Many details of Quaderna's upbringing correspond to Suassuna's own. Both have grown up on family plantations in the *sertão* and have become fascinated by the popular culture of the region, and the details of life in Taperoá that appear in the novels are based on the author's own recollections of the childhood years he spent in that town in the 1930s. Particularly vivid are Quaderna's memories of the political violence and

251

persecution suffered by his family when he was still very young, which he recounts to the *Corregedor* in the final *folhetos* of *Ao Sol da Onça Caetana*, and which are drawn from Suassuna's personal experience. The author and narrator share the same birthday, June 16th, Quaderna in 1897 and Suassuna in 1927. As a child, Suassuna received instruction from two uncles from opposing sides of the political spectrum, like the Professors Clemente and Samuel who educate Quaderna. Quaderna's father is killed, and the murder of his godfather, Dom Pedro Sebastião Garcia Barretto, occurs in the same year, 1930, in which Suassuna's own father was killed. Both author and narrator have been deeply marked by that violence and its effect on their families, and just as Quaderna, through his religious, political and literary practices, attempts to piece together his broken world and recover a sense of harmony, so does Suassuna through his writing, reconciling contradictions and creating an alternative universe with the symbols and images of the *sertão* culture of his childhood, as suggested by Maximiano Campos:

> His early childhood was marked by the assassination of his father, a gentleman of the *sertão* who became President of Paraíba, and by the struggles of his family and the persecution they suffered, and it all gave him a tragic vision of the world. That vision is laden with symbols and myths, codes of honour and life-and-death struggles. It's with that vision that Suassuna builds his castle of dream and beauty; it is the child, now an adult and turned into a writer, who tries to interpret, and live in harmony with, that untamed beast; his land. (177)

The novels certainly cannot be read as an autobiography of Ariano Suassuna, however. There are many significant differences between author and narrator. Throughout both works Quaderna is mocked, the ridiculousness of many of his attitudes and ideas fully exposed, but overall he is treated sympathetically. Through his dreams he yearns to construct something more fulfilling, beautiful and harmonious, but is constantly frustrated by a real world that does not understand, and operates according to different standards and values. It is an effort which is seen as tragically futile and yet heroic, full of both humour and sadness. It is this, Quaderna's personal struggle, which is of central interest in the novels, and a wide range of popular forms are used to express it, necessarily adapted for the new context created.

ix]   Quaderna's search for harmony

In Suassuna's novels, the principal social conflict that characterises life in the *sertão*, and with which Quaderna struggles to come to terms, is not that between peasant and landowner, as is common in the *folheto* poetry of the region, but rather that between the traditional landowning families of the interior, to whom the *sertão* peasantry is allied, and the rising bourgeoisie, whose power is based in the cities rather than on the land, and in industry rather than in agriculture and the raising of livestock. Sinésio symbolises the alliance between aristocracy and peasant, being the son of Dom Pedro Sebastião Garcia-Barretto, one of the most powerful landowners of the *sertão*, and yet also embodying the peasants' hopes for a new, more just social order; hopes which are given concrete expression in the political campaign organised around him, the *Demanda Novelosa*. In *Folheto LXII* of *A Pedra do Reino*, following the arrival of Sinésio's cavalcade into Taperoá, Dr. Pedro Gouveia, spokesman for the troop, calls to the people to support Sinésio in his attempt to regain his lost inheritance and family rights of which he has been deprived by his enemies:

> Sozinho contra todos, raptado, perseguido, encarcerado, maltratado, orfão, agora ameaçado de morte, com quem poderia ele contar, senão com o Povo, esse Povo bom, sofredor e pobre, do Sertão? Foi sempre ao lado desse Povo que ele esteve, foi sempre a seu lado que ele apareceu, e é isso que os seus inimigos não perdoam! (178)

Alone against them all, kidnapped, persecuted, imprisoned, mistreated, orphaned, and now threatened with death, who can he count on if not the people, the good, poor and long suffering people of the sertão? He was always on the side of the people, always appearing alongside them, and that's what his enemies won't forgive! (178)

Likewise, Quaderna frequently emphasises his own links with the poor. Unlike his mentors, Clemente and Samuel, who continually speak about the *sertanejos* but are incapable of understanding them or of communicating with them, Quaderna claims that he, who due to his family circumstances has never been integrated into the relatively privileged social circles into which he was born, has acquired a unique insight into the lives of the poor, and has shared their vision of the world and their forms of cultural expression. Despite their economic and social differences, Quaderna sees his family and the peasantry of the backlands united by a broad, common *sertão* culture, a common way of life. Describing his godfather, Dom Pedro Sebastião Garcia-Barretto, to the *Corregedor* in *Folheto XVI* of *Ao Sol da Onça Caetana*, he says:

> Era austero, tinha dignidade, compostura, coragem,
> devoção aos seus princípios ortodoxamente religiosos, a
> segurança e a sobriedade de maneiras com que
> executava seu código de honra, estreito mas firme. E,
> por paradoxal que isso possa parecer a Vossa Excelência,
> era, assim, muito mais aproximado do Povo e do Reino
> de fraternidade pobre e justiça com que sonho do que os
> Burgueses ricos e corrutos da Cidade. (179)

He was austere. He had dignity, decorum, courage, devotion to his orthodox religious principles, and he put his code of honour into practice in an assured but strict way, exact and firm. And, no matter how paradoxical it may seem to Your Excellency, he was really much closer to the people, and to the poor but just kingdom of fraternity which I dream about, than to the rich and corrupt bourgeoisie in the city. (179)

The common enemy is thus identified as the urban bourgeoisie which, extending its political and economic interests, threatens the traditional patterns of *sertão* life. Above all, it is the attachment to the land that links landowner and peasant. Thinking back through his childhood, Quaderna recalls moments when such feelings of fraternity found clear expression, as in *Folheto XX* of *Ao Sol da Onça Caetana*, when he tells the *Corregedor* of one occasion when he and his family, out hunting, stopped by a river to eat, and ended up sharing the meal with some peasants fishing nearby:

> (...) meu Tio Alfredo pegou uma galinha assada, chamou
> os homens para perto de nós, e terminamos todos
> comendo juntos, fraternalmente, numa grande alegria e
> contentamento, os filhos do Sertão e da mesma terra
> sagrada da Bruna Castanha do Brasil, com um dia
> honesto de trabalho e de vida ganho para frente - os
> filhos do mesmo Deus. (180)

(...) my Uncle Alfredo picked up a roast chicken, called the men over, and we all ended up eating together, fraternally, all happy and contented, sons of the "sertão" and of the same sacred, dark brown land of Brazil, and an honest day of work and life ahead - all sons of the same God. (180)

The new social order which Quaderna visualises, particularly through his adherence to Sebastianism, will reaffirm the unity of all the *sertão* population. He seeks harmony and human fulfilment through the traditional, rural patterns of life in the North East, which must resist the corrosive influence of expanding urbanisation and industrialisation. This is the area of conflict that is of paramount importance to Suassuna himself. As seen in chapter 2, the concerns of the popular poet generally lie elsewhere.

Also of interest to the author, and discussed within the novels, are the ideological divisions which polarised Brazilian politics in the 1930s, and which continue to do so today to a considerable degree. These are clearly represented in the frequently acrimonious arguments between Samuel and Clemente which regularly occur in *A Pedra do Reino*. Samuel, affiliated to the *Integralistas*, the Brazilian Fascist Movement, represents the extreme right, extolling the virtues of government by monarchy, with a traditional nobility in support. He constantly emphasises the Iberian roots of Brazilian culture, expressing contempt for the role played by Indians, negroes and *mestizos* in its development. Clemente is the complete opposite. From a poor, black family, he holds communist sympathies, arguing for a revolution that will see the oppressed sectors of society assume power. For him, the basis of authentic Brazilian culture is provided by the Indians and negroes. The extreme arguments each adopts, and the dogmatism with which they express them, are satirised by Quaderna in the novels. In *Folheto XXXIX* of *A Pedra do Reino*, for example, he mentions how everything, including all forms of scholarship and artistic creativity, is automatically divided into right and left by the two men:

> A sociologia era da Esquerda, e a Literatura fortemente suspeita de direitismo. O "riso satírico e a realidade" eram da Esquerda, a "seriedade monolítica e o sonho", da Direita. A prosa era da Esquerda e a Poesia, da Direita; mas, mesmo ainda dentro do campo da Poesia, tomavam partido, pois a lírica era considerada "pessoal e subjetiva, e portanto direitista e reacionária", enquanto que a satírica, "social e moralizante, didática", era considerada progressista e da Esquerda. (181)

Sociology was left wing, and literature very suspiciously right wing. "Satirical laughter and reality" belonged to the left, and "monolithic seriousness and dreams" to the right. Prose was left wing and poetry right wing. Even in poetry, however, they took sides, for lyrical verse was considered to be "personal and subjective", and therefore right wing and reactionary, whilst satirical poetry, "social, moralising and didactic", was progressive and left wing. (181)

It is in this *Folheto* that the differences of opinion between the two professors reach their climax, with Samuel insulting Luís Carlos Prestes, a major figure of the Brazilian Communist Party and a national hero as far as Clemente is concerned, and refusing to retract his comments. They decide to settle their disagreement by fighting a duel. Again, this evokes the ancient romances of chivalry, but, typically, it is treated humorously by Suassuna. Elements of farce predominate in the description of the duel itself, fought by the two inept professors on old horses and with chamber pots as the weapons, and of Clemente's victory parade through the town afterwards. Inspired by his triumph, which he sees as a moral victory for the left, Clemente declares his house and garden to be a free territory, a popular socialist republic with its own flag and constitution, and with Clemente himself as Head of State. Samuel and Quaderna quickly follow the example. Samuel declares his home to be a fascist republic, *"uma República integralista, unitária e centralizada"*, and Quaderna establishes his home as the promised kingdom envisaged in Sebastianist belief, where, he imagines, all Brazilians will be united in fraternity. The three men thus live out their individual dreams, each creating his own imaginary, ideal society. Quaderna is enthralled by the idea, describing it in *Folheto IX* of *Ao Sol da Onça Caetana* as:

> (...) aquela idéia maravilhosa de fundarmos, em nossas respectivas casas, *Reinos e territórios livres*, realizando nossos sonhos (...) Que outras alegrias, que outros sonhos poderíamos ter senão esses, com o Brasil e o mundo vivendo os tristes, miseráveis e inquietantes dias que estávamos vendo? Clemente tivera uma idéia genial! (182)

(...) that marvellous idea of establishing, in our respective houses, "kingdoms and free territories", and so fulfilling our dreams (...) What other joys, what other dreams could we have apart from these, with Brazil, and the world, living through those sad, miserable and disturbing days that we were seeing? Clemente had had a brilliant idea! (182)

Again, Quaderna's imagination provides him with a palliative for his sadness and discontent.

Suassuna, therefore, uses his novels as a forum for discussion of a wide range of issues relative to twentieth century Brazilian politics, culture, society and art, developing themes which are extraneous to the popular literary tradition of the North East. In *Folheto XXIX* of *A Pedra do Reino,* for example, Samuel and Clemente present their differing views of literary production, with Samuel extolling the role of individual creativity, and Clemente arguing that the greatest literary works are essentially collective creations of the masses, stories and poems which have developed gradually as they have been passed down through the generations, before finally being appropriated by individual erudite writers. In *Folheto LXXIX* of the same novel, two other characters, Adalberto Coura, a political activist who advocates revolutionary socialism, and Arésio, the violent, self-seeking half-brother of Sinésio, discuss possible ways for Brazil to confront the expanding imperialism of the United States, which, they both agree, is intent on imposing its materialistic values and narrow beliefs on the Brazilian people. However, the argument ends in violence when Arésio, having contemptuously rejected Adalberto's request for support for the revolutionary struggle, and declaring that the will and impulses of the individual will always be more powerful than the aspiration for liberty and the concern for the common good, strikes Adalberto to the ground and carries off his fiancée, Maria Inominata. As elsewhere in Suassuna's novels, dreams of a different social order are shown to be thwarted by destructive forces.

Facing conflict at all levels in the society around him, Quaderna desperately seeks to restore a sense of harmony. He attempts to fuse opposing attitudes and arguments in order to create an ideal synthesis, but his efforts continually result in absurdity. Because he remains politically in the centre, rejecting the arguments of both the left and the right, Clemente and Samuel nickname him *a Diana Indecisiva* (indecisive and wishy-washy). Instead of aligning himself with either of the political camps, Quaderna selects those ideas from both which most attract him, and describes himself as a left-wing monarchist, persisting in his dreams of a Brazil that is socially, politically and culturally united. He declares in *Folheto XL* of *A Pedra do Reino,* for example:

> Meu sonho é fundir os Fidalgos guerreiros e cangaceiros,
> como Sinhô Pereira e Jorge de Albuquerque Coelho, com
> os Fidalgos negros e vermelhos do Povo, fazendo uma
> Nação de guerreiros e Cavaleiros castanhos, e colocando
> esse povo da Onça-Castanha no poder! (183)

My dream is to fuse together the warrior and bandit noblemen, like his Lordship Pereira and Jorge de Albuquerque Coelho, with the black and brown noblemen of the people, to make a nation of dark-skinned warriors and Cavaliers, and putting the brown puma people in power! (183)

Deep down, Quaderna recognises that his dream is impossible. He is unable to envisage any alternative way forward, however. As has already been seen, a powerful determinism underlies his view of life, and ultimately he sees humankind as helpless in the face of inexplicable hostile forces waged against it. In the final *folhetos* of *Ao Sol da Onça Caetana*, he recalls how, even as a young child, secure and content in the midst of his family, he felt a strong sense of foreboding, as if the happiness he experienced in those early years was inevitably doomed to destruction, and the same notion is frequently repeated in both novels.

It is the same desire for harmony which determines the nature of the work Quaderna is creating, his literary masterpiece. It has already been seen how he rejects the divisions commonly made between popular and erudite literary tradition, and merges together elements of both in order to relate his own story and convey his own concerns. He also attempts to develop his own literary style by combining what he describes as the *oncismo* advocated by Clemente, essentially a stark and realist style, with the *tapirismo* of Samuel, elaborate, exalted and romantic. This, he claims, enables him to present a more complete picture of the life and history of the *sertão*, revealing the harshness and poverty of the region, but also what he sees as its epic quality, namely the courage and creativity of its people. Thus, in *Folheto III* of *A Pedra do Reino*, he explains to his readers how his unique style permits him to give a full and vivid description of the entry of Sinésio's cavalcade into Taperoá, with the idealistic vision of his *tapirismo* magically embellishing reality:

> (...) parti, oncisticamente, "da realidade raposa e afoscada do Sertão", com seus animais feios e plebeus, como o Urubu, o Sapo e a Lagartixa, e com os retirantes famintos, sujos, maltrapilhos e desdentados. Mas, por um artifício tapirista de estilo, pelo menos nessa primeira cena de estrada, só lembrei o que, da realidade pobre e oncista do Sertão, pudesse se combinar com os esmaltes e brasões tapiristas da Heráldica. Cuidei de só falar nas bandeiras que se usam realmente no Sertão para as procissões e para as Cavalhadas; nos gibões de honra, que são as armaduras de couro dos Sertanejos; (...) e em homens que, estando de gibão e montados a cavalo, não são homens sertanejos comuns, mas sim Cavaleiros à altura de uma história bandeirosa e cavalariana como a minha. (184)

> (...) *I started off with the "oncismo", of the mystic and opaque reality of the "sertão", with its ugly and lowly animals, like the vulture, the toad and the*

lizard, and its migrants fleeing the drought, hungry, dirty, ragged and toothless. But, using a stylistic device from "tapirismo", at least with this first scene that takes place on the road, I only recalled those elements of the harsh, stark reality of the "sertão" which could be combined with the bright colours and tapirista crests of the heraldic arts. I took care only to speak about the flags which they really use in the "sertão" for the processions and cavalcades, the doublets proudly worn by the backlanders, like leather armour (...) and men who, dressed in doublets and mounted on horseback, are not ordinary backlanders, but rather cavaliers worthy of a heroic and chivalric story like mine. (184)

The prime objective of Quaderna's work is not to convey the poverty and suffering of the *sertão*, but imaginatively to recreate the region into a new, idealised realm. It is the creative power of the popular poet, he believes, that can enable him to do this. Popular literary tradition provides him with the inspiration for his *estilo régio*, an exuberant, exalted style with which he aims to give his narrative a heroic, epic tone. Exaggeration is a major characteristic of all great epic literature, he decides. However, just as Quaderna's ego is constantly deflated, so his imagination is frequently curbed by the impositions of the social world around him. His tendency to exaggerate and embellish events when giving his testimony, for example, brings sharp reproval from the *Corregedor*, who reminds him that he is participating in an official, legal investigation, and is therefore required to give his evidence as accurately as possible.

The most striking feature of Suassuna's novels, therefore, is the combination of so many diverse materials and influences found within them. Of particular importance is the popular poetic tradition of the North East, providing the novels with many of their major themes, aspects of style and much of their tone. However, this chapter has attempted to show how such popular materials assume radically different meanings within the context of the novels, where they are refashioned in order to convey Suassuna's own vision of the world and debate the issues that are of chief concern to him.

x]   Suassuna's abandonment of literature and subsequent return

To conclude this chapter, mention must be made of Suassuna's decision, taken in 1981, to abandon his literary career and his involvement with popular culture.

Significant political developments occurred in Brazil in the late 1970s. There was a marked deterioration in the national economy, and a notable strengthening of the opposition to the military government. In 1978 and 1979, trades unions organised a series of strikes, which had long been suppressed by the dictatorship, and sectors of the middle classes voiced demands for political reform. In March 1979, General João Baptista Figueiredo became president, promising to carry out the process of *abertura*, the redemocratisation of the political life of the nation. Political groups began to reorganise, and new discussions on social, economic, political and cultural issues gathered momentum.

The question of popular culture was also reviewed in the light of these changing circumstances, and increasingly bitter criticism was made of Suassuna by opponents of the dictatorship for his work with popular culture during the most severe years of military repression. The *Movimento Armorial* had lost much of its early dynamism, and some of the original participants had left the group or dissociated themselves from it.

On August 9th, 1981, in a brief article entitled *Despedida* in the *Diário de Pernambuco*, where he regularly wrote a weekly column, Suassuna announced his abandonment of public life and of his literary career. He admitted that he had made mistakes in his work, but above all expressed bitterness towards the political leaders who had expressed support for his project for a national, popular art, but who, he claimed, had finally shown they had no genuine interest in the Brazilian people or Brazilian culture:

> I thought that Brazilian culture could only be carried out
> in the way I had dreamed of within the context of a
> policy which was truly based in the people. The political
> leaders of the Brazilian ruling class said they agreed
> with me. Later, embittered and perplexed, I gradually
> discovered that, in truth, they had no regard for culture,
> nor for the Brazilian people. (185)

He expressed the hope that a new government would be able to initiate policies of real benefit to both national culture and the Brazilian people. Finally, he announced that he would no longer be available for public engagements or interviews, and would produce no more novels, for literature no longer held any purpose for him:

> I am a man troubled by dreams, wild fancies and
> visions, sometimes even utopian visions of life and
> reality. After I wrote certain parts of the novel which I'm
> leaving unfinished, I began to free myself from some of
> the phantoms that persue me; now, perhaps I can also
> begin to escape the fearful and verbose chaos of
> literature - both my own and that of others. Please don't

ask me to produce more books, because I'm no longer
writing and I've lost all interest in it. One of the things
from which I have to free myself is precisely the huge
vanity of literature. (186)

His writing, it seems, had satisfied some of his personal needs, but all
his efforts had achieved little with regard to the broader aim of
developing a national, popular artistic expression. The contradictions in
the thought underlying Armorial art were never resolved, and the
problematical nature of the whole concept of national culture, which this
study has attempted to highlight, was either never fully appreciated or
never given sufficient attention. The political circumstances of the nation
made Suassuna's involvement in Brazilian popular culture in the 1970s
all the more controversial.

Suassuna clearly became increasingly aware of all these
problems, and increasingly disillusioned. His *Despedida*, however, ended
on a typically enigmatic note:

(...) what I had to say, write or do in public life, has now
been done. Enough of such grandeur. The rest is a
secret, a secret between me and my God. For one more
time I'll turn to the well used and consoling stock of
literary phrases and will bid farewell with a quotation:
"The matter is concluded. I'm all square with life. It's
pointless to go over one's sorrows, one's misfortunes
and the wrongdoings we've committed against one
another. May you all be happy". (187)

The restoration of democratic government in Brazil, and the resulting
opportunities that were opened up with regard to new directions in
cultural policy, eventually persuaded Suassuna to resume his literary
career in the late 1980s. Now one of Brazil's most acclaimed and highly
respected writers, he became a member of the Brazilian Academy of
Letters in 1989, and Secretary of Culture in the Pernambuco State
Government in 1994. His works remain extremely popular today, with
new editions and television adaptations being planned. The position of
Minister of Culture has enabled him to launch a new programme of
support for North East popular art. Under the name of *Projeto Cultural
Pernambuco - Brasil*, it seeks to diffuse expressions of that art through the
region in order to consolidate support for it, and provide the basis for
the establishment of centres for popular culture, the organisation of
festivals and publishing programmes for popular literature. A number
of erudite writers and artists condemned it as too restrictive, accusing

Suassuna of using his position to impose his own aesthetic tastes, and favouring some forms of art whilst disadvantaging others. (188) Meanwhile, two hundred popular artists demonstrated in his defence in Recife, in July 1995. Arguments over the question of popular culture show no sign of abating in the North East. Suassuna's career has been eventful, varied and often controversial. Perhaps more clearly than that of any other writer, it highlights the polemical and problematical nature of the ongoing debate on high culture and popular culture in Brazil.

Notes

1   Ariano Suassuna in an interview given to the author in Recife, May 29th, 1981.

2   Ariano Suassuna, 'Almanaque Armorial do Nordeste', in *Jornal da Semana*, Ano 1, No 20, Recife, April 29th, 1973

3   Many different interpretations of the 1930 Revolution exist among political scientists and historians, and an evaluation of these is obviously beyond the scope of this work. For a debate on the subject see *Movimento*, Edição Semanal 277, Rio de Janeiro, October 29th, 1980. It is generally accepted however, that the movement led by Vargas signified the end of the political and economic dominance of the coffee-producing rural proprietors, and opened the way for the development of a new power structure involving new economic groups, which would lead in turn to significant changes in political and economic policies.

4   Ariano Suassuna, dedication in *Romance d'A Pedra do Reino* (José Olympio, Rio de Janeiro, 1976)

5   Ariano Suassuna, *O Movimento Armorial* (Dept. de Extensão Cultural, Universidade Federal de Pernambuco, Editora Universitária, Recife, 1974), p.69

6   See Ariano Suassuna, 'Notas sobre o Romanceiro Popular', in *Seleta em Prosa e Verso* (José Olympio, Rio de Janeiro, 1974) On page 163, Suassuna states: "The best thing is that that erudite literature which is developed from popular roots is not imposed by theories, programmes or ideologies: it emerges naturally through love and identification."

7   He asserts, for example, that: "Today, it is only the ordinary people who preserve those distinctly Brazilian characteristics, which we now seek to defend and recreate." In Ariano Suassuna, *O Movimento Armorial*, p.68

8   The term *Civilização do Couro* has been employed by many Brazilian historians, e.g. Erani Silva Bruno, *História do Brasil,*

Listening to the People's Voice

Geral e Regional. 2: O Nordeste (Cultrix, São Paulo, 1967), to refer to the particular patterns of social life that developed as a result of the expansion of cattle production in the North East *sertão* from the eighteenth century onwards, to provide meat and work animals for other regions of the country. It was based on a very simple social structure, with a small number of families owning vast *latifúndios* for pasture, and crop production where possible, whilst the majority worked as cattle hands or agricultural workers and owned no land at all.

9 Ariano Suassuna, 'Notas', p.162

10 Ibid, p.165

11 Ariano Suassuna, 'Almanaque Armorial do Nordeste', in *Jornal da Semana*, Ano 2, No 1, Recife, December 16th, 1973

12 Suassuna states that the 1930 Revolution : "It was a natural consequence of the conflict between the urban bourgeoisie of businessmen and state employees, represented by the Pessoa family, and the rural landowning families, represented by the Suassunas, José Pereira, the Dantas family from the *sertão*, and the Cunha Limas." Ariano Suassuna, 'Almanaque Armorial do Nordeste', in *Jornal da Semana*, Ano 1, No 52, Recife, December 9th, 1973, p.15

13 Ariano Suassuna, 'Almanaque Armorial do Nordeste', in *Jornal da Semana*, Ano 1, No 46, Recife, October 28th, 1973, p.15

14 Ibid

15 Josué de Castro, *Death in the North East* (Vintage Books, New York, 1969), p.21

16 Ariano Suassuna, *O Movimento Armorial*, p.68

17 Ariano Suassuna in interview given to the author, Recife, May 29th, 1981.

18 Ariano Suassuna, 'Notas', p.172

19 Ibid, p.172

20 Ariano Suassuna, 'Almanaque Armorial do Nordeste', in *Jornal da Semana*, Ano 1, No.23, Recife, May 20th, 1973

21 Ariano Suassuna, quoted in José Augusto Guerra, 'El Mundo Mágico y Poético de Ariano Suassuna', in *Revista de Cultura Brasileña*, May 1973, p.59

22 Ariano Suassuna in interview with the author, Recife, May 29th, 1981, stated that: "The novel of the modern era is perhaps the literary genre that best permits the blending of poetry, essay and fiction. So you see that in *Pedra do Reino* poetry has a strong presence, since that has always been an interest of mine, but the essay is also present. I make an attempt to interpret certain things, in the way essay writing does. And there is also fiction."

23   In a newspaper article, 'Almanaque Armorial do Nordeste', in *Jornal da Semana*, Ano 1, No 31, Recife, July 15th, 1973, p.15, Suassuna writes: "The Ceará novels of Rodolfo Teófilo and Manuel de Oliveira Paiva are clearly naturalist. The regionalism of José Lins do Rego or Jorge Amado is neo-naturalist, but in both cases there is not much difference between them and the theories of Zola, for example, a fact which Jorge Amado has admitted. Both writers seek to approach the reality of the North East through a scientific and sociological vision, even though the regionalist analysis, linked to a more sophisticated sociology which emerged from *Os Sertões* and *Casa Grande e Senzala*, is much more advanced and less restricted than that found in the Ceará novels."

24   Ariano Suassuna in interview with the author, Recife, May 29th, 1981.

25   Ariano Suassuna in interview with the author, Recife, May 29th, 1981.

26   In interview with the author, in Recife, May 29th, 1981, Suassuna commented on the influence of García Lorca on his work: "The influence of García Lorca was decisive for me, precisely because, in my opinion, he pointed out the way which freed me from the narrowly sociological path of 1930s regionalism."

27   His friend Hermilo Borba Filho once wrote of him: "He would like to believe in God like children believe, but he believes with anguish and with fervour, and is full of questions (...) He faces both art and religion in the same fundamental way." Hermilo Borba filho, in José Laurêncio de Melo, 'Nota Bibliográfica', in Ariano Suassuna, *O Santo e a Porca / O Casamento Suspeitoso* (José Olympio, Rio de Janeiro, 1976), p.xiv

28   Ariano Suassuna, in interview with Gilse Campos, 'As Aventuras de um Cavaleiro do Sertão', *Jornal do Brasil*, Rio de Janeiro, September 9th, 1972

29   Hermilo Borba Filho, 'Teatro, Arte do Povo' (April 13th,1946) in *Arte em Revista*, Ano 2, Número 3, p.60

30   Ibid, p.60

31   Ibid, p.62

32   Ibid, p.61

33   Ibid, p.61

34   See Augusto Boal, *Documentos on the Theatre of the Oppressed* (Red Letters, London, 1984)

35   Joel Pontes, *O Teatro Moderno em Pernambuco* (Coleção Buriti, DESA, São Paulo, 1966), p.37

36   Ibid, p.37

37 José Laurêncio de Melo, 'Nota Bibliográfica', in Ariano Suassuna, *O Santo e a Porca / O Casamento Suspeitoso* (José Olympio, Rio de Janeiro, 1976), p.vii

38 Ariano Suassuna, 'Notas', p.165

39 Ariano Suassuna, 'A Compadecida e o Romance Nordestino' in *Literatura Popular em Verso*, Tomo 1 (Fundação Casa de Rui Barbosa, Rio de Janeiro, 1973), p.155, from the original interview by Ariano Suassuna, *Folha da Manhã*, Recife, 1948

40 Ariano Suassuna, *Uma Mulher Vestida de Sol* (Impresa Universitária, Recife, 1964), p.23

41 Mário Guidarini particularly emphasises that Suassuna abandoned the tragic form and plot after this work (Mário Guidinari, *Os Pícaros e os Trapaceríos de Ariano Suassuna*, Ateniense, São Paulo, 1992, p.12) and Ligia Vassallo states that this play is significantly different from Suassuna's 'mature work', and quotes his own comments of dissatisfaction with it. (Ligia Vassallo, *O Sertão Medieval: Origens Européias do Teatro de Ariano Suassuna*, Fransisco Alves, Rio de Janeiro, 1993, p.22)

42 Ariano Suassuna, *Auto da Compadecida* (Agir, Rio de Janeiro, 1981), p.22

43 See Mark Curran, 'Influências da Literatura de Cordel na Literatura Brasileira', in *Revista Brasileira de Folclore*, Ano IX, No.24, Ministério de Educação e Cultura, Departamento de Assuntos Culturais, May-August 1969

44 Enrique Martínez-López, 'Guia para lectores hispánicos del 'Auto da compadecida', *Revista do Livro*, No.24, 1964, p.91

45 Ariano Suassuna, *Auto*, p.174

46 Ibid, p.203

47 See Angel Rama, 'El teatro y la narrativa popular nacional', in *Literatura y clase social* (Folios Ediciones, Mexico, 1983). In a more recent study, Ligia Vassallo argues that the most striking characteristic of Suassuna's plays is their dependence on elements of medieval drama, which are obtained from two sources: firstly, from the vestiges of medieval culture still found in the North East popular art and cultural expression which Suassuna uses, and secondly from the structures and techniques of sixteenth century Iberian drama, read by the playwright. See Ligia Vassallo, *O Sertão Medieval*, p.22

48 Enrique Martínez López, 'Guia', p.95

49 Ibid, p.92

50 Ariano Suassuna, *Auto*, p.185

51 This point is also made by Mário Guidarini, who writes: "(...) the symbols used in his theatre are drawn more from the mysteries

of communities that are either extinct or on the way to extinction, than from current social practice." Mário Guidarini, *Os pícaros*, p.10

52   Ariano Suassuna, *O Santo e a Porca* (José Olympio, Rio de Janeiro, 1976), p.81

53   Ibid, Introduction, p.5

54   Ariano Suassuna, *O Casamento Suspeitoso* (José Olympio, Rio de Janeiro, 1976), p.145

55   Ariano Suassuna, *A Pena e a Lei* (Agir, Rio de Janeiro, 1975), p.205

56   Ariano Suassuna, *Farça da Boa Preguiça* (José Olympio, Rio de Janeiro, 1974), p.xxiii

57   Joaquim Quartim describes in detail these developments, writing: "The popular forces had begun to escape the control of the populist politicians. In the late fifties the forty-year quiescence of the peasantry was ended by the Peasant Leagues founded by Francisco Julião, which were particularly strong in Pernambuco and the North East. The last year of Kubitschek's presidency also saw a break-through towards a real autonomy for the working-class movement (...) By the time Goulart took office in 1961 the Cuban revolution had already renewed the strength of popular forces all over Latin America. In Brazil, the impact of Cuba drew the embryonic Peasant Leagues into an unprecedented mass movement for agrarian reform, strengthened the radical forces within the working class, and inspired a new wave of nationalism among the intelligentsia and sections of the army-junior officers, NCO's and lower ranks." Joaquim Quartim, *Dictatorship and Armed Struggle in Brazil* (NLB, London, 1971), p.44

58   Luis Mendonça, 'Teatro é Festa para o Povo' in *Arte em Revista*, Ano 2, Número 3, p.74

59   Ariano Suassuna, 'Manifesto do Teatro Popular Nordestino' (Recife 1961), in *Arte em Revista*, Ano 2, Número 3, p.65

60   Ibid, p.65

61   Ibid, p.65

62   Ibid, p.64-65

63   Ibid, p.65

64   Suassuna quoted in Ligia Vassallo, *O Sertão Medieval*, p.31

65   Augusto Boal, 'Que Pensa Você da Arte de Esquerda?', in *Latin American Theatre Review* (University of Kansas, Kansas, 1970), p.47

66   See Augusto Boal, *Documentos*.

67   Boal comments: "The repeated attacks on manichaeism always

come from the right, from people who want, at any price, to set up a third position, one of neutrality, impartiality, equidistance, and employing all kinds of concepts which deliberately mystify. The truth is that we know that good and evil exist, as do revolution and reaction, the left and the right, the exploited and the exploiters." Augusto Boal, 'Qué Pensa Vocé da Arte de Esquerda?', p.49

68 Yan Michalski refers to the effect this suppression had on the theatre: "It was a sophisticated system of censorship, which was imposed on texts and on performances, and which serve to prevent, with increasing severity, the presentation of any work which could be interpreted as a critical vision of the present, or as an expression of ideas which ran counter to the philosophy of the regime, or a position which was incompatible with the conservative moral code of the authorities. This situtation, which intensified after 1968, transformed the theatre into a battle field for over a decade, with the desire for free expression of the artists on one side, and the repressive spirits of the regime on the other." Yan Michalski, 'Introducción al teatro brasileño', in *Conjunto*, No.54, 1982, Casa de Las Américas, Havana, p.9

69 Ariano Suassuna, 'Ariano Suassuna: Movimento Armorial em Nova Fase Criadora', an interview with José Mário Rodrigues, *Jornal do Commércio*, Caderno 4, Recife, July 25th, 1976

70 Política Nacional de Cultura, Ministério de Educação e Cultura, 1975, reproduced in *Arte em Revista*, Ano 2, Número 3, p.6

71 Ibid, p.6

72 Ibid, p.6

73 Renato de Silveira, 'Uma Arte Genuína, Nacional e Popular?, in *Arte em Revista*, Ano 2, Número 3, p.6

74 Política Nacional, p.6

75 Ariano Suassuna, 'Arte Armorial', programme of concert, 'Tres Séculos de Música Nordestina: do Barroca ao Armorial', Recife, October 18th, 1970

76 Ariano Suassuna, *O Movimento Armorial*, p.18

77 Ibid, p.61

78 Ibid, p.62

79 Ibid, p.68

80 Ariano Suassuna, 'Almanaque Armorial do Nordeste', in *Jornal da Semana*, Recife, Ano 1, No.22, Recife, May 13th-May 19th, 1973

81 Ariano Suassuna, 'Almanaque Armorial do Nordeste', in *Jornal da Semana*, Ano 1, No 15, Recife, January 14th, 1973

82 Ariano Suassuna, *O Movimento Armorial*, p.12

83 Ibid; p.62-63

84   Ariano Suassuna, 'A Visão Mágica do Nordeste de Ariano Suassuna', in *Correio da Manhã*, Rio de Janeiro, September 8th, 1971

85   Ariano Suassuna, *O Movimento Armorial*, p.32

86   Ariano Suassuna, 'Almanaque Armorial do Nordeste', in *Jornal da Semana*, Ano 1, No 21, Recife, May 6th-May 12th, 1973

87   Ariano Suassuna, 'Almanaque Armorial do Nordeste', in *Jornal da Semana*, Ano 1, No 20, Recife, April 29th-May 5th, 1973

88   Ariano Suassuna, *O Movimento Armorial*, p.59

89   Ariano Suassuna, 'Almanaque Armorial do Nordeste', in *Jornal da Semana*, Ano 1, No 21, Recife, May 6th-12th, 1973

90   Ariano Suassuna, 'Almanaque Armorial do Nordeste', in *Jornal da Semana*, Ano 1, No 20, Recife, April 29th-May 5th, 1973

91   Cussy de Almeida, 'Movimento Armorial, a Cultura do Nordeste', in *Jornal do Brasil*, June 1st 1971, Rio de Janeiro

92   Ariano Suassuna, 'Almanaque Armorial do Nordeste', in *Jornal da Semana*, Ano 1, No 20, Recife, April 29th-May 5th, 1973

93   Ariano Suassuna, 'A Visão Mágica do Nordeste de Ariano Suassuna'

94   Ariano Suassuna, *O Movimento Armorial*, p.8

95   Ariano Suassuna, in interview with the author, Recife, May 29th, 1981

96   Candace Slater, 'Folk Tradition and the Artist: The Northeast Brazilian Movimento Armorial', in the *Luso-Brazilian Review*, No 16:2, 1979, p.166

97   Ariano Suassuna, in interview with Gilse Campos, 'As Aventuras de um Cavaleiro do Sertão', in *Jornal do Brasil*, Rio de Janeiro, September 20th, 1972

98   Ariano Suassuna, 'Almanaque Armorial do Nordeste', in *Jornal da Semana*, Ano 1, No 12, Recife, March 4th, 1973

99   Candace Slater indicates that of the groups original nineteen members, only one quarter actually grew up in a town of significant size, but that all now live in the city - mainly Recife - on incomes well above the minimum for the region. Candace Slater, *'Folk Tradition'*, p.175

100   Marcos Accioly, 'Quadrão', in Ariano Suassuna, *O Movimento Armorial*, p. 39

101   Janice Japiassu, 'Cirino', in Ariano Suassuna, *O Movimento Armorial*, p.38

102   See Luís da Câmara Cascudo, *Dicionário do folclore Brasileiro* (Edições de Ouro, Rio de Janeiro, 1972), p. 768

103   Janice Japiassu, 'Poema', in *Canto Amargo* (Universidade Federal de Pernambuco, Recife, 1970), p.106

104   Ariano Suassuna, 'Japiassu, Musa do Sertão', preface to Janice Japiassu, *Canto Amargo*, p.18

105   Deborah Brennand, 'Poema do Sertão', in Ariano Suassuna, *O Movimento Armorial*, p.37

106   Raimundo Carrero, *O Bordado, a Pantera Negra*, in Ariano Suassuna, O Movimento Armorial, p.44

107   Ibid, p.41

108   Ibid, p.44

109   Suassuna commented: "Graciliano Ramos, realist, skeptical, restrained, a type of Machado de Assis of the Brazilian scrublands, could never open up the universe of his novels in the broad, epic and poetic manner of *Grande Sertão* by Guimarães Rosa." Ariano Suassuna, 'Almanaque Armorial do Nordeste', in *Jornal da Semana*, Ano 1, No 32, Recife, July 22nd-July 28th, 1973, p.15

110   Ariano Suassuna, 'Almanaque Armorial do Nordeste', in *Jornal da Semana*, Ano 1, No 36, Recife, August 8th-August 15th, 1973, p.15

111   Maximiano Campos, *O Grande Pássaro*, in *As Sentenças do Tempo* (Universidade Federal de Pernambuco, Recife, 1973)

112   Ariano Suassuna, 'Almanaque Armorial do Nordeste', in *Jornal da Semana*, Ano 1, No 36, Recife, August 8th-15th, 1973, p.15

113   Ariano Suassuna, 'Nôvo Romance Sertanejo', preface to Maximiano Campos, *Sem Lei nem Rei* (O Cruzeiro, Rio de Janeiro, 1968), p.130

114   Maximiano Campos, *Sem Lei nem Rei*, p.58

115   Ibid, p.57

116   Ariano Suassuna, 'Almanaque Armorial do Nordeste', in *Jornal da Semana*, Ano 1, No 32, Recife, July 22nd-28th, 1973, p.15

117   Ariano Suassuna, 'Almanaque Armorial do Nordeste', in *Jornal da Semana*, Ano 1, No 28, Recife, June 24th-30th, 1973, p.15

118   Ariano Suassuna, 'Nôvo Romance', pp.129-130

119   Maximiano Campos, *Sem Lei*, p.100

120   Ibid, p.87

121   Ibid, p.86

122   Ariano Suassuna in interview given to the author, Recife, May 25th, 1981.

123   Ian Watt, *The Rise of the Novel* (Pelican, London, 1979), passim

124   Idelette Muzart Fonseca Dos Santos, 'Uma Epopéia do Sertão', preface to Ariano Suassuna, *Ao Sol da Onça Caetana* (José Olympio, Rio de Janeiro, 1977), p.xiii

125   Ariano Suassuna, quoted in 'A Visão Mágica do Nordeste de Ariano Suassuna', in *Correio da Manhã*, Rio de Janeiro, September 8th, 1981

126   George Rudolf Lind, 'Ariano Suassuna, Romancista', in *Colóquio/Letras*, Número 17, Lisbon, January 1974, p.32

127   See Maria Odila Leal-McBride, *Narrativas e Narradores em "A pedra do reino"* (Peter Lang, New York, 1989)

128   Ibid, p.188

129   Ariano Suassuna, *Romance d'A Pedra do Reino* (José Olympio, Rio de Janeiro, 1976), p.6

130   Ariano Suassuna, *Ao Sol da Onça Caetana*, pp.48-49

131   Ariano Suassuna, *Romance d'A Pedra do Reino*, p.65

132   Ibid, p.7

133   Ibid, p.6

134   Quaderna's tutor in popular poetry is clearly based on a real poet of the same name, João Melquíades Ferreira Silva (1869-1933), from Paraíba. After a period in the army, during which he served in the Canudos campaign in 1897, he earned his living as a poet and *cantador*.

135   Ariano Suassuana, *Romance d'A Pedra do Reino*, p.68

136   Ibid, p.68

137   Ibid, p.139

138   Ibid, p.296-297

139   Ibid, p.285

140   Ibid, p.66

141   Ibid, p.179

142   Ibid, p.590

143   George Rudolf Lind, 'Ariano Suassuna', p.34

144   Ariano Suassuna, *Romance d'A Pedra do Reino*, p.588

145   Ibid, p.589

146   Angel Rama, 'Ariano Suassuna: el teatro y la narrativa popular y nacional', in *Literatura y clase social* (Folios Ediciones, México DF, 1983), p.78

147   Maria Odila Leal-McBride, *Narrativas e Narradores*, passim

148   Ariano Suassuna, *Romance d'A Pedra do Reino*, p.269

149   Ibid, p.49

150   Rachel de Queiroz, 'Um Romance Picaresco?', preface to Ariano Suassuna, *Romance d'A Pedra do Reino*, p.xi. Queiroz writes: "The book is picaresque - or rather, the picaresque element is very much present in the novel, or treatise, or work or simply book; I really don't know what to call it, because *A Pedra do Reino* transcends all those genres. It's a novel, an odyssey, a poem, an epic, a satire, and apocalypse."

151 Wilson Martins, 'Romance Pitoresco?', in *O Estado de São Paulo*, Supplemento literário, São Paulo, January 9th, 1972

152 Ariano Suassuna, *Romance d'A Pedra do Reino*, p.311

153 Ibid, p.37

154 Angel Rama, 'Ariano Suassuana', p.192

155 Candace Slater, *Ariano Suassuna's 'A Pedra do Reino': A Case Study in Cultural Nationalism* (Ph.D. for Stanford University, August 1975), p.154

156 Ariano Suassuna, *Romance d'A Pedra do Reino*, p.179

157 Ibid, p.246

158 Ibid, p.44

159 Ibid, pp.444-445

160 Ibid, pp.455-456

161 Ibid, pp.447-448

162 Ibid, p.461

163 Ibid, pp.461-462

164 Ibid, pp.468-469

165 Ibid, p.15

166 Ibid, p.378

167 See Wilson Martins, 'Romance Pitoresco', and Candace Slater, *Ariano Suassuna's 'A Pedra do Reino'*.

168 Reported in 'A chave da Pedra do Reino', in *Jornal do Commércio*, Recife, December 5th 1993

169 Ariano Suassuna, *Ao Sol da Onça Caetana*, p.94

170 Ibid, p.85

171 Ibid, p.68

172 Ibid, p.67

173 Ibid, pp.62-63

174 Ariano Suassuna, in interview with Gilse Campos, 'As Aventuras de um Cavaleiro do Sertão', *Jornal do Brasil*, Rio de Janeiro, September 9th, 1972

175 Ibid

176 Ariano Suassuna, in interview with José Augusto Guerra, 'El mundo mágico y poético de Ariano Suassuna', *Revista da Cultura Brasileña*, No 35, Madrid, May 1973, p.68

177 Maximiano Campos, 'A Pedra do Reino', postscript to Ariano Suassuna, *Romance d'A Pedra do Reino*, p.630

178 Ariano Suassuna, *Romance d'A Pedra do Reino*, p.358

179 Ariano Suassuna, *Ao Sol da Onça Caetana*, p.88

180 Ibid, p.107

181 Ariano Suassuna, *Romance d'A Pedra do Reino*, p.196

182 Ariano Suassuna, *Ao Sol da Onça Caetana*, p.56

183 Ariano Suassuna, *Romance d'A Pedra do Reino*, p.215

184   Ibid, pp.1920
185   Ariano Suassuna, 'Despedida', in the *Diário de Pernambuco*, Recife, August 9th, 1981, p.A13
186   Ibid
187   Ibid
188   Poet and painter Montez Magno, for example described Suassuna as a 'new Zdnânov' (*O Globo*, July 15th 1995), and the artist Bete Gouveia commented: 'I'm in favour of the universalisation of art, not Armorial dictatorship' (*Jornal do Commércio*, Recife, July 16th, 1995)

5
CONCLUSIONS

The determined efforts made by erudite writers to assimilate expressions of popular culture and folklore into their work has long been, and continues to be today, a major dynamic force in the development of Brazilian literature. It is a process which can only be understood in the context of, firstly, the sustained employment of literature as an instrument for forging cultural nationalism, and, secondly, the continuance of regionalism as a vital factor in literary production in Brazil.

The concept of literature as a means of affirming national identity obviously has its roots in the experience of colonialism shared by all the nations of Latin America, but it retains its validity today on account of the region's persisting state of economic, political and cultural dependency. Hence many contemporary Brazilian writers still speak in terms of developing a distinctly national form of artistic expression to counteract the influence of foreign cultural models.

As regards regionalism in Brazilian literature, some critics have pointed to its decline as a force under the impact of social and economic transformation and modernisation that has taken place during the course of the present century. However, regionalism has proved to be resilient in Brazil, capable of constantly adapting and reemerging in new forms. Just as *Grande Sertão: Veredas*, by Guimarães Rosa, was hailed by some as signifying the revitalization of Brazilian regionalist literature in the 1950s, so the work of Ariano Suassuna and the other members of the Armorial Movement was commonly seen as representing a regeneration of North East regional artistic expression in the 1970s. These facts demonstrate the continued significance of acute regional disparities in Brazil's uneven pattern of development, even to the present day, when regionalism continues to find expression in the work of such writers as João Ubaldo Ribeiro.

The constant process of reaffirmation of North East cultural values that has been traced through this study can be viewed as both a defensive and an offensive reaction to change at the national and international level. On the one hand, it expresses the desire to defend what are perceived as specifically North East cultural traditions and attributes which appear to be threatened by the increasing advance of cosmopolitan values, and, more recently, of the mass media. On the other, it demonstrates the need felt by successive generations of North Eastern artists and intellectuals to reassert the value of North East culture as the Centre-South of Brazil has consolidated its status as the cultural axis of the nation. It is these circumstances that provided the vital impetus for the regionalist thinking of both Gilberto Freyre and Ariano Suassuna, for example.

Popular literature in all its forms - oral or written, in prose or in verse, as story or song - has been a vital factor in this long process of regional affirmation. Numerous North Eastern artists and writers have perceived it as the embodiment of the experience and world view of the mass of the region's population, and hence of the distinctive qualities which characterise and differentiate the region.

However, though both cultural nationalism and regionalism have remained considerable forces in North East literature throughout the present century, changing circumstances have considerably modified their forms of expression through the decades. In the 1930s, for example, the tension generated by accelerated economic and social change was expressed in conflict at numerous levels, between the traditional oligarchy and the rising bourgeoisie, between the town and the countryside, between traditional and modern patterns of life, and in the increasing political polarisation between right and left, and such an atmosphere stimulated ideological debate and the critical study of social forces. Within this context, the *Geração de Trinta* produced their works of social realism and social protest, aiming to document the strife in the North East, especially in the rural interior, and expose the injustices and exploitation underlying it. The vision conveyed in many of the works that resulted is of a way of life in decline under the impact of changes that appear to aggravate rather than ameliorate injustice.

Conditions in the 1970s were very different. Social strife was suppressed by a military government, and under President Medici, between 1969 and 1974, oppression reached its height. During the early phase of the dictatorship, industrialisation, economic modernisation and foreign investment all registered accelerated, though extremely uneven, growth. An indication of this was the expansion of the mass media and culture industry throughout the North East, with an increase in television broadcasting, advertising propaganda, and even new types of popular literature in the form of American-style comics translated into Portuguese, whilst at the same time artistic expression, including literature, was censored, severely limiting its capacity to examine critically all the social, economic and cultural changes occurring in the region. It was under these conditions that the *Movimento Armorial* was formed in 1970, essentially a group of urban based artists and writers who looked back with nostalgia at the rural North East where most of them had their roots. It was no longer critical realism like that of the 1930s that they advocated, but rather the free play of the literary imagination to recreate for an essentially urban public the traditional culture of the rural North East.

Through the movement, Ariano Suassuna, very much the

motivating force behind it, aimed to reaffirm the values of that traditional culture within the context of accelerating change. In this, he followed a long line of North Eastern writers and artists who, in one form or another, have attempted to create in their work a rural arcadia. Their efforts must be understood essentially as the expression of the vision of that sector of the region's dominant classes linked to the old landowning aristocracy, responding to the advance of industrialisation, modern work practices and the mass media, which have all played a part in accelerating the process of disintegration of the traditional patterns of rural life determined by patriarchal plantation or ranching society.

The *Movimento Armorial* also provided Suassuna with the opportunity of putting into practice some of his own theories on artistic production. In opposition to rationalism and academicism he emphasised the power of the creative imagination, and instead of the study of the concrete, social reality of the North East, concentrated on the popular mythology and legends associated with the region, what he termed its magical reality, which, he argued, expressed the underlying spirit of its inhabitants. Earlier writers had documented the expressions of the region's popular culture, but the Armorial artists used those expressions as their basic raw materials, the constituent elements for the creation of new erudite forms, and the products that resulted were often striking, inventive and highly original. Although strictly concerned with North East cultural expression, the movement combined regionalist objectives with those of cultural nationalism, arguing that in reaffirming regional culture they would reaffirm national culture, and that good regional art provided the basis for successful national, and even universal, art.

Many of the ideas embodied in the *Movimento Armorial*, which, as has been seen, were essentially those of Suassuna himself, were deeply conservative, and it is not surprising that the movement caused considerable controversy, and met with vitriolic criticism from some quarters, when the development of the debate on popular culture in the North East over the previous decades is examined. That debate reached a level of considerable intensity in the early 1960s, stimulated by the vibrant political atmosphere in the North East during those years, with the State Government of Pernambuco, under Miguel Arraes, attempting to launch a programme of radical reform, within which education and the arts were given a major role. The *Movimento de Cultura Popular* developed a whole series of cultural activities, encouraging the participation of the poorest sectors of society, aiming to politicise them, encourage them to develop initiatives for themselves and help prepare them for the fight for social change. Ariano Suassuna participated in some of the activities organized.

The 1964 military coup dramatically ended the MCP. Under the dictatorship that followed, popular culture became an extremely sensitive issue and virtually all cultural activity was depoliticised. In 1970, with political repression at its height, the *Movimento Armorial* was launched by Suassuna in Recife, turning the spotlight on to the issue of popular culture again, but now in significantly different terms. Whereas the MCP viewed popular culture as based on social class, rooted in the lives of the poorest sectors of North East Society, the Armorial Movement tended to merge popular culture into a broader concept of regional culture, a whole way of life, essentially rural, which transcended conditions of social class. The political implications of the artist's involvement with popular culture were cast aside by the Armorial artists, who emphasised instead what they perceived as the fantastic and mystical qualities of regional popular expressions and folklore, which, they argued, were to be defended against cosmopolitan influences, and recreated into new erudite works as a contribution to the broader process of cultural nationalism. Many of Suassuna's contemporaries recalled the 'cultural activities of the early 1960s and resented his new movement, which to them seemed a betrayal of the principles and objectives established ten years before, a simple accommodation to new political circumstances.

Suassuna avoided political issues, arguing that he was only interested in promoting national culture. As has been seen, however, his thought was fraught with contradictions, and those contradictions eventually overwhelmed him. He finally found himself stranded, on the one hand disowned by the more radical artists who rejected his whole approach to popular culture, and, on the other, reaching the conclusion that those elements of the establishment who had supported his project in the early years had little genuine concern at all for the development of the truly national and popular art he envisaged. In August 1981 he announced his withdrawal from public life, and a halt to his literary career, expressing total disillusionment. He finally resumed writing some eight years later, when changing political circumstances eased the controversy.

The *Movimento Armorial* represented another attempt to formulate a theory of national culture and suggest a way forward for achieving it. However, like others before it, that theory was unable to deal adequately with the reality of Brazil's pattern of development, with its extreme inequalities and the resulting divisions at all levels of society. It could not be said to offer any positive approach to the problem of how exactly the poor, still rurally dominated North East can fit into the nation's overall pattern of modernisation and industrialisation. Nor could it be said to deal convincingly with the problem of dependency and its cultural implications. In response to the propagation of cosmopolitan values, Suassuna and the other Armorial artists searched for what they perceived to be pure Brazilian forms of expression, where in fact none exist. The very popular literature Suassuna has used in all his work has undergone significant changes through the present century, no longer monopolised by the traditional themes he prefers, but incorporating urban questions, international issues and material adapted from the mass culture industry which Suassuna rejects. Armorial art, conceiving popular culture as a repository of traditional values, can only understand such changes in terms of distortion or corruption of those values. Within such a view, freezing the process of cultural development, the popular cultural material presented in Armorial art frequently appears as folklore associated with a past age, rather than as a living, dynamic force.

This work has argued that it is within the context of such perceptions that the novels of Ariano Suassuna must be considered. Beginning as a poet and establishing himself as a major dramatist in the 1950s, Suassuna's decision to dedicate himself to the novel in the 1960s and 1970s, when his ideas on national and popular culture were crystallizing, highlights the problems inherent in his thinking. Of all genres, it is perhaps the novel which is the most alien to the poor masses of the Brazilian North East. The question as to whether it can ever break out of its exclusivism to really express popular perceptions and aspirations, rather than remaining the expression of the vision of a privileged sector of society and a reaffirmation of individualism, is never dealt with by Suassuna. It is a particularly problematical question in underdeveloped societies, where the gap between the erudite artist and the mass of the population appears particularly acute.

A Pedra do Reino, immensely ambitious and enormous in scope, has been rightly acclaimed as a major literary achievement. It is undoubtedly a novel of high quality and considerable originality. Most of that originality derives from the unique distillation Suassuna has achieved of so many varied sources and materials, particularly popular cultural expressions, in one novel. Yet merely employing popular forms does not mean that the resulting work embodies the popular perceptions and aspirations which created those forms in the first place. This is the major difficulty of Suassuna's objective of creating erudite art from popular roots, an art that will be both national and popular, for no such grafting is possible without a radical change in significance in the original material. Cut away from the social environment which produced them, popular forms, reshaped according to Suassuna's own vision of the world, necessarily assume radically new meanings.

It is noticeable, for example, how selective Suassuna has been in

277

his choice of popular material for his work. Set in the 1930s, when *cangaço* and messianism still flourished in the North East *sertão*, *A Pedra do Reino* looks back to a way of life that had changed significantly in the intervening decades. Contemporary issues frequently dealt with in the popular literature of the North East, such as the inflation, unemployment or labour problems which affect the daily lives of the poor, are avoided by Suassuna, who chooses instead the most traditional themes of popular poetry. It was argued in the first chapter of this work that, above all, the *folheto* narratives can be seen as symbolic expressions of the lived reality of those who produce and consume them, essentially the poorest sectors of North East society, and that the magical world they frequently present cannot be separated from the everyday social experience of those sectors. Through the magical universe of their poetry, the poor represent and discuss their daily struggles and conflicts. This vital significance of *folheto* verse is considerably diminished when the original material is transplanted into Suassuna's writing, where it is used to emphasise universal themes, particularly man's eternal hope for redemption. It is the mystical aspects of popular literature that Suassuna develops, rather than its value as a symbolic expression of immediate, daily problems.

The result is that substantial sections of *A Pedra do Reino* give the reader an exotic, folkloric view of the North East, presented through Quaderna's magical recreation of the poverty-stricken region. His flights of fantasy produce rich and colourful passages of description, as with the cavalcade that enters the town of Taperoá, examples of popular farce and visions of mythical beasts. The rich colours and elaborate designs of the emblems and symbols associated with the heraldry, pageantry and ritual of Quaderna's mythical *sertão* world are constantly emphasised throughout the work. It is a vivid and exuberant narrative style, which offers a striking contrast with the prose of the social realist writers of the 1930s, particularly that of Graciliano Ramos, in whose work the *sertão* is presented through such stark and brutal images that it is impossible to recognise it as the same region being dealt with by Suassuna.

What particularly attracts Suassuna, and his main character Quaderna, to *folheto* verse is its capacity to transform the world imaginatively, turning ugliness into beauty and banality into grandeur. In this sense, it offers a means of coming to terms with the world and its problems. As has been seen, a more radical position emphasises instead the capacity of popular culture to express resistance to the dominant culture of society, questioning its basic assumptions and at least glimpsing alternatives.

However, if Suassuna is attracted to *folheto* literature, he is also distanced from it. He views it critically, never accepting it at face value.

Conclusions

The seriousness and dedication with which Quaderna participates in popular traditions, including his involvement with popular poetry, is presented with irony by the author. The *folhetos* bring temporary pleasure for Quaderna by offering him a fantasy, dreamlike world as an alternative to harsh reality, but he is aware of the illusion. His dreams cannot really change the world. Ultimately, he appears a tragicomical figure, hopelessly caught between the enchanting, magical realm he creates from traditional popular expressions and the objective environment within which he lives, torn by suffering and strife. Quaderna longs to restore harmony to the world about him and find some solution to his own existential problems, and the novel places as much emphasis on his personal search for redemption and release from anguish as it does on examining North East society or culture.

Suassuna claims that what distinguishes his work, and that of other Armorial artists, is that it derives its inspiration from regional popular culture rather than from cosmopolitan artistic influences, yet, ironically, some of the most memorable aspects of his writing result from his use, perhaps unconscious, of forms and techniques characteristic of the modern novel, and which are not found in popular literature at all. Quaderna, though resembling a popular poet in his style of narration, and the popular anti-hero, or *pícaro*, common in *folheto* verse, in the trickery he uses to deal with difficult situations, is above all a problematical character in conflict with the world about him, the type of anguished protagonist common to many contemporary novels, but significantly different from the central characters of popular poetry. The irony with which Suassuna treats his character is also rarely found in *folheto* narratives, whilst the complexity of the work's form, particularly with its constant changes in angle of vision, clearly distinguishes it as a contemporary novel. As has been argued, it makes little sense to speak in terms of pure Brazilian forms and to deny the influence of external models and techniques in the development of Brazilian literature. On the contrary, the most powerful works of contemporary Brazilian fiction, perhaps typified by *Grande Sertão: Veredas*, by Guimarães Rosa, have derived much of their success from their free incorporation of cosmopolitan currents and vanguard forms, reworking them to provide new tools for analysing Brazilian reality through fiction.

None of the above detracts from Suassuna's literary achievement. Within the structure of the novel he has blended elements that typify popular literature, such as legend, farce and burlesque, to produce one of the most original works of Brazilian literature of recent decades. What Suassuna's writing and literary theories fail to do, however, is provide convincing solutions to the questions concerning the development of a national, popular literature in Brazil, and which are likely to continue to play a central role in the production of Brazilian literature for the foreseeable future.

BIBLIOGRAPHY

Primary Sources

Erudite Literature

Accioly, Marcus, *Nordestinados* (Editora Universitária, Recife, 1971)

Alencar, José de, *Obra Completa*, 5 Vols (José Aguilar, Rio de Janeiro, 1959)

Almeida, José Américo de, *A Bagaceira* (União Editora, Paraíba, 1969)

---- *Memórias* (Francisco Alves, Rio de Janeiro, 1976)

Amado, Jorge, *Cacau* (Martins, São Paulo, 1968)

---- *Terras do Sem Fim* (Martins, São Paulo, 1961)

---- *Jubiabá* (Martins, São Paulo, 1961)

---- *Mar Morto* (Martins, São Paulo, 12th edition, undated)

---- *Gabriela, Cravo e Canela* (Martins, São Paulo, 1958)

---- *Dona Flor e Seus Dios Maridos* (Martins, São Paulo, 1961)

---- *Capitães da Arreia* (Martins, São Paulo, 1967)

---- *Os Pastores da Noite* (Martins, São Paulo, 1965)

---- *Teresa Batista Cansada de Guerra* (Martins, São Paulo, 1972)

Andrade, Mário de, *Obras Completas* (Martins, Brasília, 1972)

---- *Macunaíma* (Martins, São Paulo, 1965)

Andrade, Oswald de, *Poesias Reunidas de Oswald de Andrade* (Gaveta, São Paulo, 1945)

Azevedo, Aluísio, *O Mulato* (Edições de Ouro, Coleção Clássicos Brasileiras, Rio de Janeiro, undated)

Bandeira, Manuel, *Poesia Completa e Prosa* (José Aguilar, Rio de Janeiro, 1967)

Bopp, Raul, *Poesias* (Ariel, Rio de Janeiro, 1972)

Brennand, Deborah, *O Cadeado Negro* (Universidade Federal de Pernambuco, Recife, 1971)

Campos, Maximiano, *Sem Lei nem Rei* (O Cruzeiro, Rio de Janeiro, 1968)

---- *As Sentenças do Tempo* (Universidade Federal de Pernambuco, Recife, 1973)

Carrero, Raimundo, *Romance de Bordado, a Pantera Negra*, in Ariano Suassuna, *O Movimento Armorial* (Dept de Extensão Cultural Universidade Federal de Pernambuco, Editora Universitária, Recife, 1974)

Castro Alves, Antônio de, *Poesias Completas* (Companhia Editora Nacional, São Paulo, 1969)

Coelho Neto, Henrique Maximiano, *Obra Seleta, Vol 1: Romances* (José Aguilar, Rio de Janeiro, 1958)

Couto, Ribeiro, *Poesias Reunidas* (José Olympio, Rio de Janeiro, 1960)

Cunha, Euclides da, *Obras Completas* (José Aguilar, Rio de Janeiro, 1966)

Japiassu, Janice, *Canto Amargo* (Universidade Federal de Pernambuco, Recife, 1980)

Lima, Jorge de, *Obra Completa* (José Aguilar, Rio de Janeiro, 1958)

Lins, do Rego, José, *Menino de Engenho* (José Olympio, Rio de Janeiro, 1980)

---- *Doidinho* (José Olympio, Rio de Janeiro, 1960)

---- *Banguê* (Livros do Brasil, Lisbon, undated)

---- *O Moleque Ricardo Ricardo* (José Olympio, Rio de Janeiro, 1935)

---- *Usina* (Livros do Brasil, Lisbon, undated)

---- *Fogo Morto* (José Olympio, Rio de Janeiro, 1965)

---- *Poesia e Vida* (Editora Universal, Rio de Janeiro, 1945)

---- *Pedra Bonita* (Edição Livros do Brasil, Lisbon, undated)

---- *Cangaceiros* (José Olympio, Rio de Janeiro, 1956)

Matos, Gregório de, *Obras Completas*, 2 Vols (Editora Janaína, Salvador, 1969)

Melo Neto, João Cabral de, *Morte e Vida Severina e Outros Poemas em Voz Alta*, (José Olympio, Rio de Janeiro, 1983)

Olímpio, Domingos, *Luzia-Homem* (Editora Ática, São Paulo, 1980)

Picchia, Menotti del, *Seleta em Prosa e Verso* (José Olympio, Rio de Janeiro, 1972)

---- *Poesias* (Martins, São Paulo, 1958)

Queiroz, Raquel de, *O Quinze* (Editora Universal, Rio de Janeiro, 1967)

---- *Quatro Romances* (José Olympio, Rio de Janeiro, 1960)

---- *Lampião* (José Olympio, Rio de Janeiro, 1953)

---- *A Beata Maria do Egito* (Serviço Nacional de Teatro, Rio de Janeiro, 1973)

Ramos, Graciliano, *São Bernardo* (José Olympio, São Paulo, 1947)

---- *Viventes das Alagoas* (Martins, São Paulo, 1955)

---- *Vidas Secas* (José Olympio, Rio de Janeiro, 1947)

---- *Angústia* (Portugália Editora, São Paulo, 1962)

Suassuna, Ariano, *Uma Mulher Vestida de Sol* (Imprensa Universitária, Recife, 1964)

---- *Auto da Compadecida* (Agir, Rio de Janeiro, 1981)

---- *Farsa da Boa Preguiça* (José Olympio, Rio de Janeiro, 1974)

---- *O Santo e a Porca / O Casamento Suspeitoso* (José Olympio, Rio de Janeiro, 1976)

---- *A Pena e a Lei* (Agir, Rio de Janeiro, 1975)

---- *Romance d'A Pedra do Reino* (José Olympio, Rio De Janeiro, 1976)

---- *Ao Sol da Onça Caetana* (José Olympio, Rio de Janeiro, 1977)

Távora, Franklin, *O Cabeleira* (Editora Ática, São Paulo, 1977)

Teófilo, Rodolfo, *A Fome* (Impresa Inglesa, Rio de Janeiro, 1922)

Bibliography

Popular Poetry

Antologia da Literatura de Cordel, 2 Vols (Secretaria de Cultura, Desporto e Promoção Social de Ceará, Fortaleza, 1978)

Areda, Francisco Sales, *As Aventuras do Amarelo João Cinzeiro Papa Onça* (Folheto, Folhetaria Borges, Bezerros, undated)

---- *A Embolada da Velha Chica* (Folheto, Folhetaria Borges, Bezerros, undated)

Assis, Manoel Tomaz de, *O Fim do Mundo está Próximo* (Folheto, no details)

Athayde, João Martins de, *Proezas de João Grilo* (Folheto, Joazeiro do Norte, 1980)

---- *Roldão no Leão de Ouro* (Folheto, Joazeiro do Norte, 1980)

---- *Estória da Princesa da Pedra Fina* (Folheto, Joazeiro do Norte, undated)

---- *Estória da Donzela Teodora* (Folheto, Joazeiro do Norte, undated)

Barros, Leandro Gomes de, *A Força do Amor, ou Alonso e Marina* (Folheto, Joazeiro do Norte, 1980)

---- *O Cachorro dos Mortos* (Folheto, Luzeiro, São Paulo, undated)

Batista, Sebastião Nunes, (ed) *Antologia da Literatura de Cordel*, (Fundação José Augusto, Natal, 1977)

Carvalho, Elias A. de, *História do Rei Pelé* (Folheto, no details)

Cavalcante, Rodolfo Coelho, *ABC da Minha Terra* (Folheto, UFAL, Maceió, 1978)

---- *Quem Era que Não Chorava Quando Jesus Padecia* (Folheto, Salvador, undated)

---- *O Rapaz que Virou Burro em Minas Gerais* (Folheto, Salvador, undated)

---- *A Mulher que Deu a Luz uma Cobra porque Zombou do Bom Jesus da Lapa* (Folheto, Salvador, 1976)

---- *A Chegada de Lampiã no Céu* (Folheto, São Paulo, undated)

---- *Antônio Conselheiro e a Guerra de Canudos* (Folheto, Luzeiro, São Paulo, undated)

Costa Leite, José, *A Pobreza morrendo a Fome no Golpe da Carestia* (Folheto, Casa das Crianças, Olinda, undated)

---- *A Mulher que Enganhou o Diabo* (Folheto, Casa das Criaças, Olinda, undated)

---- *O Homem que Era Pobre porque Não Sabia Ler* (Folheto, Tip Pontes Guaribira, undated)

---- *Carta Misteriosa do Padre Cícero Romão* (Folheto, no details)

Cristovão, José Severino, *O Rico e o Pobre* (Folheto, no details)

Emiliano, João Vicente, *Um Matuto na Cidade* (Folheto, Casa das Crianças, Olinda, undated)

Fernandes de Oliveira, João, *O Filho que Matou a Mãe* (Folheto, no details)

Freire, João Lopes, *A História de Carlos Magno e os Doze Pares de França* (Folheto, Rio de Janeiro, undated)

Melo, Rennan, *Satanás contra a Cremação* (Folheto, no details)

Meyer, Marlyse (ed), *Autores de Cordel*, (Abril, São Paulo, 1980)

Molia, João Vicente, *O Clamor da Caristia* (Folheto, Vitória, undated)

Moreira, Flávio Fernandes, *História do Feijão Preto de o Sofrimento do Pobre* (Folheto, no details)

Nascimento, Edmundo Matos, *O Tabaréu que Perdeu a Mulher na Estação Rodoviária* (Folheto, Salvador, undated)

Oliveira, Severino Gonçalves de, *A Moça que Virou Cobra* (Folheto, no details)

Pacheco, José, *A Chegada de Lampião no Inferno* (Folheto, no details)

Pedra, Francisco, *A Volta do Vaqueiro* (Folheto, no details)

Ramalho, Chico, *O Polvo Desembestado* (Folheto, Universidade Federal do Rio Grande do Norte, Natal, 1980)

Rodrigues, Jota, *A Dor qui mais Doi no Pobre é a Dor a da Umilhação* (Folheto, no details)

---- *O Brasil e o Estudante Pobre* (Folheto, no details)

Saldanha Menezes, José, *O Brasil Prometido aos Pobres na Época de Eleição ou os Amigos do Voto e Inimigos dos Eleitores* (Folheto, Universidade Federal do Rio Grande do Norte, Natal, 1981)

Santos, Antônio Domingos dos, *Nascimento, Vida e Morte do Padre Cícero Romão Batista* (Folheto, Joazeiro do Norte, undated)

Santos, Apolônio Alves dos, *O Divorcio* (Folheto, GED, Rio de Janeiro, undated)

---- *O ABC do Feijão e os Tumultos nas Filas* (Folheto, Guarabira, undated)

---- *Nosso Mundo Moderno* (Folheto, Rio de Janeiro, undated)

---- *Os Ultimos Dias de Getúlio Vargas* (Folheto, Rio de Janeiro, undated)

---- *Os Nordestinos no Rio e o Nordeste Abandonado* (Folheto, Rio de Janeiro, undated)

---- *A Morte do Ex-Presidente Juscelino Kubitschek de Oliveira* (Folheto, no details)

---- *A Mulher que Rasgou o Traveseiro e Mordeu o Marido Sonhando com Roberto Carlos* (Folheto, Guarabira, no details)

---- *O Sacrifício do Pobre no Mundo da Carestia* (Folheto, Guarabira, undated)

Santos, José João (Azulão), *Azulão Canta Dizendo como é o Nosso Folclore* (Folheto, Rio de Janeiro, 1978)

---- *O Artista Injustiçado* (Folheto, 1979)

---- *Brasil chorando* (Folheto, no details)

Bibliography

----   *O Trem da Madrugada* (Folheto, no details)

----   *Os Namorados de Hoje* (Folheto, no details)

Santos, Manoel Camilo dos, *Viagem a São Saruê* (Folheto, no details)

----   *Autobiografia do Poeta Manoel Camilo do Santos* (Editora Universitária, UFPB, João Pessoa, 1979)

Sena, Bernardino de, *O Problema do Camelô no Recife* (Folheto, Casa das Cianças, Olinda, undated)

----   *Estória de Matuto que 'Enricou' com a Loteria Esportiva* (Folheto, Casa das Crianças, Olinda, undated)

Silva, Delarme Monteiro, *O Sino de Torre Negra* (Folheto, Joazeiro do Norte, undated)

Silva, Expedito F, *Os Clamores da Carestia* (Folheto, Rio de Janeiro, no details)

Silva, José Camilo da, *O que Padre Cícero diz* (Folheto, no details)

Silva, Manoel Caboclo e, *O Sonho de Frei Damião com o meu Padrinho Cícero do Juazeiro do Norte* (Folheto, Joazeiro do Norte, undated)

Silva, Olegário Fernandes da, *O Filho que Matou a Mãe Sexta Feira da Paixão por Causa de um Pau Macaxeia* (Folheto, Caruaru, undated)

----   *O Exemplo da Crente que Profanou de Frei Damião e Virou Macaca* (Folheto, Caruaru, undated)

Soares, José Francisco, *Acabou a Gasolina? Ou a Gasolina Acabou?* (Folheto, Recife, 1977)

----   *A Cheia do Capibaribe* (Folheto, Casa das Crianças, Olinda, undated)

----   *Exemplo da Menina Peluda de Paranatama* (Folheto, no details)

----   *A Tragédia de Jaboatão, 13 Mortos e 35 Feridos* (Folheto, no details)

----   *A Chegada do Santo Papa* (Folheto, Recife, 1980)

----   *A Cobra de 2 Pés e a Porca que Deu Cria a um Cachorro* (Folheto, no details)

----   *O Tarado de Palmares e o Monstro de Gameleira* (Folheto, no details)

----   *A Lamentável Morte do Santo Papa Paulo VI* (Folheto, no details)

----   *Zé do Brejo, O Caipora* (Folheto, Casa das Crianças, Olinda, undated)

----   *A Vitória da Arena* (Folheto, Recife, undated)

----   *A Chegada de Arraes* (Folheto, Recife, 1979)

----   *O Rapaz que Casou com uma Porca no Estado de Alagoas* (Folheto, no details)

Soares, Marcelo, *Literatura de Cordel (O Prenúncio do Fim)* (Folheto, Rio de Janeiro, 1980)

Tenório, Manoel Rodrigues, *A Morte de Meu Padrinho Cícero* (Folheto, 1979)

Torres, José Antônio, *O Velho que Enganhou o Diabo* (Folheto, no details)

Secondary Sources

Works and articles on Brazilian history, culture and literature

Aderaldo Castello, José, *A Literatura Brasileira, Vol 1: Manifestações Literárias da Era Colonial* (Editora Cultrix, São Paulo, 1965)

Adonias Filho, *Modernos Ficcionistas Brasileiros* (Edições O Cruzeiro, Rio de Janeiro, 1958)

Aires, F, *O Piauí na Poesía Popular* (Artenova, Rio de Janeiro, 1975)

Albuquerque, Ulisses Lins de, *Um Sertanejo e o Sertão* (José, Olympio, Rio de Janeiro, 1976)

Almeida, Cussy de, 'Movimento Armorial, a Cultura do Nordeste', in *Jornal do Brasil*, Rio de Janeiro, June 1st, 1971

Almeida, José de Nascimento, 'Cantadores Paulistas de Porfia ou Desafio', in *Revista do Arquivo Municipal* (São Paulo), 13 (1947)

Almeida, Mauro W.B. de, 'Leituras de Cordel', in *Arte em Revista* (Kairos, São Paulo), 2(2) (1980)

Almeida, Renato, *A Inteligência do Folclore* (Companhia Editora Americana, Rio de Janeiro, 1974)

Almeida, Ruy, *A Poesia e os Cantadores do Nordeste* (Imprensa Nacional, Rio de Janeiro, 1947)

Andrade, Manuel Correia de, *Cidade e Campo no Brasil* (Editora Brasiliense, São Paulo, 1974)

---- *A Terra e o Homem no Nordeste* (Editora Brasiliense, São Paulo, 1974)

Antologia da Literatura de Cordel, 2 Vols (Secretaria de Cultura, Fortaleza, 1978)

Arantes, Antônio, *O Trabalho e a Fala* (Editora Kairós, São Paulo, 1982)

Araújo, Alceu Maynard, *Folclore Nacional*, 3 Vols (Melhoramentos, São Paulo, 1964)

---- *Cultura Popular Brasileira* (Melhoramentos, São Paulo, 1973)

Araújo, Raimundo, *Cantador, Verso e Viola* (Editora Pongetti, Rio de Janeiro, 1974)

Arraes, Miguel, *Brazil: The Power and the People* (Pelican, Harmondsworth, Middx, 1972)

Assis, Machado de, *Obra Completa* (José Aguilar, Rio de Janeiro, 1959)

Azevedo, Carlos Alberto, *O Heróico e Messiânico na Literatura de Cordel* (Edicordel, Recife, 1972)

---- 'O Realismo Mágico na Literatura Popular de Zona dos Canaviais do Nordeste', in *Brasil Açucareiro* (Rio de Janeiro), 82 (1973):43-46

Azevedo, F. de, *Brazilian Culture* (Hafner, New York, 1971)

Bibliography

Azevedo, Luis Heitor Correia de, 'A Arte de Cantoria', in *Cultura Política* (Rio de Janeiro), 4 (1944):183-87

Azevedo, Sânzio de, *Literatura Cearense* (Academia Cearense de Letras, Fortaleza, 1976)

Azzi, Riolando, *O Catolicismo Popular no Brasil: Aspectos Históricos* (Petrópolis, Vozes, 1978)

Bandeira, Manuel, *Brief History of Brazilian Literature*, translated by R.E. Dimmick (Pan American Union, Washington, 1958)

---- *Apresentação da Poesia Brasileira* (Casa do Estudante do Brasil, Rio de Janeiro, 1972)

Baptista, Maria Edileuza, 'A História do Poéta-Repórter que Não Foi Agricultor, Não deu Para Pedreiro e Vive Feliz Escrevendo Cordel', in *Jornal do Commércio*, Recife, February 1st, 1978

Barreto, Luis Antônio, 'A Bíblia na Literatura de Cordel: Primera Versão do "Gênesis" ', in *Revista Brasileira de Cultura* (Rio de Janeiro), 7 (1971):137-55

Barros, Manoel de Souza, Arte, *Folclore e Subdesenvolvimento* (Editora Paralelo, Rio de Janeiro, 1971)

Barroso, Gustavo, *Ao Som da Viola: Folclore* (Livraria Editora Leite Ribeiro, Rio de Janeiro, 1921)

Barroso, Haydeé M. Jofré, *Esquema histórico de la literatura brasileña* (Editora Nova, Buenos Aires, 1951)

Barta, Eli, 'Retorno de Um Mito: A Arte Popular', in *Arte em Revista* (Kairós, São Paulo), 2(2) (1980)

Bastide, Roger, *O Candomblé na Bahia: Rito Nagó*, translation by Maria Isaura Pereira de Queiroz (Companhia Editora Nacional, São Paulo, 1961)

Batista, Sebastião Nunes, *Antologia da Literatura de Cordel* (Fundação José Agosto, Natal, 1977)

---- 'Carlos Magno na Poesia Popular Nordestina', in *Revista Brasileira de Folclore* (Rio de Janeiro), 30 (1971):143-70

Beltrão, Luis, *Folkcomunicação dos Marginalizados* (Cortez Editora, São Paulo, 1980)

Benjamim, Roberto Câmara, 'Breve Notícia de Antecedentes Franceses e Ingleses da Literatura de Cordel Nordestino', in *Revista Tempo Universitário* (Recife), 6 (1980):171-88

---- 'Os Folhetos Populares e Os Meios de Comunicação Social', in *Symposium* (Recife), 11(1) (1969):47-54

---- *Literatura de Cordel: Produção e Edição* (Universidade Federal Rural de Pernambuco, Recife, 1979)

Boal, Augusto, 'Que Pensa Você da Arte de Esquerda?', in *Latin American Theatre Review*, University of Kansas, Kansas, Spring 1970

----   *Documents on the Theatre of the Oppressed* (Red Letters, London, 1984)

Bopp, Raul, Vida e Morte da Antropofagia (Civilização Brasileira, Brasília, 1977)

Borba Filho, Hermilo, 'Teatro, Arte do Povo', in *Arte em Revista* (Kairós, São Paulo), 2(2) (1980)

----   *Apresentação do Bumba-Meu-Boi* (Imprensa Universitária, Recife, 1966)

Bosi, Alfredo, *História Concisa da Literatura Brasileira* (Editora Cultrix, São Paulo, 1970)

----   *O Pré-Modernismo*, Vol 5 of *A Literatura Brasileira* (Editora Cultrix, São Paulo, 1968)

Bradford Burns, E, *Nationalism in Brazil, a Historical Survey* (Frederick A. Praeger, New York, 1968)

Brito, Mário da Silva, *História do Modernismo no Brasil* (Civilização Brasileira, Rio de Janeiro, 1964)

Britto da Motta, Alda, 'Notas Sobre a Visão de Mundo do Camponês Brasileiro', in *Revista de Ciências Sociais* (Universidade Federal de Ceará, Fortaleza), X(1&2) (1979)

Caldeira, Clóvis, *Mutirão: Formas de Ajuda Mútua no Meio Rural* (Companhia Editora Nacional, São Paulo, 1965)

Calmon, Pedro, *História da Literatura Bahiana* (José Olympio, São Paulo, 1949)

Campos, Renato Carneiro, *Ideologia dos Poetas Populares do Nordeste* (Instituto Joaquin Nabuco, Recife, 1977)

Cândido, Antônio, *Formação da Literatura Brasileira*, 2 Vols (Martins, São Paulo, 1964)

----   'Literatura y subdesarrollo en América Latina', in Alfredo Chacón (ed), *Cultura y dependencia* (Monte Avila, Caracas, 1975)

----   'Literature and the Rise of Brazilian National Self-Identity', in *Luso-Brazilian Review* (Wisconsin), 5(1) (1968)

----   *Literatura e Sociedade* (Editora Nacional, São Paulo, 1980)

Cantel, Raymond, *Temas da Atualidade na Literatura de Cordel*, translated by Alice Mitika Koshiyama, Universidade de São Paulo, Escola de Comunicações e Artes, São Paulo, 1972)

Carvalho, Ronald de, *Pequena História da Literatura Brasileira* (Editora Itaia, Belo Horizonte, 1984)

Cascudo, Luis da Câmara, *Cinco Livros do Povo* (José Olympio, Rio de Janeiro, 1953)

----   *Vaqueiros e Cantadores* (Ouro, Rio de Janeiro, 1968)

----   *Literatura Oral no Brasil* (José Olympio, Rio de Janeiro, 1978)

Bibliography

---- *Diccionário do Folclore Brasileiro* (Editora de Ouro, Rio de Janeiro, 1972)

Castro, Josué de, *Death in the North East* (Vintage Books, New York, 1969)

Cavalcanti Proença, M, *Estudos Literários* (José Olympio, Rio de Janeiro, 1974)

Cirano, Marcos and R. de Almeida, *Arte Popular e Dominição* (Editora Alternativa, Recife, 1978)

Countiho, Afrânio, *A Tradição Afortunada: O Espírito da Nacionalidade na Crítica Brasileira* (José Olympio, Rio de Janeiro, 1968)

---- *Conceito da Literatura Brasileira* (Vozes, Petrópolis, 1981)

---- *Euclides, Capistrano e Araripe* (Editora de Ouro, Rio de Janeiro, 1967)

Curran, Mark, *A Literatura de Cordel* (Universidade Federal de Pernambuco, Recife, 1971)

---- 'Influência da Literatura de Cordel na Literatura Brasileira' in *Revista Brasileira de Folclore* (Rio de Janeiro), IX(24), (1969):111-123

Diégues, Manuel Júnior, 'Ciclos Temáticos na Literatura de Cordel' in *Literatura Popular em Verso*, Tomo 1 (Casa de Rui Barbosa, Rio de Janeiro, 1973)

Ellison, Fred, *Brazil's New Novel* (University of California Press, Los Angeles, 1954)

Facó, Rui, *Cangaceiros e Fanáticos* (Civilização Brasileira, Rio de Janeiro, 1976)

Fausto Neto, Antônio, *Cordel e a Ideologia da Punição* (Vozes, Petrópolis, 1979)

Ferreira, Jerusa Pires, *Cavalaria em Cordel* (Hucitec, São Paulo, 1979)

Freyre, Gilberto, *Região e Tradição* (José Olympio, Rio De Janeiro, 1943)

---- *Manifesto Regionalista* (Instituto Joaquim Nabuco, Recife, 1979)

---- *Casa Grande e Senzala* (José Olympio, Rio de Janeiro, 1943)

Guerra, José Augusto, 'El Mundo mágico y poético de Ariano Suassuna', in *Revista de Cultura Brasileira* (Madrid), 35 (1973):59-70

Guidinari, Mário, *Os Pícaros e os Trapaceríos de Ariano Suassuna* (Ateniense, São Paulo, 1992)

Henfry, Colin, 'The Hungry Imagination: Social Formation, Popular Culture and Ideology in Bahia', in S. Mitchell (ed), *The Logic of Poverty* (Routledge & Keegan Paul, London, 1981)

Inojoso, Joaquim, *O Movimento Modernista em Pernambuco* (Tupy, Rio de Janeiro, 1972)

Julião, Francisco, *Cambão - The Yoke* (Pelican, Harmonsworth, Middx, 1972)

Lambert, Jacques, *Os Dois Brasis* (Companhia Editora Nacional, São Paulo, 1967)

Lara, Cecília de, *Nova Cruzada: Contribuição para o Estudo do Pré-Modernismo* (Instituto de Estudos Brasileiros, São Paulo, 1971)

Leal-McBride, Maria Odila, *Narrativas e Narradores em 'A Pedra do Reino'* (Peter Lang, New York, 1989)

Lessa, Orígenes, *Getúlio Vargas na Literatura de Cordel* (Editora Documentário, Rio de Janeiro, 1973)

Lidmilová, Paula, 'Transformações da Ficção Regionalista Brasileira', in *Algumas Temas da Literatura Brasileira* (Editorial Nórdica, Rio de Janeiro, 1984)

Lind, George Rudoff, 'Ariano Suassuna, Romancista', in *Colóquio/Letras* (Lisbon), 17 (1974):29-44

Luyten, Joseph Maria, *A Literatura de Cordel em São Paulo* (Edições Loyola, São Paulo, 1981)

Magalhães Júnior, R, *Rui o Homem e o Mito* (Editôra Civilização Brasileira, Rio de Janeiro, 1965)

Martínez-Lopez, Enrique, 'Guía para lectores hispánicos del "Auto da Compadecida"', in *Revista do Livro*, 24 (1964):85-103

Martins, Mario, 'Arte Poético dos Cantadores Nordestinos em Ariano Suassuna', in *Colóquio/Letras* (Lisbon), 40 (1977)

Martins, Wilson, *O Modernismo* (Editora Cultrix, São Paulo, 1965)

---- 'Romance Pintoresco?', in *O Estado do São Paulo*, Suplemento Literário, São Paulo, 9th January, 1972

Maxado, Franklin, *O que é a Literatura de Cordel?* (Editora Codecri, Rio de Janeiro, 1980)

---- *O Cordel Televivo* (Editora Codecri, Rio de Janeiro, 1984)

Mazarra, Richard A, *Graciliano Ramos* (Twayne, New York, 1974)

Melo, Verissimo de, 'Origens da Literatura de Cordel', in *Tempo Universitário* (Natal), 1(1) (1976):51-56

Mendoça, Luis, 'Teatro é Festa para o Povo', in *Arte em Revista* (Kairós, São Paulo), 2(3) (1980)

Mendonça Teles, Gilberto, *Vanguárdia Européia e Modernismo Brasileiro* (Vozes, Rio de Janeiro, 1972)

Merquior, José Guilherme, *De Anchieta a Euclides* (José Olympio, Rio de Janeiro, 1979)

Michalski, Yan, 'Introducción al teatro brasileño', in *Conjunto* (Casa de las Américas, Havana), 54 (1982)

Moisés, Massaud, *Machado de Assis: Crônicas-Crítica-Poesia-Teatro* (Editora Cultrix, São Paulo, 1961)

Montello, Josué, *Para Conhecer Melhor José de Alencar* (Bloch, Rio de Janeiro, 1973)

Moreira Leite, Dante, *O Caráter Nacional Brasileiro* (Livraria Pioneira Editora, São Paulo, 1976)

Bibliography

Mota, Carlos Guilherme, *Ideologia da Cultura Brasileira* (Atica, São Paulo, 1980)

Mota, Leonardo, *Padaria Espiritual* (Edésio, Fortaleza, 1938)

Moura, Clóvis, *O Preconceito de Cor na Literatura de Cordel* (Editora Resenha Universitária, São Paulo, 1976)

Nabuco, Joaquim, *Minha Formação* (Instituto Progresso Editorial, São Paulo, undated)

Nist, John, *The Modernist Movement in Brazil* (University of Texas Press, Austin, 1967)

Noblat, Ricardo, 'A Literatura de Cordel' in *Fatos e Fotos*, Gente, Rio de Janeiro, January 1971

Nunes, Benedito, *João Cabral de Melo Neto* (Vozes, Petrópolis, 1971)

Oliveira, José Osorio de, *História Breve da Literatura Brasileira* (Editora Cultrix, São Paulo, 1945)

Paulilo, Maria Ignez de, 'A Parceira no Sertão Paraíbano: uma Análise de Ideologia', in *Boletim de Ciências Sociais* (Universidade de Santa Catarina, Florianópolis), 24 (1982)

Peregrino Júnior, 'Modernismo', in *Tres Ensaios* (Livraria São José, Rio de Janeiro, 1969)

Peregrino, Umberto, *Literatura de Cordel em Discusão* (Presença, Rio de Janeiro, 1984)

Pereira, V, 'Cantadores: Do Alpendre das Azendas às Agências de Turismo', in *Jornal do Brasil*, Rio de Janeiro, 28th September, 1974

Pinto, Luiz, *A Influência do Nordeste nas Letras Brasileiras* (José Olympio, Rio de Janeiro, 1961)

Pontes, Joel, *O Teatro Moderno em Pernambuco* (Coleção Buriti, DESA, São Paulo, 1966)

Pontes, Mário, *Doce como o Diabo* (Editora Codecri, Rio de Janeiro, 1979)

Pragana, Maria Elisa Collier, *Literatura do Nordeste em Torno de sua Expressão Social* (José Olympio, Rio de Janeiro, 1983)

Quartim, Joaquim, *Dictatorship and Armed Struggle in Brazil* (NLB, London, 1971)

Queirós, Maria Isaura Pereira de, *Os Cangaceiros* (Livraria Duas Cidades, São Paulo, 1977)

Rama, Angel, 'Ariano Suassuna: el teatro y la narrativa popular y nacional', in *Literatura y clase social* (Folios Ediciones, México DF, 1983)

Ramos, Leo, 'Cultura Popular: Cordel e os Poetas Famintos', in *Tribuna da Imprensa*, Rio de Janeiro, 29th December, 1975

Ribeiro, Darcy, *Os Brasileiros: 1 Teoria do Brasil* (Editora Vozes, Petrópolis, 1978)

Rodrigues, José Honório, *História, Corpo do Tempo* (Editora Perspectiva, São Paulo, 1975)

Romero, Sílvio, *História da Literatura Brasileira*, 5 Vols (José Olympio, Rio de Janeiro, 1960)

---- *Cantos Populares do Brasil*, 2 Vols (José Olympio, Rio de Janeiro, 1954)

---- *Estudos Sobre a Poesia Popular do Brasil* (Vozes, Petrópolis, 1977)

---- *A América Latina: Análise do Livro de Igual Título do Manuel Bomfim* (Chandrar, Oporto, 1906)

Rowland, Robert, 'Cantadores del nordeste brasileño: estructura y cambio social en el nordeste del Brasil', in *Aportes* (Paris), 3 (1967)

Scott Loos, Dorothy, *The Naturalist Novel of Brazil* (Hispanic Institute in the United States, New York, 1963)

Silva Brito, Mário da, 'Metamorfoses de Oswald de Andrade', in *Revista Civilização Brasileira* (Rio de Janeiro), IV(17) (1968)

Silva Bruna, Erani, *História do Brasil, Geral e Regional 2: O Nordeste* (Cultrix, São Paulo, 1967)

Silveira Bueno, D, 'Leitura de Cordel', in *Jornal do Comércio*, Recife, 19th November, 1982

Silveiro, Renato de, 'Um Arte Genuína, Nacional e Popular?', in *Arte em Revista* (Kairós, São Paulo), 2(3) (1980)

Skidmore, Thomas, *Black into White, Race and Nationality in Brazilian Thought* (Oxford University Press, New York, 1974)

Slater, Candace, 'Folklore and the Modern Artist: The North East Brazilian Movimento Armorial', in the *Luso-Brazilian Review* 16(2) (1979)

---- *Ariano Suassuna's 'A Pedra do Reino: A Case Study in Cultural Nationalism'*, PhD Submitted to Standford University, USA, August 1975

---- *Stories on a String* (University of California Press, Los Angeles, 1982)

Souza, Liêdo Maranhão de, *Classificação Popular de Literatura de Cordel* (Vozes, Petrópolis, 1976)

Souza Barros, *A Década 20 em Pernambuco* (Gráfica Editora Académica, Rio de Janeiro, 1972)

Suassuna, Ariano, 'Notas sobre o Romanceiro Popular do Nordeste', in *Seleta em Prosa e Verso* (José Olympio, Rio de Janeiro, 1974)

---- *O Movimento Armorial* (Universidade Federal de Pernambuco, Recife, 1974)

---- 'Manifesto do Teatro Popular do Nordeste', (1961), in *Arte em Revista* (Kairós, São Paulo), 2(3) (1980)

Tavares Júnior, Luis, *O Mito na Literatura de Cordel* (Edições Tempo Brasileiro, Rio de Janeiro, 1980)

Vassallo, Ligia, *O Sertão Medieval: Origens Europeias do Teatro de Ariano Suassuna*, (Francisco Alves, Rio de Janeiro, 1993)

Bibliography

Veríssimo, José, *História da Literatura Brasileira* (José Olympio, Rio de Janeiro, 1954)

Vila Nova, S, 'Profesor Vê Fim da Literatura de Cordel', in *Diário de Natal*, Natal, 13th November, 1975

Wagley, Charles, *An Introduction to Brazil* (Columbia University Press, New York, 1971)

Werneck Sodré, Nelson, *História da Literatura Brasileira* (Civilização Brasileira, Rio de Janeiro, 1969)

Other works of literature, literary criticism and cultural studies

Arnold, Matthew, *Culture and Anarchy* (Cambridge University Press, Cambridge, 1984)

Arguedas, José María, *Formación de una cultura nacional indoamericana* (Siglo Veintiuno, México DF, 1977)

Craig, D. (ed), *Marxists on Literature* (Pelican, Harmonsworth, Middx, 1975)

Cummings, J.G, *The Spanish Traditional Lyric* (Pergamon Press, Oxford, 1977)

Fanon, Franz, *The Wretched of the Earth* (Penguin, Harmonsworth, Middx, 1978)

Franco, Jean, *The Modern Culture Of Latin America* (Pall Mall, London, 1967)

Griffin, C.C. (ed), *Concerning Latin American Culture* (Russell and Russell, New York, 1967)

Hall, S. and T. Jefferson (eds), *Resistance Through Rituals* (Hutchinson, London, 1976)

Hobsbawm, E.J, *Bandits* (Pelican, Harmonsworth, Middx, 1972)

Hobsbawm, E. and T. Ranger (eds), *The Invention of Tradition* (Cambridge University Press, Cambridge, 1983)

Hoggart, R, *The Uses of Literacy* (Penguin, Harmonsworth, Middx, 1963)

Gramsci, Antonio, *Selections from Prison Notebooks* (Lawrence and Wishart, London, 1982)

---- *Selections from Cultural Writings* (Lawrence and Wishart, London, 1985)

García Calderón, V, *La venganza del cóndor* (Mundo Latino, Madrid, 1922)

Jay, M, *The Dialectical Imagination: A History of the Frankfurt School and the Institute of Social Research 1923-50* (Little Brown, Boston, 1973)

Leavis, F.R, *Mass Civilization and Minority Culture* (The Minority Press, Cambridge, 1930)

López Albújar, E, *Cuentos andinos* (Juan Mejía Baca, Lima, 1965)

Lord, Albert, *The Singer of Tales* (Atheneum, New York, 1976)

Lukacs, G, *The Meaning of Contemporary Realism* (Merlin Press, London, 1978)

---- *Studies in European Realism* (Hillway Publishing Company, London, 1959)

Mariátegui, José Carlos, *Siete ensayos de interpretación de la literatura peruana* (Editorial Universitaria, Santiago de Chile, 1955)

Menéndez Pidal, Ramón, *Estudios sobre el romancero* (Espasa-Calpe, Madrid, 1973)

Ortega y Gassett, José, *La rebelión de las masas* (Espasa-Calpe, Argentina SA, Buenos Aires, 1941)

Pascal, R, *The German Sturm and Drang* (Manchester University Press, Manchester, 1955)

Rama, Angel, *Transculturación narrativa en América Latina* (Siglo Veintiuno, Mexico, 1982)

Redfield, R, *Tepoztlán, a Mexican Village: A Study of Folk Life* (Chicago University Press, Chicago, 1930)

Shanin, Teodor (ed), *Peasants and Peasant Societies: Selected Readings* (Penguin, Harmonsworth, Middx, 1979)

Smith, C.C, *Spanish Ballads* (Wheaton, Exeter, 1978)

---- 'On the Ethos of The Romancero Viejo', in N.D. Shergold (ed), *Studies of the Spanish and Portuguese Ballad* (Tamesis Books, London, 1972)

Thomsom, George, *Marxism and Poetry* (Lawrence and Wishart, London, 1980)

Watt, Ian, *The Rise of the Novel* (Pelican, Harmonsworth, Middx, 1979)

Williams, Raymond, *Keywords* (Fontana, Glasgow, 1979)

---- *The Country and the City* (Chatto and Windus, London, 1976)

Index